A HISTORY OF
SOUTHERN AFRICA

PALGRAVE ESSENTIAL HISTORIES

General Editor: Jeremy Black

This series of compact, readable and informative national histories is designed to appeal to anyone wishing to gain a broad understanding of a country's history.

Published

A History of the Low Countries (2nd edn) *Paul Arblaster*
A History of Italy *Claudia Baldoli*
A History of Russia *Roger Bartlett*
A History of Spain (2nd edn) *Simon Barton*
A History of the British Isles (4th edn) *Jeremy Black*
A History of France *Joseph Bergin*
A History of Israel *Ahron Bregman*
A History of Ireland (2nd edn) *Mike Cronin & Liam O'Callaghan*
A History of Greece *Nicholas Doumanis*
A History of the Pacific Islands (2nd edn) *Steven Roger Fischer*
A History of Korea (2nd edn) *Kyung Moon Hwang*
A History of the United States (5th edn) *Philip Jenkins*
A History of Denmark (2nd edn) *Knud J. V. Jespersen*
A History of the Baltic States (2nd edn) *Andres Kasekamp*
A History of Australia (2nd edn) *Mark Peel and Christina Twomey*
A History of Poland (2nd edn) *Anita J. Prazmowska*
A History of India (2nd edn) *Peter Robb*
A History of China (3rd edn) *J. A. G. Roberts*
A History of Germany *Peter Wende*

A HISTORY OF SOUTHERN AFRICA

Alois S. Mlambo and
Neil Parsons

First published 2019 by
RED GLOBE PRESS

Red Globe Press in the UK is an imprint of Springer Nature Limited,
registered in England, company number 785998, of 4 Crinan Street,
London N1 9XW.

Red Globe Press® is a registered trademark in the United States,
the United Kingdom, Europe and other countries.

ISBN 978–0–230–29410–3 hardback
ISBN 978–0–230–29411–0 paperback

This book is printed on paper suitable for recycling and made from fully
managed and sustained forest sources. Logging, pulping and manufacturing
processes are expected to conform to the environmental regulations of the
country of origin.

A catalogue record for this book is available from the British Library.

A catalog record for this book is available from the Library of Congress.

Contents

List of Maps

Introduction

The release of Nelson Mandela from 27 years in prison, on 11 February 1990, followed the fall of the Berlin Wall in the previous November. The two events were widely seen as opening up a new world era of peace and democracy. Not for the first time, Southern Africa played a key role in world history.

Why study Southern African history? For most readers, it will locate the history of South Africa in its regional context, without which that country's present and past cannot really be understood. The earliest history of southern Africa, for the first time covered in some detail in this book, is also the earliest history of all modern human beings.

Over most of the past two millennia, the sub-continent was connected to an Indian Ocean world economy dominated by Islamic trade and then by European powers. The history of the last century and a half clusters around the production of two essential commodities of the capitalist world economy – diamonds and gold. In the mid-20th century, most of Southern Africa bucked the universal trend towards liberal democracy. Instead, it suffered reinforced racial discrimination and oppression. The history of later twentieth-century Southern Africa encompasses inspiring stories of liberation from colonialism and apartheid, both peaceful and violent, with human rights restored to face new challenges in the new millennium.

The history of Southern Africa is also the history of interaction between traditional, Christian, Islamic, and secular belief systems. The region has ancient links with Asia as well as intimate links with Europe and North America – and its past bears parallels with the histories of other indigenous peoples in South and North America, Australasia, and the Pacific. Readers will also note the importance given in this book to changing climates and physical environments.

Chapters 1–4 are about a world that has largely disappeared but has left the region with peoples, languages, and cultures that are critical to the understanding of today. Chapters 5–6 focus on fundamental changes that brought into being a racial-political and economic hierarchy of territories defined by modern borders. Chapters 7–11 pick up on the urban-industrial history that has shaped capital and labour, rich and poor in the region – conditions that still persist today.

'Southern Africa' with a capital 'S' applies to the more or less coherent region bound together by capital investment and labour migration, railways and roads and close air links, and by politics both white settler and black nationalist – with its hub on the Witwatersrand around Johannesburg. The term 'southern Africa' with a small 's' applies more generally to the southern part of Eastern Africa and to history before the later nineteenth century. (This highlights the importance of the nineteenth century as a period of crucial change.) Usage of ethnic terms in this book also varies over time. The most commonly used recent terms are 'black' for indigenous Bantu-speaking Africans; 'white' for people of European ancestry, including white Afrikaans-speakers; 'Indian' for all people of South Asian ancestry; and 'Coloured' for people of indigenous Khoe and San and of other ancestry – Muslim Malay (Indonesian), Eurafrican, Malagasy, East or West African, etc.[1]

This book opens up and outlines current knowledge, but the story of the past – particularly of the remote past – is constantly being questioned and rewritten by new findings and debates in many disciplines. Readers are encouraged to pursue their personal interests in libraries and on the internet. More details of people and places named in this book may be found through general index searches. Details of the latest debates and scholarship can be discovered through specialist search-engines such as 'Google Scholar'. Each chapter in this book has a bibliography of key books and a videography of films (at some time available on DVD, partially on 'YouTube', etc.), with a general bibliography and videography at the end of the book.

Alois Mlambo, University of Pretoria
Neil Parsons, London, Gaborone, & Cape Town
April 2018

---

1 *A note on dates in this book*: CE is used for 'Common Era' (i.e. Christian Era after the birth of Christ, otherwise known as AD), and BCE for 'Before Common Era' (otherwise BC). CE is understood and omitted from the year CE 500 onwards. The abbreviation 'kya' used for very remote times means 'thousands of years ago', e.g 5500 kya is equivalent to BCE 3500.

1 Middle and Later Stone Age

During the past two or three decades there has been a revolution in our understanding of the remote human past. There have been scientific advances in genetics, ecology and climatology, and new techniques for dating the age of remains, as well as advances in historical-linguistics and cultural analysis. History as the continuous story of human identities, actions, ideas, customs and crafts is pushing its way deeper and deeper back into prehistory.

The Stone Age refers to the period of the past when people's tools, notably knives and arrow heads, were crafted from stone. Middle Stone Age 'industries' emerged out of the Early Stone Age roughly 300 kya (300,000 years ago), and merged with the Later Stone Age roughly around 35 kya (35,000 years ago). It was during the Middle Stone Age that modern humans like us first appeared. The typical tools made by people in the Middle Stone Age were blades – flakes of rock that were twice as long as broad, with parallel sharp sides. During the Later Stone Age the characteristic stone tool was the microlith: a pear-shaped miniature flake not much larger than a finger nail, attached as barbs on the heads of arrows and harpoons or used as a sharp scraper on wood, bones, and grass twine.

HOMO SAPIENS AND OTHER EARLY MODERN HUMANS

Every person on Earth today is a member of the same biological species, Modern Humans or *Homo sapiens* – we vainly call ourselves sapient or 'wise' in Latin. *Homo sapiens* developed out of earlier humans known as Heidelberg Man or *Homo heidelbergensis* – named after Heidelberg in Germany, where a skull and bones were first discovered and classified. These people originated in Africa and spread into Asia and Europe. Middle Stone Age tools of Heidelberg people excavated at Twin Rivers, south of Lusaka in Zambia, are dated between 400 kya and 350 kya. A Heidelberg skull, found by mining north of Lusaka at Kabwe (Broken Hill Man), dated around 300 kya, is heavy-boned with a prominent brow-ridge and evidence of strong neck muscles to support a heavy head.

By contrast, Modern Humans developed a thinner-boned and more globe-shaped skull, compressed during childbirth and then expanding. The brain was not bigger but better, giving us increased power of speech and manual dexterity using our fingers. Creases in the brain gave it more power of thought and expanded working memory (analogous to computer memory-doubling). Rapid talking was enabled by a thick and highly mobile short tongue and by the voice-box dropping as a child grows older.

Language became more complex as it drew on memory and shared meanings with other people. People could tell complex stories and sing and dance. They could also love, believe, and joke. They could certainly run fast, and over long distances, because of their relatively lightweight bones and long, strong muscles. Hairless bodies enabled people to keep cool by sweating, and relatively thin skulls prevented the brain overheating.

At the time when this book is being written, the earliest known remains of *Homo sapiens* have been found at Jebel Irhoud in Morocco (dated around 315 kya) and at Florisbad in South Africa (around 260 kya). *Homo sapiens* remains in Israel (Misliya) and Ethiopia (Omo) have been dated around 186 kya and around 178 kya. No doubt other and earlier examples can and will be found.

Modern Humans slowly developed out of Heidelberg humans. Early childhood nutrition was essential. Fatty acids like Omega-3 have been identified as essential brain food for infants in the womb and in breast milk. Fatty acids could be obtained by mothers sucking the marrow out of animal bones or from a heavy diet of shellfish such as mussels. The other great advance was improved cooking, making high-energy foods easy to digest. Meat and root crops retain nutrition by being basted on slabs of rock over a fire – using animal dung as flambant – rather than burnt dry in the wood ashes.

From Heidelberg people there also developed other species of early modern humans. Neanderthal people developed in North Africa and Eurasia. Denisovan people and Flores ('hobbit') people developed in Asia. Discovered in a deep cave near Johannesburg, the remains of 18 lightweight and small-headed Naledi people have been dated as late as 236 kya. Also in Southern Africa, Boskopoid early modern humans were robust and heavily built.

But all of these species except *Homo sapiens* have since disappeared from the Earth.

SCIENTIFIC DATING AND CLIMATES: 244 KYA–PRESENT DAY

Radio-carbon dating is the cheapest and most common form of scientific dating for organic remains. It measures the wasting or declining ratio of

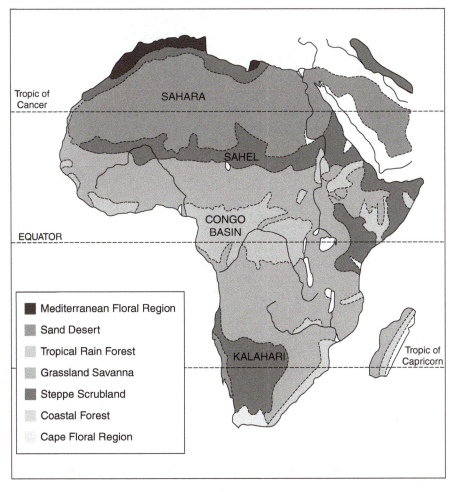

Map 1.1   Africa: Vegetation

radioactive Carbon-14 to stable Carbon-12 in wood or bone, showing its age back to about 45 kya.

Earlier dates than 45 kya can now be obtained from (1) luminescence dating of quartz and sand grains buried in the dark, (2) potassium-argon dating of volcanic rocks, (3) uranium series dating of former living organisms, (4) amino-acid racemization and protein diagenesis measuring protein deterioration in eggs etc., and (5) electron spin resonance measuring electrons in tooth enamel. Sometimes the dates from different techniques disagree, which gives rise to

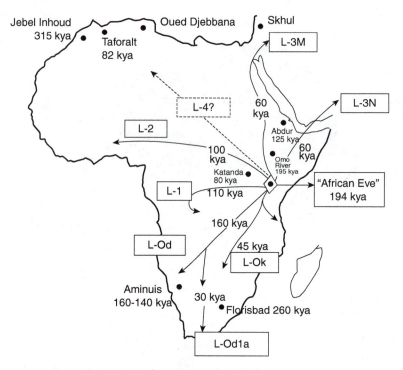

Map 1.2   Modern Human (mtDNA) Migrations

controversies and potential revisions among archaeologists. Hence, some of the dates given in this and other chapters may yet be revised by future research.

The world's climate periods have been dated by the drilling of cores into the Arctic and Antarctic ice caps. Changes in climate affected vegetation and animal life, and the culture or ways-of-living of humans was profoundly influenced by changing environment. Seven main climate periods, known as marine isotope stages (MIS) or oxygen isotope stages (OIS), are numbered backwards from today. All dates are approximate:

MIS/OIS-7	244 kya to 190 kya	Warm climate
MIS/OIS-6	190 kya to 130 kya	Cold climate
MIS/OIS-5	130 kya to 74 kya	Very warm climate
MIS/OIS-4	74 kya to 60 kya	Very cold and dry climate
MIS/OIS-3	60 kya to 24 kya	Warm climate
MIS/OIS-2	24 kya to 12 kya	Cold climate
MIS/OIS-1	12 kya until the present day	Warm climate

Map 1.3   Middle & Later Stone Age Archaeological Sites

GENETICS AND 'AFRICAN EVE': 244 KYA–190 KYA (MIS/OIS-7) & 190 KYA–130 KYA (MIS/OIS-6)

In 1987, three Californian geneticists traced back the maternal ancestry of 147 people from all over the world. They compared and traced back all the female genes (mitochondrial DNA or mtDNA) to one original source – a woman living at about 194 kya. We are all descended from her, and she most likely lived somewhere on the upland plateaux of Africa. The press started calling this mother-of-us-all African Eve. The American magazine *Newsweek* featured her on its cover as a beautiful brown-skinned woman – looking African, European, Asian, and above all American!

Since 1987 many geneticists have calculated and mapped how the daughters and female descendants of African Eve spread across the world.

The oldest known mtDNA gene type has been numbered L-0. It became distinct between 160 kya and 110 kya, as its group of people moved away from the main African Eve population. Today, it is mostly found among Northern San/Bushmen people living in the northern Kalahari. (These people, like everyone alive, also carry traces of other mtDNA gene types as well.)

The second oldest mtDNA gene type (L-1) originated around 110 kya. It is mostly found among Twa/Pygmy people in the eastern Congo Basin. The third oldest mtDNA gene type (L-2) originated around 100 kya. It is mostly found among people speaking Niger-Congo (or Niger-Kordofanian) languages, notably the Bantu languages. The fourth mtDNA gene type (L-3) is mostly found among people speaking Afro-Asiatic languages, notably Somali, Amharic, and Semitic languages. Around 60 kya, the L-3 gave rise to new genetic types that are numbered L-3M and L-3N. All the other mtDNA types in the world today are descended from L-3M and L-3N.

All the original mtDNA gene types overlap in East Africa, from where it appears that L-3M and L-3N must have spread along and across the Red Sea into the Middle-East and into Asia and Europe. This is the picture presented by our *matri-lineages* (or mother's-mother's-mother, etc.). Our *patri-lineages* (father's-father's-father, etc.) are much more difficult to plot, as the paternal genes evolve and change much more from generation to generation.

The only archaeological remains of the African Eve group of Modern Humans so far known in East Africa is probably a *Homo sapiens* skull found on the Omo River in Ethiopia, dated around 168 kya (195–160 kya). Middle Stone Age stone tools found at Aminuis Pan in Namibia, probably also made by Modern Humans, are lunette (quarter-moon) shaped and are dated 160 kya–140 kya. At Herto in the Afar depression of Ethiopia, archaeologists have found human skulls, around the same age, that were polished before burial. This suggests reverence for the spirits of the dead.

Geneticists suggest that around 144 kya, Modern Humans were reduced to perhaps less than 10,000 people by a mega-drought of cold and dry centuries. The mega-drought reduced the Great Lakes of East Africa almost to puddles. At one time Lake Malawi fell 600 metres lower than its level today, reducing it to 10 kilometres across and 200 metres deep. But this 'population bottleneck' of rapidly declining numbers was followed by quick recovery as the climate improved once again.

The rapid rise in temperature and rainfall towards the end of MIS/OIS-6 resulted in strings of lakes, great and small, covering the Kalahari. Today's Etosha and Makgadikgadi salt pans, Okavango and Chobe marshes, were brimful with water between 140 kya and 130 kya. Lake Makgadikgadi alone was bigger than today's Lake Michigan in North America. The south coast of South Africa, which had stretched up to 25 kilometres further than today when so much sea-water was frozen around the Antarctic, retreated back to cliffs and bluffs pounded by the sea.

At Pinnacle Point caves in quartzite cliffs near Mossel Bay, today under a golf course, the gathering and eating of shellfish by people is dated from about 164 kya to 120 kya. (Mossel Bay takes its name from its proliferation of mussels.) Quartzite stone tools dated around 132 kya include small blades that were hafted (connected) and probably glued onto spear shafts. Shellfish remains include brown mussels, limpets, and periwinkles. The Blombos cave, west of Pinnacle Point, has more evidence of shellfishing around 140 kya. The Pinnacle Point caves were sealed off by sea incursion around 120 kya – and were blocked off by sand dunes between 90 kya and 40 kya.

SHELL BEADS AND OCHRE PIGMENTS: 130 KYA–74 KYA (MIS/OIS-5)

Middle Stone Age sites proliferated across the continent during the warmer and wetter MIS/OIS-5 period. At Abdur on the Red Sea coast of Eritrea, the remains of oysters, clams, sea snails, and scallops have been found with Middle Stone Age tools and dated about 125 kya. In the Cave of Pigeons at Taforalt, 40 kilometres inland from the coast in Morocco, mollusc shells deliberately perforated to be strung as beads are dated about 82 kya. Similar perforated seashell beads, with comparable dates, have been found at sites along the Mediterranean coast at Oued Djebbana in Algeria and at Skhul in Israel. The Middle Stone Age site on a river at Katanda in the Congo Basin, with barbed stone tools such as are used for fish-harpoons, is dated 80 kya.

The northern Kalahari lakes were full of water again during two periods within MIS/OIS-5. At White Paintings Shelter in the Tsodilo hills, a Middle Stone Age occupation – with chert and silcrete stone tools that must have been brought from a distance – is dated between 120 kya and 100 kya. Sharp bone-tips for spears and ostrich eggshell beads from a subsequent occupation are dated around 80 kya. People combined to hunt large herds of migrating wildlife, such as waterbuck and other antelopes, splashing across the rivers and marshes. There was also use of specularite iron ore, ground into powder and mixed with fat for a sparkling hair or body dressing. One hundred kilometres away to the southwest of Tsodilo at a place called ≠Gi!, people hunted buffalo, bush-pigs, and zebra in open countryside. Ostrich eggshell remains there, found together with red ochre staining, are dated around 77 kya by no less than three types of scientific dating.

On the coastline around the Cape of Good Hope, there are still today some great piles of discarded shells from shellfish, though much has been removed to be crushed for cement. These piles are the remains of tens of thousands of years of human effort collecting shellfish at low tide. The abalone shells at Pinnacle Point caves have been dated from 100 kya.

Sharp bone tools were used to drill holes in seashells and ostrich eggshells, to be strung for bangles and necklaces, or sewn with bone needles as decorations onto leather. Animal skin blankets and clothing, necessary to keep warm during the winter of southern Africa, appear to be very ancient. The **lice** that infest human bodies in clothes became genetically separated from head-hair lice by around 170 kya.

There is much evidence for the use of red and black pigments. Red ochre (haematite: 'blood-stone') was mixed with animal fat for body adornment and protection from cold, while sparkling black ochre (specularite: 'reflective-stone') was also used as hair cosmetic. (Heating red ochre in a fire made it even redder.) The iron content in these pigments was a powerful astringent that acted as an antiseptic for wounds. Ochre mixed with fat or urine was also used to soften animal skins (for blankets and clothing) when they dried out and became stiff. Mixed with plant gum, ochre became a strong glue used to haft bone or stone points onto spears and arrows. More than 300 pieces of pigment found at Twin Rivers in Zambia suggest that other colours besides red and black were being used during the Middle Stone Age.

It is open to question how far *Homo sapiens* valued ochre pigments for personal adornment, for its medicinal magic, or for its practical uses. But its use has been seen as proof that *Homo sapiens* was developing a 'modern mentality'. Painting with ochre pigments was also used, as we shall see, to create the symbols of rock art.

Scholars debate how much we can find modern mentality in the remote past – evidence of people thinking like us. During the latter part of the Middle Stone Age, there is evidence of 'house-keeping' on archaeological sites with different areas for living and sleeping. Diet was also becoming more varied. (Grinding grass-seeds and dry fruit on grindstones, presumably for boiling into porridge, predates 100 kya at Ngalue in northern Mozambique.) How much does this also indicate emerging gender roles – *matriarchy* (mother-dominance) inside the home, and *patriarchy* (father-dominance) outside?

Increased population and competition for resources may help to explain the earliest known crime scene, dated 90 kya, at Klasies River: the bones of at least five people killed at the same time, their remains chopped up and burnt. Cannibalism?

WORLDWIDE DISPERSAL OF MODERN HUMANS: 74 KYA–60 KYA (MIS/OIS-4)

Around the beginning of MIS/OIS-4 the human population was reduced, and in some places eliminated, by a sudden climatic downturn into very cold and very dry millennia without warm Indian Ocean rainfall. This mega-drought, culminating around 70 kya, resulted in another 'population bottleneck' among Modern Humans. The fall in population was followed by climatic improvement and extraordinary population recovery. It was this population boom that resulted, around 60 kya, in people of genetic types L-3M and L-3N flooding out of East Africa into the rest of the world.

What caused the mega-drought around 70 kya? The favourite explanation is the explosion of Mount Toba in Sumatra, Indonesia, south of Singapore, in 74 kya – the biggest volcanic event on Earth in the last two million years. The eruption drove plumes of volcanic dust and a million tons of sulphuric acid aerosol 30 kilometres high, spread westwards by prevailing winds over the Northern Hemisphere – the Indian sub-continent, the Middle-East, and North Africa. Acid rain depleted vegetation and wildlife, and the dust in the atmosphere blocked off sunlight for photosynthesis of plants. Food shortages reduced to a bare minimum, or eliminated, human occupation of the Northern Hemisphere in the cold dark centuries that followed.

Africa around the Equator and southwards appears to have been spared the worst effects of Toba. Drilling into sediments at the bottom of Lake Malawi has shown no evidence of Toba volcanic dust deposited or of the lake level dropping appreciably. Sunlight also penetrated the atmosphere more directly over the Equator and between the two Tropics, and it permitted Modern Humans to survive in sufficient numbers in East Africa.

Genetic dating confirms the rapid population growth of *Homo sapiens* after 60 kya. Over the next 10,000 years, L-0 type people expanded over the northern Kalahari, while L-1 type people began to settle in the tropical forests of the Congo Basin. L-2 type people spread from East Africa along the northern edge of the Congo Basin into West Africa. L-3M type people crossed the Red Sea and circled the Indian Ocean coast as far as Australia. L-3N type people spread down the Nile or along the Red Sea, in greater numbers, through the Middle-East and Mediterranean as far as East Asia and Western Europe. Some ancestors of all these groups remained in East Africa.

By contrast, there is good evidence of genetically unclassified (Boskopoid?) people who survived and indeed thrived on the hills and coastal plains of the winter-rainfall region on the south coast – not dependent on summer rainfall from the Indian Ocean. Archaeologists there find increased consumption of shellfish and use of red haematite during the Still Bay and Howieson's Poort industries of the Middle Stone Age.

The Still Bay industry is dated from 78 kya onwards. Leaf-shaped two-edged quartz blade tools were manufactured in abundance. The blades were trimmed or repaired by pressure flaking (rather than hammer-blows) after being heated in a fire. The Still Bay site at Pinnacle Point shows that shells were collected from the beaches for their beauty and colour. Patterns of bead necklaces and bracelets may indicate 'modern' awareness of family pride or individual identity. Were they also devices helping memorization or for counting numbers?

Archaeologists at the Still Bay site in Blombos cave, dated around 75 kya, found numerous sea-snail beads with holes made by bone-point tools, plus hard blocks of red ochre haematite – methodically scratched with parallel and hatched lines. What these patterns mean, no one knows. But they do seem to be evidence of 'modern mentality'. Perhaps they were graffiti scratched in leisure time, simply meaning that this is 'mine' or 'ours'. Or were they products of complex artistic imagination – the first symbolic rock art?

The Still Bay industry flourished around 72 kya–71 kya and spread hundreds of kilometres inland. Confirmed sites include Sibudu Rock Shelter in KwaZulu-Natal and Apollo XI cave in the Hunsberge mountains of southern Namibia. Archaeological sites inland as far as Zambia and the Congo, at one time identified as Still Bay, need to be re-investigated with the aid of scientific dating.

MIDDLE TO LATER STONE AGE TRANSITION: 60 KYA–24 KYA (MIS/OIS-3)

Middle Stone Age (MSA) and Later Stone Age (LSA) industries in southern Africa overlapped during the MIS/OIS-3 climatic warm period. Demographers from Stanford University and the Russian Academy of Sciences have argued that Africa south of the Sahara 'experienced a population explosion around 35,000 years ago' – associated with the emergence of new LSA technology and ways-of-life that increased life expectancy and birth rates. (Though, in the southern Cape, the final stage of the MSA can be dated from around 59 kya to as late as 12 kya.)

The first known bows-and-arrows may be found among MSA people of the Howieson's Poort industry. (Bows-and-arrows are in a sense the first machine, articulating different parts together in one function.) This industry was named after a site near Grahamstown in the Eastern Cape, discovered in the 1920s. It lasted from about 65 kya to 59 kya in the southern Cape. The Howieson's Poort tool-kit included microliths – small crescent-shaped stone blades, used as spearheads and arrowheads hafted with gum and twine, or used as barbs on fish-harpoons. Stone for microliths was often imported from a distance, which implies long journeys or exchanges with neighbours.

Howieson's Poort sites in the southern Cape include Klasies River and Diepkloof rock shelters. The Diepkloof site has numerous pieces of ostrich eggshell, engraved with identical or similar patterns – implying an agreed decorative style for a group of people. In KwaZulu-Natal, Sibudu rock shelter (lasting until about 49 kya) has evidence of 'sedentary' or relatively stationary settlement of family groups. Microliths covered in traces of resin glue were probably hafted onto the tips of arrows. People were hunting small animals in the local Yellowwood forest – hyrax (rock-rabbit), giant edible rats, and duiker (miniature antelope). Other Howieson's Poort sites are Rose Cottage Cave near the Free State border with Lesotho and Border Cave on the Swaziland border with KwaZulu-Natal (maybe beginning as early as 75 kya).

On the Zambia-Tanzania frontier, the major MSA site at the bottom of the Kalambo Falls, 235 metres high, is dated about 57 kya–41.5 kya. Hunters waited for animals that came to drink in the pools below the falls. They dug hip-hollows for sleeping, and they built a hunting blind or windbreak with brushwood anchored in a semi-circle of stones. Archaeologists have found waterlogged wood remains of their sticks and spears. Comparable final MSA sites in Kenya are Norikiushin and Enkapane ya Muto, dated around 46 kya.

On the Zimbabwe plateau, there are important final phase MSA (Oakhurst complex) sites at Nswatugwi, Pomongwe, and Tshangula in the Matopo hills, which await re-investigation with new archaeological techniques. Final MSA occupations in the northern Kalahari are seen at the White Paintings Shelter in the Tsodilo hills. People in relatively large groups hunted migrating herds of antelopes and zebras. A number of late MSA phases have been identified at Apollo XI cave in Namibia, just north of the Orange River.

The 'population explosion' around 35 kya, identified by Stanford and Russian scientists, followed the adoption of Later Stone Age microlith technology and new styles of living. We can also see the adoption among the ancestors of the Northern San/Bushmen living around the Tsodilo hills in the northern Kalahari. The local lakes were full during the warm and wet MIS/OIS-3 climate, and the Lower Fish level excavated at Tsodilo's White Paintings Shelter is full of discarded fish bones. The period of MSA-LSA transition here is dated 48 kya–30 kya.

Stone blade tools grew smaller over time, into the size we call microliths. Spears and arrows became lighter to carry, and hunters ranged further afield in pursuit of browsing animals. Instead of assembling to intercept migrating herds with spears, people with bows-and-arrows began to disperse in small family groups throughout the year. In the northern Kalahari, some typical LSA microliths were being manufactured from about 38 kya, and the transition to bow-and-arrow culture was complete by 24 kya. People at the ≠Gi hunting site, in open countryside to the southwest of Tsodilo, used microlith arrow-heads the size of a thumb nail – less than two centimetres long. They wore lots of ostrich eggshell beads and hunted a wide variety of species, including now-extinct large hartebeest.

In the southern Cape, there had also been a 'sudden pulse' of population growth around 32 kya among late MSA (Robberg and Albany industries) people. The warm and wet climate caused ocean levels to rise, driving wildlife and hunters from the coastal floodplains back to something like today's shoreline. The change in climate also opened up to human settlement the Namib and Karoo north of the Cape. The MSA-LSA transition at Apollo XI cave near the Orange River is dated 30 kya–22 kya.

TWA, KHOE, AND SAN HUNTER-GATHERERS

Twa/Southern Pygmy hunter-gatherers occupied sites of the LSA Nachikufu industry in the dense woodlands of northern Zambia and Malawi, even as late as the nineteenth century. (Nachikufu itself is a cave in northern Zambia, with rock paintings now covered in tourist graffiti.) The industry dates from 25 kya or 18 kya onwards. The people had a varied diet, including wild fruit and nuts and honey and wild nuts and seeds – ground between upper and lower grindstones. They made much use of wood and wood by-products: gum or sap, string and rope, brush fences to herd wild animals towards spring-traps, and bark cloth woven with bone needles for clothes and blankets.

Khoe people and San people come from the same L-0 group genetic origin. Geneticists date the splitting between Northern San (L-0d group) and Khoe (L-0k group) between 43 kya and 25 kya. The split was probably originally between San ancestors of the Khoe living around Tanzania and San people in the northern Kalahari. They would have been cut off from each other when a 'population explosion' of Twa/Southern Pygmy created a wedge between them, by spreading out of the Congo Basin into northern Zambia and Malawi. (Maybe it is Twa ancestry that explains the 'matrilineal belt' still stretching from Angola to Malawi, where inheritance of wealth and status by men passes through the mother.)

Similar dates, 30 kya–25 kya, are suggested by geneticists for the division of Southern San from Northern San people. Ancestors of today's Southern San ≠Khomani people (L-0d1a group) settled in the southern Kalahari between the Molopo and Orange Rivers. From there, other Southern San ventured further south, and became well-established in the Cape region by about 22 kya. It remains to be established by genetics, archaeology, and linguistics how Southern San people interacted with MSA (Boskopoid?) people already at the Cape.

The LSA technology of the San is known among archaeologists as the Wilton industry (named after LSA rock-shelters on a farm called Wilton near Alicedale, west of Grahamstown in South Africa.) Its spread can be dated from 38 kya onwards in the White Paintings Shelter of the northern Kalahari and from 24 kya onwards on the Robberg peninsula of the Cape's Plettenberg Bay. Some archaeologists have also used the term Wilton for LSA sites as far north as Kenya and Ethiopia that may be associated with San ancestors of the Khoe.

The typical Wilton tool-kit included bone tools and microliths used for scraping, cutting, and cleaning animal skins, for sewing skins together for leather blankets, for cutting the sinews from meat for use as twine, and for carpentering of bows-and-arrows or spears. Adult men used bone-tipped arrows smeared with poison on long hunting expeditions. Women's work digging up tubers and termites was made easier by Wilton doughnut-shaped stone weights slipped onto digging sticks. Such weights could also be used for holding down fibre-woven hunting nets.

DIVERSIFICATION OF THE WILTON LSA: 24 KYA–11.5 KYA (MIS/OIS-2) & 11.5 KYA–TODAY (MIS/OIS-1 HOLOCENE)

During MIS/OIS-2, around 20 kya, a slight shift in the Earth's orbit increased solar radiation. World temperatures rose, melting the polar ice caps and raising ocean and lake levels. But then, between about 18 kya and 11.5 kya, there was an extremely cold and arid period. The Kalahari lakes dried up. The sand dunes of the Namib spread so far up the Orange River that they cut off people to the south from people to the north.

On the Cape coast, there was a final flourish of MSA industry, ending with LSA Wilton tradition predominance – seen in the rising number of fish-bones on coastal sites. People had shifted from collecting shellfish on the shore to trapping and spearing fish. Wilton tidal fishing pools, made by piling rocks in curving lines, can still be seen on the coast today.

The Wilton site at Rhino Cave in the Tsodilo hills (dated around 14.5 kya) contains evidence of trade in stone tools with other people hundreds of kilometres away. Imported fine-grained stone tools include multi-coloured chert, jasper, and chalcedony – chosen for their flaking qualities or for their colours. Ostrich eggshell beads were drilled and polished in great quantity, presumably for trade. Marshland antelopes, zebra, and even white rhino were hunted seasonally. Smaller game such as tortoise and springhare were trapped and hunted year-round.

Around 11.5 kya, the world climate entered the present-day period of MIS/OIS-1, more commonly known as the Holocene. The Holocene climate was warm but mild, and rainfall was more plentiful. The ocean level on the Cape coast continued to rise until 5 kya – reaching a level two metres higher before it fell back to today's levels. High tides covered where Cape Town's airport, shanty-towns, and suburbs now lie. There was a burst of new Wilton sites around 8 kya–7 kya in Lesotho and the Northern Cape, Eastern Cape, and Free State provinces of South Africa. The lakes of the Kalahari reached their highest water levels, but by 4 kya (2000 BCE) hot and dry conditions had set in. Lakes became marshes and seasonally flooded saltpans, the Kalahari became parched bush and grassland, thearoo became scrub once again.

The Wilton industry tradition developed many regional variants. On the Atlantic coast near Cape Town, the Wilton-like LSA sites of Elands Bay, dated between from about 4.3 kya, show hunter-gatherers often using inferior stone tools made from local black quartz pebbles. They combined hunting on land with hunting for seals and stranded whales on shore, as well as beach-combing for shellfish.

The Smithfield industry was a variation of the Wilton on the Highveld of the Free State. People quarried ridges in the Seacow (i.e. hippopotamus) valley for *hornfels* rock that could be easily flaked – notably for 'backed monoliths' used as knives, spearheads, and arrowheads. Campsites along watercourses were abandoned for new ones when they became too smelly, tick-infested, and verminous from human pollution. Smithfield people made hunting blinds or windbreaks with bush branches stuck into stone semi-circles. Summer camps were small and dispersed. Winter camps brought together people sheltering from bitter winds that drove night temperatures below freezing.

On the grassy flats of the Kafue floodplain in central Zambia, the Wilton site at Gwisho Hot Springs was a semi-permanent settlement year-round, targeting wildlife that came to drink. Archaeologists have found the burials of no less than 35 San-like skeletons, as well as stone semi-circles for hunting blinds and waterlogged pieces of wooden bows – and *Swartzia* poison pods used for arrow-tips.

POTTERY, SHEEP & CATTLE FROM EAST AFRICA

Something new was happening in the Upper Fish sites at White Paintings Shelter in the Tsodilo hills between 8.4 kya and 7 kya. As well as Wilton tools and bream or catfish bones, the sites contain bone crescent-shaped barbs from harpoons, like those also found at Lake Turkana (Rudolf) in Kenya. Geometric white paintings on the rock walls of the White Paintings Shelter are also like those found in East Africa.

To understand what was beginning to happen in Southern Africa, we must first go to East Africa. Like the Kalahari, East Africa and the Sahara were full of lakes and marshes during the early Holocene. Nilotic people spread from the Sahara and upper Nile into East Africa, taking with them their so-called Aquatic culture. They lived by fishing with bone-tipped harpoons and by making bag-shaped pottery of clay hardened around woven reed bags. The first people who brought Aquatic harpoons and white paintings to the Tsodilo hills may have been Khoe people coming from south-western Tanzania through the area of Zambia, to live with their Northern San relatives in north-western Botswana.

Between about 7.5 kya and 4.5 kya, there were great droughts that began to turn the Sahara and Arabia into the sand dune deserts we know today. Meanwhile, former lakes and marshlands in East Africa became grasslands suitable for grazing animals. Cattle were first herded into East Africa in the years between 5 kya and 3 kya. Nilotic (Nilo-Saharan) people brought in big-horned Sanga-type (Saharan ox) cattle. Cushitic (Afro-Asian) people brought in sheep and smaller Zebu-type (Arabian or Taurine) cattle from their relatives across the Red Sea. A new culture of livestock herders arose in East Africa, known to archaeologists as the Kenya-Capsian, combining both Nilotic and Cushitic roots.

Kenya-Capsian people rejected the old Aquatic fishing culture by adopting the Cushitic fish taboo, i.e. refusing to eat fish. Cattle were given a god-like status and rarely slaughtered, but their milk, blood, urine, and manure were used. Fat-tailed ('five-legged') sheep were more often slaughtered for meat and fats. People made clay pots with pointed bases and rippled rims, for milk and water to be kept cool hung on branches. They also carved bowl-shaped stones, probably to cook mutton stew. Hence the Kenya-Capsian is also known as the Stone Bowl industry.

The southward expansion of Kenya-Capsian cattle-keepers came to a halt around the gap between the south end of Lake Tanganyika and the north end of Lake Malawi. The way was blocked for most of each year by the infestation belt of tsetse-fly (*Glossina*), whose bite is ultimately fatal to cattle and people. But Kenya-Capsian Khoe herders managed to get through the tsetse belt. They took with them sheep and the making of pottery probably hundreds of years before successful trekking of cattle. Linguists show that the Khoe language adopted Nilotic or Cushitic words for sheep (*-ku*) and cattle (*-xomo*). Geneticists have found both Nilotic and Cushitic male and female genes among Khoe people dating from intermarriage about 2.4 kya.

There are many questions open to more research about early Khoe settlement, expansion, and influence in Southern Africa. Who was responsible for the stone bowls of Kenya-Capsian type that have been found near Windhoek in Namibia, near Kanye in Botswana, and near Kimberley in South Africa? Who was responsible for making a type of clay pottery known as Bambata ware – dating from 2.1 kya and deriving its name from a cave site in the Matopo hills? Bambata ware from the next 500 years has been found at Toteng near the Okavango swamps, at Skeurkrans in the Waterberg hills, Jubilee Shelter in the Magaliesberg, and Mirabib and Falls Rock in Namibia. Bambata bowls and jars were thin-walled and well-fired, in a variety of shapes for carrying and storing water (some with spouts for pouring), cooking meat stew or porridge, and possibly for fermenting and drinking beer made of honey or fruit.

Sheep and cattle bones dating from the last centuries BCE have been found at Toteng and Lotshitshi in northern Botswana. The gene for tolerance in the human gut of non-human milk (numbered -14010*C), inherited from Cushitic/Nilotic ancestors, became widespread among livestock herders. The new milk supply relieved women from breast-feeding older babies. Women could bear more children, since lactation inhibits fertility. Babies were more likely to survive weaning off mother's milk. New ways-of-living, and intermarriage with Northern San, led to a population boom among Khoe people in northern Botswana. The Showa, the Deti, and other 'black Bushmen' around the Makgadikgadi pans (and Victoria Falls) grew tall on cow's milk and continued to herd cattle and sheep.

On the other hand, the Khoe-speaking Buga or so-called river Bushmen of the Okavango remained fishing people without livestock. (They believed that a cave in the Tsodilo hills was the womb from whence they came.) The ancestors of G/ui and G//ana hunter-gatherers in the central Kalahari also adopted Khoe language without adopting livestock culture.

The archaeologist Karim Sadr has argued that *acculturation* between groups of people, rather than *migration* by large numbers of people, explains how Khoe language, pot-making, and Kenya-Capsian livestock were spread southwards. Genetic evidence shows that Khoe-speaking people from the Orange River southwards were basically of Southern San ancestry. But there were at least a few male migrants from the north, as Southern San people carry some Nilotic/Cushitic as well as Khoe male genes.

The earliest making of pottery and movement of sheep can be traced southwards down the Atlantic coast. Just south of the Orange River, at Spoegrivier, thin-walled and well-fired pottery bowls have been dated about 2.4 kya. Sheep bones have been excavated, and dated a few hundred years later, at Spoegrivier, at Die Kelders near Cape Town, and in Blombos cave on the south coast. The Kasteelberg and Witklip sites north of Cape Town show that 'hunters-with-sheep' were well established by CE 200. Relatively few cattle bones of that time have been found.

The main settlement of Southern Khoe keeping cattle, for maybe 1,000 years, was in the Orange-Vaal basin. These Southern Khoe – also known as Einqua and Xiri – made thin-walled and well-fired pottery jugs that were distinct from the pottery bowls of hunters-with-sheep. The crude pots of 'Smithfield ware', made by hunters-with-sheep in the Seacow valley between about CE 400 and 1100, were made from thick slabs of wet clay, lightly fired in pits. Most were flat-bottomed cooking bowls. They were suitable for people living a nomadic life – easily made, easily abandoned.

ROCK ART: PAINTING & ENGRAVING

According to pioneer archaeologist John Desmond Clark, rock art in Southern Africa is 'generally of such a high order' that it must have been made by 'consummate artists, whose mastery of line and skill with colour place this among the most vital and most pleasing the world has ever seen.' But rock art is very difficult to date, as pigment colours fade, particularly under rain and sun.

The oldest and most widespread form of rock art was 'cupules' – cup-shaped holes engraved out of the rock. Cupules in South India and Australia have been dated almost 50 kya. In Southern Africa, there are hundreds or thousands of cupules in rock walls in the Tsodilo hills that remain undated. Cupules on horizontal surfaces could have been used for grinding ochre or seeds. On vertical walls, cupules have no obvious purpose, though freshly-cut quartz or granite cupules can twinkle like stars in firelight or moonlight.

The earliest dated rock painting is at Apollo XI cave in Namibia, preserved under a rock fall. The painted slab of a wildcat with human legs has been dated around 26 kya, but it is in a style unknown elsewhere. Scientific dating of paint and engraving is technically very difficult, and rock art is usually dated by its association with other materials. Thus, some rock engravings at Tsodilo have fish-bone patterns that are also etched on animal bones dated 8.4 kya–7 kya. The earliest dated rock painting south of the Orange River is dated around 3.6 kya in Steenboksfontein cave, at Lambert's Bay on the Atlantic coast near Cape Town.

Without dated chronology, scholars have differed widely on classification and interpretation of rock art. The 'art history' approach concentrates on naturalistic representations of wildlife as the products of individual artists. An 'ethnic' approach is to see the art as graffiti expressing possession of the land and its wildlife by groups of people. 'Symbolic' interpretations seek deeper meanings, with visible features standing in for ideas known, unknown, or unknowable. 'Shamanistic' interpretations see the art as products of trance-dancing or drugged fantasy. All these approaches are useful.

Rock engravings were etched with stone or bone tools. Rock paintings were made either by finger-painting or with some kind of soft stick or brush. A rock painter shot dead in Lesotho during the nineteenth century CE was found to be wearing a belt with pods for different colour pigments. Finger-painted red and white circles, half-circles, and parallel lines, found on rock faces from Angola across to Mozambique and northwards up Lake Tanganyika, have been interpreted as Twa art. Other geometric art has been attributed to Khoe people. Some finger-painted white dots and lines in caves are relatively recent, made by young boys at secret circumcision camps on the rocks, and also on their own bodies. The rock art tradition continues up until today with graffiti written or sprayed on brick walls in industrial cities.

Finely drawn engravings of rhinos and other wild animals on rocks in the Orange-Vaal area, including Kimberley, have been attributed to the Southern Khoe. They have much in common in design with beautiful naturalistic rock paintings by Southern San artists in the southern Cape and around the Drakensberg and Lesotho.

Much rock art is associated with rain magic and the rain snake – a long tubular black cloud moving through the sky spitting lightning from its mouth, with rain-legs trailing behind. Also associated with rain and good times is the noble eland. It is the largest antelope, grazing alone rather than in herds. Evidence of religious belief in a spirit world, inside the rocks and waters, may be seen in symbolic figures denoting ghostly creatures and in 'entopic' images produced inside the eyes during trance. (Close your eyes, particularly during a migraine, and you will see something like the grids and zigzags found in some rock paintings.)

Has all development and change necessarily been 'progress' – i.e. for the better? The counter-argument is that change has only been necessary when and where there has been failure. Social and economic structures last as long as they meet people's needs. Changes come about because of environmental crisis, human intervention, or sheer chance and misadventure.

FURTHER STUDY

BIBLIOGRAPHY

Blundell, Geoffrey (2005), *Fragile Heritage: A Rock Art Field Guide*. Johannesburg: Witwatersrand University Press.

Blundell, Geoffrey, ed. (2006), *Origins: The Story of the Emergence of Humans and Humanity in Africa*. Cape Town: Double Storey Books for Origins Centre Johannesburg & London: Global.

Bonner, Philip, Himla Soodyall &c., eds. (2007), *A Search for Origins: Science, History and South Africa's 'Cradle of Humankind'*. Johannesburg: Wits University Press.

Campbell, Alec C. & David Coulson (2001), *African Rock Art*. New York: Harry N. Abrams.

Deacon, Hilary. J. & Janette Deacon (1999), *Human Beginnings in South Africa: Uncovering the Secrets of the Stone Age*. Cape Town & Johannesburg: David Philip.

Ehret, Christopher (2001), *An African Classical Age: Eastern and Southern Africa in World History, 100 B.C. to A.D. 400*. Oxford: James Currey, & Charlottesville, VA: University of Virginia Press.

Garlake, Peter Storr (1995), *The Hunter's Vision: The Prehistoric Art of Zimbabwe*. London: British Museum Press.

Mitchell, Peter (2002), *The Archaeology of Southern Africa*. Cambridge & New York: Cambridge University Press.

Parkington, John (2002), *The Mantis, the Eland and the Hunter: Follow the San*. Cape Town: Credo Communications for Krakadouw Trust/Living Landscape Project.

Smith, Ben W. & Geoffrey Blundell (2018), *Rock Art in Sub Saharan Africa: The Art of the Other World of Hunters and Gatherers*. Johannesburg: Wits University Press.

Soodyall, Himla, ed. (2006), *The Prehistory of Africa: Tracing the Lineage of Modern Man*. Johannesburg & Cape Town: Jonathan Ball Publishers.

VIDEOGRAPHY

DVDs and Downloads:

The Great Dance: A Hunter's Story (Earthrise Productions, 2000. 90 minutes): filmmakers Craig Foster & Damon Foster record hunting with bows and spears in the Kalahari, without dogs or guns.

The Human Family Tree (National Geographic Genographic Project, 2009. 90 mins): geneticist Spencer Wells tracks the DNA of two hundred New Yorkers back to Africa.

The Incredible Human Journey (BBC, 2009. 5 × 60 minutes): palaeontologist Alice Roberts follows Modern Human origins from East Africa up to the maritime crossing to Australia.

The Search for Adam (National Geographic Genographic Project, 2006. 52 mins): geneticist Spencer Wells tracing Modern Humans back to East Africa, visits the (semi-Khoe-San) Hadza and Sandawe.

2 Early & Middle Iron Age to c.1300

The early centuries of the Common Era (CE) saw a gradual revolution of life-styles in Southern Africa. People still hunted wildlife and gathered wild roots and berries. Many Later Stone Age people also began to herd livestock. Khoe-speaking people spread their language together with knowledge of livestock. The Early Iron Age began when people made and used metal tools, and cereal crops were planted and harvested. Bantu-speaking peoples spread their languages together with the knowledge of crop farming and the use of metals.

Later Stone Age settlement continued in the southern Cape winter-rainfall zone, and in the arid area of the summer-rainfall zone south-west of the 500 mm isohyet (line) of annual rainfall – the arid Kalahari, Namib, and Karoo. Early Iron Age settlement developed north of the 500 mm isohyet, where there were sufficient rains for annual planting and harvesting during the Indian Ocean monsoons that came between about November and February.

When farmers expanded into the territory of herders and hunter-gatherers, the latter were either incorporated by marriage or servitude or were obliged to go elsewhere. Relations between Bantu-speaking farmers with Khoe herders and even San hunter-gatherers were relatively harmonious, so long as only small numbers of farmers occupied only the best cultivable soils or areas around iron deposits.

This chapter raises questions about cultural change and population movement. How much can such changes be explained by (a) the inventions of local people; (b) the coming of migrants with new ideas to replace or to teach local people; and (c) the learning of new ideas from others without much migration being involved?

BANTU ORIGINS IN WEST AFRICA C.2250 BCE

Bantu words combine a root (such as -ntu in Zulu, meaning 'person') with a prefix (such as ba- in Sotho, for the plural). Today between 300 and 500 Bantu languages cover one-third of the African continent. All Bantu languages can be traced back to one ancestor language spoken in West Africa that was part of the Niger-Congo (or Niger-Kordofanian) language family. The original Bantu people were Later Stone Age crop farmers in northern Cameroon. They used stone tools for cultivating food crops originating both from their Nilo-Saharan neighbours in the Sahel and from their Niger-Congo neighbours in the tropical forests of West Africa.

The domestication of previously wild food crops began at least 8,000 BCE and continued until at least 3,000 BCE. In the 'food cradle' of the Sahel and eastern Sahara, Nilo-Saharan people domesticated sorghum (African corn), pearl-millet (*Pennisetum*), cotton (*Gossypium herbaceum*), water-melons, types of beans (*Voandzeia subterraneana*) and peas (*Vigna unguiculata*), bottle-gourds, and possibly a type of yam. In the 'food cradle' of the tropical forests, Niger-Congo people domesticated red-skinned swamp-rice (*Oryza glaberrima*), black-eyed peas, coco-yams, palm-oil, the raffia-palm (for cloth), and the kola nut.

The original LSA Bantu farmers grew this variety of crops in a 'mosaic' of different types of environment – savannah woodlands and grasslands, tropical forests, and mountain valleys. They herded and milked goats that had been adopted from their Nilo-Saharan neighbours – originally domesticated in the Atlas Mountains north of the Sahara. They also made a distinctive type of clay pottery. (Pottery in the eastern Sahara dates from about 10,000 BCE.)

The population grew rapidly in northern Cameroon and was followed by migration of Bantu farmers to the south and east. The possible date and trigger that set off these migrations has been discovered in the genes of Bantu farmers who remained in northern Cameroon. Geneticists have found a surprising number of male (Y-chromosome) genes of Afro-Asiatic people from central Arabia among the descendants of the original Bantu – dating from about 2,250 BCE. This is also about the same date as smelting of copper began in the Sahel. This suggests that invaders with copper-tipped weapons, squeezed out of Arabia by desiccation and desertification, helped to push many LSA Bantu agriculturalists out of their homeland.

These early Bantu migrants opened up new farmlands in woodland clearings, by slash-and-burn agriculture (swidden or *citemene* cultivation) – growing crops on fertile wood-ash and moving on to virgin territory when fertility declined. Over the course of the next millennium, early Western and early Eastern Bantu farmers adopted Iron Age technology – which would have given them more effective iron knives for slashing and iron hoes for cultivation.

Early Western Bantu farmers appear to have learned iron making in the area of Nigeria, where iron smelting dates from possibly 500 BCE. These Early Iron Age farmers, with their goats and maybe thin-tailed sheep, migrated southwards near the Atlantic coast towards the mouth of the Congo River.

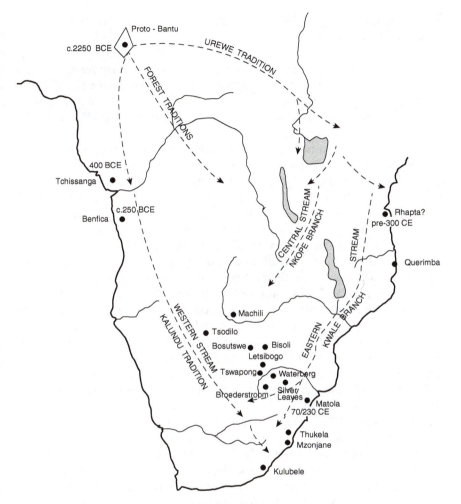

Map 2.1   Early Iron Age: Spread of Pottery Traditions

Iron objects have been found at Tchissanga East, on the lower Congo River, dated sometime after 400 BCE.

Meanwhile, Eastern Bantu farmers ventured eastwards along the savannah as far as Lake Victoria-Nyanza. They settled on the south side of the lake with Nilo-Saharan people, who had been making iron weapons and tools since 950–750 BCE. (This was long before the Iron Age reached Ancient Egypt from Anatolia or Eastern Turkey.)

EARLY IRON AGE PEOPLE OF THE WESTERN STREAM C.250 BCE–CE 700

Archaeologists identify a distinctive pottery style among early Western Bantu famers that is called the Western Stream type (or sometimes the Kalundu Tradition of the Early Iron Age). Western Stream pottery is dated from around 250 BCE at Benfica near Luanda in Angola, and at Madingo-Kayes on the lower Congo maybe a century later.

Western Stream Bantu farmers crossed the plateaux of Angola southwards into Western Zambia. Their pottery has been found at Situmpa on the upper Zambezi and at nearby Machili Forest Station – though their radiocarbon dates as early as 300 BCE (obtained in the 1950s) need re-evaluation. Western Stream farmers were the first Early Iron Age people in the Tsodilo hills, at Divuyu, between 550 CE and 750 CE. They worked small quantities of iron, copper, and ivory, as well as drying salt from saline marshes. Living off sheep and goats, wildlife meat, and fish from the Okavango, they were also importing marine shell-beads from their relatives on the Atlantic Ocean.

A larger site in the Tsodilo hills, Nqoma, dated 660–1090, shows cultivation of millet and sorghum, herding of more cattle than sheep or goats, greater use of iron and copper tools and ornaments, and trading in glass beads from the Indian Ocean as well as Atlantic shell beads. Nqoma was a centre of transcontinental trade, strongly linked to the upper Zambezi. There were also Northern San hunter-gatherers living at Tsodilo, making and using stone tools.

The Western Stream even further southwards can be seen on each side of the Limpopo valley in the dating of iron-smelting furnaces in the Waterberg hills (about CE 135) and Tswapong hills (CE 180). In East Griqualand, just south of Lesotho, Western Stream pottery is dated from about CE 360. In the Thukela valley and the coast of KwaZulu-Natal, the Msuluzi type of Western Stream pottery was widespread by 650. People there cultivated sorghum and millet on riverside alluvial soils, and herded sheep – and small numbers of cattle.

The southward extension of the Western Stream along the Indian Ocean coast reached its limit around about 800, in the Ciskei area where the summer-rainfall zone gives way to the winter-rainfall zone. Sorghum and millet needed warm nights for germination and semi-continuous rainfall for plant growth. The Msuluzi type of Western Stream pottery has been found at sites such as Coffee Bay, Kulubele on the Great Kei River, and Canasta Place outside East London.

Meanwhile, in the Limpopo valley the so-called Happy Rest culture of Western Stream pottery (named after a site dated CE 500–750) developed among Early Iron Age farmers in the Waterberg and Tswapong Hills who combined with local Khoe herders making Bambata pottery. Happy Rest people farmed sorghum and millet. They had fewer cattle than sheep and sometimes grazed them down the valley as far as what is now the Mozambique border. Khoe herders on the south-western Zimbabwe plateau were incorporated into farming communities making the Bisoli type of Western Stream pottery (650–1000).

EARLY IRON AGE PEOPLE IN EAST AFRICA

The interaction between Eastern Bantu and Nilotic/Cushitic peoples around Lake Victoria-Nyanza can be seen in iron and agricultural technology, genetics and language, in traditions of cattle-keeping, and also in architecture. While Western Bantu people made rectangular houses with four walls, Eastern Bantu people adopted Nilotic/Cushitic conical-roofed round houses.

Over the course of hundreds of years there was a build-up of Eastern Bantu mixed-farmer population among Nilotic/Cushitic herders, from Lake Victoria-Nyanza to the southern end of Lake Tanganyika. This was about the limit of the twice-yearly rainy seasons of the East African climate, before sorghum and millet had to adapt to the once-yearly rains of the summer-rainfall zone in southern Africa.

Archaeologists have identified two Streams of Early Iron Age pottery (sometimes called the Urewe Tradition) spreading out of the southern Lake Tanganyika area. An Eastern Stream (also known as the Kwale Branch of the Urewe Tradition) went eastwards to the Indian Ocean coast around Cape Delgado on the Tanzania-Mozambique border. A Central Stream (also known as the Nkope Branch of the Urewe Tradition) took longer to move directly south, through tsetse-fly country, from Lake Tanganyika down the Luangwa valley towards the Zambezi and Limpopo Rivers.

EASTERN STREAM EARLY IRON AGE PEOPLE

While some Eastern Stream people – ancestors of the Swahili – spread along the Tanzania coast, others went along the Mozambique coast until they reached Matola, just outside Maputo in Delagoa Bay. The site at Matola has been dated CE 70 or CE 230, depending on which researcher you accept. Inland on the Drakensberg escarpment in South Africa, the site called Silver Leaves is dated between CE 250 and 430.

The Mzonjani type of Eastern Stream pottery on the KwaZulu-Natal coast north of Durban, dated between CE 410 and 750, began with small numbers of people slashing and burning the thin forest on sand dunes, to grow crops within a few kilometres of the ocean – moving on after a few years when the fertility of fields was exhausted. Later sites, when Mzonjani sites moved inland to Swaziland and beyond, contain the remains of finger millet, pearl millet, sorghum, cowpeas, and ground beans on better soils – where haematite and specularite deposits were also exploited for iron ore.

West of Pretoria, the Early Iron Age site at Broederstroom, dated CE 450–750, shows a mixture of Eastern Stream (Mzonjani) culture and Western Stream (Happy Rest) culture. Thatched houses were dome-shaped like Khoe houses. Remains of many iron and copper rings and beads show that Broederstroom was a centre for metal-working. Seashells show trade with the Indian Ocean coast. Ostrich eggshell beads and stone tools suggest close contact with local Khoe or San people. Sheep and goat bones greatly outnumber cattle bones, in the ratio of 42:1, which suggests that people did not have great wealth in cattle or rarely killed and ate them. But they did use cow-dung mixed with clay in house floors. There is relatively little evidence of crop cultivation.

With the exception of copper mines at Phalaborwa, which flourished between 750 and 900, Eastern Stream sites largely disappear in South Africa by 750. Its people were absorbed into Western Stream communities.

CENTRAL STREAM EARLY IRON AGE PEOPLE

The Nkope type of Central Stream pottery in southern Malawi was closely related to Ziwa pottery on the northern Zimbabwe plateau, dated about CE 300–550. Ziwa people and local Bambata people made what is known as Gokomere pottery (dated 550–750). Gokomere pottery has been found at the base of the hill at Great Zimbabwe. It appears to have been Gokomere people who developed the first chiefdoms south of the Zambezi, with the power of chiefs based on wealth in cattle and sheep and on control of trade with the coast.

After Central Stream people came into contact with Western Stream people, Gokomere pottery developed into Zhizo pottery (750–1050). The Zhizo culture (including Taukome) stretched from Great Zimbabwe through Bulawayo into Botswana. It was a network of trading chiefdoms, with village capitals based on hilltops. The chiefdoms were connected with the Indian Ocean, exporting mainly ivory and importing glass beads. Trade routes extended inland to the Shashe-Limpopo confluence, as far south as Lydenburg, and as far west as the Makgadikgadi saltpans – at the Zhizo site on Bosutswe hill near Orapa.

Larger villages on hilltops, with housing around the big chief's livestock kraal, were circled by the smaller villages of headmen and by even smaller settlements on crop fields. An example of a smaller Zhizo village is Letsibogo on the Motloutse river (dated 775–890). Cattle and sheep, penned on hilltops to preserve them from night-time predators, were taken downhill to watercourses at dawn or dusk – and left dung many metres deep on their hilltop kraals for later archaeologists to find.

KHOE-SAN HISTORY DURING THE EARLY IRON AGE

The histories of Khoe and San people are so tied up with each other that it is often best to refer to them together as Khoe-San or Khoisan.

Northern San had networks of *xharo* exchange, exchanging goods over hundreds of kilometres, that could become the beginnings of wider trade. Some Northern San hunter-gatherers – notably the Ju (Zhu//kwansi) and !Kung – withdrew north of Tsodilo from contact with Khoe herders. Other Northern San hunter-gatherers (Nharo in the west, G/ui, G//ana, and Kua in the centre, and Hietshware in the east) accepted Khoe dominance and became Khoe-speakers.

Southern San hunters-with-sheep, notably the ≠Khomani and the Tuu or/Xam, retained their San language. Those living in the Karoo between the Orange River and the Cape escarpment mountains also, as we have seen in the previous chapter, made thin-walled Smithfield bowl pottery. It is open to debate whether, in the coastal zone around the Cape of Good Hope, makers of thin-walled spouted clay jugs between about CE 400 and 850 were Southern San hunters-with-sheep or pioneer Southern Khoe cattle herders.

Among the Northern Khoe, the Buga or 'river Bushmen' of the Okavango and Chobe marshes kept to their fishing way-of-life, while the ancestors of Shoa and Deti cattle-herders on the Nata and Boteti rivers continued to make clay jugs with 'lugs' (ear-shaped handles for hanging on twine from a branch) for almost 1,000 years after CE 700. The Kwadi group of Northern Khoe herders retreated west to the Kunene river near the Atlantic coast.

The Southern Khoe of the Orange-Vaal Basin (Einqua or Xiri, Nama etc.) had a mixture of Khoe and San origins. Hunter-gatherers might be incorporated into herder societies looking after sheep and cattle, in return for milk and meat. They were thus converted to Khoe language and culture but with a low social status. The Dama or Berg-Dama group of Southern Khoe, who had significant Nilotic/Cushitic ancestry, opened up copper mining in the mountains of Namibia. They maintained Later Stone Age technology, and used blast-pipes (tuwers or *tuyères*) made of stone instead of clay for smelting.

The histories of Khoe-San people became ever more entangled with Bantu-speaking people. We can see overlaps between them in genetics, language, and culture. Many Bantu-speakers in Southern Africa carry L-0d and L-0k genes from maternal Khoe-San ancestry, and most carry an immunoglobin gene (Gm 1, 13, 17) from Khoe-San ancestry. Conversely, many Khoe-San carry the Y-gene M2 of paternal ancestry brought from West Africa by Bantu-speakers. In the central Kalahari, both Bantu-speaking Khalagari cattle-herders and Khoe-speaking G/ui hunter-gatherers share exactly the same maternal gene (L-0d1c).

Bantu languages have adopted Khoe-San vocabulary as well as click-consonants. All Bantu-speakers south of the Limpopo adopted Khoe words – originally Cushitic/Nilotic – for sheep and cattle: *mvu* and *nkomo* in Nguni languages and *nku* and *kgomo* in Sotho-Tswana languages. Nguni languages (Zulu, Xhosa, Swazi, Ndebele, etc.) took three click-consonants from Khoe-San: the clicks written as C (/ in Khoe, sucking the tongue behind top teeth), Q (! in Khoe, plucking the tongue off the roof of the palate), and X (≠ in Khoe, clicking the sides of the tongue inside the cheeks).

Common Khoe-San and Bantu culture in Southern Africa can be seen in similar Khoe/Nguni traditional architecture (grass-mat covered, stick-framed dome-houses), and in the similar folklore, music, and dance of Sotho-Tswana and Khoe-San peoples. The *Hlonipa* speech pattern of Khoe wives, with ultimate Nilo-Sudanic origins, was adopted among Nguni wives and South Sotho wives. *Hlonipa* speech identifies the wife with her husband and his clan by avoiding utterance of their proper names. Rhymes and synonyms for the names are used instead – analogous with Cockney or Australian 'rhyming slang'.

Khoe herders grazed large herds of cattle and fat-tailed sheep, while Bantu mixed-farmers initially had goats and thin-tailed sheep. An old Khoe-San name for Bantu-speaking people was *biri-kwa*, meaning 'goat people'. The earliest domesticated hunting dogs, the yellow or black *Canis africanus*, built for speed with a body like a greyhound, also appeared about this time, though we do not know how they were introduced from the north.

Over the centuries, Bantu-speaking farmers incorporated Khoe herders and their cattle, rather than the other way around. How and why remains to be better explained. It is true that the farmers held the secrets of iron-making. Probably much more important in the long run, their crop harvests increased food supplies and accelerated population growth. Cultivation tied them to the land, resulting in more settled and more complex societies – with layers of patriarchal authority ranging from family heads up to clan or village chiefs.

The marriages of Khoe women who became Bantu-speaking wives might be sealed by the transfer of cattle to the wife's family. San women more likely became servant-concubines than 'wives-with-cattle'. Many San hunter-gatherers retreated into lands left alone by farmers and herders – dry deserts, marshlands, and mountain ranges. They had meeting places where goods were traded with herders or farmers. Their distinctive art in caves and rock shelters suggests that San people were expressing a renewed sense of identity as hunters – proudly distinct from their herder and farmer neighbours.

There was a general growth of trade and contact between peoples towards the end of the Early Iron Age. The rock paintings that portray violent conflict between hunters on the one hand, and herders and farmers on the other hand, were most likely made during the Later Iron Age rather than the Early Iron Age.

THE MEDIEVAL WARM EPOCH C.900–1300

The period of cultural and social transformation from Early to Later Iron Age is sometimes called the Middle Iron Age. This more or less coincided with what is called the Medieval Warm Epoch of world climate history – though it included at least one short cold period, and the Cape coastline remained more or less constant like it is today.

From about 900 we see the rise of chiefdoms based on the accumulation – and redistribution to loyal followers – of wealth in cattle and in imported trade goods such as woven cloth, cowrie-shells, and glass beads. As cattle herds increased in size, there was greater wealth to be controlled and possessed by groups and individuals. There was also rising demand for export of ivory and copper to ships on the Indian Ocean coast.

We begin to see chiefdoms laid out on what archaeologist Tom Huffman calls the Central Cattle Pattern of settlement. The houses of wives and children were clustered around the husband's cattle kraal. Subordinate households clustered around the household and great kraal of the clan chief. Bigger herds of cattle meant that rich men could acquire more wives by payment of *lobola* (*bogadi*) cattle to their wives' fathers. More wives meant more sons who would break away as adults or would dispute inheritance and succession among themselves.

In KwaZulu-Natal, the farming cultures of the Western, Eastern and Central Streams combined to produce the Ndonondwane (750–950) pottery culture and then the Ntshekane culture (950–1050) – within 80 kilometres of the coast, from southern Mozambique and Swaziland in the north to as far south as the Transkei. A site near Durban, called KwaGandaganda (after the engine noise of the archaeologists' yellow mechanical digger), was a large village with the remains of iron-smelting, iron and copper beads, and cattle as well as sheep. Meanwhile, the nearby Thukela valley was depopulated probably because of overgrazing and over-cultivation and maybe because of tsetsefly infestation.

In the Limpopo valley, the Happy Rest culture grew into the Diamant culture (750–1000) in the Waterberg and Tswapong hills and into the Malapati culture between Musina and the Mozambique border. Their villages overlapped with those of the Zhizo (Central Stream) people from the north. At a prominent hill called Baratani ('the lovers'), near Lobatse in Botswana, a Romeo-and-Juliet story is told about two young lovers from warring villages (Diamant and Zhizo?) who were last seen running hand-in-hand up the hill to disappear in the sky. The Diamant site at Baratani is dated 850–1000.

The Doornkop culture is famous for its Lydenburg heads, dated 750–1000, in the foothills of the northern Drakensberg mountain ridge near Lydenburg. These terracotta clay pots in the shape of young women's heads appear to have been deliberately smashed at the end of an initiation school celebrating the graduation of girls into womanhood. Art historians see the Lydenburg heads as the forbears of art at Great Zimbabwe, but such naturalistic sculptures have rarely been found south of the Limpopo.

INDIAN OCEAN TRADE BEFORE C.945

Pottery made in India, dated around 500 BCE, has been found in caves at Mafia island on the Tanzania coast. There was a trade boom across the Indian Ocean from about 200 BCE to about CE 300. Trade with India was opened up by Pharaoh Ptolemy V of Egypt, and it continued into the period of Roman rule in Egypt. Much of what we know about this period comes from a shipping guide to the Indian Ocean, published in Latin around CE 156 and titled *Periplus Maris Erythraei* ('The Periplus of the Erythrean Sea').

Persian ships travelled from the Hadramaut (Yemen) coast of Arabia to what they called the Zanj coast ('Azania' in Latin and Greek). Zanj was the Persian name for black people. It was Persians who founded a port they called Rhapta, probably around the Rufiji delta on the Tanzania coast. The *Periplus* tells us that 'a great quantity of ivory' was taken from Rhapta – also rhino horn, high-quality tortoiseshell, coconut oil, and exotic animal furs such as those of leopard. Ivory from East African elephants was valued in India, as it was less brittle for carving than smaller tusks from Indian elephants. High-value luxury goods – for rich Indians in the east and Romans or Greeks in the west – were exchanged on the coast for iron lances and hatchets, daggers, awls, and items made of glass such as beads. But Rhapta declined and disappeared after CE 300, and Persian traders turned instead to Adulis on the coast of Ethiopia for their elephant ivory.

Ships sailed around the Indian Ocean, near the coastline, from as far as Indonesia. Up to 50 tons, these *mitepe* ships, with woven raffia sails, were made of bundles of reeds and wooden planks sewn together. Demand for African ivory, hippo teeth, and rhino horn in India and China remained strong. There was constant demand in India for ivory carved into brides' wedding bangles. African chiefs were paid in glass beads from about 300 BCE until CE 1200. So-called Indo-Pacific Trade Wind glass beads, including inferior ones with bubbles in the glass, were manufactured in India, Sri Lanka (Ceylon), Vietnam, and Thailand – later on being mass manufactured in China. Archaeologists also find glass beads manufactured at al-Fustat (Old Cairo) in Egypt between 640 and 1168.

Sailors from North Borneo came direct across the ocean in sailing canoes with outrigger floats, like those of their Polynesian relatives who ventured across the Pacific. Some of them settled in the Comoros islands, the northern tip of previously uninhabited Madagascar, and probably the Querimba islands of northern Mozambique. They were the first Malagasy. They brought with them banana trees – as well as chickens and domestic pigs previously unknown in Africa. They contributed wooden xylophones and zithers to the music of Africans – who were already playing wooden drums and the metal-tongued *mbira* ('thumb-piano').

Bananas may have been grown in Africa as early as 500 BCE, but did not become the staple crop in Uganda until after CE 400. Other foodstuffs brought from Asia to be planted in Africa were coconut palms, Indus valley sorghum, South-East Asian rice, sweet-reed (sugar-cane), chickens, and domestic pigs ultimately from New Guinea.

With the coming of Islam out of Arabia in the seventh and eighth centuries, the Indian Ocean turned into a thriving international 'common market'. Muslim Arab and Persian dhows made the long voyage further south to the new port of Sofala, near Beira in central Mozambique. Dhows with lateen (triangular) sails found the winds difficult in the Mozambique-Madagascar channel and could take six months to one year to return home.

Some Arab and Persian traders settled on the Zanj coast, intermarrying with local Swahili people. In the year 740 they were joined by Shia-Muslim refugees under a leader named Zaide, fleeing Sunni-Muslim rule in the Hadramaut (Yemen). Their descendants (often carrying 'Cohen haplotype' genes) eventually moved far south as craft-workers – known as Vashambadzi on the Zimbabwe plateau and as Lemba in the Limpopo valley.

Zanj people were kidnapped to be sold as slaves across the Indian Ocean. The story is told of an Arabian prince from Oman who tricked Zanj children into slavery by offering them dates to eat. By 724, Zanj slaves in Asia included pearl-divers, prized in China for holding their breath for long periods, and musicians in the royal courts of the Buddhist kingdom of Srivijaya in Sumatra.

The largest number of Zanj slaves laboured on the sugar-cane fields around Basra on the Tigris-Euphrates delta of Iraq. In the year 871, Zanj slaves who had become Shia Muslims staged a great revolt against their Sunni masters and sacked the city of Basra. This gave Zanj slaves a ferocious reputation, such that the slave trade from East Africa declined.

Malagasy people living on the coast of East Africa, disparagingly called Waq-Waq by the Arabs (imitating their alien tongue), were defeated and expelled by the Muslims in 945. They retreated to Madagascar where they could continue with their 'pagan' customs, such as eating pork. Malagasy people remaining in the Comoros converted to Islam, exporting cowrie shells and soapstone bowls to the Zanj coast. Cowrie seashells lay in great heaps on the beaches of Indian Ocean islands, and they became valued currency on the African mainland. Larger and more rare conus shells, worn on a neck cord, became symbols of chiefly or royal power.

In the year 969 the Fatimid rulers of Egypt made gold currency their standard measure of value. Demand for gold greatly increased in the world economy. The gold mines of South India suffered when mines reached down to the water table. Muslim traders looked for new gold supplies across the Sahara in West Africa and to the costal ports of the Zanj coast and the Sofala coast to the south.

Prevailing winds and currents prevented Arab dhows from venturing further south than Inhambane Bay. The most southerly port on the Sofala coast was Chibuene, an important archaeological site near the Bazaruto archipelago. Chibuene began trading inland across the plains to the Shashe-Limpopo Basin in the eighth and ninth centuries. The finding here of Indian glass beads, and fragments of Persian glazed pottery, shows that such imports were being exchanged for elephant or hippo ivory and for iron or copper bars. The growth of gold exports in the tenth century gave the coastline of Mozambique the name Sofala-al-tibr, the shoal of the golden sand.

IVORY, IRON, & COPPER TRADE C.790–1020

The Shashe-Limpopo Basin (where Zimbabwe, Botswana, and South Africa today meet) became important because of its proximity to supplies of ivory, gold, and other minerals. Great herds of elephants roamed the Limpopo valley, and hippos inhabited the rivers and pools. The Shashe river contained alluvial gold nuggets in its sands and gravels, which had been washed down from gold reefs on its headwaters. In the Shashe-Limpopo Basin, we see the growth of important Middle Iron Age chiefdoms into states or small kingdoms, controlling trade and political authority in central villages or towns.

The Zhizo culture village at Schroda, on the Limpopo near its confluence with the Shashe, is dated about 790–1020. Schroda housed up to 500 people and great herds of cattle and sheep. Archaeologists have uncovered the remains of ivory bangle manufacture and the casting of iron and copper beads. There is also evidence of adolescent initiation schools within the village: small clay figurines of giraffes, birds, cattle, and human genitals. Schroda and other Zhizo sites contain 'snapped cane' glass beads (more usually cut from a glass cane), opaque dark blue or yellow beads, and a few green beads.

Iron from Africa was prized among sword-smiths in Asia, because it was strong but malleable – and could be continuously folded and re-hammered, to make the finest thin but strong sword blades. It was a mild form of steel, alloyed with up to 2 per cent carbon. Iron came to the port of Chibuene from the Tswapong and Waterberg hills on either side of the Limpopo valley. At Moeng and Makodu in the Tswapong hills, at least 300 iron-smelting furnaces have been counted – evidence from a Diamant culture community dated 650–1350. Raw iron ore was found in sand and pebbles ('bog-iron') or was mined in the form of red haematite, black specularite, and yellow limonite. Primary smelters, made of puddled clay, were two-metre-tall natural-draught chimney furnaces, used for a number of times at temperatures up to 1200 degrees centigrade. Secondary smelters were squat little bowls, aerated by the forced-draught of tuwers (blow-pipes) and bellows, and broken apart after use. Smelters were seen as female objects giving birth to iron ore, but they were tended by men only.

No less than 500 Iron Age copper mines have been located around the Shashe-Limpopo Basin. The oldest known copper mining, at Phalaborwa, is dated about 770, with later copper mining by Malapati culture people (750–1000) around Musina. The mines were probably opened with the skills of miners from the Katanga copperbelt north of Zambia, where people of the Sanga and Chondwe cultures (Western Stream) had opened up extensive mines from about CE 400 onwards. Sanga and Chondwe people had spread as far as Chonoyi on the Zimbabwe plateau by 800. Rock was cracked open and broken by applications of fire and water, and the copper ore vein was then hacked out with picks. Trenches many metres long, hacked through solid rock, were so narrow that they must have been mined by adolescents or slim young women.

GOLD TRADE & THE MAPUNGUBWE KINGDOM C.950–1300

Rulers originating from the Doornkop (Lydenburg heads) culture, attracted by the wealth of trade with the Sofala coast, seized control of the Shashe-Limpopo Basin around 950. They were joined by other Western Stream people from the south and set themselves up with a capital on a rise above the flood-plain, at a place called Bambadyanalo – more familiarly known to archaeologists as K2. A state was formed by clustering together subordinate chiefdoms under a ruling chief and his clan. Commoners were taught loyalty to the new state by initiation in youth as members of age-cohorts.

The K2 state took tribute in ivory and cattle, received gold nuggets panned from the Shashe river, and smelted gold for export. Tribute cattle and trade goods were accumulated by the rulers or re-distributed to loyal chiefs and sub-chiefs. The large size of the central cattle and sheep kraal, next to the king's courtyard, reflected the wealth and power of the rulers. Subordinate chiefs had smaller kraals and courtyards. Senior men were assembled and justice was dispensed in courtyards next to livestock kraals.

There is much evidence of trade and production at K2, including ivory shavings and chunky green cylinder beads (so-called 'garden-rollers') – locally manufactured after boiling down imported glass. Spindle-wheels are evidence of weaving from local cotton – often interleaved with imported Indian cotton – from about 1100. Gold was melted and beaten into sheets. Stone walls date from about 1150. Almost 100 human skeletons (with mixed Khoe-Bantu characteristics) were excavated from the site in the 1930s. Khoe-speakers of the former Bambata culture and Bantu-speakers of the Zhizo culture were incorporated in the state. There is also evidence of Khoe-San hunter-gatherers maintaining a separate lifestyle a mere two kilometres from K2.

Farming on the floodplain grew more productive as the climate grew warmer and wetter. This may explain why the Zhizo people of Schroda moved their village closer to the floodplain in about 1020, to a hill known to archaeologists as Little Muck. The sluggish Shashe spilled its wide banks in wet years, leaving behind nuggets of gold when it subsided, while floods backed up in the Limpopo river's narrow gorge upstream of Little Muck.

Prospecting for gold moved up the Shashe to the gold-bearing quartz around the Tati river and on the western Zimbabwe plateau. Using techniques borrowed from copper mining, extensive mining of gold in shafts and trenches, pits and 'scoops', was begun by people of the Kutama or Leopard's Kopje tradition (Mambo culture 1000–1250 and Woolandale culture 1250–1400). Kutama settlements near gold mines include Taba-zika-Mambo in Zimbabwe and Domboshaba in Botswana. (Glass beads at Kutama sites include cylinders with heated ends of many colours, as well as Indo-Pacific Trade Wind beads – red to opaque blue-green, green, yellow, light orange – plus a few Chinese beads and locally made green 'garden-roller' beads.)

Around the year 1200 – leaving K2 intact under their control – the rulers of K2 suddenly moved about a kilometre away to the hill of Mapungubwe, where the hilltop was already used for rain-making rituals. The state had become a kingdom in which royal power was linked to a sacred cult. The king with his royal wives lived in seclusion within stone-walled enclosures, on top of the steep-sided hill, accessible only by narrow passages that could be easily guarded. His noble (or bureaucrat) relatives at the bottom of the hill were royal mediators with the chiefs and sub-chiefs at K2. Traders no doubt went to the K2 courtyard, where exports were exchanged for imported goods that went – in due proportions – to royalty, nobility, chiefs and headmen, and commoner elders. We are beginning to see Huffman's Zimbabwe Pattern of settlement: society is segregated, with priestly kings hidden from their people, and noble (royal relative) households are distinct from commoner (former Zhizo) households.

Three royal burials, two male and one female, have been excavated on Mapungubwe hill. The graves included 12,000 gold beads and 26,000 glass beads, and pieces of Chinese celadon pottery of the Sung dynasty (961–1279). Most famous of all were wooden objects covered in gold leaf, including a small rhino sculpture and a short staff of office. As well as old al-Fustat beads from Egypt, the glass beads found at Mapungubwe (subsequently also at Great Zimbabwe) were opaque black, blue-green, and plum coloured Indo-Pacific Trade Wind beads and other lozenge-shaped beads.

By 1300 both K2 and Mapungubwe disappear off the archaeological map. Why? Wet and warm years could have resulted in floods washing away good soils and the advance of tsetse-infested woodlands out of the lower Limpopo valley, restricting cattle to hilltops during the daytime when the flies were active. Rats from Indian Ocean ships have also been found by archaeologists in granary remains far inland: did they carry plague as they did in Asia and Europe around this time? Most dramatic of all, though we do not know the date, was when a small earthquake made a large rock fall from Mapungubwe hill into the K2 courtyard. Such unforeseen disaster could have fatally undermined the religious power of a king and his nobles. The rulers fled south-westwards, where they built and survived in an isolated small, stonewalled palace at Lose near Mahalapye (1300–1420).

The underlying reason for Mapungubwe's collapse was the shift of gold production, and the rise of new rulers controlling trade on the central Zimbabwe plateau during the thirteenth century. Western Zimbabwe mines may also have been flooded by rising water tables. Also about this time, Arab and Swahili dhows began to sail from the sea, up the Save river to its confluence with the Runde or Lundi river (on the later Mozambique-Zimbabwe border) – where they were met by canoes and carriers on foot from the goldfields.

OTHER MIDDLE IRON AGE CHIEFDOMS C.1030–1450

Copper miners of the Malapati culture at Musina moved northwards from the Limpopo onto the central Zimbabwe plateau, to begin gold mining on the central Zimbabwe plateau around 1030. Their Gumanye culture (1030–1250), in the area of future Great Zimbabwe, took control of the trade routes that ran from Musina and the central Zimbabwe plateau to the Sofala coast north of the Bazaruto archipelago.

Meanwhile, Doornkop people around Lydenburg grew apart from their relatives who had seized the Shashe-Limpopo Basin around 950. Doornkop developed into distinctive Klingbeil (1000–1200) and Maguga cultures (1200–1450) that spread from Lydenburg south into Swaziland.

The Eiland tradition of pottery (1000–1300) is named after a salt manufacturing centre on a saline spring near Tzaneen in South Africa's Northern Province. It originated as an outgrowth of the Diamant culture and spread south-westwards over the related Baratani culture area, beyond Gaborone in Botswana. (The best-known sites around Gaborone are at Moritsane and the Broadhurst sewage ponds.) The historical importance of the Eiland tradition is that it continued to be the pottery style of Khalagari people until recently. The Khalagari language is now considered a dialect of Sotho-Tswana, but it shows evidence of having originated as a separate language with click-consonants.

Many Zhizo people remained under K2-Mapungubwe (950–1300) as commoners – some as sub-chiefs, rain-priests, and metalworkers. Other Zhizo people retreated west up the Motloutse river into formerly arid pastures improving during the Medieval Warm Epoch. They founded chiefdoms laid out on the Central Cattle Pattern clustered around the chief's livestock kraal and central courtyard. Around the year 1000 there was a virtual doubling of such sites in east-central Botswana. The former Zhizo culture developed into a new Toutswe culture by about 1050.

There were three large kraal-centred hilltop villages within the Toutswe culture – at Toutswe north of Palapye, Taukome north of Serowe, and Sung at Shoshong. Each large village was surrounded by smaller villages on isolated hilltops, which served as overnight refuges for livestock from predators on the plains – and as vantage points for spotting herds of wildlife such as elephants at a great distance. (These sites can be seen on aerial and satellite imagery as yellowish patches of *silicon-rich* grass, growing on top of up to six metres deep of vitrified cattle dung and sheep urine. The silicon sand within the dung was baked by fire after lightning struck the hilltops.)

In general, Toutswe culture sites have no evidence of Indian Ocean trade. There is, however, a notable exception on a small site on open plains at Kgaswe (dated 1020–1210), between Palapye and Serowe. Archaeologists here found a deliberately buried clay pot containing hundreds of Indian Ocean glass beads. Was this the hoard of an itinerant trader, or of a thief?

Further inland than the Toutswe culture, between Serowe and Orapa, Bosutswe hill is the longest known continually occupied site in southern Africa. It lasted 1000 years, from about 700 until 1700. It was originally a Zhizo-type settlement but remained isolated from K2 and Mapungubwe. It was strategically located for trade between the western Zimbabwe plateau and the Makgadikgadi salt-pans, the Boteti river, and the Okavango marshes – all major sources of ivory and wildlife furs. Bosutswe manufactured Later Stone Age tools, employing Khoe-San craft-workers to manufacture Later Stone Age tools for exchange with hunter-gatherers for ivory and wildlife furs. Ostrich eggshells were manufactured into beads or used as water-containers.

Production of larger-sized ostrich eggshell beads increased at sites all over southern Africa from about 1100. Larger eggshell beads used in trade were often unpolished and crudely cut – such as are still today sold to tourists. Greater skill was needed to cut and polish fragile small beads, and they were more comfortable to wear on the skin, while larger beads were sewn onto leather clothing. Indian Ocean traders were no doubt pleased when Africans valued little beads made of glass over bigger ones.

NGUNI & SOTHO-TSWANA ROYAL ANCESTRY

Nguni and Sotho-Tswana royalty or traditional rulers have strong traditions of ultimate ancestors in the far north. The Nguni claim origins 'among the reeds' – lakes, marshlands, and river deltas. The Koni, probably the most ancient Nguni group, explicitly specify their ancestors having travelled along the coast from 'somewhere near the Zambezi'. Venda rulers, of partial Sotho-Tswana descent, similarly record their ultimate ancestors coming from 'many rivers which all join and in one body rush to the sea' – adding that 'not far to the east were long pools of silent water', and that it was a warm climate 'with many forests and fruit, of bananas growing in many groves and of tubers and pea-nuts in great variety.' Taken together, these traditions most likely all refer to East Africa and to crossing the Zambezi delta and other marshlands near the coast.

We will see in the following chapter that the royal ancestors of the Nguni are associated with the Blackburn pottery tradition of the Later Iron Age, while the royal ancestors of the Sotho-Tswana are associated with the Moloko pottery tradition. Both of these traditions appear to have originated in the Eastern Stream of the Early Iron Age north of the Zambezi. But how and why these ancestors came south remains unexplained.

The answer may lie in other population movements during the disruption of the Indian Ocean trade boom from the tenth century onwards. Around 945, Muslim incomers expelled Malagasy settlers from the vicinity of Cape Delgado (Tanzania-Mozambique border) and the Querimba islands.

This suggests that the ancestors of Nguni and Sotho-Tswana royal clans once lived in the coastal region of northern and central Mozambique. But they came under pressure from inland people coming to the coast from the interior during the Indian Ocean trade boom from the tenth century onwards – Chewa-speaking people (Zimba) north of the Zambezi and Shona-speaking people south of the Zambezi were attracted from the interior towards the coast by the gold trade. This could have been the incentive for the migration south of the Limpopo valley by Nguni royal ancestors. Sotho-Tswana royal ancestors appear to have followed later – maybe pushed out by the migrations of Nyanga Shona-speaking people from the Zimbabwe plateau, pulled in by new goldfields in the Inyanga mountains on the Zimbabwe-Mozambique frontier.

KHOE-SAN TRANSFORMATION C.850–1250

> In ancient times the whole nation of Hottentots [Einqua or Xiri] lived close together along the banks of the Vaal and Orange Rivers...But in consequence of a great quarrel which arose amongst them, they divided. One part of the nation [Khoekhoe] went in the direction of Cape Town and settled there; another part [Nama] went down the Orange River, and...the greatest and richest tribe, remained [in the Vaal-Orange area].

This oral tradition of Southern Khoe origins was related in 1858 by an old man named !Korab to a German missionary, Rev. Carl Wuras. The Southern Khoe of the Orange-Vaal Basin are remembered as Einqua or Xiri people. 'Einqua' means people of the Great River (*Groot Rivier*). Until the later nineteenth century the Vaal and Lower Orange were seen as one river, with the Upper Orange a mere tributary. Floods today sometimes reveal Einqua Khoe skeletons buried on river banks. A skeleton with iron earrings found at Koffiefontein on the Riet River has been dated around 1060.

Archaeologists have studied ruins of Einqua semi-circular stone kraals stone on the Riet tributary of the Vaal, south of Kimberley. The kraals protected cattle from predators and enabled herders to keep lambs separate from their mothers to ensure regular milk supply. What is called Type-R stone walling is mostly dated thirteenth and fourteenth centuries, but maybe starting earlier. Southern Khoe pottery jugs had small (monkey-ear) lug-holes, unlike Northern Khoe jugs that had large (elephant-ear) lug-holes.

We do not know the date of !Korab's 'great quarrel' among Einqua in the Orange-Vaal Basin – after which Nama and Khoekhoe dispersals to the west and south occurred. Two dates are suggested by changes in pottery types further south. People at the Cape of Good Hope around the year 850 began to make and use undecorated, thick-bodied clay jugs. By around 1250 they were making and using decorated or incised, thick-bodied clay jugs – of the same type later seen in illustrations when European ships began calling at the Cape of Good Hope.

The undecorated jugs at the Cape from 850 onwards were most likely introduced by Nama migrants, who had migrated west down the Great River and south along the Atlantic coast. Similar jugs with similar dating have been found in Namibia at Hungarob, Kaiseb, and Geduld. Meanwhile, we may suggest that ancestors of the Khoekhoe, who made decorated jugs, moved south in two stages. During the first stage, roughly around 850, they migrated to settle in the Camdeboo ('green hippo pools') south of the Sneeubergen ('frost mountains') escarpment mountain chain – approximately where the Eastern and Western Cape provinces today meet. During the second stage, Khoekhoe arrived and took charge around the Cape of Good Hope by the year 1250.

Traditions of the Khoekhoe at the Cape, collected in the seventeenth century, tell us that they once recognized the Inqua chiefdom in the Camdeboo-Karoo as their senior ancestor. Khoekhoe identity emerged under one senior Inqua chief on the pastures of the Camdeboo. Calling themselves Khoekhoe (i.e. Khoe-Khoe) reinforced their identity as *khoen*, meaning people. The word 'San' meaning 'others' rather than 'us' was applied to Southern San hunter-gatherer neighbours. San people were often seen by Khoekhoe as being thieves of livestock grazing on good pastures. The relative prosperity of Khoekhoe herders, secured from hunger by ready milk and meat, attracted some San hunters to attach themselves as servants. Conversely, drought and starvation might impel Khoekhoe herders to join San in hunting and gathering of wild plant foods.

Khoekhoe clans spread out to new pastures, both east and west, as people and livestock increased in numbers. The Cochoqua clan settled around the Cape of Good Hope, their chief living in the mountains near later Stellenbosch. Cochoqua family groups took their herds seasonally around pastures – carrying their lightweight mat-houses on the backs of oxen. They came together for ceremonies such as the exchange of brides and the initiation (without circumcision) of boys. During dances, a rotating circle of men, blowing on reed flutes and facing outwards, was surrounded by an inward-facing counter-rotating circle of rhythmically clapping women. All-night dances might culminate in dramas imitating wild animals, before sheep were slaughtered at dawn by hungry men howling like wolves.

The Khoekhoe of the Cape continued to trade and interact with their relatives in the north. Copper beads and bangles from Dama copper-smiths came via the Nama in the north-west. Iron goods came from the Sotho-Tswana they called Birikwa (goat-herders) on the Great River. Old !Korab told Rev. Wuras that Einqua people first heard from their southern relatives about long-haired men landing from the sea – an obvious reference to European sailors.

During this Middle Iron Age period there was much cultural overlap and exchange between Khoe-San and Bantu-speakers. In the Seacow valley after about 1100, hunters-with-sheep began to decorate their Smithfield bowls with lines of impressed dots like Bantu decorated pottery. Bantu-speakers employed Khoe-San to hunt, with spears and arrows, for the animal furs prized in Indian Ocean markets. Khoe-San people were even employed, as we have seen at Bosutswe, in 'factory' groups making stone tools or weapons and ostrich eggshell beads for exchange. Rather than use stone or bone, Khoe-San began to purchase iron for the tips and blades on their weapons. Communities combined to drive wildlife into avenues of brush walling erected on rough stone foundations, funnelling to a great *hopo* pit where the animals could be speared. Khoe-San individuals were prized as medical practitioners and diviners because they were the original 'owners' of the land.

There was also influence inland from coastal Swahili and Arabs, Malagasy and Persians. Persian and Arabic words like *-fundi-* (knowledgeable), *mali* or *madi* (silver), and *ndalama* (gold) have been widely accepted by the Bantu languages of Southern Africa. The four tablets made of wood or bone (representing old man, old woman, young man, and young woman), which became widespread among African diviners, are the same as in Yemen. Wooden xylophones that originated among the Malagasy became the basis of Venda music and dance. Khoe music shared singing by call-and-response with

Sotho-Tswana, as well as instruments like the metal-stringed musical bow and the *mbira* thumb-piano. By contrast, Nguni music and dance were more martial and male-oriented, with heavy drumming by hands rather than a stick.

The expansion and migration of human populations, and the adoption of new foodstuffs, had long-term effects on health. It is thought that tuberculosis originated with the grinding of wild wheat and barley in Egypt from maybe 16,000 BCE. *Bilharzias schistosomiasis* travelled south from the Upper Nile, spread by human urination – though the type of mollusc that hosts bilharzia has also been dated as early as 36,000 BCE in Southern Africa.

Malaria (*Plasmodium falciparum*) is believed to have 'jumped species', from wild animals in the Congo Basin into human blood as its 'reservoir of infection'. It began spreading as a human disease as long ago as 55,500 BCE. The *Trypanosomiasis* vector of Rhodesian sleeping-sickness carried by tsetse-flies on savannah grasslands, more fatal to humans than the Gambian variety found in West Africa, found its 'reservoir of infection' in the blood of wild vertebrates, particularly buffalo. It has been spread both by climate change and by bush encroachment following farmers' over-cultivation of soils.

People generally had longer lives in southern Africa, with its relatively dry and healthy climate, than in lower lying parts of Africa with wet tropical forest – where generations passed more quickly. Oral traditions and customs were kept alive over centuries by some men and women living into and beyond their seventies.

FURTHER STUDY

BIBLIOGRAPHY

See also books recommended in previous chapter.

Deacon, Hilary J. & Janette Deacon (1999), *Human Beginnings in South Africa: Uncovering the Secrets of the Stone Age*. Cape Town & Johannesburg: David Philip.

Ehret, Christopher (1982), *The Archaeological and Linguistic Reconstruction of African History*. Berkeley, CA: University of California Press.

Ehret, Christopher (2001), *An African Classical Age: Eastern and Southern Africa in World History, 1000 B.C. to 400 A.D.* Charlottesville, VA: University of Virginia Press.

Ehret, Christopher (2002), *The Civilizations of Africa: A History to 1800*. Charlottesville, VA: University of Virginia Press.

Hall, Martin (1987), *The Changing Past: Kings & Traders in Southern Africa, 200–1860*. London: James Currey.

Hall, Martin (2006), *Great Zimbabwe*. Cape Town: Oxford University Press.

Hammond-Tooke, David (1974), *The Bantu-Speaking Peoples of Southern Africa*. London: Routledge & Kegan Paul.

Huffman, Thomas Niel (2007), *Handbook to the Iron Age: The Archaeology of Pre-Colonial Farming Societies in Southern Africa*. Pietermaritzburg: University of KwaZulu-Natal Press.

Lane, Peter, Andrew Reid, & Alinah Segobye, eds. (1998), *Ditswa Mmung: The Archaeology of Botswana*. Gaborone: Pula Press for the Botswana Society.

Leslie, Mary & Tim Maggs, eds. (2000), *African Naissance: The Limpopo Valley 1000 Years Ago*. Claremont: South African Archaeological Society (Goodwin Series vol. 8).

Lewis-Williams, J. David (2011), *San Rock Art*. Auckland Park: Jacana Pocket Books.

Phillipson, David W. (1977), *The Later Prehistory of Eastern and Southern Africa*. London: Heinemann & New York: Africana Publishing.

Phillipson, David W. (2005), *African Archaeology*. Cambridge & New York: Cambridge University Press.

Smith, Andrew Brown (1992), *Pastoralism in Africa: Origins and Development Ecology*. London: C. Hurst.

Smith, Andrew Brown, ed. (1995), *Einiqualand: Studies of the Orange River Frontier*. Cape Town: University of Cape Town Press.

VIDEOGRAPHY

DVDs and downloads:

The Tree of Iron (Documentary Educational Resources, 1988. 57 mins): archaeologist Peter Schmidt documents ancient iron forging techniques near Lake Victoria-Nyanza.

Wonders of the African World (Wall to Wall for PBS, 1999. 6 × 57 mins): historian Henry Louis Gates travels to and comments on Mapungubwe etc.

Africa's Great Civilizations (Inkwell Films etc. for PBS, 2017. 6 × 57 mins): Henry Louis Gates's second voyage of discovery at Mapungubwe etc.

3 Later Iron Age Societies to c.1685

Later Iron Age 'industries' emerged by the time that the Medieval Warm Epoch had ended. Southern Africa was experiencing a cooler and drier climate from about 1350 until about 1640. There was then a warmer and wetter period from about 1640 to 1675. This coincided with the further growth of trade on the east and south coasts.

North of the Limpopo, the Early Shona linguistic group is represented in archaeology by Zimbabwe pottery traditions. Early Nguni and Early Sotho-Tswana linguistic groups south of the Limpopo are represented in archaeology by the Blackburn and Moloko pottery traditions. There were many overlapping dialects within and between each language group. (The standard dialects of each language taught in schools today usually date from the later nineteenth century.)

BLACKBURN POTTERY & NGUNI ORIGINS

The Blackburn pottery tradition is named after an archaeological site at Blackburn near Eshowe in northern KwaZulu-Natal, dated around 1160. (A nearby site at Mpambanyoni is dated even earlier, at 1025.) The most northerly Nguni descendants (the Koni) identify the first place of the ancestors – after coming from the far north – as having been around the copper mines of Phalaborwa in north-eastern Limpopo province. Nguni and related Tsonga ancestors then moved southwards – on either side of the Lebombo hill chain that marks the Mozambique border with South Africa. The Tsonga spread along the coast as far as Delagoa Bay, while Nguni penetrated further south.

Between about AD 1050 and 1500, the Blackburn pottery tradition in KwaZulu-Natal absorbed and replaced the previous Ntshekane (Western Stream) culture. Blackburn pottery is found on the Lowveld, including in shell middens on the seashore, before it spread up valleys into the Middleveld. Homesteads – of less than 40 houses – were built on valley ridges overlooking agricultural fields. During summer, cattle were sent upstream to cooler

Highveld 'sour' grazing, and during winter, downstream to warmer Lowveld 'sweet' pasture.

The Moor Park culture (about 1350–1750) developed out of the Blackburn tradition and spread first over KwaZulu-Natal. It is named after a site in the Middleveld near Estcourt. Moor Park culture spread southwest across the Mtamvuma river into the Eastern Cape province (Transkei), where it inter-acted with Khoekhoe herders and is known by archaeologists as Umgazana ware (1350–1700). (As we shall see below, around 1450 the Moor Park culture also spread through the Drakensberg escarpment to the Highveld.)

The Southern Nguni making Umgazana pottery were ancestors of people today identified as Xhosa speakers. West of the Kei river, the Gona (Gonaqua or Gqunu-khwebe) Khoekhoe intermarried with ancestral Xhosa and culti-vated cereal crops, but they kept Khoe language and loyalty to their Khoe ancestors. Other Khoekhoe communities resisted conversion to the language and culture of mixed-farmers.

Northern Nguni (Koni, Kekana, Swazi, Hlubi, Ndebele, Mphahlele, etc.) and neighbouring Sotho-Tswana in Limpopo/Mpumulanga/Swaziland have inter-related archaeology and oral traditions. Swazi and Hlubi traditions identify Dlamini and Langa as the names of their ancestral founders, who lived up to 29 generations before 1900 – i.e. possibly as far back as 1100. In KwaZulu-Natal and Transkei, the traditions of the Ntungwa clans (including the later Zulu core) claim direct descent from a founding ancestor named Malandela (not Mandela!) who lived 22 chiefly reigns before 1900. The Ntungwa regard themselves as 'pure' Nguni, while other Central Nguni, the so-called Lala and Mbo clans, are pre-Nguni in origin.

Through what 'magic' did small numbers of Early Nguni immigrants incor-porate pre-existing populations? It was evidently through male dominance. Nguni marriages were exogamous. Men had to find wives from outside their paternal clan. Men and women slept together but otherwise ate and lived separately. Women were responsible for making pots and things from clay, and they drank from pots made by women. Men were responsible for tending cat-tle, including milking. Men drank from baskets woven by men, and they were responsible for weaving grass-cloth or reed mats and thatching roofs.

Women became Nguni in culture by adopting their husband's language and by making pottery in the Blackburn tradition of their husband's clan. But women kept the Khoe tradition of using *hlonipha* rhyming language, avoiding mention of their husbands. Families continued to live in Khoe-type domed or igloo-shaped mat-houses – a framework of bent and tied sticks, covered by reed mats under a network of ropes. Nguni languages retained old Khoe or San words and click-consonants. Ideas of bodily health and medicine included

Map 3.1   Later Iron Age Archaeological Sites

semi-nudity and facial and body scarification, as well as ideas of personal pollution that required regular purgation – especially by vomiting.

MOLOKO POTTERY & SOTHO-TSWANA ORIGINS

The Moloko and Blackburn pottery traditions were closely related, as also are Sotho-Tswana and Nguni languages and cultures. Both Sotho-Tswana and Nguni held onto old East African beliefs – the taboo against eating fish and respect for cattle given a religious status as 'the god with the wet nose'.

The Moloko tradition appears to be dated from a couple of hundred years younger than the Blackburn. The earliest known evidence of the Moloko tradition is found around a site named Icon, dated between 1250 or 1300 and 1500 – in the Middleveld above Phalaborwa where the Nguni originated.

Out of the Icon culture, three new Moloko pottery cultures of mixed-farmers spread between about 1500 and 1700: (a) the Letsibogo culture – associated with early North Sotho people – covering the old Icon heartland in Limpopo and eastern Botswana; (b) the Olifantspoort culture – associated with early Tswana and South Sotho people – around the Limpopo headwaters in Gauteng and southern North-West province; and (c) the Madikwe culture – associated with southern Tswana people around the Marico headwaters in North-West province.

The archaeology and oral traditions of the North Sotho area are complex and sometimes contradictory. To the north, Icon/Letsibogo culture became mixed up with the cultures of southern Zimbabwe as well as with Eiland pottery making. To the west, Eiland tradition pottery continued to be made by Khalagari people in the eastern Kalahari, from 1300 until as late as 1900. There were also significant numbers of Khoe-San people hunting and herding in the Icon/Letisibogo area, possibly 'protected' by the tsetse-fly belt that expanded after wet years and contracted after drought.

The Olifantspoort culture, dated from 1500 in Gauteng, is associated with the Rolong clans of southern Tswana, whose traditions trace origins to an ancestor living as far back as 1300. That ancestor, a man named Morolong, lived at Mosega near Mafikeng. He had a son named Noto, meaning a blacksmith's hammer. The Rolong clan adopted iron (*tshipi*) as their emblem or 'totem'. The clan probably increased in cattle wealth and power by introducing iron and marrying among local Khoe herders.

The Madikwe culture, west of Gauteng and north of Mafikeng, is originally associated with the ancient Phofu clan (its emblem being *phofu* or eland) that was ancestral to the two other major groups of Tswana clans besides the Rolong – the Kwena clans and the Kgatla clans.

Phofu origins are traced a man named Masilo and his son Masilo, living before 1500 at a place named Rathateng at the confluence of the Marico river with the Limpopo. The house of Phofu later split in two, when Mohurutshe was rejected as its head – one tradition says that Mohurutshe was a woman. Most people followed a brother called Mokwena with a *kwena* (crocodile) emblem. Thereafter the Hurutshe chiefs descended from Mohurutshe retained ritual seniority by being offered the first fruits of the annual harvest by the chiefs of the many Kwena chiefs descended from Mokwena.

Meanwhile, Kgatla clans recognized Malope's son Mokgatla as their eponymous founder. He rejected the *phofu* and adopted the *kgabo* (blue monkey or 'flame of fire') as his emblem. Kgatla people spread eastwards in the Middleveld. Extensive mining of red iron ochre at Rhino Mine near Thabazimbi, dated 1485–1615, may have been by such ancestral Kgatla.

Clans of Rolong, Kwena, and Kgatla called each other 'Tswana' – the very word *tswana* meant coming from the same origin. Tswana incorporation of earlier people differed from that of the Nguni because marriages among Tswana rulers were endogamous – i.e. chiefs and headmen married their first cousins as 'great wives', thereby keeping big cattle herds 'in the family' while also marrying non-Tswana as junior wives – producing daughters whose marriages sealed alliances with subject (*motlhanka* or vassal) headmen who paid cattle as bride-wealth. The cattle were 'loaned' back to the subject headmen so long as they were loyal.

Tswana rulers brought non-Tswana subjects together as multi-cultural subordinate 'wards' within villages. While Nguni family homesteads were scattered across hills and dales, Tswana villages grew like flower petals around a stem, with their wards arranged around a large royal cattle kraal. Houses consisted of cylindrical clay walls topped by Khoe-style matted domes or by East African-type conical thatched roofs.

NGUNI INVASIONS ONTO THE HIGHVELD

Archaeologists trace the first incursion of Nguni-speaking people onto the Highveld of the eastern Free State around 1450. The Moor Park pottery culture – with people of Mbo rather than Ntungwa (original Nguni) stock – spread up the Buffalo valley over the Drakensberg escarpment to give rise to the Ntsua-na-tsatsi culture. (Ntsuanatstatsi hill near Vrede is today sliced through by the N3 Durban-Johannesburg expressway.)

The Ntsua-na-tstatsi culture (1450–1650) retained Moor Park-type pottery but otherwise saw the rise of a new people – called Fokeng – created by the interaction of Mbo-Nguni with Khoe or San and South Sotho people. (The name Fokeng was given them by the South Sotho, from the verb *ho foka* meaning to blow around like smoke.) Oral traditions claim that Fokeng origins lie in marshy reeds near Ntsua-na-tsatsi hill.

Fokeng people built stone-walled kraals to protect their cattle from the icy winds that blew across the Highveld grasslands in winter, as well as domed 'lion houses' of piled flat rocks – to shelter herdsmen from the night attacks of predators roaming on the open grasslands, as well as to keep them warm in winter. Since people of the Moor Park culture in upland KwaZulu-Natal and Khoe herders of the Orange-Vaal confluence made similar walls to those of the

Ntsua-na-tsatsi culture around the same time, it remains controversial as to who first built such stone walls.

The warmer climate around 1640–75 (with night temperatures above 15 degrees centigrade in the growing season) promoted sorghum (*mabele*) harvests on sunny grasslands and sweet grass for grazing cattle. This encouraged population movement and growth on the Middelveld and Highveld. (It is also possible that maize or American corn was temporarily cultivated in this period – but as an exotic or medicinal crop, not a regular food crop.)

Fokeng people from the Ntsua-na-tsatsi culture migrated north to the Madikwe culture area around the Marico-Limpopo confluence. The migrants adopted Tswana language but their cultural inheritance was so strong that – according to archaeologists – the Uitkomst pottery culture (1650–1820) that replaced the Madikwe was more Blackburn rather than Moloko in character. Tlokwa clans among the Tswana and South Sotho can be traced to the intermarriage of these Fokeng with Kgatla Tswana in the seventeenth century.

More Nguni speakers crossed the Drakensberg in the seventeenth century, this time across the Vaal into Mpumulanga province. These Nguni are known to historians as Transvaal-Ndebele, to distinguish them from Zimbabwe-Ndebele under Mzilikazi two centuries later. Transvaal-Ndebele immigrants of Central Nguni origin traced descent from a common ancestor named Musi. Other Transvaal-Ndebele of Northern Nguni (Hlubi-related) origin, who came up to a century later, traced their descent from a man called Langa.

Some Transvaal-Ndebele became miners and metalworkers for Tswana employers, but were also happy to use their spears in warfare. They appear to have earned the name Matebele, which became Ndebele in their own language – after they were engaged as mercenary fighters by a Hurutshe Tswana chief named Motebele in the mid-eighteenth century.

INDIAN OCEAN TRADE

Muslim Persian and Arab ships dominated trade on the Zanj and Sofala coasts until about 1500, when they were challenged by Christian Portuguese ships rounding the Cape of Good Hope into the Indian Ocean. The main port on the coast from the eleventh century onwards was Kilwa in Tanzania. Its sultan built a great mosque and issued his own gold currency. The Arab geographer Ibn Battuta, who visited the town in 1331–32, called it 'one of the most beautiful and well-constructed towns in the world.'

By 1300, small Arab or Swahili dhows were sailing up the Save (Sabi) river in central Mozambique to its confluence with the Runde (Lundi), where there was a small port known as Mambone. These dhows took gold from the Zimbabwe plateau down river to a bigger port on the Sofala coast for ocean-going dhows. Arab-Swahili merchants harvested crops and planted trees such as coconuts while they waited for annual winds to blow their dhows north to Kilwa.

Sofala's exports included iron and copper bars as well as gold. Most of its copper came from the Katanga copperbelt – where the Luba kingdom was also trading with the Kongo kingdom on the Atlantic coast. Katanga rocks with veins of green malachite copper were sliced open by fire and water and broken by axes and hammers to a depth of many metres – at least in one case, a cut 750 metres long and 7 metres wide. Katanga copper ingots were H-shaped or, later, X-shaped.

South of the Limpopo, copper mining was less extensive. Phalaborwa copper ingots were shaped like dried flowers with studded heads. Musina copper ingots looked like small top-hats studded with heavy nails. Other metals mined include tin known as 'white iron' at Rooiberg in the Waterberg hills. Tin was mixed with copper to make bronze, while brass (a copper and lead alloy) appears to have been imported and then reworked locally.

A Chinese world map of 1402 included the Zanj coast as K'un-lun Ts'eng-chi. Few Chinese ships, however, ventured into the ocean beyond Indonesia. In 1417–19 and 1421–22, Admiral Chengo Ho led naval expeditions as far as Malindi on the Kenya coast, taking back with him a giraffe as a present for his emperor. But Cheng Ho was subsequently dismissed from service by the emperor, and no more such voyages were permitted.

The great historian Ibn Khaldun, who died in 1406, was himself a Muslim North African and thought that Islamic world power had reached its peak and was now declining. But it was not to be China in Asia, but Portugal in Europe, that was to challenge Islamic control of the Indian Ocean.

GREAT ZIMBABWE & SHONA ORIGINS

The kingdom of Great Zimbabwe in south-central Zimbabwe dates from about 1300 among people of the Middle Iron Age Gumanye culture, which had become distinct from the local Early Iron Age Zhizo culture by 1000.

Great Zimbabwe stood at the head of the Runde (Lundi) river, dominating the trade route from interior gold mines to the Sofala coast. It may also have been the centre of a rainmaking priesthood. The area attracted people from the Luangwa pottery tradition of eastern Zambia and Malawi to share in its prosperity. The standard dialect of the Shona language, Karanga, appears to have originated in the ancestral language of southerners (Early Kalanga) modified by the Early Chewa language of these northerners.

From the north, the rulers of Great Zimbabwe adopted the 'bells of kings' from Luba and Lunda royalty in Katanga – copper double-gongs beaten by a royal courtier, with varying tones imitating spoken speech, which were used to announce a royal procession. From the south, Great Zimbabwe adopted Mapungubwe's priestly kingship and divisions of caste or class. The king and his royal wives lived in seclusion in a hilltop palace that was also a rainmaking and ancestral shrine, with magnificent stone walls straddled between great rocks. At the heart of the palace or temple on the hill, there were sculptures of eagles or other raptor birds, carved from soapstone. They may have represented ancestors who had since flown away.

Great Zimbabwe was surrounded by good soils for cultivation and excellent grazing for large numbers of cattle and lesser numbers of sheep and goats. The town grew rapidly in size, covering the valley below the hill with the housing of aristocrats and commoners. The courtyard (*dare*) beneath the hill was a place of assembly and probably also the market place for salt and beeswax, furs and skins, and cotton for spinning. Archaeologists have found evidence of coastal trade in glass beads and marine shells, locally produced chert-stone tools that were traded with hunters, and the remains of foreign ships' rats that plagued granaries inland.

By about 1350, we may even call Great Zimbabwe a city. Around that time an enormous circular wall was built on the plain, consisting of nearly a million stone blocks piled without mortar. This Great Enclosure could have been a new palace, if the king had left the hilltop to rainmakers. Alternatively, it was built to screen the housing of royal wives, enabling them to hold court over other women. Its conical tower, shaped like a granary, could have symbolized royal wealth and generosity. The tower was topped with crocodile patterning that symbolized older men, i.e. the king's ancestors looking on.

Beyond Great Zimbabwe there were 47 outlying *zimbabwe*'s or stone-walled hilltop palaces of regional rulers. Royal relatives and chiefs sent tribute to the capital in metals, skins, salt, livestock etc. and in return received a share of trade wealth (glass beads etc.) and the loan of royal cattle. Cattle exchanges sealed marriages and created political alliances. More wives meant more fields to feed court officials (councillors, guards, messengers) and to provide visitors with hospitality, adding to the prestige of rulers as patrons of their people.

In the north, at Ingombe Ilede on the Zambezi river 50 kilometres upstream from the Kafue, archaeologists have found the burials of rich local people – dated between 1300 and 1500. They were probably trading with Great Zimbabwe, but independent from it because their pottery is that of Kangila culture in southern Zambia. They wore clothing woven of bark cloth and local cotton, but also fine cotton cloth from India. They had copper and iron arm bangles, thousands of glass beads from overseas, some local gold beads, and gold foil. The chief wore a large conus seashell, with 'bells of kings' buried nearby. Craft-workers were buried with iron tools for making copper wire, as well as pieces of copper wire and X-shaped copper ingots.

In the far west, a remote site of the Great Zimbabwe culture at Kubu (Ga'nnyo) island in the Makgadikgadi salt pans has scores of flat stone cairns without burials beneath. It has been suggested that each one was made as a graduation exercise by boys' initiation schools. Similarly, the Great Enclosure at Great Zimbabwe may have given privacy to girls' initiation schools.

The *zimbabwe*'s of the Great Zimbabwe kingdom covered an area from Toranju collecting salt on the Makgadikgadi in the west, to Manekweni on the Sofala coast near the Bazaruto archipelago. Shona people migrated from the plateau to live among Chopi-speaking people on the coastal plains – giving rise to the Ndau dialect of Shona language. Swahili or Arab merchants came to Manekweni *zimbabwe* to buy gold and iron and copper brought overland from the Limpopo valley. South of the Limpopo, it is unclear how far Great Zimbabwe controlled or took tribute in iron and tin from the Tswapong and Waterberg hills and copper from Musina and Phalaborwa. But the *zimbabwe* at Thulamela (occupied between 1240 and 1700) – in South Africa where today's Kruger game park meets the Limpopo – was a gold-processing site under the control of Great Zimbabwe.

After Great Zimbabwe reached its peak of prosperity, it appears to have suffered from civil strife. The land around was becoming over-cultivated and over-grazed. The city was abandoned around 1450 (not earlier than 1405 and not later than 1465). Loss of resources in outlying areas is confirmed by the oral tradition that the city was abandoned because of a shortage of salt. The Save river was silting up with soil loosened by agriculture upstream, and much of the Sofala coast was being swamped with sand dunes by the sea. Gold mining was shifting to the north-eastern plateau, using new trade routes into the lower Zambezi valley. Arab and Swahili dhows discovered how to sail upriver through the coastal swamps of the Zambezi delta.

Two new states replaced Great Zimbabwe. In the north, the new Munhumutapa kingdom controlled gold mining and trade into the lower Zambezi valley. In the west, the new Khami state kingdom controlled not only salt supplies from the Makgadikgadi but also the Limpopo valley trade route through Manekweni to the Bazaruto archipelago.

Oral traditions complete the picture. The last ruler of Great Zimbabwe, King Mutota, fled north and died near the Zambezi – because he was 'an evil king who disregarded sacred precepts, and that is why Great Zimbabwe came to an end.' Thereafter, the site of Great Zimbabwe was occupied sporadically by minor chiefdoms. But the making of Great Zimbabwe pottery continued within the Munhumutapa kingdom at least until 1700.

PORTUGUESE INCURSIONS

In 1427, the Christian king of Ethiopia sent an appeal for help against Muslim invaders to the Christian king of Aragon in Spain. This opened the eyes of Spanish and Portuguese to ideas of reaching the riches of India by sailing around Africa and bypassing the Islamic Middle-East. The Portuguese started sailing southwards along the Atlantic coast, first importing gold and slaves from West Africa in 1441. By 1482 Portuguese ships had reached the Kongo kingdom at the mouth of the Congo river. Meanwhile the Spanish decided to sail to India and the East Indies (the islands of Indonesia) the other way around the world – not knowing that the Americas stood in the way, arriving in the West Indies (Caribbean islands) in 1492.

The captain of the first ship to round the southern end of Africa, Bartholomeu Dias in 1488, reached the mouth of the Keiskamma river (Ciskei). On the way back home he saw the Cape of Good Hope – Cabo da Boã Esperança – for the first time. (It also became known as Cabo Tormentosos, the Cape of Storms.) The first Portuguese man on the Sofala coast was an envoy or spy who went there via Egypt and returned that way in 1491. Meanwhile the Portuguese were already allied with the Kongo kingdom on the Atlantic coast, which sent envoys to Portugal in 1489–91.

Preparations were made for a Portuguese naval expedition to sail around Africa into the Indian Ocean. The expedition, under admiral Vasco da Gama, set out in 1497 and – guided by a Gujerati Indian pilot – sailed across the Indian Ocean from Malindi to India and returned home to Portugal in 1499. In 1503, a captain named Saldanha explored and reported back on the area around the Cape of Good Hope. For centuries thereafter the land around the Cape was known to Europeans as Saldania.

In 1505, Portuguese ships launched surprise artillery bombardments on Swahili ports, taking over the Sofala export trade in gold and ivory by receiving tribute from Kilwa. Many Kilwa Muslims fled to Malindi and the Comoros islands. This was seen as part of a Christian crusade against Muslims, revenging Muslim jihads against the Christian kingdoms of Ethiopia and the northern Sudan – where Christian Nubia was finally conquered in 1529.

The Portuguese king appointed a viceroy or governor named Almeida, to rule the Indian Ocean on his behalf. Almeida attacked Khoekhoe people in Saldania with musket fire after they refused to sell livestock. His men then stole cattle and kidnapped Khoekhoe women and children as slaves. Khoekhoe men successfully counter-attacked (with trained oxen answering to whistles) in the first recorded battle at the Cape of Good Hope – at the mouth of the Salt River on Table Bay, now an industrial area of Cape Town, on 1 March 1510. Almeida himself was killed. The Khoekhoe of the Cape reported to their relatives on the Great River that men with hair resembling a bush with long green fibres had come from the sea and had fought with them.

Thereafter, the Portuguese usually steered clear of the Cape of Good Hope, for fear of the Khoekhoe. Instead, the Portuguese opened up trade between Sofala and India. But Sofala traders refused to accept European glass beads[1], considering them oversized and inferior. Instead, the Portuguese had to acquire glass beads from India, bringing in Indian merchants from Portuguese Goa (founded in 1510 on the west coast of India). Portuguese ships also brought in blue-on-white Chinese porcelain, great quantities of cowries and other seashells, and faked porcelain reproductions (even with factory marks on the back) of the *ndoro* conch-shells prized by Shona chiefs. The gold mines on the Zimbabwe plateau were kept secret from the Portuguese, who failed to find them on a venture inland in 1514.

Meanwhile around the Congo river mouth on the West Coast, the Portuguese alliance with the Kongo kingdom turned sour. King Nzinga Mvemba (1506–43) had been converted to Christianity, taking the Christian name Afonso. His son Henrique went to Rome and was made a bishop by the Pope in 1518. But the Kongo kingdom was a military aristocracy ruling over tens of thousands of slaves captured in war. From 1514 onwards the Portuguese began to export Kongo slaves to work on sugar plantations on offshore islands such as Sao Thomé – from where some were shipped across the Atlantic to Portuguese Brazil.

After the death of Afonso in 1543, the Portuguese encouraged civil wars that increased the number of captives that they could buy as slaves.

From 1594 onwards, Portuguese slaving ships sailed out of Luanda port in the Ngola (Angola) kingdom of their allies – where slave exports topped 10,000 per year by 1612. This was the beginning of the Atlantic slave trade, which over the next three centuries was to take millions of Africans to the Americas, and on Sao Thomé was not to end until the twentieth century.

MUNHUMUTAPA & THE PORTUGUESE

The Munhumutapa kingdom was situated in the Dande area at the northern end of the Zimbabwe plateau, around the headwaters of the Mazowe river that ran down to Muslim seasonal trading posts (fairs or *feiras*) on the Zambezi at Tete and Sena. The kingdom combined Great Zimbabwe traditions – notably 'divine kingship' – with the local Musengezi culture. It was founded by a man called Nyatsimbe, given the praise-name Munhumutapa – usually translated as 'master pillager'.

In about 1490 the kingdom experienced a successful revolt by Changa, the keeper of the king's cattle herds on the plateau. Changa had the Arabic honorific title of Amir (conqueror), thus becoming known as Changamire – the title being perpetuated by his descendants. Munhumutapa Chikuyo (ruled 1494–1530) seized the kingship back from Changamire in 1494. Ruling until 1530, he maintained excellent relations with Muslim traders. Gold exports from the Sofala coast probably reached a peak of approximately 8,500 kilograms per year around 1500. The royal court rang with the sound of the 'bells of kings' as royals and aristocrats paraded, showing off their wealth by wrapping rich Indian cloth around themselves, so long that it dragged behind them on the ground.

In 1528, the Portuguese made direct contact with the Munhumutapa kingdom. Soon after the death of Munhumutapa Chikuyo in 1530, they seized the trading posts at Sena and Tete, and expelled Muslims from Quelimane and Delagoa Bay on the coast. In 1552, the Portuguese consolidated their hold on the coast by building a strong fort at Msambiji (Mozambique), a small island north of the mouths of the Zambezi. Out of this seed eventually grew the colony of Mozambique or Portuguese East Africa.

In 1560, a Portuguese Jesuit priest named Father da Silveira tried to convert Munhumutapa Nogomo (1560–89) to Catholic Christianity, in competition with Sunni Muslim mullahs. Silveira was murdered in 1561. The Portuguese response was furious vengeance. Their first attack on

Munhumutapa failed in 1565, and the Portuguese instead raided for slaves northwards from their posts at Sena and Tete.

These slaving raids started a chain reaction north of the Zambezi in 1571–88, with people attacking their neighbours around Lake Malawi. Marauding bandits remembered as 'Zimba' helped to supply ever greater numbers of slaves to the Portuguese. Meanwhile, on the West Coast in the Kongo kingdom and northern Angola, there was a similar response to Portuguese slave raiding. So called 'Jaga' marauders from the interior caused widespread chaos and enslavement in wars of 1571–90 and 1623.

The Munhumutapa kingdom was eventually beaten into submission by increasingly humiliating treaties with Portugal. In the treaty of 1578, Munhumutapa Nogomo allocated to the Portuguese territory around Tete and Sena on the Zambezi – land that was then divided into riverside estates called 'prazos', under Portuguese settlers called 'prazeros'. The second treaty of 1609 handed over gold and silver mines near the Zambezi, though the Portuguese still recognized the sovereignty of Munhumutapa Gatsi Rusere (ruled 1596–1627) by paying him annual tribute for these land and mine concessions. The third Portuguese-Munhumutapa treaty of 1629, conceded by Munhumutapa Mavura, freed Portuguese citizens from paying any tax or tribute. In effect, the concessions were now under Portuguese sovereignty. However, the gold mines of the Zimbabwe plateau were still kept secret from the Portuguese.

Portugal's wealth and world power declined in the middle of the seventeenth century, when French and Dutch and English ships entered the Indian Ocean around the Cape. Muslims also regained complete control of the Zanj coast north of Mozambique by 1698. Sofala gold exports declined, and Portuguese coastal forts fell into disrepair. Gold exports dropped from 7,650 kilograms in 1506 to 716 kilograms by 1591 – rising again to 1,488 kilograms in 1667, but dropping away thereafter to less than half that. Arab-Swahili dhows continued to trade periodically along the coast as far south as Delagoa Bay, as did Portuguese ships from their Mozambique island base that mainly served as a stop for ships on their way to Portuguese India (Goa).

The main export from Delagoa Bay was elephant ivory. The Ronga (southern Tsonga) kingdom of Nyaka (Inyaka) stretched from the bay to as far south as St Lucia Bay in KwaZulu-Natal, where – as it was reported in 1589 – there were great herds of elephants. Meanwhile the small Ronga chiefdom of Mfumo – located on the site of the future city of Maputo – became valued by the Portuguese as a supplier of slaves from upstream in the Nkomati marshes.

Prazeros, some of them Portuguese Indians from Goa, enjoyed close relations with local Chewa people, including the Maravi (Malawi) kingdom that had brought peace after the Zimba wars. The prazeros hunted and raided with private armies of Chikunda men, and they kept large numbers of women as workers and concubines. Over the generations many prazos were owned by powerful women of mixed ancestry known as the 'black donnas'.

KHAMI (BUTWA) KINGDOM

Some rulers from Great Zimbabwe migrated to the south-western Zimbabwe plateau, where they were known to local people as Torwa – meaning 'foreigners'. They founded a small but complex stone-walled city on a hill at Khami (Kame) near later Bulawayo, which has been dated around 1450 to exactly 1685. The king or Mambo and his priests sacrificed black bulls on Khami hill as rain offerings. Instead of soapstone birds as at Great Zimbabwe, each succeeding Mambo appears to have been symbolized by a great spear planted inside a sacred hut.

The common people of the Khami kingdom were from the Woolandale culture of the Leopard's Kopje pottery tradition. Like Woolandale buildings, Khami stone walls and adobe (clay) buildings were built on stone platforms. The Torwa rulers adopted the language of the local people, but called it Kalanga – the local pronunciation of Karanga.

Khami lay on one of the headwaters of the Gwayi (Gwaai) river that runs north to the Zambezi below the Victoria Falls. The kingdom extended over an area called Butwa (meaning 'south'), extending from the Makgadikgadi salt pans in the west to the *zimbabwe* at Manekweni near the coast. The city itself probably had a population up to 13,000 living within or near its stone walls. There is evidence of cotton spinning and weaving and of the carving of soapstone, wood, bone and ivory. As well as salt and gold trade, the Khami kingdom controlled ivory hunting in the Limpopo valley and copper and tin trade from further south. (This regional economic strength probably predated, and indeed helped to cause, the demise of the Great Zimbabwe kingdom.)

The Khami kingdom was split by civil war in 1644, when a younger brother of the Mambo invited Portuguese gunmen from the Zambezi to attack the capital. (You can still see at Khami ruins a large Maltese cross on the ground, made by a Dominican priest to celebrate the victory.) Khami was burned down, and the capital moved eastwards – to what are now called the Regina ruins (near Fort Rixon). Civil war continued over the next 40 years under warlords based in villages on small hilltops, with beautiful stone walling, such as Naletale and Danongombe (later called Dhlo-Dhlo).

The most powerful warlord was Mengwe (the 'teeth' of the Mambo), who controlled great herds of cattle and salt trade from the Makgadikgadi. The last Mambo of the Torwa dynasty, named Tshibundule, attempted to rule the kingdom from Danongombe. Here he was attacked and killed by Rozvi raiders who came from the east in 1685.

EARLY VENDA & COASTAL CHIEFDOMS

The Soutpansberg (Saltpan hills) mountain chain stood out above the Lowveld south of the Limpopo valley. It was occupied by a mixture of Icon (North Sotho) and other pottery culture people called Ngona (mushroom totem) by Shona-speaking people who settled among them. The Tavashena pottery culture in the Soutpansberg (1450–1600) can be attributed to the influx of Shona refugees from the wars on the Zimbabwe plateau. The mountains became part of the Khami kingdom in Butwa under so-called Singo rulers with distinctive Letaba-type pottery (1600–1840). After the collapse of the Khami kingdom, and the death of its conqueror Mambo Dombo, the Singo of Soutpansberg were to assert their independence as the new kingdom of Venda from the 1690s onwards.

Other Shona refugees from the civil wars around 1450 invaded the territory of Tonga-Chopi people on the coast around Inhambane Bay. They then set up the kingdom of Wutonga. The new Shona rulers introduced the worship of the Supreme Being, Mudzimu, and at some time stopped the local practice of male circumcision. The Wutonga kingdom lasted for about two centuries, until the reign of its last king called Gwambe.

Portuguese ships, with a combination of different types of sails, were able to sail more freely up and down the Sofala coast than Muslim dhows with a single lateen (triangular) sail. The first Portuguese ship to trade at Delagoa Bay, in the 1540s, was captained by a man named Lourenço Marques. The Portuguese then sent a ship once a year from Mozambique island to trade with Wutonga and Delagoa Bay, buying ivory, beeswax, copper, and slaves. The Wutonga kingdom was united under its greatest ruler, Gwambe, but broke up thereafter into a number of smaller so-called Gwambe-Tonga chiefdoms.

Archaeological evidence suggests that there were adolescent initiation schools (with circumcision for boys, not girls) from eleventh-century Bambadyanalo-Mapungubwe through Great Zimbabwe to the seventeenth-century Khami kingdom. When the Shona-speaking Singo settled in the Soutpansberg in the late seventeenth century, and complained that Ngona people already living there did not know how to 'make fire', we may assume that they meant practising male circumcision. But there is no evidence of initiation schools in the Munhumutapa kingdom, or at Khami after the Rozvi conquest of 1685. There is also no tradition among Shona-speaking people today of there ever having been boys' circumcision. By contrast, south of the Limpopo both Nguni and Sotho-Tswana continued to practise circumcision.

The answer to this conundrum may lie in the rise and fall of Muslim influence in the interior between the eleventh and seventeenth centuries, as male circumcision was an Islamic practice. Early Muslim trade was concentrated in the middle Limpopo valley, and there was a strong connection with Yemen in south-east Arabia. We have seen in the previous chapter that Shia-Muslim refugees fled Yemen as early as the eighth century to settle as far south as the Limpopo valley. These Lemba craft-workers and Vashambadze hawkers married with local women, but their descendants maintained old customs and beliefs – including prayers and shaving their heads every new moon. How far did they influence other people living around them? Were they responsible for the taboo among North Sotho against eating pork? Did they teach male circumcision to people south of the Limpopo already holding adolescent initiation schools?

The impact of early 'globalization' through overseas trade was greatest in the Limpopo valley and then on the Zimbabwe plateau. Trade goods, notably glass beads or cowrie sea-shell currency and cotton cloth, enhanced the visible wealth and prestige of rulers, but economic–political power was stored and redistributed in cattle wealth – attracting subjects by a kind of 'cattle feudalism'. Subjects paid tribute to their chief in grain and milk and meat for communal feasts and in metals from mines and the hides and horns from wildlife that were sold in long-distance trade.

Chiefly dynasties might rise and fall because of the vagaries of familial disputes over *lobola* (bride-price), or because climate change opened up and reduced pasturelands. But the ultimate wealth and strength of a chiefdom lay in the number of people it ruled. Age-regiments composed of former graduates of adolescent initiation schools were organized for communal labour, hunting, and minor warfare to capture women and children as well as cattle from rivals.

More complex and hierarchical societies reinforced gender roles. Wives were obliged to adopt the pottery styles, bead patterns, and customs of their husband's ethnic group. Though widows and women past childbearing might exercise some political power, most women were restricted to the spheres of domesticity, collection of wild foods, and hoe-agriculture.

FURTHER STUDY

BIBLIOGRAPHY

See also books recommended in previous chapters.

Beach, David N. (1980), *The Shona and Zimbabwe, 900–1850: An Outline of Shona History*. London: Heinemann.

Beach, David N. (1993), *The Shona and Their Neighbours*. Oxford: Blackwell.

Beach, David N. (1994), *A Zimbabwean Past: Shona Dynastic Histories and Oral Traditions*. Gweru: Mambo Press.

Birmingham, David. (1981), *Central Africa to 1870: Zambezia, Zaire, and the South Atlantic: Chapters from the Cambridge History of Central Africa*. Cambridge: Cambridge University Press.

Birmingham, David (1983), *History of Central Africa*. Harlow, London: Longman.

Boxer, Charles Ralph (1977), *The Portuguese Seaborne Empire, 1415–1825*. London: Hutchinson.

Garlake, Peter Storr (1973), *Great Zimbabwe*. London: Thames & Hudson.

Garlake, Peter Storr (1983), *Early Zimbabwe: From the Matopos to Inyanga*. Gweru: Mambo Press.

Huffman, Thomas Niel (1996), *Snakes and Crocodiles: Power and Symbolism in Ancient Zimbabwe*. Johannesburg: Wits University Press.

Huffman, Thomas Niel (2005), *Mapungubwe: Ancient African Civilisation on the Limpopo*. Johannesburg: Wits University Press.

Huffman, Thomas Niel (2007), *Handbook to the Iron Age: The Archaeology of Pre-Colonial Farming Societies in Southern Africa*. Scottsville, KwaZulu-Natal: University of KwaZulu-Natal Press.

Mudenge, Stan I.G. (1986), *Christian Education at the Mutapa Court: A Portuguese Strategy to Influence Events in the Empire of Munhumutapa*. Harare: Zimbabwe Publishing House.

Mudenge, Stan I.G. (1988), *The Political History of Munhumutapa c.1400 to 1902*. Harare: Zimbabwe Publishing House.

Pikirayi, Innocent (2001), *The Zimbabwe Culture: Origins and Decline of Southern Zambezian States*. Walnut Creek, CA: AltaMira Press.

Ravan-Hart, Rowland (1967), *Before Van Riebeeck: Callers at South Africa from 1488 to 1652*. Cape Town: Struik.

Swanepoel, Natalie, Amanda Esterhuysen & Philip Bonner, eds. (2008), *Five Hundred Years Rediscovered: Southern African Precedents and Prospects*. Johannesburg: Wits University Press.

VIDEOGRAPHY

DVDs and downloads:

Africa's Great Civilizations (Inkwell Films etc. for PBS, 2017. 6 × 57 mins): Henry Louis Gates's second voyage of discovery at Great Zimbabwe etc.

Africa: A Voyage of Discovery (Channel 4, 1984. 6 × 57 mins): the late historian Basil Davidson travels to and comments on Great Zimbabwe etc.

4 Early States & European Colonies c.1600–c.1790

Warm wet years between about 1640 and 1675 gave way to cold dry conditions – the so-called Little Ice Age – until about 1750. The return of warmer wetter years from about 1750 saw the rise of Nguni and Tswana dynasties, with lineage roots that can be traced back to the earlier warm period. These dynasties competed with other chiefdoms to capture burgeoning populations of cattle and people into new chiefdoms or small states.

Increased cattle population from about 1750 can be attributed to the opening up of sweet grazing on the Highveld (grasslands above 1,000 metres from sea-level). At the same time, wetter years in the Lowveld (woodlands below 1,000 metres) increased bush encroachment and tsetse-fly infestation and pushed cattle and people onto the Middleveld. The Middleveld became intensively cultivated and was the main locality of human population growth and political development.

Harvest sizes and food supplies were effectively doubled in the mid-eighteenth century by a new second-harvest crop. Maize (*milho* or *mielies*) from South America was an exotic type of corn that benefitted from good rains and warm nights for germination. It was planted and reaped at different times in the agricultural season to the drought-resistant indigenous crops of sorghum or millet. The grains of multi-colour maize were regarded as medicinal charms to be strung round the neck as beads.

Maize was imported by the Portuguese to the Mozambique coast, while cassava was imported to the Angola coast. Sailors reported that maize was already being grown alongside melons, beans, gourds, medicinal roots, and two types of millet among the Xhosa on the Xhora River of the Transkei coast in 1635. But maize disappeared from cultivation (except around Delagoa Bay) during the mid-seventeenth century drought years of the Little Ice Age. When maize cultivation was revived in the mid-eighteenth century, some people resisted, perhaps on the grounds that it was bad medicine that caused drought. But it was now reddish rather than multi-coloured maize (not white or yellow as in the twentieth century), and its cultivation spread rapidly among Middleveld and even Highveld cultivators.

Historical sources become richer in detail in the seventeenth and eighteenth centuries. This explains the increasing proliferation of new ethnic and personal names in the next two chapters. Oral traditions record the names and deeds of chiefly ancestors. Such traditions legitimize the ruling lineages of successful states, and they also record the names of age-regiments that were essential to state structures. Written records found in overseas archives become increasingly important. Large numbers of ships from the Atlantic nations of Europe began to stop in Africa on their way to and from Asia.

FRENCH, ENGLISH, DUTCH & DANISH SHIPS CALL AT THE CAPE

Other Atlantic European nations began to challenge the world sea power of the Spanish and Portuguese during the 1580–1640 period, when Portugal came under the rule of Spain. Ships from northern Europe were smaller than Portuguese ships, and they could come closer into the shelter of Table Bay. The first recorded French ship at the Cape of Good Hope was in 1530, and the first recorded English ship in 1579. The first Dutch ship came in 1595 – 14 years after the Netherlands had declared itself independent from Spanish rule.

Three years later, in 1598, 13 Dutchmen were killed in a quarrel with local Khoekhoe. By contrast, an English captain in 1601 – bargaining for 'beeves and shepe' by using *moo* and *baa* sounds – was pleasantly surprised that 'we lived in so great friendship and amitie' with these 'countrey people...contrary to that which lately had befallen the Hollanders'.

Northern European nations awarded state monopolies in overseas trade to powerful companies of merchants. England's East India Company was founded in 1600, the Netherlands' East India Company (VOC or Verenigde Oostindische Companie) in 1602, France's East India Company in 1604, Denmark's East India Company in 1614, the Netherlands' West India Company in 1621, Sweden's Royal African Company in 1647, and the England's Royal African Company in 1660.

Ships called in Table Bay, known to the Cochoqua Khoekhoe as Camissa – 'the place of sweet waters', to collect fresh water from the fast streams running off Table Mountain (Hoerikwaggo), and to barter for sheep and cattle killed for fresh meat. Those Cochoqua who herded and fished and gathered shellfish on the coast became known as Gorinhaiqua, while beachcombers or *strandlopers* among them were known as Goringhaikona.

On May 21, 1613, a Khoekhoe man called Gora or !Kora, known to the English and French as Corey or Corée, was kidnapped in Table Bay by an

English ship's captain named Gabriel Towerson.[1] Corey was taken to London, where he lived for six months in the household of Thomas Smythe – both governor of the East India Company and treasurer of the Virginia Company trying to colonize North America since 1609. (One wonders if Corey met any 'Indians' from North America in the Smythe household.) He is said to have 'had good diet, good clothes, good lodging'.

Corey was given a crash course in English language and manners, plus a complete suit of armour in his favourite metal of 'bright Brasse'. Yet, 'when he had learned a little of our Language, he would daily lie upon the ground, and cry very often thus in broken English, Coorie home goe, Souldania goe, home goe...'. On his return home in June 1614, Corey 'threw away all his Clothes, his Linnen, with all his Covering, and got his sheeps skins upon his back [again], guts about his neck, and such a perfumed Cap...upon his head'. (The dried intestine of a sheep, full of semi-digested herbs and grasses, was worn as a medicinal sash around the chest.)

Despite this, Corey became the local agent (*comprador*) of the English East India Company and leader of a people known after him as the Gora-choqua. He founded a village of 100 houses on the Liesbeeck and Swart rivers – the first substantial settlement in the area of future Cape Town. It was described with some exaggeration in February 1617 by a sailor arriving on what is now the Groote Schuur hospital ridge:

> ...when we were come to the top of the hill, some four miles from our tents, we saw in the valley below about 10,000 head of cattle, and by judgment about 5,000 people which fled not for fear of us.

Corey was a hard-bargainer, knowing the true value of European goods. At one time, he taught 'his countrymen to despise bits of copper – so that for a long time afterwards it was impossible for ships that called to find a supply of fresh meat.' Corey grew wealthy and got into fights with his Cochoqua relatives. Eventually he bargained too hard. In the words of a Welsh visitor of 1627, remarking on the Khoekhoe at the Cape of Good Hope: 'They hate the dutch-men since they hanged one of the blackes called Cary who was in England & upon refusall of fresh victuals they put him to death.'

The English and the Danish were the first to attempt colonial settlement in Table Bay. In 1615 the English tried to set up a trading base on Robben Island in Table Bay with a small gang of London ex-convicts – who either killed each other or were executed on their return to England. In 1619, four Danish ships arrived in Table Bay – after capturing two French ships – and built a turf-covered earth fort to resist any French counter-attack. The fort was abandoned when they sailed on.

The Netherlands' West India Company seized Portuguese Brazil between 1630 and 1654 and Portuguese Angola between 1641 and 1648, in order to control the extremely lucrative South Atlantic slave trade between them. Ships of the Netherlands' East India Company (VOC) stopped for fresh water and foodstuffs at Luanda in Angola, and at Mauritius in the Indian Ocean, on their way to and from the main VOC trading base at Jakarta (renamed Batavia in 1619) in Indonesia. Meanwhile, the French (1642) and English (1645) were content with small victualling stations on the coast of Madagascar.

After the Dutch lost possession of the port of Luanda in 1648, the VOC decided to set up a victualling station for their ships at Table Bay in 1652. Survivors of the wreck of a ship named Haarlem in 1647 had identified the vicinity of the Cape peninsular as the most attractive place to grow vegetables and cultivate crops and to corral livestock. (The quest to find a local equivalent for ginseng, a medicinal root imported dearly from China, proved to be a failure.)

DUTCH SETTLEMENT AT THE CAPE

Over the protests of the its sister West India Company, the VOC decided to build an earth fort on the Atlantic side of the Cape peninsula, in the vicinity of the abandoned Danish fort where the Platteklip (Varsche) stream flowed into Table Bay. VOC ships, under the command of a surgeon named Jan van Riebeeck, arrived in Table Bay in April 1652.

Two English-speaking Goringhaikona *compradors*, Doman and Autshumao (who the English called Harry and the Dutch called Herry), were brought from shore for dinner on the night before Van Riebeeck landed with them. (Paintings made 200 years later, reproduced in many books, are completely inaccurate.) Autshumao sent his niece Krotoa to be a spy in the household of Jan and Maria van Riebeeck. Krotoa was subsequently christened Eva, when she was married to a Danish barber-surgeon in VOC employment. (Some white families in South Africa, like people in North America who claim descent from Princess Pocahontas, now claim descent from Princess Krotoa.)

Van Riebeeck released some VOC soldiers to become 'free burghers' (citizens) – to cultivate land with slaves on the Liesbeeck river, from which the Khoekhoe retreated. By 1658 there were 80 VOC soldiers and 51 free burghers, 98 VOC-owned slaves, and 89 slaves owned by free burghers. There were vegetable gardens growing cabbage, carrots, and beets, and four taverns next to the VOC fort. The first slaves were West African boys and girls from a captured Portuguese ship, but they were too young for hard work. Instead, the first school at the Cape was created for them.

After Van Riebeeck left in 1662, the Cape of Good Hope military post grew in size as a port for passing ships of all nations. More and more slaves were captured from Portuguese slaving ships sailing out of Mozambique and Madagascar, or they were taken from the islands of Indonesia or the Malabar coast and Bay of Bengal (India). The Slave Lodge, without windows in its walls (today a museum with windows), was built in 1671. It provided overnight accommodation for harbour slaves and passing sailors who slept with slave washerwomen. Construction of the large stone fort or Castle of Good Hope, on the shore next to the main stream, began in 1674.

The first female slave imported from the East in 1657 was an Indian woman known as Groote Catrijn – only the 14th woman among all the men at the VOC fort. She washed clothes by day and slept with the men at night, giving birth to a son named Christoffel Snyman – after his German soldier father (originally Schneider). In 1671 Groote Catrijn became a free woman when she married a 'free black', Anthonij Jansz from Bengal. The couple died apparently in a house fire, but 13-year-old Christoffel was taken on by Mooij ('kind') Ansela, an ex-slave who was married to an enterprising free burgher named Arnoldus Willem Basson. We will return later to Christoffel's story.

Sporadic Dutch-Khoekhoe warfare first erupted in 1656–59, over slaves who had escaped to live among the Khoekhoe. A second war followed in 1673–77 when Dutch hunters and traders ventured beyond the Liesbeeck, across the Cape Flats, to confront the Khoekhoe chiefdom in the Cochoqua mountains, which the Dutch named Hottentots-Holland. The VOC decided to turn the military post into a permanent colony. In 1679 a governor named Simon van der Stel – himself of part Indonesian ancestry – was appointed governor. He authorized settlement by free burghers in the conquered Cochoqua lands around the mountain valley, which became known as Stellenbosch after him. Over the next 20 years, many more land grants were given to free burghers to start arable farms, including vineyards.

In 1688, Dutch settler numbers were boosted by 400 Huguenot Protestants – a tiny percentage (0.4) of the refugees who fled Catholic France after persecution of Protestants began in 1685. The Huguenots brought capital and skills to found a thriving settler farming economy, based on production of wine and wheat in and beyond Stellenbosch. Huguenot men and their wives propagated Christian ethnicity and religiosity among the settlers. Rich families such as De Villiers, Du Toit, Du Preez, and Marais kept their French names and pedigrees, while others adopted Dutch identity (e.g. Villon became Viljoen).

Khoe-San workers and slaves on the farms were controlled by the ringing of bells to signal working hours, and also by addiction to alcohol. Workers were 'paid' by the *dop* system after work: a *dop* (slug) of cheap brandy-wine, made from the remains of grapes after their juice had been stamped out.

One of the first farms in the Drakenstein valley beyond Stellenbosch was a sheep farm named Meerlust – later famous as a vineyard. It was owned by Arnoldus Willem Basson, the adoptive father of Christoffel Snyman (1687). Young Christoffel married the French-born daughter of a Huguenot immigrant. He purchased a neighbouring wine farm after its owner – guilty of murder – escaped into the interior. The Snymans became one of the leading Dutch settler families.[2]

The response of one Khoekhoe man to these new white farmers in 1695 is recorded:

> You people eat grain grass and cabbages that would be better fed to your oxen. We would rather starve. Your habits are disgusting. We never belch or fart. In your stupidity you value a necklace of tiny beads (pearls?) more than you do a sheep. You know no gods and have no respect for ours, since you dump your excrement on the graves of our ancestors.

The Korana descendants of the Gora-choqua have an elaborate story of how Dutch settlers tricked them with artillery fire out of their lands around Stellenbosch – to which they had previously fled from the Liesbeeck valley. To avoid the Dutch altogether, all the Korana fled to the far north. While the Left-Hand (Links) Korana fled north up the Atlantic coast to their Khoe relatives on the Great River (Gei-Garliep or lower Orange), the greater number of Right-Hand Korana fled east to shelter with the Inqua – the most senior Khoekhoe clan – on the Camdeboo plains south of later Graaff-Reinet.

ROZVI & VENDA KINGDOMS

After decades of civil war, the Butwa grasslands of the south-west Zimbabwe plateau were invaded by the army of the Rozvi ('destroyers') around 1680. The last Mambo of the Torwa dynasty in the Khami kingdom was killed and replaced at his Danongombe capital by the leader of the Rozvi – Dombo-la-kona-Chiswango. Himself a descendant of the old Changamire dynasty, Mambo Dombo brought the Torwa warlords of Butwa under his control.

In 1684, Mambo Dombo, in alliance with Munhumutapa, led his Rozvi army back east, where he defeated a Portuguese force at the battle of

Maungwe. The Rozvi army, armed with bows and arrows as well as with spears, clubs, and battle-axes, surrounded the enemy with the chest-and-horns (front and two wings) battle formation – to be made famous two centuries later by the Zulu army.

Mambo Dombo broke with the Munhumutapa and diverted his gold exports direct to Afro-Portuguese or Muslim traders on the Zambezi at Zumbo. In order to stop the Munhumutapa state exporting its own gold, Dombo attacked the Portuguese *feiras* around the Mazowe river in 1693 and 1695.

When Mambo Dombo died around 1696, his sons competed to succeed him. Old Torwa chiefs, such as Mengwe in the far south-west, re-asserted their power. The kingdom has thus become known among historians as the Rozvi confederacy – an alliance under the Mambo rather than a unitary state.

It may have been one of the sons of Dombo who migrated and founded the Venda kingdom among the Singo and others in the Soutpansberg south of the Limpopo. By the year 1730 the Venda kingdom under King Thovela was based in the town of Dzata, with splendid dark blue stone walling. Daughters of Dombo or later Mambos were married further south into the chieftaincies of the North Sotho. Other sons and daughters of the Mambos gained power as chiefs over North Sotho clans – including the Lobedu, Birwa, and the Mujaji people. These clans were often ruled by women priests of Mambo lineage with rain-making magic. (The most famous 'rain queen' in the nineteenth century was Queen Mujaji, probably the inspiration for Rider Haggard's novel *She* – that word being word-play between *she*, the Shona term for chief or ruler, and the English female pronoun.)

TSONGA & NGUNI NEAR DELAGOA BAY

Portuguese ships sailed round Africa from Angola to the Sofala or Mozambique coast. Few ships tried to land along the coastline before Delagoa Bay, because of the currents and rough seas. A boy from a Portuguese ship wrecked in 1593 was eventually found in 1635 living as a rich man with three wives and many children among the Xhosa.

The Ronga (southern Tsonga) kingdom of Nyaka (Inyaka), on the south side of Delagoa Bay, continued to trade in elephant ivory with passing ships during the seventeenth century. The Tsonga kingdom of Wutonga to the north also traded in slaves, until the death of its great king named Gwambe (hence its people are called Gwambe-Tonga). Thereafter the smaller Ronga kingdom of the Mfumo, on the west side of the bay, became the main slave traders – with the reputation of being powerful witches and re-introducing male circumcision.

By about 1700, the Northern Nguni kingdom of the Tembe overtook the Nyaka as successful ivory traders. The Tembe succeeded in creating a powerful new kingdom on the south side of Delagoa Bay. They took tribute in ivory and cattle from a wide area around the bay and controlled the export of copper from the Olifants valley – as well as selling some slaves to passing ships. At its height, the Tembe kingdom controlled more than 250 kilometres of coastline and ruled over 27 regional chiefdoms inland, including Ronga (Tsonga) and Northern Nguni and maybe Sotho.

Northern Nguni subjects of the Tembe kingdom included Dlamini and Hlubi clans. (Swazi elders today recall that their Dlamini ancestors were once known as 'bakaTembe'.) From the Tembe, the Northern Nguni learned sacred annual ceremonies of planting and harvesting, secret ideas of 'divine kingship', and military tactics probably inspired by Rozvi successes further north.

The Dlamini and Hlubi also mixed with Sotho ('those who sink beneath their shields') on the Highveld – also known as 'those found ahead' (*emakhandzambili*). The Sotho taught them the secrets of adolescent initiation, including male (not female) circumcision. The lodge of the boy initiates at the school was thereafter known as *isutu*. Also from the Sotho, the Dlamini and Hlubi adopted the idea of the king's mother as being second in power to the king. They also, like the Tswana, sometimes abandoned Nguni exogamy to marry cousins within their paternal lineage.

NGUNI DESCENDANTS IN THE INTERIOR

Fokeng people of mixed Nguni-Sotho origin readily adopted Tswana dialects in North-West and Gauteng provinces. Their influence among the Tswana can be seen in Uitkomst-culture pottery (more Blackburn than Moloko in style) replacing Madikwe pottery among Tswana from about 1650. It has also been argued that maybe it was the Fokeng who introduced the building of extensive stone walls in Tswana settlements.

The Koni in and around Mpumulanga province, at the head of valleys that ran down to Delagoa Bay, were Sotho-speakers with ancient Nguni origins. Archaeologists call their pottery from about 1650 onwards the Morateng culture. Their best-known sites are the Badfontein terraced stone walls and cattle lanes stretching many kilometres along the hills for many kilometres south of later Lydenburg. This is the 'mist belt', where clouds from the Indian Ocean hit the escarpment, rendering warm moisture lacking elsewhere in the interior during the Little Ice Age.

Most Transvaal-Ndebele chiefdoms kept Nguni language. Those descended from Musi as their common ancestor divided into a number of chiefdoms: the Kekane around the Waterberg, the Ndzundza around the Steelpoort hills in Limpopo province, and the Manala and Hwaduba in Gauteng province. The Hlubi-related Kobe and Seleka chiefdoms – the descendants from Langa – invaded the upper Limpopo valley as far as the Tswapong hills.

Transvaal-Ndebele traders and metal-workers turned their spears to good use in hunting and warfare. The Kekane (Rooiberg pottery culture) fortified villages with stone-walling and domed stone houses along ridges in the Waterberg hills. The Manala or Hwaduba (Klipriviersberg pottery culture) near Johannesburg had houses with heavy wooden sliding-doors – protection no doubt against predators, both wild animal and human. The Lete (MaLete), after working for Kgatla masters in the copper mines of the Dwarsberg hills near the Ngotwane, earned sufficient cattle wealth to be recognized as a Tswana chiefdom with its own hereditary chief.

Oral tradition in the Tswapong hills blames Transvaal-Ndebele invaders for ending local production of iron for hoes, spears, bangles, and bow-strings. But more fundamental explanations may be offered for the decline in southern African production of 'black iron' and 'white iron' (tin) and 'red copper' during the early eighteenth century. Little Ice Age droughts dried up springs of water used in smelting and stunted the regrowth of the hardwood trees on hill-sides used for charcoal. (A typical smelt needed 180 kilograms of wood to convert raw iron into iron bloom, at 1100–1300 centigrade – achieved in the blazing base of a chosen tree or in a clay oven.) Probably even more drastic, the Asian market for African metal exports collapsed, because of the industrialization in Europe that mass-produced and exported cheaper base metals.

TSWANA & PEDI STATES IN THE INTERIOR[3]

We have seen in the previous chapter how Rolong, Kgatla, and Kwena dynasties traced common ancient origins and identified themselves together as Tswana. Dynasties came to power in larger chiefdoms through intermarriage and the profits of hunting, metalwork, and trade, or as doctors and rain-makers – earning them large herds of cattle, farmed out to followers in return for loyalty. Elephant ivory, wild animal furs, and metals were sold to traders from the coast, in return for beads and other imports – either down the Limpopo valley and across the coastal plains to Inhambane or down the headwaters of the Lepelle (Olifants) River to Delagoa Bay.[4]

The government (*bogosi*) of Tswana states was centred on a chief or king (*kgosi*) in a royal village. Tswana endogamy – marrying first cousins as 'great wives' – ensured political continuity through the succession of *bogosi* to the senior son of the senior wife. People of other clans and ethnicities were incorporated into the state. They were clustered together in commoner wards or smaller villages around the royal courtyard (*kgotla*). All men and women were organized in age-regiments formed during adolescent initiation schools – loyal to each other and hopefully to the *kgosi*.

Aerial photographs and satellite imagery show the remains along the Transvaal Middleveld of an east-west chain of stone-walled villages or towns, in mountain kloofs (gorges) or on northern slopes warmed by the winter sun. The chain stretches from Mpumalanga and Gauteng provinces in the east to North-West province and Botswana in the west. Archaeology reveals that these sites, rarely occupied for more than one generation, were built between about 1750 and about 1830. Oral traditions and written records tell us how the villages and towns were occupied by Tswana and related Nguni dynasties.

The growth of stone-walled Tswana towns after about 1750 has been explained as 'defensive aggregation' against Transvaal-Nguni or neighbouring Tswana cattle-raiders. The east-west chain of towns also marks an eastern trade route towards the Mozambique coast via the Pedi Kgatla kingdom, competing with the traditional northern route down the Limpopo valley. Trade to the south with the Cape coast had also opened up, at least among western Tswana. Competition for new wealth was complicated by crises of 'over population' by people and cattle during the droughts around 1800. The Tswana anthropologist Isaac Schapera points to both fission and fusion at the same time: dynasties splitting up, new chiefdoms bringing people together.

The oldest Tswana dynasty, that of the Rolong, had a long history of interaction with neighbouring Einqua and other Khoe herders in the Orange-Vaal Basin. This probably accounts for the seventeenth-century stone-walled ruins of Dithakong (Lattakoo) being re-occupied by the Tlhaping in the later eighteenth century. The previous chapter has noted the Type-R stone walls built around the thirteen and fourteenth centuries by Einqua herders on the Riet River near the Vaal.

Some Rolong people, who broke away towards Kalanga country in the north in the eighteenth century, became known as Kaa (*baKaya*, 'let them go'). Other Rolong people who settled in the south on the Vaal River, and married among Korana-Khoe herders, broke the old taboo against eating fish (*tlhapi*) – and thereby became known as Tlhaping people. They were joined later in the eighteenth century by more Rolong people fleeing dynastic warfare. As we

shall see, the Tlhaping founded a strong kingdom at Dithakong, trading indi-
rectly with the Cape.

The Phofu (eland) or main Kwena dynasty, strategically settled at the head
of Limpopo valley trade route around its confluence with the Marico River,
split up around 1700. The junior Mogopa-Kwena and Kgabo-Kwena dynasties,
who held onto the *kwena* (crocodile) totem, split from the senior Hurutshe
dynasty, which converted to the *tshwene* (baboon) totem. While the Kgabo-
Kwena stayed in the same area, the Mogopa-Kwena moved eastwards through
the Middleveld towards Gauteng. Some other Kwena migrated far south to
settle with the cattle-rich Fokeng in the Ntsua-na-tsatsi area – hence the royal
family of Lesotho today traces itself from a Koena (Kwena) lineage.

During the later eighteenth century, the Hurutshe kingdom prospered
and built a number of stone-walled towns, in the vicinity of the later town
of Zeerust (which 'borrowed' some of the stones for its buildings). The best
known of these sites, Kaditshwene (Kurechane), was described in detail by a
missionary visitor, John Campbell. The kingdom sent hunters for ivory and
furs deep into the Kalahari, where some Hurutshe hunters known as Tlharo
settled down and stayed on the Molopo River. Other Hurutshe went north
into Kalanga lands, where they became known as Khurutshe.

Many of the stone-walled villages and towns of Gauteng and the
Magaliesberg can be attributed to the populous Mogopa-Kwena dynasty and
its offshoots. (It gave rise to the Modimo-mosana dynasty, subsequently
divided into competing Ramanamela, Maake, Mma-Tau, and Mma-Tlhaku
dynasties). The old stone town of Molokwane at Selonskraal near Rustenburg
was occupied by Mma-Tau and Mma-Tlhaku people. The old stone town of
Motlako-tsotswe at Olifantspoort, on the Hex River south of Rustenburg,
was the capital of the Kubung-Kwena. (The Kubung later built a village of clay
walls underground, in the Lepalong cave of the Gatsrand near Potchefstroom,
to shelter from the *difaqane* wars.)

The Ngwaketse dynasty of south-east Botswana was an early eighteenth-
century off-shoot from the Kgabo-Kwena. The Ngwaketse founded a militarily
strong kingdom, exploiting local copper resources and ruling local Khalagari
people, who paid tribute in labour and hunting products. Ruins of old stone
villages near Lobatse bear witness to the eighteenth-century Ngwaketse kingdom, which settled its capital at Kanye around 1800.

Confrontations over cattle and wives led to further breakups among the
Kgabo-Kwena. In the later eighteenth century, the Ngwato dynasty broke
away. It was a long-established royal lineage descended from MmaNgwato
(Ngwato's mother), which had adopted the *phuti* (duiker) as its emblem.
Around the 1770s, the Ngwato followed previous Kaa and Khurutshe

migrants north into the Shoshong hills of east-central Botswana. The Ngwato themselves soon split in two: the minority under Tawana ('little lion') leaving for Ngamiland, to settle among Yei people on the south side of the Okavango delta.

The Kgatla dynasty engaged in mining and metallurgy on the Middleveld and herded cattle up to the margins of tsetse-fly belt in the Lowveld of the Limpopo valley. The MmaKau group of Kgatla, under *kgosi* Tabane, settled on the Limpopo headwaters (at Schilpadfontein) around later Pretoria, trading northwards through Transvaal-Ndebele intermediaries. Sometime around the beginning of the eighteenth century, Tabane's grandson *kgosi* Diale went north to the Soutpansberg, where the Venda kingdom under Dzata was trading with Tsonga merchants coming across the Mozambique coastal plains. Diale then settled instead in the Leulu mountains of the escarpment, where trade from the Olifants River headwaters was in more direct contact with Delagoa Bay.

The MmaKau-Kgatla settled as new rulers among Northern Sotho people commonly known as BaPedi or BaPeri – recorded as Biri on a European map around 1730. Diale's son Thobela Lelleteng (the man who 'cries inside') founded a kingdom among the Pedi on the Thubatse (Steelpoort) tributary of the Olifants River. The Pedi kingdom rejected the *kgabo* emblem of the Kgatla and first chose *phuti* (duiker) and then *noku* (porcupine). During the eighteenth century, the Pedi incorporated cattle-rich Koni people. They traded between Tswana lands in the west and Tsonga and Europeans at Delagoa Bay in the east.

The Tlokwa dynasty – apparently of mixed Fokeng and Kgatla origin – also came to prominence among the Tswana in the seventeenth and eighteenth centuries. Tlokwa (Tlokoa) clans south of the Vaal among the South Sotho can be traced to the intermarriage of Fokeng with Kgatla in the seventeenth century. The main Tlokwa dynasty north of the Vaal developed at the place named Tlokwe (later Potchefstroom) and then split up. The eastern Tlokwa of Marothodi traded with the MmaKau-Kgatla rulers of the Pedi kingdom. The western Tlokwa (later of Gaborone in Botswana) also maintained close relations with local Kgatla.

The old stone town of Marothodi, near Sun City in the Pilansberg north of Gauteng, is dated between about 1780 and 1827. It had a population of up to 7,000 people. There is much evidence of iron working and of intensive copper mining nearby. The town appears to have had two centres, with two large cattle kraals next to two royal residences. One was the court of the Tlokwa *kgosi* of the town; the other may have been that of an Ndzundza-Ndebele *nkosi*. They would have been brought together by common interests: relaying ivory and furs from the Kalahari towards the Pedi kingdom, and producing metals such as copper that were valued at Delagoa Bay.

DELAGOA BAY SHIPPING & NORTHERN NGUNI STATES

Under attack from Arab-Swahili in the north and from Dutch in the south, Portuguese colonial power on the East Coast declined during the seventeenth century. Portuguese ships in the Mozambique channel were joined by French and English as well as Arab or Persian and Dutch ships – trading and raiding for ivory and slaves. The English port on the island of Nosy Boraha set up in 1649, 20 kilometres north-east of Madagascar, became a notorious haven for pirate ships from the Caribbean and North America. Pirate captains such as Thomas Tew from New Providence (Rhode Island), William Kidd from New York, John Bowen from Barbados, and Edward England from Ireland raided treasure-laden ships crossing the Indian Ocean. They were not averse to slave-trading on occasion: Robert Drury from England bought 74 boys and girls in the Bay of Natal (later Durban) in the year 1719.

The Dutch maintained and then abandoned a trading post at Delagoa Bay in 1721–30. The Portuguese rebuilt their fort further north, at Inhambane in 1761, and gave protection to local Gwambe-Tonga and Chopi people resisting Tsonga domination from the south. Beginning in the 1770s, there was a boom in slave exports from the Mozambique coast supplying labour for sugar and coffee plantations on the French colonial islands of Mauritius, Réunion, and the Seychelles in the Indian Ocean. Merchants from the Austrian-Italian port of Venice took advantage of the slave boom to set up a base ('factory') on Nyaka island in Delagoa Bay – until they were attacked and expelled by Portuguese invaders in 1781–82.

From the 1780s onwards, increasing numbers of European and North American whaling ships landed at Delagoa Bay – to butcher the whales they had caught and to extract the oils needed for lubricating new industrial machines overseas. The whalers were not averse to buying ivory or slaves when they could not catch enough whales. But the main trade with local Africans was now in cattle slaughtered for meat.

The demand for cattle as well as slaves increased raiding and military activity around Delagoa Bay. During civil war that began in the 1770s, the power of the old Tembe kingdom waned. The Mfumo chiefdom increased its trade in slaves from the valley of the Nkomati River. In 1794 a junior Tsonga chiefdom, the Maputo, seized power from the Nyaka on the south side of Delagoa Bay. Among the Northern Nguni, the Ndwandwe on the Lowveld, trading in ivory and cattle and slaves with the Maputo at Delagoa Bay, became powerful raiders of other peoples' young men and women, cattle, and harvests.

Under its kings Yaka and his son Zwide, the Ndwandwe was the first large centralized state or kingdom among the Nguni peoples. They adopted Tsonga ideas of 'sacred kingship' and military organization. During the annual *incwala* or 'first fruits' ceremony, the king was cleansed by his doctors and reinvigorated in secret as the embodiment of his people. Young men from scattered homesteads were brought together in military regiments, and they were circumcised like the age-cohorts from neighbouring Sotho people. Long throwing spears were replaced by short stabbing spears, and soldiers were drilled in chest-and-horns battle formations. Zwide elevated his mother (one of Yaka's widows) to the status of Indhlovukati or queen-mother, with the right to shelter people from the king's wrath.

Kings Yaka and Zwide of the Ndwandwe ruled over the Mthethwa chiefdom of Dingiswayo in the south. To the west, they controlled various Ngwane chiefdoms. Zwide gave his daughter Thandile to the chief of the Dlamini-Ngwane (later Swazi), along with three clever doctors who taught the secrets of *incwala* and of beadwork with sacred meanings. The cattle-rich Hlubi-Ngwane on the Highveld edges of the upper Phongolo (Pongola) river prospered after adopting maize as a food crop. Rich Hlubi women wore cowhide skirts, while poor women wore goatskin skirts. Under Bhungane as their chief, the Hlubi defiantly held their own *incwala* separate from Zwide's.

CAPE COLONIAL SETTLEMENT

During the eighteenth century, the Cape of Good Hope became an important crossroads between Western Europe and Southern Asia. Ships of many nationalities, notably French and English as well as Dutch, called at the Cape on their way to and from the Indian Ocean. By the latter part of the century the settlement around the VOC fort was known as De Kaap or Cape Town. Ships brought new diseases as well as new people, animals, and goods. The first outbreak of smallpox at the Cape was in 1713.

After the arrival of the Huguenots, few women and children arrived from Europe. Richer and better educated Huguenots established themselves as the social élite of white-settler grape and grain farmers and town-dwellers. Individual male white settlers, mainly from parts of Germany, continued to arrive. Some were ordinary soldiers recruited by the VOC, others were sailors who jumped ship and decided to stay. Young white men without capital or skills to sell in town gravitated towards the frontiers. While young men from all classes often went on three-month hunting trips, those with a firearm and a horse might continue as hunter-traders and herders – in time acquiring a wagon and a family. By 1705, at least 191 German males were recorded as married or cohabiting with women of Khoekhoe or mixed ancestry. One of these 'van der Caap' wives was the grandmother of later Boer leader Paul Kruger.

As well as slaves brought by the Netherlands West India Company from the Gold Coast (later Ghana) and Angola, slaves were brought by the VOC from the Mozambique coast, Madagascar, Bengal, and most consistently from VOC Indonesia. The Malays from Indonesia included skilled craft-workers, such as builders, and political prisoners sentenced to exile. Slaves were distinguishable by their dress, women had to wear chintz or striped cotton cloth, and all slaves were forbidden to wear shoes. But some slaves in town bought their freedom with their earnings from craftwork, and even became Christians. These 'free blacks' came to be seen as a threat by European settlers.

Racial distinctions between black and white began to replace distinctions between slave and free. Whites on the frontier called themselves Christians and regarded all others as heathens. From 1765 onwards, free black women were forbidden to wear earrings, silk clothing, or hooped skirts in the streets. Islam also became widespread among Malays after the preaching of Abdullah Kadi Abdu Salaam, an exiled Indonesian prince who had arrived in 1767.

Dutch language was initially reserved for slave-owners only. Town slaves and Khoesan farmworkers communicated in Portuguese créole (colonial dialect), which had already taken words from Arabic such as *kafir* (heathen) and *assegai* (spear). The local Dutch dialect (*taal* or tongue), the foundation for later Afrikaans, developed slowly over the course of a century or more. It incorporated the créole that emerged strongly among frontier people and free blacks in town. It picked up Khoesan words such as *gogga* (flying insect), *kudu* (a type of antelope), *kwagga* (a type of zebra), *gecko* (lizard), *dagga* (cannabis), *kaross* (skin blanket or fur), and *kierie* (stout stick). Town talk incorporated Malay kitchen words such as *atjar* for hot fruit sauce and *piri-piri* for pepper spicing.

EXPANDING CAPE FRONTIERS

When the Korana fled north from the vicinity of Stellenbosch around the 1670s, the Left-Hand or Links Korana travelled due north up the Atlantic coast to join their Khoe relatives on the Great River (Gei-Gariep). Nama Khoe from around the Great River were already trading with the Dutch at the Cape, who had remarked in 1661 on the great number of copper beads worn by Nama envoys – sewn in their hair or onto their leather clothing, strung around their necks, or wound up to 16 times round their arms and legs.

The Dutch were anxious to find the source of Nama copper, but the aridity of the Atlantic coastal lands prevented much contact. Dutch envoys were sent north in 1705. They gave symbolic staffs of office to three southern Nama chiefs in Little Namaqualand, but they failed to locate the copper mines. In fact, while the Nama smithed copper and even iron, the metals were actually mined and smelted across the Great River by the Dama (Berg Dama) in the mountains of Namibia. The Dutch continued to import copper and brass from Europe. VOC brass buttons became a form of currency in interior trade.

From 1701, Dutch free-burghers (white male citizens) settled as Boers (the Dutch term for small farmers) around Tulbagh north of Stellenbosch, supplying livestock to the Cape market. They met with strong resistance from local Soanqua San, who attacked and killed cattle. In response, frontier Boers organized themselves into raiding parties, killing San men and capturing San women and children.

Boer raiders were organized as official 'commandos' under the control of the 'landdrost' (magistrate) at Stellenbosch. A large typical commando might consist of 12 mounted Boers and 12 mounted Khoekhoe auxiliaries – nominated by their Boer masters to ride in their stead. With their own horses and firearms but supplied with gunpowder and ammunition by the landdrost, the commando took to the field for a month or more. Military service on commando was often rewarded by the official grant of 'loan-farms' (VOC retained freehold ownership) to free-burghers.

The lone Soaqua survivor of a commando attack in 1731 shouted from atop a rocky outcrop, 'We Bushmen still have more people; we shall give the Dutch no rest.' But by 1739 the Soaqua were effectively destroyed as a people after a commando attacked them in their last refuge in the Onder Bokkeveld hills.

Small numbers of Boer men continued to spread out from Stellenbosch, to trade and herd and afterwards to settle in the Hantam area to the north and the Roggeveld area to the east. Many Khoekhoe herders surrendered their cattle and became servants of the Boers. A new landdrost was posted at Swellendam on the eastern frontier in 1745.

The Right-Hand main body of Korana who had retreated to the far northeast in the 1670s lived among their seniors, the Inqua Khoekhoe on the Camdeboo plains. The plains were at the head of the Sundays river, south of the Sneeuberg mountains of the Great Escarpment – beyond which lay the interior of the continent. The Korana were followed in 1689 by Boer hunter-traders who bought 500 cattle from King Hijkon of the Inqua. In 1702, Boer 'freebooters' attacked the Inqua and Korana on the Camdeboo – capturing 2,000 cattle and more sheep. Though the VOC authorities protested at this lawlessness, in 1719 they authorized an official commando raid that killed many Inqua.

The Korana survived the attack, possibly because they were out hunting in the mountains to trade ivory back to the Cape. Around the 1730s–40s, their *khoeseb* or chief Eiyakomo was killed by an elephant. The Korana decided to migrate with their cattle across the escarpment mountains to the north – before Boer settlers could claim the Camdeboo. They fought pitched battles with resisting San people on the way. The Korana eventually reached the land in the Orange-Vaal Basin of their Khoe relatives, who kept their cattle in stone-walled kraals. Here the Korana settled around the waterholes later known as Griquatown.

Migrant male Boer hunters and herders spread eastwards within the coastal climatic zone, south of the escarpment mountains, and were followed by 'trekboers' – Boers living, often with families, in their wagons. Trekboers began to settle in the Camdeboo after an official VOC expedition of 1752 concluded that the Camdeboo was now 'empty' of people. Some Inqua had sought shelter in the south around the Suurveld – seasonal 'sour' grassland north of later Port Elizabeth. Boer hunter-traders and commandos followed them down the Sundays River to the grazing lands where Khoekhoe, Gonaqua, and Xhosa were rich in cattle. The Western Cape winter and Eastern Cape summer rainfall zones overlapped around the Suurveld. Competition for seasonal pasturage among Khoekhoe, Gonaqua, Xhosa groups, and now Boers from the 1760s resulted in armed conflict, particularly when rains failed. San hunters also attacked the herders and mixed farmers, who were stealing good grazing for wildlife.

Scattered groups of western Xhosa mixed farmers were united in one chiefdom or kingdom by a remarkable individual leader named Phalo. When he died, in 1795, Phalo left his sons Rarabe in the east and Gcaleka in the west to face the Boers.

In 1775 the Cape Colony declared its western borders extended up to the western Suurveld. The first of many Cape-Xhosa frontier wars broke out in the Suurveld in 1779–81, with sporadic fighting over grazing. Soon after, however, Rarabe died, leaving a succession dispute between his son Ndlambe and his grandson Ngqika – a dispute exploited by neighbouring Boers equipped with muskets and horses, determined to seize the Suurveld for themselves. Second and third Cape-Xhosa wars followed in 1789–93 and 1799–1803.

DESTRUCTION OF THE MOUNTAIN SAN

Boer hunters were initially welcomed by the Sun e'i San hunter-gatherers of the Camdeboo, the Great Escarpment, and the plains around the Seacow (hippo) River that ran north towards the Great River. Boer musket fire provided the San with fresh meat. But Boer livestock herders then began to occupy San hunting lands, and so they were resisted by these 'Bushman raiders'. In 1768 the first Camdeboo loan-farms were registered by Boers, spreading thereafter towards the Sneeuberg mountains.

Between the 1770s and the 1790s there was sporadic but bitter warfare between Camdeboo Boers and Sun e'i San. Tradition records that hostilities began after a servant of the Boers named Andries Jacobs stole the wife of a swift-running San hunter known as Hacqua (the Horse). This led to a commando raid into the Sneeuberg in April 1770 under veld-corporal Adriaan van Jaarsveld. By 1773, San armed resistance had spread all along the Great Escarpment mountain chain – from the Sneeuberg in the east, through the Nuuweveld, to the Roggeveld in the west. San raiders killed or maimed Boer sheep and cattle and some Boers and their servants.

In 1774 the landdrosts at Stellenbosch and Swellendam recruited a general commando, 'entirely to destroy' if necessary every San in the escarpment mountains. Three commando units of 100 Boer men and 150 servants (Khoekhoe, or of mixed race), all on horseback, killed 499 San and captured 231. At Blaauwbank on the Seacow River, 122 San men were lured forward with tobacco and then shot down. San wives and children were seized to swell the number of Boer servants.

Sun e'i survivors regrouped in clusters of up to 300 people under warrior chiefs in the mountains. They built defensive stone walls near watercourses for protection against commandos. Boer loan-places in the Sneeuberg were periodically abandoned as Sun e'i raiders attacked isolated cottages at night with fire and poisoned arrows, killing horses and stealing firearms. Some farm servants joined the raiders rather than be killed. The Sun e'i also raided Boer farmers south of the escarpment. When unable to get close enough with bows and poison arrows, they fought musket firepower by setting light to the dry veld and burning out their enemies.

A mounted commando was berated in the Sneeuberg by a Sun'ei man known as Koerikei the bullet-escaper: 'What are you doing in my land? You have taken all the places where the eland and other game live. Why did you not stay where the sun goes down, where you first came from?' The great eland antelope was a symbol of San good fortune that often featured in dance-dramas and rock paintings – together with honeybees and honeycombs, fat locusts, rain clouds, falling stars, and the rising sun as symbols of good luck.

In 1786 the VOC posted a new landdrost at Graaff-Reinet in the Camdeboo. San extermination increased after the Van Reenen family – the biggest meat contractors at Cape Town – started running sheep on the Sneeuberg and Camdeboo. In 1792 the Van Reenens lost 6,000 sheep and 253 cattle on the Gamka river, and Boer commandos took San 478 lives and captured a further 66 in revenge. Boer families such as Viljoen, Potgieter, Prinsloo, and Botha sent their sons north to join the Pretorius and other families on the Camdeboo and Sneeuberg. The cash-strapped VOC lost control of its frontier settlers – who refused to pay rent for their loan-farms. In the years between 1786 and 1795, 19,000 cattle and 84,000 sheep were lost, but at least 2,504 San were killed and 669 captured.

CAPE RAIDERS IN THE INTERIOR

The Korana, who settled around the Orange-Vaal confluence in the mid-eighteenth century, were the bow-wave of Cape expansion. They acquired a few muskets and horses and used the Dutch frontier *taal* as their second language. They raided their Nama Khoe and San neighbours for cattle and women – and came into serious conflict with Rolong Tswana to the north.

The Rolong had been brought together in a powerful kingdom by Kgosi Thibela, whose son Tau ruled ruthlessly at Taung on the Harts river north of the Vaal – raiding for cattle and ivory as far as Namibia and trading eastwards in ivory and furs towards Delagoa Bay. Kgosi Tau came into conflict with Khoeseb Kunapsopoo of the Korana. Tau treacherously killed Kunapsopoo on an ostensibly friendly visit, and bitter warfare followed.

After a number of battles, Tau died of his wounds and Taung was captured and destroyed by the dead Khoeseb's brother Taaibosch. Korana large bows and poisoned arrows succeeded against Tswana spears and battle-axes. This was around the year 1760. Thereafter the Rolong became divided between the five sons of Tau – four of whom gave rise to separate Rolong dynasties that last until today (Rratlou, Tshidi, Seleka, and Rrapulana).

The Korana of Taaibosch dominated the Orange-Vaal Basin for the last four decades of the eighteenth century – trading with the Cape in ivory and cattle exchanged for tobacco, beads, and brandy. Wherever the Korana went, they were followed by Boer hunters and cattle traders. Boer elephant hunters reached Gu-daos (later anglicized as Goodhouse) on the river in 1760 and 1761–62, finding that smallpox brought into the Cape by ships had already spread to people thereabouts. People of mixed ancestry calling themselves Oorlams (wise guys) or Bastards started to arrive in the Orange-Vaal Basin in 1769. They settled into a lifestyle of hunting and raiding with their muskets and horses. Prominent among them was Adam Kok, who arrived on the river in 1771. Kok attracted subjects and allies among Khoe and San and Tswana. They acquired enough muskets and horses by 1800 to challenge Korana ascendancy. Kok was persuaded to re-name his people the Griqua – the name of his Khoekhoe ancestors nearer the Cape.

One of the new loan-farms of the 1770s in Namaqualand, near the Atlantic coast towards the Great River, was held by a Boer named Petrus Pienaar. Among his employees were a German ex-sailor named Jan Bloem (Johann Blüm), wanted for murder at the Cape, and a man of colour named Klaas Afrikaner. The Stellenbosch landdrost lost all control of Namaqualand by 1791. Bloem left to lead the Springbok clan of the Korana on the Great River – marrying 8 or 10 wives and having many sons. In 1796 Klaas Afrikaner shot Pienaar dead in 1796 in a dispute over a woman, and also escaped northwards. His group of Oorlam bandits controlled the western part of the Great River, based at Warmbad in later Namibia, where his son Jager Afrikaner succeeded him on his death around 1800. (His people were known as Afrikaners until, as so-called non-whites, the apartheid government forced them to abandon that name in the mid-twentieth century.)

By the 1820s, some frontier Boers became men of property, with multiple grazing farms for their large herds of sheep and cattle. They held onto the distinctive identity of being Christians surrounded by heathens, or they began to see themselves as whites among blacks. The frontier Boers imported white wives and slaves from the Cape, and they employed other Boers and large numbers of Khoekhoe servants. The frontier village of Graaff-Reinet grew in size and importance, with a small 'petty bourgeoisie' of small businessmen and officials, lawyers, preachers, and land speculators.

Drawing comparisons with American, Russian, and Australian history, historians have debated about the nature of the advancing South African colonial frontier. Was it a reversion to barbarism, growing ever more remote from coastal civilization? Or was it the spearhead of Christianity, commerce, and civilization into the interior of the Dark Continent? Was it a zone of conflict between cultures and societies or a zone of interaction where new forms emerged? Economic historian Daniel Neumark argued against frontiersmen being seen as loners and losers, disconnected from the Cape of Good Hope. Clothing, horses and saddles, wagons and wagon parts, firearms and gunpowder, iron pots and pans, tools and nails, Bibles, coffee and brandy, were all from the Cape. Ivory and skins or furs, livestock and lard (for soap and candles) or butter, and indentured labourers, were all sent to market at the Cape.

FURTHER STUDY

BIBLIOGRAPHY

See also books recommended in previous chapters.

Adhikari, Mohamed (2011), *The Anatomy of a South African Genocide: The Extermination of the Cape San Peoples*. Athens, OH: Ohio University Press.

Boxer, Charles Ralph (1977), *The Portuguese Seaborne Empire, 1415–1825*. London: Hutchinson.

Delius, Peter, ed. (2007), *Mpumulanga History and Heritage*. Scottsville, KwaZulu-Natal: University of KwaZulu-Natal Press.

Delius, Peter (2014), *Forgotten World: The Stone Walled Settlements of the Mpumulanga Escarpment*. Johannesburg: Wits University Press.

Elphick, Richard H. (1977), *Kraal and Castle: Khoikhoi and the Founding of White South Africa*. New Haven, CT.: Yale University Press [*Kraal and Castle* omitted in title, Johannesburg: Ravan edition, 1985].

Elphick, Richard H. (1989), *The Shaping of South African Society 1652–1840*. Cape Town: Maskew Miller Longman.

Neumark, Solomon Daniel (1957), *Economic Influences on the South African Frontier, 1652–1836*. Stanford, CA: Stanford University Press.

Penn, Nigel (1999), *Rogue, Rebels and Runaways: Eighteenth-Century Cape Characters*. Cape Town: David Philip.

Penn, Nigel (2005), *The Forgotten Frontier: Colonist and Khoisan on the Cape's Northern Frontier in the 18th Century*. Athens, OH: Ohio University Press & Cape Town; Double Storey.

Penn, Nigel (2015), *Murderers, Miscreants and Mutineers: Early Cape Lives*. Auckland Park: Jacana Media.

Shell, Robert C.-H. (1994), *Children of Bondage: A Social History of the Slave Society at the Cape of Good Hope, 1652–1838*. Hanover, NH: Wesleyan University Press.

Thompson, Leonard, ed. (1969), *African Societies in Southern Africa: Historical Studies* London: Heinemann.

Tlou, Thomas & Alec Campbell (1985), *History of Botswana*. Gaborone: Macmillan.

Vernon, Gillian (2014), *Even the Cows Were Amazed: Shipwreck Survivors in South-East Africa, 1552–1782*. Auckland Park: Jacana Media.

VIDEOGRAPHY

DVDs and downloads:

Against all Flags (dir. George Sherman & Douglas Sirk, 1952. 161 mins): Indian Ocean pirates based at Diego Suarez in Madagascar, with Errol Flynn and Maureen O'Hara.

Captain Kidd (dir. Rowland V. Lee, 1945. 90 mins): New York ship-owner becomes pirate in the Indian Ocean, with Charles Laughton as Captain Kidd.

The King's Pirate (dir. Don Weis, 1967. 100 mins): More Indian Ocean pirates at Diego Suarez, re-make of *Against All Flags* with Jill St John.

Krotoa (Penguin Films, 2017. 122 mins): Krotoa (!Goro/gõas) is brought up in the Van Riebeeck household, to be an intermediary with the Khoekhoe. She is raped, marries and has children, and becomes embittered about the fate of her people.

Proteus (dir. John Greyson & Jack Lewis, 2003. 127 mins): Dramatic reconstruction of eighteenth-century court case over sodomy between a Khoe male prisoner and a Dutch sailor on Robben Island penal colony.

5 Coastal & Interior Frontier Wars c.1790–c.1868

Widespread warfare tore Southern Africa apart in the early nineteenth century. To quote an old man called Mabhonsa talking to Zulu chronicler James Stewart, it was like the shattering of a glass bottle into smithereens. Others have compared it to a complex pattern of numerous pool or snooker balls colliding. (This chapter is an outline; more details can be found on-line.)

Migrating armed peoples on the march ransacked the interior, gathering up populations into highly mobile states. The burning of crops and theft of cattle impelled people to move ever onwards to attack their neighbours, inevitably killing adult men but forging new nations by the impressment of women and youths. Boer farmers on the frontiers of Cape Colony invaded the interior to exploit the opportunities of capturing land and labour.

The traditional explanation of the great disruption has been to trace it back to the explosive rise of the Zulu kingdom under King Shaka. Early twentieth-century historian Eric Walker portrayed what he called the Mfecane as Zulu-initiated aggression and mass destruction. Mid-century historian John Omer-Cooper saw the Mfecane in more positive terms as a 'Revolution in Bantu Africa' that created new identities and institutions.[1] Climatologists suggest that the wars were violent competition for limited resources during and after the great droughts around 1800 known as *madhlatule*. Demographers can add that the droughts followed population growth fed by the adoption of maize cultivation. Later twentieth-century historian Julian Cobbing argued that the Zulu kingdom developed as a defensive state against raiders supplying slave traders, who were supplying European colonial enclaves at Delagoa Bay and Cape Colony.

European colonialism in Africa was enhanced during the nineteenth century by the industrial revolution of mass manufacture and communications – new machines and weapons, steamships, telegraphs, railways, etc. Great Britain emerged as the century's global economic superpower. This new 'imperialism' overseas was accompanied by ideas of 'democracy' growing among property-owning colonial settlers.

CAPE COLONY UNDER DUTCH, BATAVIAN & BRITISH RULE

The Netherlands allied with France against the British in a war of 1780–84. Cape Town was alive with French influence and was dubbed Little Paris during the sugar trade boom between Mauritius and France. Table Bay also serviced British ships on their way to and from India and Australia in 1784–94. (After losing its North American colonies, Britain considered and rejected the mouth of the Orange River as a place to export its criminals.)

By 1791 the Dutch East India Company lost its monopoly over Cape Colony commerce, and the Dutch Reformed Church lost its monopoly as local state church. Missionaries of the Moravian church from Bohemia (Czech lands) returned to revive their Genadendal mission among the Khoekhoe, which they had been obliged to abandon 50 years earlier. They taught the Christian faith and artisan skills among Khoekhoe and other people of colour.

The Netherlands once again became allies in war against Britain between 1794 and 1802. Cape Town lost control of its frontier district Boers who were engaged in 'Bushman wars'. In 1795 'Patriot' Boers expelled the land-drost at Graaff-Reinet, H.C. Maynier, and declared an independent republic. Swellendam followed suit with its own republic. The British then landed troops on the Cape peninsula, in the name of the former Netherlands government, to restore order in the colony. The two frontier Boer republics dwindled back to former district status.

The 'Bushman wars' in the Cape Colony north of Graaff-Reinet were ended only by a new official policy of 'kindness' in 1798–1800 – with gifts to the San and offers of employment as herdsmen – proclaimed by Governor Macartney on local advice. Boer occupation of the Sneeuberg was thus ensured and the way opened for seasonal grazing further and further north in the interior. In 1799 the Boers of Graaff-Reinet tried to take advantage of peace with the San by rising in rebellion, after the British appointed the same H.C. Maynier as their commissioner on the frontier. But the rebellion was nipped in the bud by the third Suurveld war (1799–1803) between Boers and Xhosa and Khoekhoe over grazing lands. One Xhosa leader, Ngqika (Gaika), allied with the Boers against the other Xhosa leader, Ndlambe, and his Khoekhoe allies. One of the Boer rebel leaders – Coenrad de Buys – married young Ngqika's mother.

Cape Town continued to develop as a centre of Western culture or 'civilization', with its first theatre founded in 1800. Its upper-class social life was recorded in the writings of Lady Anne Barnard, wife of a top British official. This period is also notable for the admission to Cape Colony in 1799 of missionaries of the London Missionary Society (LMS), who had enlightened ideas of freedom for all individuals. LMS missionary Jan Vanderkemp ('Jankanna') arrived on the eastern frontier in 1799. Already a middle-aged widower, he founded the Bethelsdorp mission among Khoekhoe and married the daughter of a former slave from Madagascar. In 1804 he printed at Bethelsdorp the first book in a Khoe language, *Tzitzika Thuikwedi mika Khwekhwe-Nama* ('Principles of the Word of God for the Hottentot Nation').

Many Khoekhoe were converted to Christianity. One evening in June 1801, the church building at Graaff-Reinet was filled with dancing Khoekhoe converts singing in Dutch: 'Behold now, praise the lord all ye servants of the Lord...Lift up your hands in the sanctuary' (Psalm 134). Angry white parishioners, referring to the converts as cursed Children of Ham (Cham) and mere 'hewers of wood', answered with Psalm 74, which is translated as: 'Lift up thy feet, that thou mayest utterly destroy every enemy which hath done evil in thy sanctuary...[They] that hewed timber...have defiled the dwelling-place of thy Name'.

The first British military occupation of the Cape lasted from 1795 until 1803, when the British withdrew after a truce between France and Britain. The Cape Colony was restored to the Netherlands, and war between France and Britain resumed. The so-called Batavian or second period of Dutch Cape history lasted from 1803 until 1806. Governor Janssens and councillor De Mist were sent out from the Netherlands as men of the Enlightenment. They reformed administration and justice, civil marriage and public education, opened up freedom of worship, and instituted the rule of law.

The British once again invaded the Cape in 1806, landing at Blaauwberg just north of Cape Town, with little Dutch resistance because Emperor Napoleon of France had imposed his brother Louis Bonaparte as king of the Netherlands. The second British military occupation was confirmed by peace treaties of 1814–15. In return for £4 million compensation paid to the Netherlands, Britain kept the Cape Colony.

Besides slaves from overseas bought and sold at Cape Town, wine and wheat farmers near Cape Town – as well as livestock farmers inland – kept Khoekhoe workers as *inboekselingen* ('booked-in') or indentured servants. *Inboekselingen* were born on the farm, or they were seized as vagrants or 'orphans' during warfare and registered under a master by a landdrost magistrate. Their indentures had originally tied them to the farm until they were 25 years old, but from 1750 the indenture could be indefinitely extended – in effect servitude for life.

The so-called Hottentot Code introduced by the British administration in 1809 referred to the *inboekselingen* as 'apprentices', with their servitude enforced by criminal law. A young Khoekhoe woman named Sarah Baartman was taken overseas in 1810 by her master, a free man of colour, to become an entertainer who danced and displayed herself as the so-called Hottentot Venus in London and Paris, where she died in 1815.

Great Britain declared the slave trade illegal in its empire in 1807. But, as slaves at Koeberg north of Cape Town discovered in 1808 when they claimed freedom, an end to slave trading did not mean an end to slavery itself. In 1813 the British authorities issued a Slave Code restricting the rights of slave owners over their slaves, and in 1817 a Protector of Slaves was appointed at Cape Town. From 1814 onwards, Britain's Royal Navy confiscated slaves from ships of all nationalities passing the Cape, where the slaves became 'prize negroes' placed in temporary apprenticeship. The West Africa Squadron of the Royal Navy, patrolling the Atlantic coast as far as Sierra Leone, was based at Simonstown on the Cape peninsula from 1832 onwards. But it was to take four or five decades more before slave trading stopped on the Indian Ocean coast.

In 1828, the Cape Colony's 50th Ordinance abolished the Hottentot Code, and thereby freed Khoekhoe workers to leave their masters. Liberal abolitionist ideas had been promoted at the Cape by John Philip, superintendent of LMS missions in southern Africa from 1822 to 1849. Philip published his book *Researches in South Africa* in 1828. Donald Moodie, who was the official Protector of Slaves, attempted to refute Philip by publishing official documents in his book titled *The Record*.

Slavery was eventually abolished in the British Empire on 1 January 1838, after a transitional period of four years during which all slaves had become 'apprentices'. Ex-slaves celebrated by marching through Cape Town, singing *Victoria! Victoria! Daar waai de Engelschen vlaag* ('Victoria! Victoria! There waves the English flag'). Queen Victoria had come to the throne only a few months before. She came to be seen as the guarantor of official benevolence towards indigenous people. Abolition of slavery was accompanied by British government compensation to slave-owners. It was estimated that the 35,745 Cape slaves counted in 1833 would be worth £3 million in compensation. Compensation was, however, delayed for three years. It was 'creamed off' by bankers, lawyers, and accountants in London and Cape Town (where the Board of Executors, 'the first trust company in the world' was founded in August 1838) – leaving perhaps one-fifth for the actual slave-owners, and less for Boer owners living on the frontiers.

Free labour migration swelled Cape Town with ex-slaves and benefitted wine farms – with a five-fold increase in production between 1810 and 1824, under 'imperial preference' (1810–60) which taxed competing French and Iberian wine imports into the British Isles. Most of the pay received by workers on the wine farms, however, consisted of 'free' accommodation, some clothing, and an addictive daily *dop* of cheap brandy.

The fourth eastern frontier war erupted on the Suurveld in 1811–12. British troops under Colonel Graham pushed back to the Great Fish River the Xhosa of Ndlambe, who had re-occupied the Suurveld four years previously. Local Boer satisfaction, however, was short-lived. A judicial commission known as the Black Circuit began touring to hear the complaints of Khoekhoe servants against their masters. Local Boers rose in rebellion during 1815. (Again, the assistance of local Xhosa was sought but refused.) The Boer rebels surrendered at a place called Slagter's Nek, but five were hanged – and Slagter's Nek became a cause of Boer grievance for later generations.

Governor Somerset raised a force of Khoekhoe and coloured troops – the Cape Corps – to police the eastern frontier. He tried to enforce Nqika over Ndlambe as paramount chief of the western Xhosa. The result was the fifth eastern frontier war of 1818–19, with a battle around the new British fort of Grahamstown, and extension of the Cape Colony to the Keiskamma river. Ndlambe's people were inspired to fight by a warrior-prophet named Makhanda (Makana), who was captured and imprisoned on Robben Island in Table Bay. On Christmas Day 1820, Makhanda and 30 others escaped by boat, but he was drowned in the surf. Many Xhosa continued to live in hope that one day he would return and set them free.

In 1820 the British government brought English and Scottish families to settle on farms around Grahamstown and the area that became known as Port Elizabeth. Many 1820 settlers remained in towns, but others imported woolly merino sheep and bought farms from impoverished Boers – who had been content with hairy sheep used for meat rather than wool. Some Boers also prospered in this new commercial age as men of property, moving large herds of sheep and cattle between their many farms. Frontier villages grew into towns with traders and officials, lawyers, and land speculators.

SLAVE RAIDING FROM DELAGOA BAY & CAPE COLONY

When Britain seized the Cape of Good Hope in 1795, the French responded by expelling the Portuguese from Delagoa Bay in 1796. The Portuguese re-took control of the Bay by the time of the 1803 truce. They built a fort in the Mfumo chiefdom that they named after the old explorer named Lourenço Marques.

The British conquered the Indian Ocean islands of Mauritius and the Seychelles around 1810 and held onto them in the peace treaty of 1814–15, which returned the island of Réunion to France. While the British stopped their own slave-trading, the sugar economy of Réunion continued to rely on slave imports until 1848. Meanwhile, the Arabic-speaking sultans of the Comoros Islands (conquered by the French in 1841) and Zanzibar continued to import slaves from northern Mozambique until 1873.

The development of farming in the Cape Colony in the 1770s–90s pushed trade frontiers deeper into the interior – in pursuit of ivory and furs for export, and cattle and slaves for the farms. In the previous chapter, we have seen the expansion to the Orange River and beyond of Korana, Oorlam-Griqua, Bloem's Springbok-Korana, Oorlam-Afrikaners, and mounted *bergenaar* (mountain-men) bandits in general, followed by pioneer Boer hunters and herders ranging seasonally as far as the Orange. Springbok raiders reached as far as Lobatse in Botswana in 1798. Jan Bloem died soon thereafter, after drinking from a poisoned well. His son Jan Bloem II continued to lead the Springboks ranging far and wide over the next two decades across the Highveld – including the spring later called Bloemfontein.

When the British crushed the Boer frontier rebellion at Slagter's Nek in 1815, the Boer leader Coenrad de Buys and his sons rode north from Xhosa country with their horses and guns. They reached the Tswana kingdoms of the Tlhaping and Hurutshe, who were trading in ivory and furs down the Limpopo Valley. Known as Moro after his Dutch morning greeting, Buys caught malaria in the Limpopo Valley and died in the Tswapong hills. Taking local Birwa and Venda wives, his hunter-trader sons founded the Buys 'tribe' in the Soutpansberg, trading with the East Coast instead of with the Cape.

Griqua ivory hunters around the Orange-Vaal Basin avoided the malaria and sleeping-sickness of the Limpopo Valley, and trekked (i.e. pulled) their ox-wagons across the Kalahari thirst-lands, eventually as far north as the Okavango Delta and the Chobe-Zambezi confluence. Meanwhile increasing numbers of Graaff-Reinet Boers took their sheep north of the escarpment mountains to seasonal pastures on the upper Orange (Ntsho or Cradock) River.

LONDON MISSIONARIES IN THE INTERIOR

The LMS began to send missionaries beyond the Cape frontiers in 1801 – to San, Nama, Xhosa, Griqua, and Tswana peoples. Cape government explorers had recently reached the land of the Booshuana (BoTswana) nation. At Dithakong (Lattakoo) they were 'not a little astonished to find, in this part of the world, a large and populous city...as large as Cape Town, with all the gardens of Table Valley'.

In the Orange-Vaal Basin, LMS missionaries were welcomed by Oorlam-Afrikaners in the west, and by Griqua and Korana of Taaibosch in the east.

The missionaries encouraged them to settle down in one place and trade with the Cape Colony. In 1813 the Griqua at Klaarwater (Griquatown) formed their own republic with a written constitution, on the advice of William Anderson of the LMS. Church leader Andries Waterboer, himself San by origin, was elected president in 1820 – but had little effective control over the Kok and Berends families, beyond leading them into battle at Dithakong in 1823 (see below).

Mission expansion led to organizational problems. John Philip was called in from Scotland to be the LMS superintendent in southern Africa (1822–49), after a bitter dispute between missionaries over their colleague James Read, who had married into a Khoekhoe family. The LMS began to hand over stations to other missions with similar theology. It handed over its Nama and Oorlam-Afrikaner missions to German (Rhenish) Lutherans, and it abandoned its San mission at Toverberg (Colesberg). Scottish (Glasgow) Presbyterians took Christianity to the Xhosa from 1824. English (Wesleyan) Methodists extended their missions to the Mpondo (Pondoland) and Rolong-Tswana people. French (Paris Evangelical Mission) Calvinists began to minister among Sotho people around Lesotho.

From 1821 onwards, Robert Moffat ran a particularly successful LMS mission at Kuruman among the Tlhaping-Tswana. Helped by local interpreters, Moffat set to work translating the Gospel of St Luke (Luka). By 1838, they had completed translating the New Testament in SeTswana, and by 1853 the complete Holy Bible (*Bibela ea boitsepho*). Other missionary societies followed in other African languages. The efficacy of translation is still debated. Did Christian texts distort African ideas of a universal God? The words *Modimo* (the one in heaven) and *Nkulunkulu* (great-great one) used for God by mission translators essentially meant Ancestor in Sotho-Tswana and Zulu languages. This ignored the most common word for God among Bantu languages – *Nyambe*, meaning Creator. An alternative, *Lesa*, meant Nourisher.

RISE OF SHAKA'S ZULU KINGDOM

Many books and even movies have been made about Shaka, the founder of the Zulu nation, and it is not always easy to separate fact from fiction. But we do know that his father, Senzangakhona, was the chief of a small clan, named Zulu after an eponymous ancestor who had lived generations before. The Zulu clan became part of Dingiswayo's Mthethwa kingdom. Dingiswayo is remembered as an inspiring leader who created a Northern Nguni kingdom independent from Zwide's Ndwandwe. Dingiswayo traded in person at Delagoa Bay but absolutely refused to sell slaves. Unlike Yaka and Zwide, who killed recalcitrant chiefs and sold their people as slaves, Dingiswayo confiscated their cattle and their men became soldiers. (It may be argued that the Mthethwa kingdom originated as a defensive state against slave-raiders.) When Senzangakhona died around 1817, Dingiswayo appointed Shaka as the chief of the Zulu clan and its army.

Dingiswayo allied with the Hlubi against Zwide's Ndwandwe and raided Matiwane's Ngwane. Matters came to a head after Zwide personally insulted Dingiswayo. At the battle of Mbuzi Hill (1817–18), Dingiswayo was captured and then killed in humiliating circumstances. The remnants of the Mthethwa were driven south almost to the Thukela river but were rallied under the brilliant command of young Shaka Zulu. The Mthethwa nation of Dingiswayo thus became the Zulu nation of Shaka.

Shaka drilled his army into unquestioning obedience. He made them run faster by banning the wearing of sandals. He forced them to fight hand-to-hand, by rejecting long throwing-spears and axes in favour of short stabbing-spears. Regiments were identified by the cowhide patterns on their shields – large shields that could be locked together against a shower of spears. Soldiers were fed on a diet of beef and cereal porridge or beer, creating the need for continual capture of cattle and grain supplies. (Either Shaka or Dingiswayo before him stopped circumcision among Northern Nguni, on the grounds that it weakened warriors who must be made fit for fighting.) Shaka attacked Zwide's Ndwandwe and defeated them twice in 1818–19 – first at Gqokoli Hill and then in the bloody battle of Mhlatuze River. The Zulu army harassed and chased Zwide's defeated army northwards towards Delagoa Bay, driving them forward by burning grasslands as well as by spear attacks.

The Zulu nation was divided into high and low castes. The higher caste of Zunda-dialect clans included Shaka's own Zulu, plus the clans of the Khumalo, Buthelezi, Sithole, and (after 1826) Qwabe. The lower caste of Tekela-dialect speakers included Lala ironworkers. Shaka ruled through his *indunas* (councillors), who were also the officers of the *amabutho* (regiments). Masculine heroism was promoted by the high chance of death among young men – in warfare, mass hunting, and rustling of livestock. Men were refused wives until they were veterans. They would then choose much younger wives – but never from their own clan. Polygamy was largely reserved for men of the higher caste. Distinctions between women were promoted through Shaka's monopoly on glass beads from Delagoa Bay. Higher caste Zunda wives, with distinctive hairstyles, wore 'black reserve' beadwork and brass rings. They were served by lower caste Tekela wives, wearing 'white reserve' beads, who were given menial tasks in the homestead.

Shaka had problems in controlling the Khumalo clan in the Drakensberg foothills of the north-west. The young Khumalo leader, Mziikazi, refused to give Shaka all the cattle that the Khumalo had raided from Sotho-Tswana

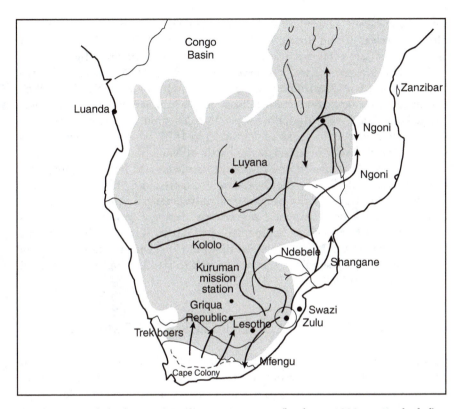

Map 5.1　Early 19th Century Difaqane Migrations (land over 1000 metres shaded)

people on the interior plateau. In 1822 Shaka sent a punitive force against the Khumalo. Mzilikazi and his people fled north into lowlands where they encountered Afro-Portuguese slave traders, 'brown-skinned men armed with guns'. Next, they took the trade route westward onto higher land, where they attacked and scattered the Pedi kingdom of King Thulare in the Leulu Mountains. The Khumalo then settled on the north-eastern Highveld among their Ndzundza-Ndebele relatives. All Mzilikazi's people subsequently became known as Ndebele (Matebele or Matabele).

To the north-east of the Zulu kingdom, by 1823 Shaka's Zulu had taken control from the Ndwandwe of all trade in ivory and cattle with the Portuguese at Delagoa Bay. Like Dingiswayo, Shaka refused to deal in slaves, while other northern Nguni continued to sell captives to slave ships on the coast. From 1824 onwards, British ivory traders came to the Zulu from Port Natal (Durban). One among them, Nathaniel Isaacs – later a slave trader in

Sierra Leone – left an account of Shaka as a bloodthirsty tyrant. By contrast, Charles Maclean (John Ross), a ship's cabin boy aged about 12 who lived at Shaka's court, left a sympathetic account of Shaka as a kind uncle figure.

The Zulu kingdom (KwaZulu) expanded southwards. A new capital town was established at KwaDukuza on the trade route to Port Natal in 1825. Southward Zulu expansion pushed Bhaca people into San hunting lands (later Griqualand East), and Mpondo people into Thembu and Xhosa territory. The kingdom reached its peak under Shaka in 1826, when the Ndwandwe in the north were finally defeated at the battle of Ndololwane. (Zwide had died one year earlier). While other Ndwandwe survivors fled north to join other Nguni armies of the march, the Qwabe were accepted into Shaka's army.

Around this time, Shaka became mentally deranged. He killed his own mother, Nandi – possibly when she was protecting a grandchild from his murderous wrath. Finally, in September 1828, Shaka was assassinated by his brothers Dingane and Mhlangane. The new Zulu king Dingane exerted control over Delagoa Bay by sending regiments north to attack other Nguni in 1828 and Portuguese in 1833.

NGONI INVASIONS ACROSS THE LIMPOPO & ZAMBEZI

Northern Nguni regiments who retreated from the first Ndwandwe defeat in 1819 attacked Portuguese traders on the coast at Inhambane in 1822. After the final Ndwandwe defeat by the Zulu in 1826, more survivors fled north to join other Northern Nguni armies on the march, who collectively became known as Ngoni.

In 1831 the Ngoni quarrelled, fought, and split into two major groupings – the Shangane southerners led by Soshangane and the Jere-Ngoni northerners led by Zwangendaba. The Jere-Ngoni army invaded the old Rozvi kingdom on the western Zimbabwe plateau. The Rozvi had been divided in civil war between its Mambo (king) and powerful regional chiefs such as Tumbare. Tumbare fended off a Jere-Ngoni attack in about 1832. But a remarkable Ngoni woman general called Nyamazuma attacked and killed the last Mambo (Chirisamhuru II), at the hill thereafter known as Ntaba-zikaMambo.

In the old Munhumutapa territory of eastern Zimbabwe, Zwangendaba's Jere-Ngoni clashed with more Ngoni coming from the south – the Msene-Ngoni and Maseko-Nguni both led by Nxaba as their general. Zwangendaba decided to take his people on the march yet farther north. The Jere-Ngoni crossed the Zambezi River in November 1835 – we know the month and year because it coincided with an eclipse of the sun. Some of Nxaba's Ngoni met their fate around 1843–45, when trying to attack the Kololo kingdom across the Zambezi River near the Great Falls. They were abandoned by boatmen on an island which they were told was the riverbank, and starved to death – after eating their leather shields and sandals.

The Jere-Ngoni moved on through Malawi and eventually settled in southern Tanzania, where Zwangendaba died in 1848. The Jere-Ngoni then splintered into a number of groupings. Mpezeni's Ngoni, near the Luangwa-Zambezi confluence, competed with Nxaba's remaining Ngoni in attacking the villages of Chewa-speaking people. Captives were sold as slaves either to Portuguese allies on the Lower Zambezi or to Yao and Swahili traders around Lake Malawi supplying Arabs on the coast.

MANTATEE RAIDERS ON THE HIGHVELD

It is difficult to untangle the separate courses of the warring parties that spread the wars of the 1820s onto the Highveld. The chaos of *difaqane* appears to have started with invading Hlubi, who had been expelled westwards by Ndwandwe and Ngoni attacks in 1821–22. The burgeoning Ndebele kingdom of Mzilikazi then expelled Mpanganzita's Ngwane and Matiwane's Ngwane from the north-east Highveld. Next, they attacked the Phuting group of Sotho-Tswana.

The Phuting led by Tshwane and Ratsebe first attacked and then persuaded Nkharahanya's Hlakwana to join them as masters of the Gauteng area. Here they replaced their previous cattle losses by raiding the stone-walled villages of Kwena or Kgatla and Musi-Nguni groups in and around Gauteng. (The metropolitan area around Pretoria has since been re-named Tshwane after the Phuting leader.)[2]

Mpangazita picked a personal quarrel with a powerful woman leader, Queen MmaNthatisi of the Tlokwa chiefdom at Kurutlele (around later Harrismith). Accompanied by her son Sikonyela, she led her own army on the march, causing mass panic that gave her the image of a giantess who suckled warriors at her breasts. Sotho-Tswana raiders on the Highveld became known as *BoMmaNthatisi* or Mantatees. MmaNthatisi's army attacked a nearby Kwena (Koena) clan named Mokoteli, headed by a man who was destined to become one of the biggest men of the century – Moshoeshoe. The Mokoteli under Moshoeshoe beat off the invaders and then moved to a fortified village on top of Thaba Bosiu hill.

When the LMS mission station at Kuruman was threatened by the invasion of Mantatees in 1824, the missionary Robert Moffat called for the aid of Griqua horsemen with firearms. The invading army was defeated and scattered at the Battle of Dithakong before they reached Kuruman. We now know that the invaders at Dithakong were not led by MmaNthatisi but were Hlakwana and Phuting raiders expelled from the east by the Ndebele. Some Sotho-Tswana refugees were given refuge among the Griqua and, further up the Vaal river, with the Korana of Taaibosch at Mpukani.

Unscrupulous traders from the south came to the Springbok base on the Modder tributary of the Vaal to buy Mantatee captives as slaves, who were taken south to farms in Cape Colony where they were sold and registered as *inboekseling* 'apprentices' – in exchange for horses, guns, and ammunition. Mounted Springbok raiders under Jan Bloem II ranged far and wide across the Highveld, riding fast at night over long distances and keeping awake on psycho-active drugs, to suddenly attack villages at daybreak. Bloem was 'notorious for his evil doings, and for his expertness in retreating and continuing to load and fire.'

Matiwane's Ngwane attacked the Taung of Moletsane, who in turn became Difaqane raiders until they were defeated in battle by Griqua horsemen with guns. Matiwane's Ngwane fought with but then came to terms with their Hlubi relatives to surrender after a five-day battle near later Ladybrand. Shaka sent a Zulu army across the Drakensberg escarpment to attack the newly united Ngwane and Hlubi. Mzilikazi followed suit with two Ndebele attacks that scattered the survivors far to the south and east. Some sought refuge in the Mpondo and Thembu kingdoms. Others marched south through Xhosa lands, causing panic among white settlers in the Eastern Cape. They were stopped by a colonial army in July–August 1828 at the Battle of Mbolompo, which dispersed them to become *inboekseling* in the Eastern Cape or Mfengu (Fingo) refugees among the Xhosa.

SEBETWANE'S KOLOLO

The Patsa clan of Fokeng people was another southern Sotho-Tswana chief-dom attacked by MmaNthatisi and Sikonyela on the southern Highveld. The young Patsa chief Sebetwane is said to have then addressed his people: 'My masters, you see that the world is collapsing...today there is no peace, no prosperity. Let us march...to find some land where we can live in peace!'

Sebetwane fell in love with a young widow among the nearby Kollo people. He named his new nation Kololo in her honour. The Kololo of Sebetwane raided villages on the Highveld until 1826, when they were pushed westward by Mzilikazi's Ndebele. They settled in south-east Botswana and attacked the Ngwaketse kingdom at Kanye – where Sebetwane received a wound that was never to completely heal. The battle was recorded by J.T. Bain, a visiting horseman (and pioneer road-maker).

The Kololo retreated northwards to the Kutswe hills, where they attacked the Ngwato clan of Kwena origin in 1827–28. The Kololo chased Ngwato survivors to the Boteti River and settled at Lake Xau with large herds of stolen cattle for a couple of years. Here they were joined by Ramabusetsa of the Phuting fleeing from the Ndebele in 1831. (Meanwhile the Ngwato *Kgosi* Kgari led a small army to raid the Rozvi kingdom in western Zimbabwe, where in the Matobo or Matopos hills they were defeated and Kgari was killed.)

Sebetwane moved westward to Lake Ngami in search of fine cattle with long horns. Venturing into Namibia, to buy firearms at Walvis Bay, his people were ambushed by Mbanderu warriors with bows and arrows. Sebetwane's young son was killed and the Kololo turned back eastwards, around 1835, to settle on the Chobe River at a place known as Dinyanti (Linyanti). Sebetwane gave a new Sotho name, Mosi-oa-Thunya ('the smoke that thunders'), to the Great Falls of the Zambezi – previously known locally as Shongwe-na-mutitima ('the pot that boils'). Four or five years later, Sebetwane led his people eastwards again, onto the southern plateau of Zambia, attacking Ila people on the way.

When the Kololo reached the area of later Lusaka, a prophet arose among them. He warned Sebetwane against venturing farther east into the land of slave-traders: 'There I behold a fire, avoid it; it may burn you'. The prophet pointed west instead, to a land of fine red cattle on the upper Zambezi, where Sebetwane was warned to treat their owners kindly as his own nation. On their way west, the Kololo beat off an attack by Ndebele raiders come from the south at the Battle of *Thaba ya Basadi* ('the women's mountain') – so named because of the valour of Kololo women warriors.

The Kololo settled on the floodplains of the upper Zambezi, where the old Luyana kingdom had been torn apart by civil war. The Luyana or Lozi (Barotse) found Sebetwane to be an approachable ruler, unlike their old priest-kings, and adopted the Kololo language as their own. Sebetwane welcomed Griqua traders from the south and Ovimbundu traders from Angola. In 1850, he decided to move down the Zambezi to once again settle at Dinyanti, to receive more directly the ox-wagon traffic coming from the south. One visitor was David Livingstone, who mourned Sebetwane's death in 1851 from his old wound of 1826.

SOTHO-TSWANA 'REFUGE KINGDOMS'

After a youthful career in cattle-rustling, Moshoeshoe (pronounced 'Mo-shwe-shwe') learned how to rule people through persuasion rather than oppression, from a wise old mentor named Mohlomi – whose motto was *khotso ke nala* (peace means prosperity). More and more Sotho took refuge on the mountains with Moshoeshoe to protect themselves from the Springboks 'who stole their children to dispose of down the river.' Moshoeshoe finally defeated the Springbok-Korana in 1836, by tricking the charging horsemen into 'hidden game-pits, into which they fell and where they were swiftly killed.' Springbok survivors retired north to the Modder River, where they paid tribute to the Griqua leader Barend Berends – and joined them in harassing Mzilikazi's Ndebele, making off with cattle and ivory.

In a short time, Moshoeshoe had attracted so many Sotho refugee followers that his nation became synonymous with a new Sotho nation known as Lesotho (Basutoland). Other Sotho-Tswana chiefdoms in mountains and thirst-lands also became refuge kingdoms, taking in people fleeing from the Highveld. The Pedi leader Sekwati, son of Thulare, who had survived the Ndebele attack by fleeing to the Soupansberg, returned home and restored the Pedi kingdom in the Leulu Mountains. He is remembered like Moshoeshoe for his wisdom in providing peace 'without shunning fighting when required.' Similarly, in south-east Botswana, the ivory-trading chiefdom of the Kgabo clan of the Kwena rose to importance under *Kgosi* Sechele – known to his people as *Botshabelo* ('the refuge'). After his conversion by David Livingstone, Sechele became a Christian and trusted that he could call on the firepower of Christian allies in the south.

MZILIKAZI'S NDEBELE KINGDOM

Around 1823, Mzilikazi was joined by Nxaba, who was leading Maseko-Ngoni and Msene-Ngoni from the lowlands. Together they attacked the Pedi kingdom that controlled trade from Gauteng towards the coast. Mzilikazi and Nxaba then quarrelled, and Nxaba took his Ngoni army northwards across the Limpopo River. Mzilikazi then turned his attention to the Gauteng area.

Mzilikazi replaced the Phuting as the master of Gauteng around 1824. Phuting led by Ramabusetsa made peace with Mzilikazi, who made Ramabusetsa one of his Ndebele generals. Other Phuting and Hlakwana fled westwards, raiding more and more people of their cattle – until, as we have seen, they were defeated at the Battle of Dithakong (1824). In Gauteng, the Ndebele were themselves attacked in 1826–27 by the Taung of Moletsane, assisted by some Griqua, Korana, and Rolong Tswana. Other attacks were to follow – by Griqua, Korana, Tswana, Zulu, and Boers. Mzilikazi explained the need for a protective ring of empty 'scorched earth' around the core of his kingdom:

> I was like a blind man feeling my way with a stick. We heard tales of great impis that suddenly popped up from underground[3], or swept down on you from high mountains, and we had a dread of the [Springbok-] Korannas, mounted and armed with rifles. I had to keep open veld around me.

Mzilikazi attacked the stone-walled villages of Gauteng and expelled their populations to the west and south. Dead bodies became so common that scavenging lions and hyenas developed a taste for human meat.

The core of the Ndebele kingdom was three military towns with rough stone walling – Kungwini (later Wonderboom near Pretoria), Dinaneni (near later Hartbeespoort Dam), and Hlahlandela (near later Rustenburg). Tswana chiefdoms – such as the Mogopa-Kwena under old chief Moré near Dinaneni – survived in this core area so long as they paid tribute in cattle and in young men for soldiers and young women for wives. When Tswana children grew up, they constituted a Nhla caste beneath the Zansi caste of the Nguni rulers. Phuting chief Ramabusetsa remained one of Mzilikazi's generals until 1830, when he fled to join the Kololo of Sebetwane in eastern Botswana.

The Ndebele state was seriously threatened in 1831. After an Ndebele army was defeated assaulting Moshoeshoe's hilltop capital, Mzilikazi sued for peace with Moshoeshoe. The Zulu exploited this new weakness by attacking the Ndebele in the Gauteng area. Another attack on the Ndebele by Griqua horsemen and their Tswana allies was beaten off at Kgetleng (Elands) River. Mzilikazi now decided to move the centre of his kingdom westwards, to Hurutshe-Tswana country on the Marico (Madikwe) River. Here, in 1834, the Ndebele beat off yet another raid by Griqua horsemen under Piet David, with Springbok horsemen under Jan Bloem II. Wagons, horses, and Davids' niece, Gertrude, were captured.

TREKKERS & NDEBELE

On the Eastern Cape frontier, drought pushed Xhosa and Boers, British and Boers, into ever greater competition for livestock grazing and hunting lands. During 1834–35, frontier Boers sent out three scouting parties along existing trade routes to spy out new lands in the interior. Andries Pretorius reached Oorlam-Afrikaner country north of the Orange. Piet Scholtz reached as far north as the ivory hunting country of the Buys clan in the Soutpansberg. Piet Uys's party on horseback crossed the numerous valleys of Xhosa and Mpondo territory, as far as the fertile country of KwaZulu. The scouts concluded that the lands occupied by the Ndebele and the Zulu were the best for livestock and for farming.

In the sixth frontier war of 1834–35, Ngqika-Xhosa under Maqoma were overwhelmed by British and Boer forces. Maqoma was captured and exiled to Robben Island. Chief Hintsa of the Gcaleka-Xhosa was then shot dead after surrendering. Xhosa territory of the Ciskei (between the Kei and the Keiskamma rivers) was annexed to Cape Colony as Queen Adelaide province in 1835 – and was promised to frontier Boers as new farmland. The Colonial Office in London, however, concluded that the Xhosa had been deliberately provoked into war by land-hungry white farmers and speculators. The Ciskei was restored to the Xhosa, and its annexation was withdrawn in 1836.

Fury and despair at British prevarication led to the migration of Boers out of the Eastern Cape that became known as the Great Trek (i.e. the long wagon-haul). Two groups of elephant hunters led by Louis Trichardt and Jan van Rensburg left for the Soutpansberg in 1835 but failed to reach Inhambane on the coast to trade in ivory and slaves. Later that same year, the first wagon-trek parties of settler families in their ox-wagons – led by Hendrik Potgieter and Sarel Cilliers – set out for the southern Highveld.

In Mzilikazi's eyes, the incoming Boers were seen as just another group of Basters come from the Cape. After the Cape of Good Hope Punishment Act of 1835 declared legal responsibility for all British subjects leaving the Cape Colony, Mzilikazi sent envoys to Cape Town in 1836 to conclude a treaty of friendship with the British.

More Boer wagon-trekkers left for the Highveld in 1836 under Gert Maritz, a prosperous Graaff-Reinet wagon-maker. They settled with their Tswana Rolong allies at Thaba Nchu. Together they went to the rescue of Potgieter-Cilliers hunters' camp, at a hill near the Vaal River called Vegkop, when it was attacked by Mzilikazi's main general Kaliphi. In December of that year the little colony's *volksraad* (adult male assembly) elected Hendrik Potgieter as commando commandant and Gert Maritz as *landdrost* (magistrate) and president.

In January 1837, Hendrik Potgieter and Piet Davids of the Griqua, with their Boer commando, Griqua, and Rolong forces, made a sudden dawn attack on the Ndebele military town of Mosega – when Ndebele regiments under Kaliphi were away campaigning in the north. The attackers captured large numbers of cattle and sheep, women, and children. Potgieter and Maritz quarrelled over their ownership when the captured children were sold to Cape slave-traders on the Modder river.

Dingane of the Zulu took advantage of Mzilikazi's new weakness by sending raiders to attack the Ndebele around the Marico river. This appears to have been what decided Mzilikazi to move northwards – like the Sebetwane had done. While Mzilikazi prepared to leave with the main body of the Ndebele, Kaliphi was sent to spy out the land as far as the Zambezi.

The Maritz-Potgieter Boers got wind of this. Together with their Rolong and Griqua allies they harassed the retreating Ndebele in a nine-day running battle (November 1837) down the Marico river towards its confluence with the Limpopo. Mzilikazi and his people retired to Photophoto waterfall (Palapye) in the Tswapong hills, in time to plant and harvest – before moving on to the Matobo hills of Zimbabwe in early 1838. The price that Mzilikazi had to pay for ruling western Zimbabwe was marriage to Queen Nyamazuma, its Ngoni conqueror. Indigenous Kalanga people were treated as a new lowest caste, the Holi, beneath the Nhla caste of incorporated Sotho-Tswana.

BOER TREKKERS IN KWA-ZULU & NATALIA

The richest man in the Eastern Cape, Piet Retief, assembled the largest party of Boer trekkers. Retief was a former commando commandant turned farm sales realtor. He published his 'Manifesto of the Emigrant Farmers' in English in the *Grahamstown Journal* in February 1837. It complained that British policies, inspired by Christian missionaries (with 'unjustifiable odium...cast upon us by interested and dishonest persons, under the cloak of religion'), had caused the security threat of roaming Khoesan 'vagrants'. The British had robbed owners of compensation for the emancipation of their slaves, and they had opened up the frontier to Xhosa cattle raids. The manifesto concluded:

> We are now quitting the fruitful land of our birth, in which we have suffered enormous losses and continual vexation, and are entering a wild and dangerous territory; but we go with a firm reliance on an all-seeing, just, merciful Being, whom it will be our endeavour to fear and humbly to obey.

When Retief reached Thaba Nchu, he found that Potgieter and Maritz were at odds with each other. Retief was unanimously elected commando commandant in place of Potgieter. A constitution for 'The Free Province of New Holland in South-East Africa' was adopted at the nearby Boer camp of Winburg in June 1837. Retief then took his trekkers to Zulu country across the Drakensberg escarpment, leaving the Maritz-Potgieter trekkers behind. In October 1837, Retief's trekkers arrived at Port Natal (Durban) where a small group of English traders paid tribute to King Dingane of the Zulu.

Retief approached the Zulu king for a land deal. Dingane insisted that first the Boers must recover his cattle raided by the Tlokwa horsemen of Sikonyela and Mma-Nthatisi. Retief achieved this by tricking Sikonyela. He gave Sikonyela bangles that snapped shut on his wrists. They were handcuffs! In return for the 'magic' key, Sikonyela surrendered 700 cattle. When Retief's horsemen (70 Boers with 30 Khoe servants) appeared at Dingane's court in February 1838, firing their weapons in the air in celebration, they brought only 300 cattle. Dingane knew about the trickery of his visitors, and – after adding his mark to a land concession document – gave his men the order to bind the 'witches' (*abathakati*) and drag them away. Zulu soldiers slaughtered the visitors on a nearby hill and then massacred Boer families and coloured servants remaining in the main trekker camp, afterwards known as Weenen ('weeping').

Potgieter, attempting retaliation against the Zulu, was defeated at the Battle of Ethaleni and repelled back to the Highveld. Meanwhile, Maritz sent for help to the Eastern Cape. Reinforcements arrived in strength under Andries Pretorius, a prominent Graaff-Reinet farmer. In December 1838, a Zulu army attacked Pretorius's army, camped in a *laager* (wagon circle) above a gully on the Ncome river. Zulu soldiers were trapped by gunfire in the gully, which ran red with their blood. As nobody was killed on the Boer side, the Battle of 'Blood River' was considered a miracle for a 'chosen people'. Pretorius claimed ownership of Natalia south of the Zulu kingdom, as the new centre of the Free Province of New Holland. The capital was named Pietermaritzburg (after Piet Retief and Gert Maritz). Its *volksraad* of burghers, elected in 1839, soon clashed with the autocracy of Andries Pretorius as commandant-general.

In 1840, Pretorius intervened in civil war between Dingane and his brother Mpande. Dingane fled north and was killed by Swazi enemies. King Mpande was considered indebted to the Boers. Zulu farm workers were registered with a wooden pass or small metal plate (*plaatjie*) strung round their necks, and 'surplus labour' was expelled southwards into a 'native reserve' of Mpondo territory. King Faku of the Mpondo appealed to the authorities at Cape Town to discipline their Boer rebels.

Britain only took action when the Netherlands and the United States threatened to recognise the Free Province of New Holland, which now had its own coastline and port, as an independent state. In 1843 Natal was annexed as part of Cape Colony, subject to the governor at Cape Town. Faced by better armed British forces, Natalia Boers retreated to the Highveld – Pretorius himself was one of the last, in 1848.

Between the Orange and the Vaal, Boers claimed ownership of land by treaties with African chiefs, written in Dutch. Land holdings of the Griqua, who had written title deeds, had to be purchased before they were sold on the market. Moshoeshoe tried in vain to expel Boer 'squatters' building clay and stone houses in Lesotho west of the Caledon River – but he made absolutely sure that Boers were never allowed to settle east of the river.

Potgieter quarrelled with his fellow Boers around Winburg, and he decided to cross the Vaal in 1839. He claimed that the land north of the Vaal River was his, by right of conquest over Mzilikazi. Conquest had been justified by the appeals to Potgieter of oppressed chiefs under Ndebele rule such as Mogale of the Po people. Potgieter himself settled at Pot-chef-stroom in good cattle country. Other Trans-Vaal Boers settled in a separate colony on well-watered farmland at Mogale's village (Rustenburg) in the Magaliesberg (i.e. Mogale's mountain).

Orangia (later Orange Free State) Boers remaining at Winburg declared their independence from Pietermaritzburg in 1842. The Transvaal Boers at Potchefstroom and Rustenburg confirmed their independence in 1844. There was also a third group of seasonal Boer sheep grazers living near the Caledon River, who retained allegiance to the British authorities in Cape Colony.

MORAVIANS, PRESBYTERIANS & ANGLICANS

When slaves were liberated in 1838, many ex-slaves remained as workers (skilled and unskilled) employed by white farmers. Many Muslim ex-slaves migrated to Cape Town. Other ex-slaves sought refuge on Christian mission stations. Three Moravian mission stations in the south-western Cape – Genadendal, Elim, and Mare – provided housing and artisan training for families who attended church. In 1843 a group of independent Protestants, whose home church was the old theatre in Cape Town, founded Pniel mission near Stellenbosch. It was run on similar communal lines to the Moravians, with market-gardens for ex-slaves. Farther afield, some ex-slaves joined the free Khoekhoe communities at LMS missions in the Eastern Cape.

The LMS required literacy in the Scriptures for church membership. The Scottish Presbyterians laid even greater stress on education. Their mission school at Lovedale was developed progressively over the decades, from elementary grades upwards. Their college at nearby Fort Hare was founded in 1841. Edward Govan was its first principal, until 1870. One of its early graduates was Tiyo Soga, the pioneer Xhosa linguist and scholar. He received higher education in Scotland and was ordained a minister of the Free Church of Scotland in 1856.

Anglicanism was split asunder in 1884 when Bishop J.W. Colenso of Natal was expelled for heresy. His collaboration with Zulu-speaking elders in translating Scriptures had convinced him that good non-Christians could go to heaven like Christians. Colenso's church held onto church property and (much later) called itself 'the Church of England in South Africa'. Hence the main Anglican church based in Cape Town responded by calling itself 'the Church of the Province'.

It had been the Evangelical and Pietist revivals among Protestants in Europe and North America – preaching Christian faith, hope of individual salvation, and charity towards others – that had sent so many missions to Africa. In retrospect, we can see the spread of Christianity as a global movement strongly linked with commerce and civilization. Christianity offered security and modernity at a time disrupted by wars, and it spread literacy and scientific knowledge through the printed word. It also opened up consumption and production for the world market, and it appealed to downtrodden or disadvantaged people – with new goods and machines including ploughs, wagons, and firearms. However, as educated and skilled African Christians grew in number, they came to be seen as a threat to the supremacy of the ruling white minority.

BRITISH CAPE & NATAL COLONIES

Survivors of the Battle of Mbolompo (1828) had settled on white farms and among Gcaleka-Xhosa in the Eastern Cape. They were joined by more refugees fleeing from the expansion of the Zulu kingdom. In the year 1836, no less than 17,000 people with 22,000 cattle sought shelter inside Cape Colony. Collectively they became known as Mfengu ('beggars') among the Gcaleka-Xhosa and as Fingo among white farmers and ranchers. The Mfengu included productive peasants and traditional doctors, and they became firm allies of the British. Many Mfengu pupils attended Christian missionary schools such as Lovedale.

Frontier clashes over land and cattle grew ever more intense between white settlers and Xhosa people. In 1844, the British built a line of forts in the Ciskei (including Fort Hare) and made many treaties with Xhosa chiefs to police the frontier. But warfare erupted again in the War of the Axe (seventh frontier war, 1846–47). Xhosa and Thembu forces were eventually defeated. Cape governor Harry Smith humiliated Ngqika-Xhosa leaders by placing his heel on the neck of Maqoma and by forcing Sandile to kiss his feet. He then exploded a wagon full of gunpowder and pieces of paper, shouting 'There go the treaties! Do you hear? No more treaties.'

The Ciskei area (west of the Kei River) was annexed as a new British colony (called Kaffraria) in 1847, and white settlers began to take up farms. Harry Smith's deposition of Sandile as Ngqika-Xhosa paramount chief in 1850 led to the eighth frontier war – a bitter civil war within the Ciskei. Anti-British

Xhosa, emigrant Thembu, and even Khoekhoe from the mission stations fought pro-British Xhosa, Mfengu, and Khoekhoe. The war threatened to spread. Moshoeshoe declared support for the 'rebels', and the Zulu declared support for the British.

A new Cape governor, George Grey, coming from New Zealand in 1854, thought he had the solution. The Ciskei was cut up into a checkerboard of small 'reserves' for free black peasants plus freehold farms for whites. This benefitted Mfengu newcomers, but it broke up traditional loyalties to Xhosa chiefs. People began to put their trust instead in religious leaders who offered miracles. A young girl named Nongqause had a vision of warriors springing up from the reeds and of a great wind sweeping the whites back into the sea. In October 1857, Nongqause's uncle Mhlakaza preached that this would only happen when Xhosa people killed all their cattle, destroyed grain supplies, and refused to plant new crops. The result of this 'great cattle killing' (or 'national suicide') was widespread starvation and death by February 1858. People begged for food in return for labour on white farms. German ex-soldiers were brought in to take up the new farms. In 1866, the Ciskei was fully incorporated into Cape Colony – with representation in the Cape parliament for African men with sufficient education or personal property.

The Cape Colony, before the addition of the Ciskei, had an estimated population of about half a million, of whom maybe 40 per cent were white people. The addition of the Ciskei considerably reduced that percentage. Britain had granted the Cape Colony 'representative government' in 1854, with a parliament of elected members advising the governor. Members were elected on a 'colour-blind' franchise, limited to male voters owning a house worth £25 or earning at least £50 per year. Under 'responsible government' after 1872, executive powers were given to a cabinet of ministers under a prime minister.

Port Elizabeth began to rival Cape Town from the 1840s onwards because of the rise in the Eastern Cape of production of wool, which was exported to the industrial mills of Britain. Wagon roads into the interior, via Grahamstown, also brought in ivory, horns, and wildlife furs from as far as the Zambezi. The same roads supplied the interior with woollen clothing and iron utensils and Brazilian coffee, as well as Bibles and cheap Cape Smoke brandy. The import and sale of mass-produced Tower muskets (typically £1 each) from the 1840s onwards began the wholesale extermination of Southern Africa's wild animals.

The biggest trading company into the interior during the 1840s–90s was Mosenthal Brothers, with main branches at Cape Town, Port Elizabeth, and Graaff-Reinet, and numerous trading connections inland. Mosenthal Brothers encouraged German Jewish immigration from the 1840s. The Solomon brothers, by contrast, were the children of orthodox Jews from the island of St Helena. The brothers were active in both the synagogue and the (LMS) Congregational church at Cape Town. Saul Solomon, a member of the Cape parliament, founded the *Cape Argus* newspaper in 1857. (His widow, Georgiana, was later a supporter of Tswana writer and politician Sol Plaatje.) Other Solomons became traders at Kimberley and farther north, and at least one married an African wife.

On the Cape peninsular, Simonstown grew in importance as a British naval base for anti-slavery patrols in the South Atlantic and Indian Oceans – intercepting ships of all nationalities taking slaves to Brazil and Cuba, Zanzibar and the Middle-East, where slavery remained legal. Many of the sailors were themselves ex-slaves – known in the Royal Navy as Kroomen, as they were often of Kru origin in West Africa. On the East Coast, freed slaves of Ethiopian origin (Oromo or Galla) were settled on the bluff at Durban. Some were educated at Lovedale mission.

Natal became a separate British colony in 1856, no longer subject to the governor at Cape Town. The most powerful man in Natal was Theophilus Shepstone, Agent to the Native Tribes and Secretary for Native Affairs until 1877. He regarded himself as the paramount-chief of all Africans in the colony, giving instructions to chiefs. The tax paid by African men in Natal was doubled in 1875 from 7 shillings per year to 14 shillings, to make the African men seek paid employment under white masters. The Transkei, occupied by independent Xhosa, Thembu, Mpondo, Bhacu, and others, was increasingly squeezed between Natal and the Cape Colony. The underpopulated part known as Nomansland (later Griqualand East) was the haunt of San mounted bandits known as amaThola, who recorded their raids in paintings on the rocks.

ORANGE RIVER & TRANSVAAL BOER STATES

The Cape of Good Hope Punishment Act of 1835 had failed to control Boers crossing the frontiers. British authorities woke up when Natalia was almost recognized internationally in 1843. The Orange Free State was restricted by the Cape government's recognition in 1843 as treaty-states, with recognized borders, of the Griqua of Adam Kok (at Philippolis) and Moshoeshoe's Lesotho. In 1845, the Cape governor also became Britain's 'high commissioner' responsible to London for the whole of Southern Africa. Cape governor and high commissioner Harry Smith responded by marching north with a small army to protect Kok's Griqua from Boer attack in 1845–46, causing more Boers to relocate to the Transvaal.

The later nineteenth-century history of the Boer colonies or states between the Orange and the Limpopo is one of continual territorial expansion and periodic warfare against Africans. Burgher citizens (all adult white males) periodically served, or sent their most trusted servants, on commandos to conquer new lands and people. But there were always tensions between burghers and their elected bosses, and between their elected bosses. Hendrik Potgieter in particular clashed with Andries Pretorius. Potgieter cut himself off from other Boers in 1845 by founding a new Transvaal colony at Ohrigstad, on the trade route to the coast via the Pedi kingdom. After an outbreak of malaria, Potgieter moved north to settle among Venda and Buys people in the Soutpansberg. There he worked with Spanish-Italian slave-trader Joao Albasini and Afro-Portuguese employees in exporting ivory and slaves to the coast.

Harry Smith's intervention in Orangia led to his declaration of the Orange River Sovereignty as a British colony in 1848, with its capital at Bloemfontein. Andries Pretorius arrived to lead Boer resistance but his commando was defeated at the Battle of Boomplats, and he retired north. There was an influx of mostly British traders from the Cape, whose stores became the centres of new villages serving the farms of the colony. Boer farm holdings in the new British colony – regardless of their legal origins – were declared to be perpetual freehold property. This led to renewed conflict with Moshoeshoe, who defeated a small British force at the Battle of Viervoet in 1851 – who then sued for peace as the victor rather than the vanquished!

In the Transvaal, Boer commando forces fell under rival commandants in the four colonies of Marico (later Zeerust) and Potchefstroom-Magaliesberg (under Andries Pretorius) in the west, Lydenburg-Ohrigstad in the east, and Soutpansberg (under Hendrik Potgieter) in the north. These Transvaalers came together in 1849 to declare themselves as the South African Republic, with a united *volksraad* (people's assembly) – but, as yet, with no president. Andries Pretorius took the lead in negotiating a treaty with Britain.

The Sand River Convention of 1852 gave the South African Republic a free hand north of the Vaal – in exchange for the abolition of slavery. Next, the Bloemfontein Convention of 1854, signed after the death of Andries Pretorius in the previous year, recognized the independence of the Orange Free State. From the 1850s until the 1870s, the British government used its army and navy to enforce the 'imperialism of free trade' on other countries, rather than using them to acquire expensive new colonies.

The Transvaal wanted to expand westward over the so-called Missionaries' Road – running from Kuruman through Mafikeng and Botswana towards the Zambezi. In 1852 the Marico commando, including a young Paul Krüger, attacked the Kwena kingdom of Sechele. The Boers demanded that Sechele return the refugees who had fled to him. David Livingstone's LMS mission at Kolobeng was destroyed, impelling Livingstone to leave on a new career north of the Zambezi, to open up routes for Christianity and to publicise the horrors of the slave trade. (Livingstone earned the opprobrium of white Afrikaners after his *Missionary Travels and Researches*, published in 1857, brought Boer slave-raiding to the world's attention.)

Led by Potgieter's sons after his death, the Soutpansberg Boers ventured south to attack the still independent Kekana-Ndebele of chief Mokopane II (Mugombane) in 1854. Thousands of Mokopane's subjects were blockaded and starved to death in a great cave later known as Makapansgat. A new village called Potgietersrust (since re-named Mokopane) was founded nearby. (Some sources confuse the Kekana of Mokopane with their relatives the Laka of Mankopane, who were also attacked by the Boers.)

Marthinus Pretorius, son of Andries, was elected president of the South African Republic in 1854. He made one of his farms, near the old Ndebele capital of Kungwini, into the meeting place of the *volksraad* – to be known as Pretoria. Marthinus Pretorius intervened unsuccessfully in the first Orange Free State war with Lesotho in 1858 and subsequently tried to unite the Free State with the SAR under his presidency. The attempt failed, and it led to Transvaal civil war in 1862–63. A new strongman emerged in this period, namely commandant-general Paul Krüger – though Marthinus Pretorius was elected SAR president once again.

The Boer republics of the Transvaal and the Orange Free State not only demanded field labour and other forms of tribute from Africans, they also tried to enforce disarmament on African chiefdoms. Africans were forbidden to carry firearms, and the production of spears was stopped by banning iron smelting. The primary use of firearms was in hunting, particularly for elephant ivory for lucrative export, but their secondary use in warfare was as vital.

The African 'refuge kingdoms' around the Transvaal and Orange Free State all developed adequate firepower to defend themselves, at least until the introduction of breech-loading rifles in the 1870s. Sporadic warfare between Boers and Venda in the Soutpansberg during 1864–67 resulted in the expulsion of Boer settlers from the northern Transvaal area for more than a generation. The Venda kingdom in the Soutpansberg, the Pedi kingdom under Sekhukhune, and the Swazi kingdom that allied itself with the Boers, all had access to firearms from southern Mozambique. The Swazi even laid siege to the Portuguese at Lourenço Marques in 1863–64.

FURTHER STUDY

BIBLIOGRAPHY

See also books recommended in previous chapters.

Dubow, Saul (2002), *Earth History, Natural History and Prehistory at the Cape, 1860–75*. Basel: Basler Afrika Bibliographien.

Elbourne, Elizabeth (2002), *Blood Ground: Colonialism, Missions, and the Contest for Christianity in the Cape Colony and Britain, 1799–1953*. Montreal: McGill-Queen's University Press.

Etherington, Norman (2001), *The Great Treks: The Transformation of Southern Africa*. Harlow: Longman.

Guy, Jeff (1983), *The Heretic: A Study of the Life of John William Colenso 1814–1883*. Johannesburg: Ravan Press.

Guy, Jeff (2013), *Theophilus Shepstone and the Forging of Natal; African Autonomy and Settler Colonialism in the Making of Traditional Authority*. Pietermaritzburg: University of KwaZulu-Natal Press.

Hamilton, Carolyn (1995), *The Mfecane Aftermath: Reconstructive Debates in Southern African History*. Johannesburg: Witwatersrand University Press & Pietermaritzburg: Natal University Press.

Hamilton, Carolyn (1998), *Terrific Majesty: The Power of Shaka Zulu and the Limits of Historical Invention*. Cambridge, MA: Harvard University Press.

Hamilton, Carolyn & Nessa Leibhammer, eds. (2017), *Tribing and Untribing the Archive: Identity and the Material Record in Southern KwaZulu-Natal in the Late Independent and Colonial Period*. Cape Town: UCT Press/Archive & Public Culture Initiative 2017.

Keegan, Timothy J. (2018), *Dr Philip's Empire: One Man's Struggle for Justice in Nineteenth-Century South Africa*. Cape Town: Zebra Press.

Laband, John (2017), *The Assassination of King Shaka*. Johannesburg: Jonathan Ball.

Legassick, Martin Chatfield (2010), *The Politics of a South African Frontier: The Griqua, the Sotho-Tswana and the Missionaries, 1780–1840*. Basel: Basler Afrika Bibliographien.

Livingstone, David (1857), *Missionary Travels and Researches in South Africa, Including a Sketch of Sixteen Years' Residence*. London: Ward, Lock.

Moodie, Donald, comp. (1838–42), *The Record; or, A Series of Official Papers Relative to the Condition and Treatment of the Native Tribes of South Africa*. Cape Town: A.S. Robertson & 1960 reprint Amsterdam: A.A. Balkema.

Mostert, Noel (1992), *Frontiers: The Epic of South Africa's Creation and the Tragedy of the Xhosa People*. New York: Knopf & London: Jonathan Cape.

Newton-King, Susan (1999), *Masters and Servants on the Cape Eastern Frontier, 1760–1803*. Cambridge: Cambridge University Press.

Omer-Cooper, John D. (1966), *The Zulu Aftermath: A Nineteenth-Century Revolution in Bantu Africa*. Harlow & Ibadan: Longman (Ibadan History Series).

Philip, John (1828), *Researches in South Africa, Illustrating the Civil, Moral and Religious Condition of the Native Tribes, etc.* London: James Duncan.

Plaatje, Solomon Tshekisho (1930), *Mhudi: An Epic of South African Native Life a Hundred Years Ago.* Lovedale: Lovedale Press & many later editions.

Rasmussen, R. Kent (1985), *Migrant Kingdom: Mzilikazi's Ndebele in South Africa.* Bloomington, IN: Indiana University Press.

Sanders, Peter Basil (1975), *Moshoeshoe, Chief of the Sotho.* London: Heinemann Education.

Ross, Robert (1983), *Cape of Torments: Slavery and Resistance in South Africa.* London: Routledge & Kegan Paul.

Ross, Robert (1999), *Status and Respectability in the Cape Colony, 1750–1870: A Tragedy of Manners.* Cambridge: Cambridge University Press.

Ross, Robert (2014), *The Borders of Race in Colonial South Africa: The Kat River Settlement, 1829–1856.* New York: Cambridge University Press.

Shell, Robert C.-H. (1994), *Children of Bondage: A Social History of the Slave Society at the Cape of Good Hope, 1652–1838.* Hanover, NH: Wesleyan University Press.

Thompson, Leonard Monteath (1976), *Survival in Two World: Moshoeshoe of Lesotho, 1786–1870.* Oxford: Clarendon Press.

Tyson, P.D. (1986), *Climatic Change and Variability in Southern Africa.* Oxford: Oxford University Press.

Volz, Stephen C. (2011), *African Teachers on the Colonial Frontier: Tswana Evangelists and Their Communities During the Nineteenth Century.* New York: Peter Lang.

Wylie, Dan (2006), *Myth of Iron: Shaka in History.* Pietermaritzburg: University of KwaZulu-Natal Press.

Wylie, Dan (2012), *Shaka.* Auckland Park: Jacana Pocket Books.

VIDEOGRAPHY

DVDs and downloads:

De Voortrekkers. Or Winning a Continent (African Film Productions, 1918. DVD Villon Films c.2000. 54 mins): silent epic Afrikaner nationalist version of the 'Great Trek' story, with a cast of thousands.

The Life and Times of Sara Baartman (dir. Zola Maseko, 1998. 53 mins): documentary film about young Khoe woman entertainer taken from Africa for exhibition first in London and then in Paris, where she died and her body was used for 'racial science'.

Shaka Zulu (dir. William C. Faure, 1986. 10 × 52 mins): Simon Sabela as Dingiswayo, Henry Cele as Shaka, and Robert Powell as narrator Henry Fynn re-live phases of Shaka's life as the amazing warrior king, building a great new nation, and facing the first European intruders.

Venus Noire/Black Venus (dir. Abdellatif Kechiche, 2010. 162 mins): Sara Bartman played by large non-Khoe woman, exploited by respectable scientists in Paris. Warning: extreme nudity.

6 Scramble for Africa Part 1, 1868–1902

The map of Africa was divided up among European powers during 'The Scramble for Africa'. The term was invented by *The Times* newspaper of London for a great conference of imperialist European states held at Berlin, in late 1884 and early 1885. Representatives of Germany and Britain, together with France and Italy, the Belgian king, and the Turkish sultan, agreed on how to carve up the continent between themselves. The scramble for new colonies in the interior was boosted by the Mineral Revolution in southern Africa that lasted from around 1867–68 into the 1890s. The 'new imperialism' out of Europe drew its impetus from the Second Industrial Revolution in Europe and North America around the same time.

New industries in Europe and North America mass-produced steel and new chemicals and introduced electricity and new medicines against diseases. The 1870s–80s saw rapid proliferation of telegraphs, railways, and steam-ships, as well as wire fencing, improved sanitation, and the adoption of modern weaponry. Breech-loading rifles like the Winchester and Martini-Henry became standard issue. The improved machine-gun invented by Hiram Maxim could kill scores of people in one sweep.

Great Britain was no longer the world's sole capitalist-industrial power. With the rise of industrial production in Germany, the U.S.A., France, Italy, Belgium, Japan, and Russia, export markets for British manufactured goods declined. During the economic 'long depression' of 1873–79, the British realized that the only markets protected from foreign competition were their overseas colonies. This gave Britain the incentive to increase the number and size of its colonies in Africa and the Pacific, an initiative followed by lesser industrial powers France, Belgian, Italy, and Russia – before Germany and the U.S.A. fully woke up to their own desire for colonies.

Production of wool in the Eastern Cape and of wine in the Western Cape were already organized along capitalist lines – with individual property and perpetual 'freehold' land ownership. By contrast, African states held onto traditional values of communal property and usufruct (provisional personal use) of land. The original property values in the Boer states of the interior, often described as 'feudal', were something between these two models. Farms were awarded to white men in return for military service on commando. Hence the demand for frontier wars, to possess land and wildlife and also to be the lord and master over people and their livestock on the land. Arable agriculture was generally limited to tribute in crops (share-cropping) or labour from the farm's pre-existing peasant farmers.

Mines and towns opened up cash markets for agricultural produce. Farms became capital assets and securities for debt. There was accumulation of land by a few magnates, and the growth of a ready market in land-deeds – speculating on what minerals lay beneath.

EUROPEAN IMPERIALISM IN AFRICA

Historians Ronald Robinson, John Gallagher, and Alice Denny have argued that Britain scrambled for territories in the interior of Africa to protect coastal colonies – guarding the sea routes to Britain's most important colonies in India and Australasia. British armies marched into the interior only to subdue military powers threatening the coastal colonies of the Cape and Natal. We will see, however, that the revelation of rich new mineral prospects gave the British an incentive to seize new colonies in the interior.

European imperialism was driven forward by the capitalist interests of industrialists, merchants, and bankers – but it also had popular appeal for workers in Europe. It offered employment in export industries, as well as new opportunities overseas for colonial settlers, soldiers, and sailors. Imperialism went hand-in-hand with militarism in what was called Jingoism – from a popular song ending 'We don't want to fight them, but by Jingo if we do...'. Jingoism damped down working-class agitation and ideas of social revolution. In the words of colonial-imperialist Cecil Rhodes:

> My cherished idea is a solution for the social problem, i.e. in order to save the 40,000,000 inhabitants of the United Kingdom from a bloody civil war, we colonial statesmen must acquire new lands to settle the surplus population, to provide new markets for the goods produced in the factories and mines. The Empire, as I have always said, is a bread and butter question. If you want to avoid civil war, you must become imperialists.

Africans were softened up to accept colonial rule by the prior arrival of European 'explorers', missionaries, and traders. Explorers mapped and reported their geographical discoveries to interested parties at the coast and overseas. Missionaries did likewise, while answering to the spiritual needs of Africans in a period of crisis and confusion. Traders sold cheap and plentiful ironwork and clothing that put local craft-workers out of business.

The first colonial administrators on the spot were military men, backed by well-equipped soldiers. They reported to senior administrators on the coast, who were in communication with Europe by the undersea telegraph network and fast ships.

The success of European technology and 'civilization' was widely assumed to be because of the biological superiority of the European race. The so-called white man's burden in British circles, *la mission civilisatrice* in France, and manifest destiny in the United States, were buttressed by 'scientific racism'. Charles Darwin's theory of 'evolution of the fittest' had been expounded in *The Origin of the Species by Means of Natural Selection or the Preservation of Favoured Races in the Struggle for Life* (1859). Even the Social Darwinists, who talked of cultures rather than biological races being superior, believed in the 'civilizing mission' over people of inferior cultures.

The new era was marked by the deaths in 1868 and 1870 of two great figures of the previous era – Mzilikazi and Moshoeshoe. In both cases, some white settlers saw advantage in intervening and backing one successor or another to the throne. Lesotho had grown steadily more powerful under Moshoeshoe. Sotho horsemen with firearms rode sturdy ponies bred in the mountains. French Protestant missionaries had bolstered the kingdom by introducing literacy and secretarial administration.

Orange Free State Boers turned their attention to Lesotho after the East Griqua abandoned Philippolis in the Free State and migrated across the escarpment into so-called Nomansland (thereafter Griqualand-East) in 1862. Occupation of the western Caledon (Mohokare) valley by Boer farmers led to the second Boer-Lesotho war of 1865–69. Moshoeshoe tried to recruit the British as allies, but the British insisted on Lesotho conceding all the 'conquered territory' to the – almost bankrupt – Orange Free State. In 1871, after the death of Moshoeshoe, Basutoland was declared part of the Cape Colony.

MINERAL REVOLUTION

During 1867–68, a German prospector named Carl Mauch found ancient gold mines in Zimbabwe and Botswana (Tati near later Francistown) and in the northern Transvaal. The South African Republic began to flex its muscles in the expectation of wealth. Transvaal Boer raids on Tswana chiefdoms in the west resumed in 1867–68, and Boer and Swazi raids on the Pedi kingdom followed in 1867 and 1869.

In 1867–68, large diamonds were discovered in the gravels of the lower Vaal river. The land lay north of the Cape Colony and west of the Transvaal and Orange Free State, and it was claimed by the West Griqua chief Nicholas Waterboer as well as by Tlhaping (southern Tswana) and Taaibosch-Korana chiefs. Around the same time, white and coloured men from the Cape Colony were settling on the Orange River, fighting on both sides of a civil war between Springbok-Korana and other Korana and San in 1867–69. The new settlers pegged out farms along the river bank, while Korana and San retreated into islands in the river. The farms became valuable after a Baster (coloured) man named Abraham September dug the first irrigation furrows from the river in the 1870s.

The opening up of the diamond fields saw an inrush of white 'diggers' from as far as Australia and America – employing local Africans to do the actual digging. In 1870 the white 'diggers' set up their own republic. Its capital at Klipdrift flew the black flag of anarchism, and it was headed by an Irish republican named Stafford Parker – who claimed to represent Korana people as the true owners of the land. The Transvaal republic tried to claim the diamond fields. British authorities intervened to demarcate a frontier (the Keate line) in 1871 that kept out both the Transvaal and Orange Free State. Later that year, claiming to represent the Griqua chief Nicholas Waterboer, Britain proclaimed the diamond fields to be its new colony of Griqualand-West.

Griqualand-West included 'wet diggings' on the River Vaal and 'dry diggings' to the south where there were four great diamond 'pipes' – the biggest being Kimberley, named in honour of Britain's colonial minister the Earl of Kimberley. A city of tents and corrugated iron shanties sprang up between the Kimberley and De Beers mines. The four mines were initially divided into 3,588 small square claims, each owned by an individual 'digger'. Some of the claim-owners in the early years were 'natives' (i.e. local Africans), Malay (Cape coloured), Indian, and Chinese. Thousands of peasants from the Eastern Cape and Lesotho flocked in to become workers, digging ever deeper into the claims of diamondiferous ground. Two to three thousand Africans came to the diamond fields every month in 1874.

Kimberley was a 'Wild West' city full of hard grafters and sore losers, cardsharps, prostitutes, and fights involving hard liquor and revolvers. Racial discrimination was introduced in 1872 by a law banning people of colour from owning a claim – on the pretext of restricting I.D.B. (illicit diamond buying). When the colony's lieutenant-governor, Richard Southey, armed his black policemen with guns, the white diggers rioted and expelled him in 1875.

African workers earned cash to pay colonial taxes and to invest back home in hoes and ploughs, wagons, cattle, and horses. Lesotho and the Free State sent hundreds of wagons to Kimberley full of maize, sorghum, and mountain wheat. An 1875 census in Lesotho revealed 2,700 ploughs, 300 wagons, and 35,000 horses. African workers from as far as the Kalahari and the Zambezi, and from the Pedi kingdom across the Transvaal, came – or were sent by their chiefs – to 'earn a gun'. Between 1871 and 1875, African workers bought 400,000 firearms at Kimberley – mostly cheap Tower brand muskets for hunting, but also some rifles good for military defence.

The two individual capitalists who profited most at Kimberley were Barney Barnato and Cecil Rhodes. The Kimberley and De Beers mines were consolidated from 3,588 claims in 1871 down to 408 in 1877, to 98 in 1885, and to just 2 in 1888. Barnato and Rhodes eventually came together in De Beers Consolidated Mines of 1890, which effectively controlled the diamond sales of the whole world. Barnato was a diamond buyer, formerly a London music-hall performer, who was always prepared to accept ownership of a concession in return for settlement of debts. Rhodes was a calculating young Englishman, who cornered the market in pumping out water-drowned concessions with his steam engine. (He believed 'every man has his price', and he bargained and bribed his way to the top.)

CONFEDERATION PLANS & TRANSVAAL ANNEXATION

Britain's Liberal government of 1868–74 believed in 'free trade' – and in reducing British responsibility for British Empire defence. It handed the duty of 'protection' over Basutoland (Lesotho) to the Cape Colony in 1871. It granted full 'responsible government' (with a prime minister and cabinet of ministers drawn from parliament) to the Cape Colony in 1872. But the 1873–79 'long recession' turned the 1874–80 Conservative government of prime minister Benjamin Disraeli away from 'free trade' into protectionism – and into rabid 'new imperialism' extending the British Empire.

Colonial settlers in Natal pressed for mounted police and soldiers to enforce disarmament on 'armed natives' on the borders. From the mid-1870s into the 1880s there were many 'gun wars' to disarm African states and people. In 1873, Chief Langalibalele and his Hlubi people resisted disarmament by Natal and fled towards Basutoland. He was captured and sentenced to life imprisonment on Robben Island off Cape Town. Bishop Colenso of Natal, a stout defender of African rights, sailed to London to protest at the injustice. Publicity around this, however, together with the state funeral given to David Livingstone in 1874, helped to inspire British media interest in Africa and the 'new imperialism'.

The Conservatives planned a South African Confederation of existing colonies and former Boer states – to bring law and order to new mines, towns, and labour supplies in the interior. At a conference in London in 1876, colonial delegates argued that independent Africans must first be disarmed by the 'imperial factor'. Britain sent out a new governor of Cape Colony and high commissioner for Southern Africa, Henry Bartle-Frere (1877–80), who struggled hard to get the Cape parliament to annex Griqualand West to the Cape Colony in 1880.

The first modernizing president of the South African Republic, Rev. Thomas Burgers, replaced M.W. Pretorius in 1872. (This was after a scandal revealing slave-trading in the northern Transvaal, resulting in the withdrawal southwards of Boer settlers in 1871.) Burgers planned railways, telegraphs, and schools, using the income of newly discovered gold. Some Boers in the western Transvaal objected to these modern ideas, and they trekked with their cattle through the Kalahari *dorstland* ('thirstland') to Namibia in 1876–77.

The Transvaal's new state income was less than expected, and Burgers had to raise loans from foreign banks. The state pledged numerous state farms as security for the loans. But most farms were on maps rather than on the ground. Farm prices were so low that some burgher families like the Krügers and Jouberts bought up large tracts of land. In the area claimed as the northern Transvaal, whites were actually paying tribute to African chiefs, not to white farm-owners.

The British government allowed Burgers to extend Transvaal borders westwards into Tlhaping territory in 1875. In the same year, Transvaal hopes were raised by the MacMahon award confirming Delagoa (Maputo) Bay as Portuguese. But the pathway for a railway to the Bay was blocked by the Swazi and Pedi kingdoms. Burgers recruited the Swazi under King Mbandzeni (ruled 1874–89) as allies in attacking the Pedi kingdom of Sekhukhune to its north. The Pedi had firearms earned by workers at Kimberley, and they were in a loose alliance with the Zulu kingdom to the south of the Swazi. Boer and Swazi attacks on the Pedi culminated in a war of 1876–77. By the time King Sekhukhune strategically made peace, after defeating the main Boer attack, the South African Republic was bankrupt. The Cape Commercial Bank in Cape Town was crying out for its loans to the Transvaal government to be repaid.

This was the moment that Natal's settler 'king', Theophilus Shepstone, was waiting for. Encouraged by Bartle Frere, he marched into the Transvaal with 24 mounted police and 8 officials (including the later writer Rider Haggard). He occupied the Pretoria capital of the Transvaal without a shot being fired. The Cape Commercial Bank took over the empty treasury, helping to raise the value of land. The Transvaal remained a British colony under Shepstone from 1877 until 1881.

CAPE COLONY, GRIQUALAND-WEST & MORE 'GUN WARS'

Under 'responsible government' from 1872, the Cape Colony was responsible for the security of white farmlands on its eastern frontier. Even beyond the colonial border, it imposed its magistrates on every chiefdom or kingdom in the Transkei area except Pondoland. In the words of one chief: 'Government is a wolf. One by one my rights are stolen from me in the dark.'

The ninth and last Cape-Nguni war in 1877–78 began with a quarrel between Cape Mfengu and Transkei Xhosa gate-crashers at a wedding party. It became full-scale war when Cape forces invaded the Transkei, to confiscate the firearms of its Xhosa and Thembu people. Their resistance was so strong that British army reinforcements were called in. The cost to the Cape government was £1.25 million. Thereafter, only the Mpondo kingdom (Pondoland) remained independent between the Cape and Natal.

The Basutoland 'gun war' began with resistance against an imposed Cape magistrate in 1878–79. The rebellion was widened by the Cape Colony's demand that everyone in Lesotho should surrender their firearms in May 1880. An invasion by Cape forces was futile, being defeated by armed horsemen at the battle of Kalabani and elsewhere in the mountain kingdom. After spending £4.8 million on hostilities, the Cape Colony government sued for peace in April 1880. The Basuto were allowed to keep their firearms, and they were promised no land alienation to whites. But there was a £1 annual tax on each firearm, and representation by elected representatives in the Cape parliament was refused. Mindful of the incompetence of Cape colonial rule, and of previous direct requests for 'protection' to Queen Victoria, the British imperial government took over full responsibility for Basutoland as a colony in 1884.

Griqualand-West, where Kimberley was located, was still a British colony under imperial control in 1871–80. Griqua claimants to the land lost their farms on both sides of the border with the Free State, and Tlhaping and Korana claimants were expelled north of the colony. Together they rose in 1878–79 to attack white farmers and traders, and the uprising spread down the Orange River. British army officers and light artillery arrived in 1878–79 to stiffen up colonial forces against Korana and San guerrilla attacks on riverbank farms from the well-wooded islands in the river. Captives were sentenced to hard labour in Cape Colony – on prison farms or on Robben Island near Cape Town.

Britain over-ambitiously even declared a 'protectorate' over central Namibia in 1878, but later restricted its claim to the fishing and whaling port at Walvis (Whale-fish) Bay in 1880. Griqualand-West was fully incorporated into Cape Colony in 1880.

The most famous 'gun war' was the Anglo-Zulu war of 1879. British imperial and Natal colonial forces invaded the Zulu kingdom from the south in January 1879, while Transvaal Boer and Swazi forces guarded the north. After Zulu victory and British defeat in the Battle of Isandhlwana mountain in that same month, a second British invasion was followed by British victory in the Battle of Ulundi, the Zulu capital, in July 1879. A newly arrived British general, Garnet Wolseley, then marched north with Swazi allies to attack and disarm the particularly well-armed Pedi enemies of the Transvaal Boers. King Sekhukhune of the Pedi was deposed and taken prisoner to Pretoria.

King Cetshwayo of the Zulu was captured and exiled at Cape Town – and was eventually permitted to see Queen Victoria in England, where he received acclaim as a noble enemy. Meanwhile, Wolseley followed Shepstone's advice and divided up the Zulu kingdom into competing powerful chiefdoms – that were to periodically engage in civil war. When Cetshwayo returned from England to Ulundi in 1883, he found himself head of only one of these chiefdoms.

RESTORATION OF TRANSVAAL INDEPENDENCE

Modern Afrikaner nationalism began to emerge among élite whites in the Cape and among Boer leaders in the Transvaal and Orange Free State. Common culture and history was promoted by *Geskiedenis van Ons Land in die Taal van Ons Volk* (History of Our Land in the Tongue of our People) by Stephanus du Toit (Toitus) in 1877. He also began to publish *Die Afrikaanse Patriot* magazine. Cape wine farmers led by Jan Hofmeyr came together in 1878, founding the Afrikaner Bond – including some members in the north – in 1880.

In Britain, the 'imperialist' Conservatives were replaced once again by the 'free trade' Liberals in government (1880–85). This encouraged Transvaal leaders Paul Krüger and Piet Joubert to strike for freedom in December 1880 – attacking the British fort at Potchefstroom. An invading British force from Natal was defeated at the Battle of Majuba hill in February 1881. The Pretoria Convention in August that year recognized Transvaal self-government, under a British resident commissioner in Pretoria.

The first large-scale gold mining in the Transvaal had begun at Barberton on the Swaziland frontier in 1881. This led to a speculative boom in land sales and sales of mineral rights that spread across the Transvaal from 1882 onwards. Boer leaders campaigned for full independence for the South African Republic, eventually recognized by Britain in the London Convention of 1884. Britain allowed its 'suzereinty', or control over external relations, to lapse. Paul Krüger became president, Piet Joubert his army commandant-general. The Transvaal began a period of aggressive territorial expansion, east and north and west. In 1884–85, the Transvaal sponsored its citizens to set up mini-republics beyond its borders, as treaty-states to be later incorporated into the S.A.R. The New Republic (*Vryheid*) was a land concession over the Transvaal border obtained by dabbling in divided Zulu politics in 1884. Among those who made their fortunes was young Louis Botha.

In Swaziland, King Mbandzeni was faced by a flood of Afrikaner and European chancers and tricksters seeking concessions (to re-sell to others). Through his agent 'Offy' Shepstone Jnr, son of old Theophilus Shepstone, his country was virtually sold off many times in return for champagne and trinkets. In the eastern Transvaal, commandant-general Joubert worked hard to win more Boer farms. In 1882, Joubert replaced Mampuru, whom the British had made Pedi king in place of Sekhukhune, and executed him at Pretoria. Joubert then attacked the powerful Ndzundza-Ndebele chiefdom that threatened the wagon road from Pretoria to Barberton. Like their Kekana-Ndebele relatives before them in 1854, the Ndzundza were blasted in their cave refuge, but this time by dynamite rather than gunpowder, during a siege.

BRITISH BECHUANALAND & GERMAN SOUTH WEST AFRICA

Beyond the Transvaal and north of Kimberley, Transvaalers exploited dynastic divisions among Tlhaping, Rolong, and Korana to obtain concessions in 1882 for two mini-republics that they named Stellaland (based at Vryburg) and Goshen. Stellaland and Goshen blocked the Road to the North – the wagon trade route (former Missionaries' Road) from Kimberley through Botswana to the Zambezi and Zimbabwe. In response, missionaries of the London Missionary Society, notably John Mackenzie, promoted the idea of a British 'protectorate' over the Tswana Christian states of Bechuanaland. In 1884 Britain warned off the Boers of Stelllaland and Goshen by declaring British Bechuanaland, north of Kimberley and south of the Molopo, to be a British protectorate. General Charles Warren was dispatched to expel the Boer 'filibusters' – who preferred instead to declare themselves loyal British subjects in order to keep their farms.

Meanwhile, in 1883, a German businessman named Adolf Lüderitz acquired a land and mineral concession, at Angra Pequena on the Namibian coast afterwards re-named Luderitz Bay. Lüderitz's concession from the Nama chief Joseph Fredericks covered a coastal stretch 250 miles long and 20 miles wide. Fredericks believed that these were normal English miles, but the concession was in German miles that were seven times bigger! Luderitz's concession was sold to a German company that surrendered it to the German imperial government by April 1884. Germany then proclaimed its 'protectorate' extended inland, over all Herero and Nama territory, in August 1884.

In March 1885 Britain announced the northward extension of its Bechuanaland 'protectorate' over the Kalahari as far as a line of longitude agreed on with Germany. The consent of the northern Tswana paramount chiefs (Gaseitsiwe, Sechele, and Khama) was belatedly obtained a few months later. Then, on 30 September 1885, British declared British Bechuanaland (later the north-western part of South Africa) south of the Molopo river to be a colony for white settlement, separate from the Bechuanaland Protectorate (later the Republic of Botswana) to the north.

Squeezed between Stellaland and the Transvaal, the Taaibosch-Korana territory of David Massouw was attacked by S.A.R. forces in December 1885. Reuters press agency reported that Massouw's hill capital of Mamusa had been stormed, and that German artillery officer Captain Schweizer had been killed. Sixty or seventy Korana men, women, and children were killed in the siege, including David Massouw. Nine Transvaalers were killed, including Field-Cornet Reneke. Transvaal patrols then went out to 'collect' Korana men, women, children, and cattle. Male prisoners were sent to Pretoria, while women and children were allocated to local white farmers as labourers. Mamusa was thereafter renamed Schweizer-Reneke.

The Cape Colony was faced by serious insurrection in 1896–97 after it incorporated British Bechuanaland in 1895. Tlhaping chiefs and people responded to the loss of their land to whites and the shooting of their cattle in rinderpest control measures. The revolt was led by Luka Jantjie (pronounced 'Yankee') – the discoverer of the second diamond found in the Vaal in the 1870s. The revolt concluded in 1897 with Jantjie's death and the deaths of hundreds of his followers in the Langeberg hills, surrounded and overwhelmed by Cape colonial forces. The surviving families were imprisoned, or they were allocated to white farmers far to the south as servile workers.

GOLD ON THE WITWATERSRAND

Prospectors, notably the Struben brothers, had previously found gold in quartz reefs on the Witwatersrand. But it was the discovery of gold in banket conglomerate (nougat-looking rock) on the farm Langlaagte in 1886 that revealed the 30-kilometre long Main Reef of the Witwatersrand. In 1886–87, three S.A.R. commissioners named Jan or Johannes pegged out the small city blocks of the place to be called Johannesburg after themselves.

Prospectors, mine managers, and skilled workers flocked from Kimberley and Barberton to the new city – with increasing numbers of unskilled workers coming direct from Natal or KwaZulu and from southern Mozambique. Mine capitalist Joseph Robinson, who had lost out at Kimberley, struck it rich by buying up much of Langlaagte farm. Multi-millionaires Rhodes and Barnato arrived too late from Kimberley to get choice pickings on the Witwatersrand. Numerous small mines pockmarked the Main Reef for five years. But costs rose as mines got deeper, needing expensive explosives and chemicals – notably dynamite and the cyanide that reduced the gold out of the ore. Forty-four mining companies went bust in 1889, and a 'group system' of successful mine-owners (known as Randlords) emerged to share costs in 1890–92. By 1893, it was discovered that the Main Reef was as deep as 750 metres, which meant that deep shafts and stopes had to be opened up and equipped.

The Randlords combined in the Witwatersrand chamber of mines to recruit black workers and reduce their wages. The first attempt to reduce black wages, from 60 shillings per month in 1889 to 45 shillings in 1890, had failed – only 14,000 miners were recruited in 1891. Pay rose again to 60 shillings per month by 1895, when 70,000 miners were recruited. The chamber of mines established the Rand Native Labour Association (RNLA) in 1896 to coordinate recruitment. Wages were then reduced to 50 shillings by 1899 – but numbers of recruits nevertheless increased, to 97,000, because of drought, killing of cattle by the rinderpest disease, and Portuguese and Boer conquests in southern Mozambique and adjacent parts of the Transvaal.

There was much hard drinking in the crime-ridden and chaotic young city of Johannesburg, with black and white miners encouraged to fritter away their incomes in 'canteens' on expensive but cheaply made spirits from the state-sponsored Hatherley distillery near Pretoria. These conditions have been described by social historian Charles van Onselen.

The S.A. Republic assisted mine labour recruitment in 1895 by increasing taxation on African men in rural areas. In addition to the regular 'hut tax' of 10 shillings per year paid by adult men, an extra wife was counted as a second 'hut', and every adult man – except those in white household employment – had to pay an extra levy of 40 shillings that year.

CAPE COLONY, NATAL & THE ZULU KINGDOM

While the Eastern Cape thrived from the production of wool and its export through Port Elizabeth and East London, the Western Cape suffered from the decline of wine production after Britain replaced 'imperial preference' for

Cape wines by 'free trade' for all foreign wines in 1860. Vineyards were almost wiped out by *Phylloxera* vine disease in the late 1880s and were only saved by vine grafts and expertise from California. Cecil Rhodes bought up bankrupt wine farms in the Drakenstein valley for production of apples and other fruit.

Cape Town remained an important port for ships travelling to and from Europe, India, and Australia, but ships had to anchor in the shallows off-shore until the construction of the stone-walled Alfred Dock began in 1860. A second dock named Victoria was added in the 1870s. The docks were built with stones cut and shaped by prisoners from the nearby Breakwater *tronk* (prison). Some of the prisoners were San men captured in the interior. A man called //Kabbo, arrested for illegal hunting in the northern Cape, was marched south to the Breakwater in about 1870. There he was recruited to teach Southern San language and culture to the family of German linguist and eth-nologist Willem Bleek, living at nearby Mowbray.

Historians often refer to a 'Cape liberal tradition' advocating human rights, regardless of race or colour, backed by the rule of law. Its early proponents were the missionary John Philip and the poet and free press campaigner Thomas Pringle, followed by journalist-politicians James Fairbairn and Saul Solomon, and John Molteno the first Cape prime minister (1872–78). The Cape fran-chise was extended to more and more middle-class African men – until the years 1887 and 1892, when the racist governments of prime ministers Gordon Sprigg and Cecil Rhodes reduced the number of Africans who could vote. However, the 'colour-blind vote' continued in the Cape, and the call for its extension elsewhere in Southern Africa continued to be the rallying cry for middle-class African nationalists even after the First World War.

In the sugar industry of Natal, the first indentured labourers were imported from India to work for the period of their indenture in the 1860s. The number and size of sugar plantations rapidly increased, as did the num-ber of workers and the fortunes of white sugar-planters. By the mid-1890s the number of Indians, who had settled after their indentures or had come as voluntary 'passengers' from India, was almost equal to the number of white settlers in Natal. In 1896, after Natal Indians were denied the vote like Natal Africans, a branch of the Indian National Congress was formed in Natal, with the young English-educated lawyer Mahatma Gandhi as its secretary.

After finding his former kingdom torn apart by civil war, Cetshwayo died a disappointed man in 1884. Great Britain annexed Zululand as a colony in 1887, and it was incorporated into Natal in 1897. Taxes on huts and wives were intended to drive Zulu men to walk and work outside KwaZulu in cash-paid unskilled employment – particularly in the Transvaal, where the Randlords were desperate for the cheapest labour in the gold mines.

FOUNDING RHODESIA

Kimberley multi-millionaire capitalist Cecil Rhodes was a dreamer, but a practical dreamer. He dreamed of linking up British colonies from the Cape to Cairo by a rail line and actually succeeded in laying a telegraph line half-way. After the discovery of a deep gold reef under the surface workings of the Witwatersrand's Main Reef, he wanted to believe that there was also a deep gold reef lying under the ancient gold-mines of Mashonaland.

During the later 1880s, Rhodes was not alone in sending envoys to obtain concessions in Matebeleland and Mashonaland from King Lobengula of the Ndebele. Lobengula had already granted a mining concession to a company exploiting the gold of Tati (Francistown) on the frontier with Bechuanaland, but now became cautious of becoming trapped and tricked by concessionaires like King Mbandzeni in Swaziland had been:

> Did you ever see a chameleon catch a fly? The chameleon gets behind the fly and remains motionless for some time, then he advances very slowly and gently, first putting forward one leg and then the other. At last, when well within reach, he darts his tongue and the fly disappears. England is the chameleon and I am that fly.

In 1888, Rhodes sent Charles Rudd to Lobengula. When Lobengula proved reluctant to put his X on a document written in English, Rev. Helm of the LMS assured him that the document would allow only a handful of Englishmen to prospect and dig for gold in his territory. In fact, the words were as follow:

> I Lobengula, King of the Matebele, Mashonaland and other adjoining ter-ritories ... do, hereby, grant and assign to the said grantees, their heirs, representatives ... the complete and exclusive charge of all metals and min-erals situated and contained in my kingdoms, principalities and dominions, together with the full power to do all things that they may deem necessary to win and procure the same and to hold, collect and enjoy the profits and revenues, if any, derivable from the same metals and minerals.

The inclusion of gold-rich Mashonaland in the Rudd Concession was a shrewd move. It justified Rhodes taking possession of territory that was claimed by Lobengula but was never really under Lobengula's rule. In return, Lobengula was to receive 'one hundred pound sterling...on the first day of every lunar month' and one thousand Martini-Henry breech rifles – as well as a steam-boat 'with guns for defensive purposes' on the Zambezi River.

Soon afterwards, Lobengula was told by rival concessionaires that Rudd and Helm had duped him into signing away his sovereignty, giving Rhodes unlimited control within his territory. Lobengula wrote letters of protest to the British government. Rhodes made sure the letters were delayed until they were too late, as also were two Ndebele *induna* (headman) envoys sent to London to see the queen.

Rhodes allied with a rival company, which had concession rights in Bechuanaland, and he used the Rudd Concession as the basis for being granted a British royal charter for his British South Africa Company. (Private companies with a royal charter over an overseas territory had previously been used to establish British colonies in North America and India – and for East Africa in 1888.) The royal charter gave the B.S.A. Company the authority to 'make treaties, promulgate laws, preserve peace, maintain a police force and acquire new concessions...make roads, railways, harbours...engage in mining or any other industry'.

In London, Rhodes recruited powerful British figures, including the husbands of Queen Victoria's daughters, to sit on the board of his company. At Kimberley, Rhodes organized his so-called Pioneer Column, a band of adventurers, to trek north and occupy Mashonaland. Each adventurer was promised over 3,000 acres of land and several mining concessions. An original plan to suddenly attack the Ndebele was abandoned as impractical. Rhodes instructed the column instead to skirt Matebeleland, so that Mashonaland could be occupied without confronting the Ndebele: 'If Lobengula looks on in silence and does nothing, the Charter[ed Company] will occupy Mashonaland...If he attacks us, he is doomed.' Armed with the latest machine-guns and searchlights to pierce the dark, the Pioneer Column left Kimberley and hoisted the British and B.S.A. Company flags at Fort Salisbury (Harare) in 1890. Rhodes's friend Dr Starr Jameson became the first administrator of the new colony of Mashonaland.

Determined to ensure the 'disappearance forever of the Matabele as a power', Rhodes and Jameson next sought a pretext for outright war with Lobengula. The pretext seized was an Ndebele raid on a vassal Shona chief near Great Zimbabwe. In 1893, Jameson raised a punitive force of volunteers, each promised 6,000 acres of land and 15 mining concessions, plus a share of any loot. While a British imperial army with Ngwato soldiers approached slowly from the south, drawing off the main Ndebele army, Jameson launched a 'flying column' of mounted troopers suddenly attacking Matebeleland from the east – like the Prussian *blitzkrieg* on Paris in 1870. As Lobengula fled northwards, he sent as a peace offering gold that was stolen by Jameson's troopers. Lobengula disappeared: neither his death nor burial place was ever recorded.

As provinces under Rhodes' company administration, Matebeleland and Mashonaland together became known as Rhodesia. In 1896, Africans in Rhodesia took up arms in the *Chimurenga/Umvukela* (armed struggle) – a determined campaign to drive out the white settlers. The uprising was unexpected. The whites believed that the war of 1893 had cowed the Ndebele into submission. As for the Shona, the settler arrival in Mashonaland had not previously provoked any armed response. Why then did the two African groups join hands in the 1896 uprising?

African grievances were the subordination and humiliation of their traditional chiefs, the imposition of taxes and the abuses of tax collectors, the loss of land to white settlers without permission or compensation, and forced labour on settler farms. The Ndebele were particularly aggrieved by the abolition of the Ndebele monarchy and by the theft of four-fifths of their cattle by Jameson's troops as war loot in 1893–94. Natural disasters – popularly blamed on the settlers – made the situation worse. Followed by locusts and severe drought destroying crops, the great rinderpest epidemic that came across the Zambezi in 1895–96 decimated herds of cattle.

Historians, notably Terence Ranger, at one time assumed that the *Chimurenga* uprising was coordinated across the land by traditional priests and spirit-mediums. Further research suggests that there were uncoordinated separate uprisings across the country that responded to local circumstance. The uprising began when many British South Africa Company troops had gone south and been captured during the ill-fated Jameson Raid in the Transvaal. The Ndebele chiefs took the initiative in March 1896, and many but not all Shona followed suit.

British imperial army reinforcements arrived, a railway from Kimberley was speedily built, and scorched-earth tactics denied food and shelter to the 'rebels'. Cecil Rhodes personally negotiated peace with the Ndebele chiefs at an *indaba* (meeting) in the Matobo Hills, south of Bulawayo, in late 1896. In Mashonaland, the war continued into 1897, ending with the capture of spirit-mediums Kaguvi and Nehanda, the latter a woman. 450 whites were killed in the uprising. There are no statistics for the number of Africans who died.

RAILWAY RIVALRY & THE JAMESON RAID

Railways were the backbones of imperialism. The rail line from Cape Town first penetrated Cape mountain ranges into the interior in 1859–63. The line reached Kimberley in 1885, Bloemfontein in 1890, and Johannesburg in

1892. By that time there were also shorter connecting rail lines from East London, Port Elizabeth, and Port Alfred on the coast of the Eastern Cape.

Cecil Rhodes became prime minister of Cape Colony in 1890, as well as head of the De Beers diamond monopoly at Kimberley and Consolidated Gold Fields Company on the Witwatersrand. Meanwhile his British South Africa Company was laying claim to the lands north of Cape Colony across the Zambezi towards Lake Tanganyika. Some now said that Rhodes had become the second most powerful individual on earth, after the Tsar of Russia.

Opposed to Rhodes, President Paul Krüger of the South African Republic (Transvaal) was determined to break away from British capitalist imperialism and from economic dependence on the Cape Colony and Natal. This meant fostering the friendship of non-British Randlord capitalists and tentative alliances with German, Portuguese, and even French imperialists. The essential part of Krüger's strategy was a new railway in the Transvaal direct from Delagoa Bay to lessen reliance on railways and wagon roads from the Cape and Natal. Backed by German finance, the Netherlands South African Railway Company was contracted in 1887. It completed the line from Lourenço Marques across flat country to the Mozambique frontier by 1890, and then had to climb dramatically onto the Highveld, reaching Pretoria in 1894. (Another rail line reached Johannesburg from Durban in 1896.)

Meanwhile, Rhodes and Jameson were planning how to capture the wealth of the Witwatersrand after a surveyor's report in 1894 had shown that there was no 'Second Rand' in Rhodesia. They proposed to repeat in the Transvaal Jameson's successful 'flying column' that had captured Matabeleland. There was much discontent among *uitlanders* (expatriate workers and managers) on the Witwatersrand about Boer misrule. *The uitlanders* – mostly British but also American and Australian – complained about being refused the vote in Transvaal elections. Randlords complained about the high costs of black labour and mine equipment under Krüger. Jameson's plan was that the *uitlanders* would rise up in armed revolt against the Krüger government and would thus justify Jameson's invasion ostensibly to protect them, in fact to take over the Transvaal government.

The South African Republic favoured its state-owned railway from Delagoa Bay by raising tariffs on all other rail routes from the coast. In response, Cape railways organized the off-loading of goods from trains north of Kimberley, to be loaded onto ox-wagons that reached Johannesburg across the Vaal drifts (fords) on the Transvaal border. Krüger therefore closed the Vaal drifts to wagon traffic in November 1895. The British threatened war, forcing Krüger to re-open the route a few days later.

This was the opportunity that Rhodes and Jameson were waiting for. The new British colonial minister, Joseph Chamberlain, refused to officially assist the Jameson plan but he arranged for the B.S.A. Company to be given a strip of land along the Transvaal border of the Bechuanaland Protectorate – for company troops to come south from Rhodesia and launch their invasion. This was after Chamberlain's negotiation in London with three chiefs from the Bechuanaland Protectorate (Khama, Sebele, and Bathoen) had further and maybe fatally delayed the arrangements of Rhodes and Jameson.

The whole enterprise proved to be an ill-managed fiasco. Jameson's raiders stayed on the border through a drunken Christmas in very hot weather, waiting in vain for an *uitlander* revolt that never materialized. Transvaal forces were waiting for them. They were captured and disarmed on 2 January 1896, on the western heights overlooking later Soweto, with Johannesburg in the far distance.

The fallout of the Jameson fiasco was considerable. Rhodes had to resign as prime minister of the Cape Colony, and his personal papers were destroyed in a mysterious fire a few months later. Four *uitlander* leaders in Johannesburg received death sentences that were commuted to hefty fines. While junior ranks among the raiders were deported, senior officers including Jameson were sent to serve prison sentences in Britain. The B.S.A. Company was punished by the British government with indefinite delay of its right to incorporate Bechuanaland as the third province of Rhodesia. Great Britain was soundly condemned by Germany, France, and Russia. Germany sent naval vessels to Delagoa Bay. For the first time, Germany was seen as Britain's potential great enemy. As Winston Churchill was to say of the war-torn twentieth century, 'I date the beginning of these violent times from the Jameson Raid.'

The Jameson Raid increased white Afrikaner distrust and suspicion of Cecil Rhodes, British imperial motives, and English-speaking whites in general. In expectation of war, the S.A. Republic had already begun stockpiling arms and ammunition in 1894, with new French and German artillery manned by German expatriates. After his re-election in 1898, Krüger signed a mutual defence pact with the Orange Free State. Commandant-general Joubert used this new military might in the re-conquest of the northern Transvaal, where the rinderpest epidemic of 1896–97 also cleared the area of blood-sucking tsetse-fly by killing off its wild buffalo hosts. The Venda kingdom in the far north was finally defeated in 1898.

Meanwhile, Joseph Chamberlain in London became convinced that British imperialism must act where private enterprise had failed to bring the Transvaal back into the British fold. In 1897, he appointed a new high commissioner in South Africa, a brilliant financial administrator named Alfred

Milner, with a mandate to bring the two Boer republics into a Cape-dominated confederation by any means necessary.

SOUTH AFRICAN WAR 1899–1902

From 1899 until 1902, Africa south of the Limpopo was seized by war between Britain and the Boer republics. The war involved all its population, black as well as white, actively or passively, in what is known as the South African War or (Second) Anglo-Boer War.

To force a showdown, Milner demanded that all *uitlander* men be given the franchise to vote for the Transvaal *volksraad*. Presidents Krüger and Steyn of the two republics presented an ultimatum demanding that Britain should stop interfering in their internal affairs. Britain rejected the ultimatum on 10 October, 1899. The South African Republic (Transvaal) and the Orange Free State declared war on Great Britain the following day. The Boer states exploited their advantage in the early phase of the war to deploy 40,000 men before British imperial reinforcements could arrive from India. By the end of October 1899, Boers had surrounded British garrisons at Ladysmith, Kimberley, and Mafeking. Some continental Europeans and Americans, and a few Englishmen, fought on the Boer side.

Most rural Afrikaners in the Cape Colony supported their Boer republican compatriots. Coloured people around Calvinia defied local white Afrikaner farmers by supporting the British army. After their leader, Abraham Esau, was assassinated, a woman named Martha Jantjies led demonstrations of women in favour of Queen Victoria that 'reached a crescendo of menacing rhythmic clapping, dancing and mocking songs to guitar and banjo accompaniment.'

Initial British reinforcements were defeated by Boer victories at Stormberg south of the Orange Free State, Magersfontein near Kimberley, and at the village called Colenso in Natal during December 1899. The War Office in London brought in General Lord Roberts from India as the new field commander. With a superior force drawn from many British colonies, Roberts marched north and captured Bloemfontein in March 1900, then Johannesburg, and finally Pretoria on 5 June 1900. Krüger escaped to Portuguese territory and ultimate exile in the Netherlands. Conventional S.A. Republic forces were 'mopped up' during August 1900. (The siege in that month of an army garrison at Elands River consisting of troops from Queensland, New South Wales, Victoria, West Australia, and Tasmania has been hailed as a founding moment for a united New Australia.)

Roberts assumed that the war was effectively won. He retired overseas when the Transvaal was once again declared a British colony in September 1900. He was succeeded by General Lord Kitchener. In fact, the war was far from over. General Christiaan de Wet began hit-and-run tactics against the British in the Orange Free State in March 1900. The guerrilla campaign of high-mobility attacks by horseback riders spread across the veld. It prolonged the war until 1902. In those two years, approximately 60,000 Boer guerrillas held their own against 200,000 British empire soldiers by fighting a hit-and-run type of war and making the maximum use of their high mobility on horseback to move across the land and harass the British military.

Kitchener's counter-guerrilla strategy was warfare by fire and fences. Crops and housing were burnt to deny the Boer guerrillas food and shelter. The open veld next to railway lines was divided into zones like a checkerboard by 8,000 kilometres of barbed-wire fence and 10,000 block-house forts overseeing the veld. Boer families and their black servants were moved into 'concentration camps' like the closed compounds of the mines – separating the guerrillas from the general populace, thus denying them access to information, food, shelter, and other help. By war's end, 117,000 whites and at least 107,000 blacks were living in overcrowded concentration camps. The death rate in these camps was very high – particularly from measles, a contagious urban disease previously little known in rural areas.

Bittereinders (Bitter-enders) were determined to fight on, even beyond the end of the war. Many Afrikaners surrendered, and some joined the British forces as National Scouts. Africans were also divided. There were armed African allies on both sides, mostly used as scouts and spies, though both sides officially denied this – and Paul Krüger made a big issue of it in his memoirs. Many peasants were loyal to the Boer farm-owners they knew, but chiefs and their followers were more likely to respect the British monarchy.

Boer guerrilla leaders operated on three fronts: Generals Jacobus de la Rey and Jan Smuts around the Magaliesberg hills of the western Transvaal, Christiaan de Wet and James Barry Hertzog in the Orange Free State, and Louis Botha on the KwaZulu frontier in the south-eastern Transvaal. It was a Zulu attack at Holkrantz on Botha's Boers, killing 56, that finally led Botha to negotiate peace with the British. Meanwhile, Smuts led a wild ride into the western part of the Cape Colony almost as far as Cape Town.

The Peace of Vereeniging in May 1902 was achieved by Milner conceding the main demands of the Boers: to keep their own rifles for protection, to allow the Nederlands language in schools and courts, for the British to fund £3 million worth of post-war reconstruction, and – above all – not to extend the Cape franchise and civil rights for black people into the Transvaal and Orange Free State. It was now Africans rather than Afrikaners who might feel betrayed by the British. Mission-educated Africans generally supported the British – in the hope that the Cape non-racial franchise would be extended to the Boer republics after conquest.

The South African War directly claimed 7,000 Boer and 22,000 British lives. There are no figures of how many black people died, though it is known that at least 20,000 died in the concentration camps. An unknown number of Africans were shot as spies.

FURTHER STUDY

BIBLIOGRAPHY

See also books recommended in previous chapters.

Beinart, William Justin (2013), *African Local Knowledge and Livestock Disease: Diseases and Treatments in South Africa*. Oxford: James Currey & Johannesburg: Wits University Press.

Couzens, Tim (2013), *South African Battles*. Johannesburg: Jonathan Ball.

Cuthbertson, Greg, Albert Grundlingh, & Mary-Lynn Suttie (2003), *Writing a Wider War: Rethinking Gender, Race and Identity in the South African War, 1899–1902*. Athens, OH: Ohio University Press.

Davidson, Apollon (2003), *Cecil Rhodes and His Time*. Pretoria: Protea Book House.

Delius, Peter Nicholas St Martin (1984), *The Land Belongs to Us: The Pedi Polity, the Boers, and the British in the Nineteenth-Century Transvaal*. Johannesburg: Ravan, London: Heinemann & Berkeley, CA: University of California Press.

Flint, John E. (1976), *Cecil Rhodes*. London: Hutchinson.

Forth, Aidan (2018), *Barbed-Wire Imperialism: Britain's Empire of Camps, 1876-1903*. Berkeley: University of California Press.

Glass, Stafford (1968), *The Matabele War [1893–94]* London: Longman.

Grundlingh, Albert (2006), *The Dynamics of Treason: Boer Collaborators in the South African War of 1899–1902*. Pretoria: Protea Books.

Guy, Jeff (1994), *The Destruction of the Zulu Kingdom: The Civil War in Zululand, 1879–1884*. Pietermaritzburg: University of Natal Press.

Guy, Jeff (2002), *The View Across the River: Harriet Colenso and the Zulu Struggle Against Imperialism*. Oxford: James Currey, Cape Town: David Philip & Charlottesville, VA: University of Virginia Press.

Landau, Paul Stuart (1995), *The Realm of the Word: Language, Gender, and Christianity in a Southern African Kingdom* [Khama's Ngwato, Botswana]. London: James Currey, Cape Town: David Philip & Portsmouth, NH: Heinemann.

Nasson, Bill (1991), *Abraham Esau's War: A Black South African War in the Cape.* Cambridge: Cambridge University Press.

Nasson, Bill (1999), *The South African War, 1899–1902.* London: Hodder Headline.

Nasson, Bill (2011), *The Boer War: The Struggle for South Africa.* Stroud: History Press.

Pakenham, Thomas (1982), *The Boer War.* London: Futura & Macdonald/Weidenfeld & Nicolson & Johannesburg: Jonathan Ball.

Pakenham, Thomas (1997), *The Scramble for Africa, 1876–1912.* Johannesburg: Jonathan Ball.

Parsons, Neil (1998), *King Khama, Emperor Joe, and the Great White Queen.* Chicago, IL: University of Chicago Press.

Plaatje, Solomon Tshekisho, ed. John Comaroff (1973), *The Boer War of Sol T. Plaatje: An African at Mafeking.* Basingstoke: Macmillan & subsequent editions.

Pretorius, Fransjohan (2013), *The Anglo-Boer War 1899–1902.* Cape Town: Don Nelson.

Pretorius, Fransjohan (2017), *Scorched Earth* [1899–1902.] Cape Town: Tafelberg.

Ranger, Terence Osborn (1979), *Revolt in Southern Rhodesia 1896–7: A Study in African Resistance.* London: Heinemann.

Ranger, Terence Osborn (1989), *Rhodes, Oxford, and the Study of Race Relations: An Inaugural Lecture.* Oxford: Clarendon Press.

Roberts, Brian (1985), *Kimberley: A Turbulent City.* Cape Town: David Philip.

Roberts, Brian (1991), *Those Bloody Women: Three Heroines of the Boer War.* London: John Murray.

Robinson, Robert, John Gallagher, & Alice Denny (1961), *Africa and the Victorians: The Official Mind of Imperialism.* London: Macmillan, 2nd edn, 1981.

Ross, Robert (1976), *Adam Kok's Griqua: A Study in the Development of Stratification in South Africa.* Cambridge: Cambridge University Press.

Rotberg, Robert I. (1988), *The Founder: Cecil Rhodes and the Pursuit of Power.* Johannesburg: Southern Book

Samkange, Stanlake (1966), *On Trial for My Country* [Lobengula drama based on official sources]. London: Heinemann.

Stassen, Nicol (2016), *The Thirstland Trek 1874–1881.* Pretoria: Protea.

Van Heyningen, Elizabeth (2013), *The Concentration Camps of the Anglo-Boer War: A Social History.* Auckland Park: Jacana Media.

Van Onselen, Charles (2001), *New Babylon, New Nineveh: Everyday Life on the Witwatersrand 1886–1914.* Johannesburg: Jonathan Ball.

Van Onselen, Charles (2008), *The Small Matter of a Horse: The Life of "Nongoloza" Mathebula, 1867–1948.* Pretoria: Protea Books.

Van Onselen, Charles (2010), *Masked Raiders: Irish Banditry in Southern Africa, 1880–1899.* Cape Town: Zebra Press.

Van Onselen, Charles (2017), *The Cowboy Capitalist: John Hays Hammond, the American West, and the Jameson Raid.* Johannesburg: Jonathan Ball.

Warwick, Peter (1983), *Black People and the South African War 1899–1902.* Johannesburg: Ravan Press & Harlow, London: Longman.

VIDEOGRAPHY

DVDs and downloads:

Blood and Glory (dir. Sean Else, 2016. 133 mins): after we see Breaker Morant revealed as a real villain, a captured Boer farmer finds redemption in the game of Rugby in a prisoner-of-war camp on the island of St Helena.

Breaker Morant (dir. Bruce Beresford, 1980. 107 mins): Australian outback troopers, led by heroic horse-breaker Morant (Edward Woodward), are court-martialled for killing Boer civilians in the Northern Transvaal in 1901–02. Were they not following official orders?

Kimberley Jim (dir. Emil Nofal, 1965. 113 mins): the only movie of American cowboy crooner 'Gentleman' Jim Reeves, strutting and singing his way as a con-man through the diamond-mining town of Kimberley.

Ohm Krüger (dir. Hans Steinhoff, 1941. 135 mins): Krüger played by the great Emil Jannings, with Rhodes, Chamberlain, Queen Victoria, and even young Churchill as villains. Goebbels' best ever drama movie.

Rhodes of Africa (dir. Berthold Viertel, 1936. 90 mins): Nostalgia DVD 2015, re-titled *Walter Huston as Rhodes*, with Oscar Homulka as Krüger. The very pro-British story made by an anti-Nazi émigré director.

Rhodes (dir. Anthony Thomas BBC/PBS/SATV, 1996. 8 × 57 mins): survey of Rhodes' life by a producer-director-author, onetime admirer of Rhodes turned sceptic. Choose the one-part movie DVD over the eight-part TV series.

The Story of an African Farm (dir. David Lister, 2004. 97 mins): dramatized version of Olive Schreiner novel set in Karoo during the 1870s. Irish confidence trickster (Richard E. Grant) disrupts Afrikaner farm life.

7 Scramble for Africa Part 2, 1902–1919

Colonialism, republicanism, and imperialism were identified in 1889 by a retiring British high commissioner at the Cape, Hercules Robinson, as the 'three competing influences at work' in Southern Africa. Robinson predicted that imperialism was 'a diminishing quantity, there being no permanent place for direct Imperial rule on any large scale.' While it was true that the economic and political might of Great Britain was being overtaken by Germany and the United States by 1900, British imperialism was to have a great burst of expansion in 1899–1905, with ripples that followed into the First World War and beyond. White settler colonialism was to flourish for much of the twentieth century. This chapter charts how British (and German) imperialism created a Southern African state system, and how white settler power created colonial segregation – between white racial aristocracy and black proletariat.

African 'primary resistance' by military means was ultimately futile, given the superiority of European technology and weapons. Africans were also divided by loyalties to rival traditional states and 'tribes'. Traditional leaders varied in their understanding and responses to colonialism. On the whole, Africans became powerless until mission-educated élites and black industrial workers became organized in 'secondary resistance' within and against colonialism.

POST-WAR RECONSTRUCTION

Between 1902 and 1905, Britain's high commissioner Alfred Milner, 'whose reputation exceeded his achievements', oversaw post-war reconstruction – assisted by a team of young British university graduates, his so-called kindergarten. Reconstruction was helped by the return to their farms of Boer prisoners of war (31,000) and concentration camp internees, as well as *uitlanders* (50,000) returning to the Witwatersrand.

The South African War left most Transvaal and Free State Boers at least temporarily impoverished, with destroyed homesteads, livestock, and crops. Some were permanently impoverished by the subdivision of property under

Romano-Dutch law, which made some farms too small to be viable. Poor white men sold their farms to rich white men, but might remain on the farm as *bywoners* (semi-employed squatters).

The post-war reconstruction project assisted the capitalization of agriculture by soil surveys for optimum crop production, agricultural research stations, and extension services to farmers. Farmers were helped in erecting barbed wire jackal-proof fencing around their land, drilling boreholes topped by windmills for water extraction, and increased mechanization of ploughs and planters. After stockholders of the Netherlands South African Railway Company were compensated, new state railway lines were extended to and through prime agricultural areas.

Agricultural reconstruction benefitted speculators on the rising value of farmland. Large farm-owners benefitted from expanding markets in mines and towns. Most Boer farmers had neither sufficient capital nor expertise to make a go of truly commercial farming. They evicted unproductive *bywoners*, often their relatives, and contracted black peasants – often the original occupants of the land – as share-croppers paying one-half or more of their harvest each year as rent. Some landless Boers were resettled in areas of the northern and western Transvaal opened up for cattle ranching by previous elimination of tsetse-fly during the rinderpest. Other white Afrikaners went to work on the mines and railways, or they emigrated to East Africa and South America.

Afrikaners in the former republics and inland areas of Cape Colony were by means reconciled with British imperialism by post-war reconstruction. Bitterness was perpetuated by Milner's Anglicization of white education and state administration. The curriculum was English-medium, with Nederlands (not Afrikaans) as a second language. Some Afrikaners responded by setting up their own schools, teaching in Afrikaans what was called a Christian-National curriculum, emphasising Afrikaner religion and national history.

Reconstruction paid little attention to Africans who, denied the franchise in the ex-republics and Natal, were not considered true citizens. It took time, after relatively good wages for wartime labour, for post-war hope and high expectations to dissipate. There was a boom of 'tribal' schools in the interior, teaching literacy and English, conducted by graduates of established Christian missions and by the proliferation of Ethiopian and independent churches (see page 146 below).

Urban racial segregation began to be enforced in coastal Cape and Natal cities during the South African War, to counteract the spread of bubonic plague brought in by hundreds of thousands of British Empire soldiers. The so-called sanitation syndrome classified some ethnicities as clean and others as dirty. Multi-racial slums were destroyed by fire and their black inhabitants expelled to new 'locations' separated by open countryside from the 'white' city. Xhosa-speakers were removed to Maitland and Ndebeni on the edge of Cape Town, or to a location near the docks for dock-workers, and to Korsten and New Brighton outside Port Elizabeth in 1901–03. Similar 'cleansing' was more difficult to implement among the shambolic shanties of Johannesburg, but the so-called Coolie location was destroyed after bubonic plague in 1904. Some Africans were removed to a camp on the Klipspruit farm – later to become the Pimville nucleus of the South-Western Townships (Soweto).

Reconstruction had to be paid for out of general taxation. The Bambatha Rebellion of 1906 in Natal was begun by chiefs resisting a new poll tax imposed in 1905–06. Two white tax collectors were killed near Pietermaritzburg. The killers were executed, and Natal colonial forces unleashed a reign of terror, looting and destroying people and property, that was to appall even the Colonial Office in London. Chief Bambatha retreated to the Drakensberg mountains to continue guerrilla warfare. Colonial forces hunted down and killed Bambatha at Mome Valley in June 1906, and the rebellion was finally crushed two months later. The Zulu king Dinizulu, Cetshwayo's successor, was arrested for sheltering tax resisters, sentenced to four years in prison, and exiled from Natal in 1910. His case was publicized internationally by the daughters of the late Bishop Colenso.

POLITICAL UNION OF FOUR PROVINCES

Resistance to Anglicization and British imperialism promoted the formation of new Afrikaner political parties. Vereeniging Het Volk (People's Party) was founded by Louis Botha and Jan Smuts in the Transvaal. Orangia Unie was established by J.B.M. Hertzog, Abram Fischer, and Christiaan de Wet in the Orange River Colony. Het Volk became the governing party of the Transvaal when the colony became self-governing in 1906. The Orange River Colony, reverting to the name Orange Free State, became self-governing in 1907.

The Earl of Selborne, who took over as high commissioner from Lord Milner in 1905, placated Afrikaners by watering down Anglicization. The Selborne Memorandum, on how a united national government for South Africa might be established, was published in January 1907. The National Convention of representatives from the Cape Colony, Natal, Transvaal, and Orange Free State met at Durban and Cape Town from October 1908 to February 1909. They agreed on a Union of South Africa, combining a central government and national assembly with provincial administrations and assemblies in each province. The main disagreement was over the Cape's objection to a common 'native policy' and a common education system. The compromise reached was to leave 'native policy' and education to each member province. There was, however, to be only one Native Affairs Department (NAD) responsible for the vast majority of Africans not privileged to vote in Cape elections.

Three African churchman or newspaper editors – Walter Rubusana, J. T. Jabavu, and John L. Dube – convened a rival South African Native (National) Convention at Bloemfontein in March 1909. The convention demanded a 'colour-blind' franchise for adult males throughout South Africa and an end to racial discrimination against Africans. Opposition to Union proposals also came from the African Political Organisation (APO) predominantly representing coloured people in Cape Town. In June 1909, a delegation, including Rubusana, Jabavu, and APO leader Dr Abdul Abdurahman, and led by Cape liberal W.P. Schreiner, travelled to Britain but could not secure support from the British government. 'No longer must we look to our flabby friends in Great Britain', concluded Abdurahman.

The British Parliament passed its South Africa Act in 1909. The Union of South Africa came into being on 31 May 1910, under the South African Party (SAP) government of Louis Botha as prime minister and Jan Smuts as his deputy.

HIGH COMMISSION TERRITORIES

Basutoland and Bechuanaland Protectorate were part of a common customs area with Cape Colony, Natal, Transvaal, and Orange River Colony, declared in 1903, to which Swaziland and Southern Rhodesia were added in 1904. The 1907 Selbourne Memorandum suggested that Basutoland and Swaziland should become part of the Union, followed by Bechuanaland Protectorate if and when Southern Rhodesia joined the Union.

Protests at plans to incorporate the High Commission Territories into the Union came from their rulers from 1907 onwards, with the support of missionary and humanitarian bodies in Britain. A number of delegations were sent to London from each of the three territories but received a cold shoulder from the Liberal party government that was determined to create the Union of South Africa as soon as possible. (Liberals had previously opposed the conquest of the Boer republics.)

The Colonial Office in London decided that because Basutoland, Bechuanaland Protectorate, and Swaziland were 'protectorates' voluntarily under the

British crown, they should not come under the governor-general of the Union (and its Native Affairs Department) but should stay under Britain's high commissioner in South Africa. Thus, the three 'protectorates' became known as the High Commission Territories.

The South Africa Act of the British parliament in 1909 included two important features. First, there was an 'entrenched clause' that the Cape non-racial franchise could only be constitutionally altered by two-thirds of the Union's senate and the house of assembly sitting together. Second, there was a schedule listing the conditions protecting African rights when the High Commission Territories were transferred to the Union. It was during parliamentary debate at Westminster on that schedule that the British government made a promise to 'consult' the chiefs of the territories before any transfer was made.

Prime minister Botha of the Union of South Africa requested the transfer of Swaziland and Bechuanaland as soon as possible in March 1913. This was countered by the Administrator of Southern Rhodesia reviving the British South Africa Company's claim to incorporate Bechuanaland Protectorate – lapsed after the failure of the Jameson Raid. Botha made a second bid, this time for Swaziland alone, in June 1919, which was also turned down.

WITWATERSRAND MINING & INDUSTRIALIZATION

The Witwatersrand mines found it difficult to recruit African workers immediately after the South African War. This was hardly surprising, as the gold mines had reduced monthly wages from the pre-war 50 shillings to 43 and then to 30 shillings, at a time when reconstruction works such as railway construction offered better wages. Mine companies looked elsewhere in the world for cheap labour, and persuaded the authorities to allow the importation of Chinese workers.

The first Chinese eventually arrived in June 1904 – ironically at a time when African men were being driven back to the mines by drought and famine. 63,000 Chinese workers were brought to the Rand in 1904–06 on four-year indentures. Their meagre wages and poor working conditions caused a scandal overseas, and the new Liberal government in Britain stopped the 'experiment'. By 1910 nearly all the Chinese workers had been repatriated to South China.

The Witwatersrand Native Labour Association (popularly known as Wenela) was responsible for recruiting labour from the region. Two-thirds of Wenela recruits came from southern Mozambique, organized by the Portuguese colonial authorities almost as a continuation of the old slave trade. Under the so-called Modus Vivendi agreement of 1901, the Portuguese supplied labour in return for the Transvaal sending an agreed proportion of its imports and exports through Lourenço Marques. The Portuguese authorities received a payment of 13 shillings per worker, plus half a shilling more for each month's service beyond the initial one-year contract period – and one-half of each worker's deferred salary was paid directly through officials in Lourenço Marques.

Nyasaland provided large numbers of migrant labourers to the Rand until 1906, when the Nyasaland government stopped labour recruitment due to very high mortality rates among 'tropical' workers in the mines. There was widespread miner's phthisis (tuberculosis) and pneumonia from chills caught from damp clothing at the end of shifts underground. This suited the Rhodesia Native Labour Bureau set up to recruit Nyasa labour for Southern Rhodesian mines and farms. Between 1912–13 and 1933 Wenela concentrated on southern Mozambique recruitment and was forbidden to recruit north of the 22nd parallel latitude (roughly the South African-Rhodesian border). In 1912, the Randlords founded a twin organization to Wenela, called the Native Recruiting Corporation (NRC), to recruit labour from the Union and south of the 22nd parallel.

Milner closed the Hatherley distillery near Pretoria in 1902–03 and declared total prohibition of alcohol for all black people – considered a necessary corollary to the reduction of black wages. Beyond the provision of basic supplies for the mining sector and packaging of local food and beverages, there was little manufacturing in South Africa before the First World War. The new Union government's Cullinan Commission of 1910 saw possibilities as long as 'infant' industries were protected from international competition by tariffs, a reasonable proportion of the raw materials came from South Africa, and employment favoured white rather than black labour. However, the South African Party government was more inclined towards free-market economics. The 1914 Customs Tariff Act giving protection to select products was insufficient to kick start the development of manufacturing industry.

It was the First World War that gave manufacturing its kick start. Import substitution was necessary during the disruption of international trade by German submarine warfare. New industries manufacturing textiles, leather, and furniture were established. By 1919 food, clothing, wood, and paper products accounted for 57 per cent of manufacturing output.

LAND SEGREGATION & AFRICAN CONGRESSES

The South African Native Affairs Commission (SANAC) of 1903–05, chaired by former Basutoland resident commissioner Godfrey Lagden, was charged with drafting a unified 'native policy' for the four colonies – paying particular attention to the Transvaal. The commission heard evidence from hundreds of witnesses, including prominent Africans, but the Lagden Report recommended what was becoming called 'segregation' – a term borrowed from the United States meaning, only in theory, 'equal facilities' for white and black. Africans should not be allowed to purchase or lease land in 'white' farming areas. The state should demarcate 'native reserves' concentrating African rural settlement. Africans should be confined to segregated 'locations' or townships outside 'white' towns, and 'native education' should equip Africans for no more than the lowest-level jobs.

The Natives' Land Act of 1913 implemented the segregationist recommendations of the Lagden Report, in all except the Cape province. It was biased towards the development of large-scale commercial farms by trying to stop share-cropping agreements between black peasants and smaller white farmers. Significant numbers of productive black peasants had emerged since the 1870s, supplying crops and livestock to mining areas. The supply of high-quality wheat from the highlands of Lesotho for Kimberley was one such crop. Peasants had benefitted from supplying British troops on the edges of the war zone, and many had moved back onto burnt-out white farms to restore agricultural production as soon as warfare was ended.

The 1913 Act pushed peasants either to become wage-employees ('farm servants') of the white farmers or to be expelled into the 'native reserves'. The Act identified 8.9 million hectares (less than 8% of the total land area) as 'native areas' where Africans could legally reside. Africans could not buy or lease land in the white areas. The 'native reserves' were to be labour pools for the white economy. Few people there could produce enough crops to sell and pay their taxes but were obliged instead to seek employment in mines, towns, and white-owned farms.

The Natives' Land Act was the major bone of contention for the newly formed South African Native Native Congress (SANNC) – later renamed African National Congress in 1923. Founded in 1912, the SANNC brought together representatives of pre-existing provincial congresses. Its president was John L. Dube from Natal; its vice-president was Rubusana from the Eastern Cape; its secretary-general was journalist Solomon T. Plaatje from the Northern Cape; its treasurer was lawyer Pixley kaIsaka Seme from the Transvaal; and the chairman or speaker of the assembly was carpenter Thomas Mapikela from the Orange Free State.

In 1914, the SANNC sent a five-man delegation to Britain to protest against the Natives' Land Act and its drastic implementation in the Orange Free State, where peasants were being expelled into the Transvaal and Basutoland. Their petition was unsuccessful, because the act was considered the legislation of another sovereign parliament. Publicity for their case was also drowned out by news of the coming war in Europe. Plaatje stayed on in England to publish his *Native Life in South Africa* (1916) detailing the effects of the act already felt by Africans: 'Awaking on Friday morning, 20 June 1913, the South African native found himself, not actually a slave, but a pariah in the land of his birth.'

SANNC and Abdurahman's APO tried to lobby the British government again during the Versailles peace talks in Paris in 1919, using the argument that non-white South Africans had served the British Empire loyally in the war. But, while admitting responsibility for the welfare of Africans in the High Commission Territories, the British government repeated that it bore no such responsibility for South Africa under the 1909 Act of Union.

Van Onselen's history of Kas Maine illustrates the life of an exceptional African peasant share-cropper in South Africa. People like him were driven out of commercial farms in the main agricultural areas into marginal white farms. As well as taking half-shares of produce, poor white farmers borrowed oxen and equipment from black peasant tenants to grow maize, tobacco, and vegetables. Long after the 1913 Act, Kas Maine prospered from unwritten share-cropping agreements with white farmers in the dry extreme south-west pocket of the Transvaal.

GERMANY & NAMA-HERERO RESISTANCE

Nama and Herero chiefs came under German colonial rule through treaties accepting German 'protection' and German traders. In 1893, the Nama village of Hornkrantz, whose chief had refused to sign such a treaty, was attacked at night by German commander Captain Curt von Françoise, killing more than 78 women and children, looting, and burning the village to the ground. As the number of German immigrants increased, Africans were expelled to marginal areas to give the vacated land to the new arrivals:

The land...must be transferred from the hands of the natives to those of the whites, [this] is the object of colonization in the territory. The land shall be settled by whites. So the natives must give way and either become servants of the whites or withdraw. (*Deutsch Sudwestafrikanische Zeitung*, 22 January 1901).

The Nama and Herero had been well-to-do pastoralists with large herds of cattle. They lost both their land and cattle through white traders' sharp practices – inflated prices for imported goods and easy credit trapping people into debt. Land and cattle were taken as payment of debt. By 1903, 80,000 Africans owned only 45,910 cattle, while the handful of Germans – who had had no cattle a few years earlier – possessed no fewer than 44,490. Grievances arose from confinement of herders and hunters in restricted 'native reserves' and from the construction of land-eating towns and railways cutting across the country – symbols that German rule had come to stay. African men suffered from racial discrimination, and African women suffered from sexual abuse.

These grievances fuelled Herero and Nama wars against the Germans. The Herero paramount chief, Samuel Maherero, urged his Nama counterpart in 1904 to join him in war because it was better 'to die fighting than as a result of maltreatment, imprisonment, or some other calamity'. The Herero rose against German rule on 12 January 1904, seized German settlers' livestock, and killed more than 100 German settlers and soldiers. The Herero held the initiative until June that year in conducting a guerrilla campaign against settler farms and businesses. The colonial government was forced to appeal back to Germany for military reinforcements. The reinforcements arrived under ruthless General Lothar von Trotha, who declared:

> I believe that the [Herero] nation as such should be annihilated, or, if this was not possible by tactical measures, have to be expelled from the country...This will be possible if the water-holes from Grootfontein to Gobabis are occupied...All Hereros must leave the country. If they do not do so, I will force them with cannons to do so. Within the German borders, every Herero, with or without weapons...will be shot. I shall no longer shelter women and children. They must either return to their people or I will shoot them. This is my message to the Herero nation.[1]

At the Battle of Waterberg in August 1904, German forces defeated the Herero and drove them, the majority being women and children, into the Omaheke desert – where thousands perished. Some survivors reached safety in the Bechuanaland Protectorate. By the end of the campaign, only 16,000 out of the original 80,000 Herero were left alive inside German South West Africa.

The Herero defeat aroused Nama resistance that lasted from 1904 until 1908. Two thousand Nama fighters evaded and ambushed a German army of 15,000 men in no less than 200 armed engagements. Nama guerrilla leader Jacob Morenga was eventually cornered at the Battle of Rooysvlei and escaped into the Cape Colony, where he was killed by Cape colonial police in June 1907. The final battle of the war in March 1908 was an unsuccessful German attempt to stop the Franzman-Nama leader Simon Kopper (Cooper) and his people escaping (successfully) across the border to refuge in Bechuanaland Protectorate. By this time, only 9,700 Nama were left alive out an original 20,000 people.

Survivors of the Nama-Herero uprisings were kept in concentration camps on Shark Island in Lüderitz Bay, for day-release as slave labour to settlers and the military. Many died from overwork, malnutrition, and disease – nearly half of them in 1908. All remaining cattle were confiscated, and chiefs were deposed. From August 1907, Africans (except those in the unconquered far north) were forbidden by law from owning land or cattle, and all over seven years of age were required to carry passes identifying their employment.

CONQUEST & RESISTANCE IN PORTUGUESE AFRICA

It was not until the second decade of the twentieth century that Portugal established control over all of Angola or Mozambique, when Portuguese troops were equipped with superior modern weapons to conquer resistance and quell uprisings.

In Angola, the Bailundo-Ovimbundu people of the Bihé Plateau, who had been under Portuguese rule for many decades, rose up in 1902 against the contract labour system imposed on them by the authorities. Led by Matu ya Kevele, the uprising targeted Portuguese tax collectors, traders, and troop bases. It took the Portuguese two years to subdue this uprising. In southern Angola, the Kwanyama-Ovambo (Cuanhama) rose in armed resistance against the 1902–04 Portuguese attempt to impose their rule. Over 300 Portuguese soldiers were killed before the Kwanyama were defeated – only to rise again during the First World War. Numerous other uprisings in different parts of Angola were suppressed by the Portuguese army up until 1919.

In Mozambique, the Portuguese intensified inland military conquest after the 1884–85 Berlin conference. In the south, King Gungunyana (Ngungunyana) of the Gaza-Nguni was encouraged by Cecil Rhodes to ally with Britain, so that Rhodesia could have its own road to the sea. But Britain stood back when the Portuguese engaged in battles with the Gaza-Nguni. Gungunyana was finally defeated in 1895 and was exiled to the Portuguese

Azores islands in the Atlantic. In northern Mozambique, the Makua of Cabo Delgado province surrendered only in 1910, and the Yao of Niassa province only in 1912. But these same areas were lost to a German army invasion during the First World War. It was not until 1918 that the Portuguese were able to say that they had gained full control of all Portuguese East Africa (Mozambique).

SOUTHERN AFRICA & FIRST WORLD WAR

When Britain declared war on Germany and Austria in August 1914, many black and coloured men offered to fight on Britain's side. The S.A. Native National Congress suspended political protest against the Natives' Land Act and declared its support for the war. The Union Defence Force (UDF), however, refused to equip non-whites with firearms. Cape coloured troops joined

Map 7.1   First World War Hostilities

the British Army overseas instead, while black troops were recruited into the unarmed South African Native Labour Contingent or Corps (SANLC). This included men from the High Commission Territories – though Khama and other chiefs boycotted recruitment. Meanwhile, black troops (Kalanga from Bulawayo, as Ndebele boycotted recruitment, and Shona from Salisbury) were recruited into the Rhodesia Native Regiment, and Nyasa and some Northern Rhodesian men were recruited into the King's African Rifles – given a fully armed combat role in German East Africa (Tanganyika).

English-speaking white South Africans rallied to the cause, but the war seriously divided Afrikaners. Louis Botha himself led the UDF invasion of German South West Africa (Namibia), and Jan Smuts later took to the field in German East Africa. Others saw the war as an opportunity to ally with Germany and restore Boer independence. General Koos de la Rey, *bittereinder* hero of the previous war, was inspired by the vague prophesy of victory by *siener* (seer or prophet) Niklaas van Rensburg. On 15 September 1914, De la Rey and co-conspirator General Christiaan Beyers, who had just resigned as head of the UDF, set off by car through Johannesburg to recruit other rebels in the south-west Transvaal. They refused to stop at a police road block, intended to catch the Foster gang of criminals, and were fired upon. De la Rey was killed. The UDF commander on the German frontier, Manie Maritz, defected to the German side, after being attacked by UDF troops loyal to Botha and Smuts. Beyers was drowned trying to cross the Vaal River in flood. General Christiaan de Wet was captured trying to join Maritz. General Jan Kemp turned back and surrendered on 4 February 1915.

Botha capitalized on his UDF victory over the Boer revolt by leading the conquest of German South Africa, capturing Swakopmund in February 1915 and Windhoek in May 1915. After the Germans surrendered, the UDF proceeded northwards to collaborate with Portuguese forces against the Kwanyama-Ovambo.

The war in German East Africa was fought on two fronts. In the south, Rhodesian forces (including the black soldiers of the Northern Rhodesia police) and the King's African Rifles from Nyasaland pushed slowly northwards, while British army units – stiffened by UDF troops under Smuts and by West African and Caribbean troops – pushed the German army of General Paul von Lettow-Vorbeck southwards from Kenya. Vorbeck led an army of 3,000 whites and 11,000 well-trained black soldiers (*askaris*). Between November 1917 and September 1918 Vorbeck withdrew into northern Mozambique, living off captured Portuguese supplies. He then led a rapid invasion around the north end of Lake Malawi into Northern Rhodesia, where only the end of the war stopped him from capturing the Katanga copperbelt. His was the only undefeated German army of the Great War.

White troops of the UDF played a notable part and suffered heavy losses at Delville Wood during the battle of the Somme on the Western Front in France (1916). The UDF's great achievement in the war was its suicidal resistance of the German counter-offensive launched in March 1918. Unarmed black troops of the S.A. Native Labour Corps handled supplies behind the front line. More than 600 of them were drowned when the troopship Mendi sank after a collision in the English-French Channel on 21 February 1917.

The failure of the Boer revolt in 1914 showed that the effective future of Afrikaner nationalism lay within, not outside, the new political system. General Hertzog broke away from Botha and Smuts's South African Party in 1914 to form his own National Party. Botha and Smuts were perceived as being too close to British or English-speaking mining capitalists. In 1918, wealthy Afrikaners, mostly in the Cape, using the *helpmekaar* (mutual aid) principle, pooled financial resources to establish the South African National Trust Company (Santam) – a credit institution, and the South African National Life Assurance Company (Sanlam) – an insurance company. In the same year, young professionals and ministers in the Dutch Reformed Church countered the non-racial international Brotherhood movement by founding the Afrikaner Broederbond to promote and protect Afrikaans culture and national assertion.

There was a cultural outburst of the new Afrikaner nationalism in the publishing of books and magazines in Afrikaans. The relative failure of English-language culture to take root among whites in South Africa can be seen in the history of the film industry. African Film Productions began with a great flourish by its founder American millionaire I.W. Schlesinger in 1915–16. It produced more than 40 movies plus weekly newsreels and hundreds of actuality or documentary films. But it failed to follow up its initial appeal for both Afrikaners and Africans, by ceasing to make movies that featured them. South African movie production disappeared under the flood of Hollywood imports in the early 1920s.

COLONIAL RULE IN SOUTHERN RHODESIA

From 1908 onwards the British South Africa Company shifted the economy of Southern Rhodesia away from mineral production towards white agricultural settlement. African peasants on better soils showed that there was a good and growing market for foodstuffs in mines and towns and export potential opened up by the new railway across the Victoria Falls to the Katanga copper-belt in the Belgian Congo and new mines of Northern Rhodesia. In 1908, the

B.S.A. Company set up an Estates Department to promote white settlement and process applications for land. This was followed by agricultural training and extension services and by the creation of a Land Bank in 1912 to provide capital for farmers.

Hand in hand with the 'white agricultural policy' came the removal of African inhabitants from white-owned land into 'native reserves'. The first reserves had been declared in 1894 in southern Matebeleland (Gwaai, Tsholotsho, and Nkai). By 1905, 60 had been established mostly in less fertile parts of the country with less rainfall, and they were demarcated and considerably reduced by the Native Reserves Commission of 1914–15. Over time the 'native reserves' became overcrowded and degraded through soil erosion. Thus was born the land issue that remained a constant source of African grievance.

White settler males were given an elected majority of representatives in the Southern Rhodesia legislative council in 1911 – with Charles Coghlan its most voluble member. The British royal charter, given in 1889 to the British South Africa Company, was due to expire after 25 years in 1914, but the charter was extended for 10 years. This enabled the company to bring in more white settlers of British and Irish origin after the Great War, selling them company land in Southern and Northern Rhodesia and in the border strip of Bechuanaland acquired in 1895. This would make Rhodesia not just a 'white man's country' but also more loyal to the British Empire than the Afrikaner-dominated Union of South Africa. Some white women were also enfranchised in 1919.

The B.S.A. Company hoped to profit from financial compensation when Southern Rhodesia became the fifth province of the Union. However, the referendum among settler voters held in 1922 rejected this possibility, despite Jan Smuts's tour of the country campaigning for a 'Yes' vote. Two out of three voters voted 'No'. Charles Coghlan became the first prime minister of the colony under 'responsible government' in 1923 when B.S.A. Company rule ended.

The African voice was muted in much of Southern Rhodesia for a generation after *Chimurenga*. The two voices most strongly heard were those of Ndebele royalists and expatriate Africans from South Africa. Among the latter, there were Mfengu (Fingo) and Basuto associations, spokesmen for the S.A. Native National Congress, and the Rhodesian Bantu Voters Association. Supporters of Lobengula's oldest surviving son, mission-educated Nyamanda, came together in the Matabele National Home Movement to protest the reduction of royal and aristocratic land rights by the 1914–15 Native Reserves Commission. Meanwhile, beginning in the 1920s there was a remarkable conversion to attendance at mission schools among Shona and Kalanga children.

COLONIAL RULE IN SOUTH WEST AFRICA

Following the crushing of the Nama-Herero uprisings, German economic development of South West Africa proceeded apace. Copper mines were opened at Otavi and Tsumeb in 1907, and diamond fields were exploited in the sands of Lüderitz Bay from 1908. In the southern two-thirds of the country, known as the Police Zone, all African males aged seven or over who did not carry passes at all times, to prove their employment by whites, were arrested for vagrancy and impressed into labour on white farms or in public works.

The northern one-third of the country (Ovamboland and Caprivi Strip) was not fully conquered until the First World War. Chief Mandume ya Ndemufayo of the Kwanyama had fled there from the Portuguese in 1915. Following their victory in the south, the South African army combined with Portuguese forces to attack, capture, and kill Mandume in February 1917. His last words were: 'I will fight until my last bullet is spent.'

The League of Nations emerged in 1920 out of the Versailles peace negotiations of 1919, inspired by President Woodrow Wilson of the United States. (The next U.S. president refused to join the League.) One of the League's remits was the disposal of Germany's overseas colonies and Turkey's Middle-East possessions as 'mandates' or trusteeship territories held 'in trust for their inhabitants' by victorious Allied powers. In Africa, France and Britain shared Togo and Cameroon. Belgium took Rwanda and Burundi, and Britain took Tanganyika – all as B-class mandates. South Africa took South-West Africa as a C-class mandate – i.e. it could be administered as part of South Africa but had to 'promote to the utmost the material and moral well-being and social progress of the inhabitants of the territory'. This was understood to be until such time as South West Africa 'reached a stage of development' like an A-class mandate that it could be recognized as an independent nation.

The new colonial régime in South-West Africa raised the age for African males to carry compulsory passes from to 7 to 14 years of age. White Afrikaner settlers flooded in to take up farms and ranches, requiring further reduction of African reserves in order to accommodate them. English-speaking capitalists took over the mines, with the Anglo-American Corporation of South Africa Ltd under Ernest Oppenheimer of Kimberley acquiring the Lüderitz diamond fields.

The new South African administration was confronted by the Bondelswarts rising in 1921. The Khoe-speaking Bondelswarts, closely related to the Nama, were upset by South Africa refusing to restore land taken forcibly by the

Germans – and this after they had fought on the South African side in the recent war. The immediate trigger of the rising was the imposition of a dog tax, limiting their ability to hunt independently. The rising was put down with exceptional brutality that involved dropping 16 bombs on the community from aircraft, killing 100 people and wounding 468 others.

Another serious uprising against South African rule was nipped in the bud. The coloured Afrikaans-speaking Basters of Rehoboth, south of Windhoek, had migrated from Cape Colony in 1868 and regarded themselves as a free people with their own government – and had been recognized as such under German overrule. The South African administration, however, regarded the well-armed Rehobothers as a challenge to its authority. Restrictions on land use, imposition of new taxes, and new cattle-branding regulations caused 400 Rehobothers and non-Rehobother 'squatters' to attempt a rebellion, which was quickly suppressed in 1925. Demonstrations of colonial military might included hostile buzzing by aircraft.

INDEPENDENT CHURCHES

The scramble for Africa was accompanied by an increasing flow into the continent of European and American Christian missionaries, who subordinated and even replaced African ministers, evangelists, teachers, and preachers already at work in the missions. This resulted in some African ministers and church leaders breaking away from established white missionary societies to found their own independent churches. The first independent churches usually began as 'tribal' state churches. There were temporary schisms among (Paris Evangelical) Calvinists in Basutoland in 1872 and (London Mission) Congregationalists in British Bechuanaland in 1886–90 – the latter restored in 1895 as the Native Independent Congregational Church.

The founder of the Thembu National Church of 1884, Rev. Nehemiah Tile, was resisting the attempt of his Wesleyan Methodist superiors to stop him engaging in politics. Other Thembu Wesleyan ministers, as far distant as the Witwatersrand, then joined his church. Anglican evangelist Joseph Khanyane Napo broke away to found his own non-tribal Africa Church at Pretoria in 1888. The Free Lutheran Bapedi Church was founded in 1889 by a faction within Pedi royalty backing a breakaway white missionary (Rev. J.A. Winter) of the Berlin Mission.

It was Wesleyan Methodist Rev. Mangena Maake Mokone who chose the name Ethiopian Church for the new church he founded with other clergy at Pretoria in 1892, inspired by the King James Bible's Psalm 68 verse 31: 'Ethiopia shall soon stretch forth her hands unto God.'[2] This brought together the Thembu Church now under Jonas Goduka (Tile's successor), Khanyane Napo's Africa Church, and a black Anglican named Samuel James Brander. They were joined in 1895 by dynamic preacher Rev. James Mata Dwane – who had quarrelled with his Wesleyan Methodist superiors over funds he had raised on a mission tour of England.

Dwane received letters from his nieces Charlotte and Kate Manye, sisters from Kimberley, who had been part of an African choir sent in 1891 to raise money in Britain for the Lovedale Institution of the Free (Presbyterian) Church of Scotland in the Eastern Cape. While other choir members went home to the Cape Colony in 1893, Charlotte and Kate Manye managed to cross the Atlantic and enroll at the Wilberforce College of the African Methodist Episcopal Church, at Xenia south of Cincinnati. The sisters became members of the AMEC – historically the oldest and most prestigious of independent black churches in the United States (founded 1787). They persuaded their uncle that the Ethiopian Church should join the AMEC. The Ethiopian Church thus became part of the AMEC's new mission in southern Africa from about 1896.

Dwane himself was persuaded to become an Anglican in 1900, heading his own Order of Ethiopia, and the AMEC mission began to fragment four years later in personal quarrels. Brander broke away from the AMEC to found his own Ethiopian Catholic Church in Zion in 1904. Other important independent churches, unconnected with the AMEC, were the Zulu Congregational Church, which broke from the American (Congregationalist) Board in 1897, and the African Presbyterian Church in 1898, when the Reverend Pambami Mzimba took most of his congregation with him after quarrelling with the Scottish Presbyterian at Lovedale over money raised on mission tour in Scotland.

Thus was born what was called the Ethiopian(ist) Movement of African independent churches, with political differences but essentially no religious differences of doctrine from the established mission churches. They can be seen as 'secondary resistance' to colonialism, expressing the political and economic ambitions of a rising educated élite or 'petty bourgeoisie'. The AMEC remained at the heart of African nationalism in South Africa.

The new century saw a great spread of Zionist and Apostolic type churches from seeds planted in southern Africa by new religious movements from America. These churches were congregations under populist individual preachers or 'prophets' who invoked the Holy Spirit and offered the masses, women in particular, freedom from the witchcraft of tradition and the diseases of modern life. Christian-Zionism originated in America with the Christian Catholic Church (CCC) of John Alexander Dowie at Zion City, north of Chicago. The CCC soon split into six groups, and the converts made in Johannesburg were taken by the Zion Apostolic Church in 1908 – taking advantage of the Transvaal's 1907 ban on the AMEC and the Ethiopianists. From about 1915, white members called themselves Pentecostalists, while blacks split up into Zionist congregations under different leaders. (The predominant Zion Christian Church or ZCC of Anglican-educated Bishop Engenas Lekganyane dates from 1924 but expanded most rapidly after 1949.)

Fears of the Ethiopian movement – with its subversive African American connections – were unfounded as a security threat to white colonial domination, except in the case of Rev. John Chilembwe, who led a revolution against British rule in Nyasaland in 1915. According to the official enquiry afterwards held, the aim of the uprising was the 'extermination or expulsion of the European population, and the setting up of a native state or theocracy of which John Chilembwe was to be head'.

John Chilembwe was one of a number of Africans who came under the influence of a radical white Australian missionary named Joseph Booth. They first met in 1892 when Booth set up an 'industrial mission' paying workers in Nyasaland six times the normal pay. Booth then tried and failed to set up a cooperative venture known as the African Christian Union in Natal in 1896 – to run mines and plantations on behalf of its black shareholders, with a shipping line linking Natal with America, and 'to pursue steadily and unswervingly the policy AFRICA FOR THE AFRICAN.' Chilembwe travelled with Booth to the United States, where he was ordained a Baptist minister. On returning to Nyasaland in 1901, Chilembwe founded his own church, the Providence Industrial Mission, in his home village of Chiradzulu. His mission was adjacent to the vast Bruce Estates, run by a white manager whose harsh treatment of African workers was legendary.

Chilembwe became increasingly critical of British colonial rule and the maltreatment of Africans on white settler-owned estates. But it was the recruitment of Nyasa soldiers into the King's African Rifles at the outbreak of war that really incensed him. He protested publicly at Africans being required to die for a cause that was not their own. The colonial government remained deaf to his protests, and Chilembwe decided to take matters in his own hands. His followers would first raid the colonial armoury at Blantyre, to capture arms and ammunition. That would be the spark that would detonate a country-wide revolt by African workers, leading to freedom and a new state free from British rule.

Chilembwe's planned uprising began as planned on 23 January 1915. The manager of Bruce Estates was decapitated by the insurgents. But the attack on the armoury failed, and colonial forces counter-attacked. Chilembwe attempted to flee to Mozambique but was captured and killed on 3 February. Most of his attack group were summarily tried and executed. Did John Chilembwe – like the American abolitionist John Brown at Harper's Ferry in 1859 – expect merely to 'strike a blow and die' and be a martyr for those who followed struggling for freedom?

Cecil Rhodes, who died in 1902, may never have used the word 'segregation' but it is difficult to disassociate his heritage from the concept. As prime minister of the Cape Colony he may have invoked 'equal rights for all civilized men' when it suited him. He summed up his political preferences more clearly as 'no liquor and no vote' for Africans. Rhodes aspired towards a dualism of parallel socio-economic and political systems kept apart by racial segregation. Rhodes' former private secretary Robert Corydon developed these ideas further after the death of his master.

As a colonial administrator, Coryndon expressed his conviction 'that [the white] man must master nature and use her for his own betterment.' In North-Western Rhodesia (1900–07), he established white farms along the railway line. In Swaziland, he converted white land leases from the Swazi king into freehold ownership, scattering 32 small 'native reserves' among white farms (1909). In Southern Rhodesia, Coryndon's Native Reserves Commission of 1914–15 demarcated the country's prime agricultural areas for commercial white agriculture. As governor of Uganda he favoured white-owned coffee plantations over African peasant production, and he opposed industrial development by local Indians. Finally, as governor of Kenya (1922–25), Coryndon favoured European enterprise in farms and towns alongside dependent African (labour) reserves. At the same time, he hid behind the pretence of 'native paramountcy' for African interests to deny property and political rights for the large local Indian population.

In order to justify his segregation policies, Coryndon used the phrase 'dual policy' – an echo of Lord Lugard's best-seller *The Dual Mandate* (1922). Economists later described the typical colony as a 'dual economy' – with a dynamic 'modern' sector and a traditional 'subsistence' sector. Few economists realized that the 'dual economy' of a colony was not a state of nature. It had been man-made by dual policies.

FURTHER STUDY

BIBLIOGRAPHY

See also books recommended in the previous chapter.

Beinart, William Justin (1982), *The Political Economy of Pondoland, 1860–1930*. Johannesburg; Ravan & Cambridge: Cambridge University Press.

Beinart, William Justin & Colin Bundy (1987), *Hidden Struggles in Rural South Africa: Policies and Popular Movements in the Transkei and Eastern Cape*. Berkeley, CA: University of California Press.

Bundy, Colin (1979), *The Rise and Fall of the South African Peasantry*. London: Heinemann, Berkeley, CA: University of California Press & Cape Town: David Philip.

Couzens, Tim (2013), *South African Battles*. Johannesburg: Jonathan Ball.

Couzens, Tim (2014), *The Great Silence: From Mushroom Valley to Delville Wood, South African Forces in World War One*. Johannesburg: Art Publishers.

Gewald, Jan-Bart (1999), *Herero Heroes: A Socio-Political History of the Herero of Namibia 1890–1923*. Oxford: James Currey & Athens, OH: University of Ohio Press.

Gribble, John & Graham Scott (2017), *We Die Like Brothers: The Sinking of the SS Mendi [21 Feb.1917]* London & Swindon: Historic England.

Grundlingh, Albert (2015), *War and Society, Participation and Remembrance: South African Black and Coloured Troops in the First World War, 1914–1918*. Stellenbosch: SUN Media.

Guy, Jeff (2005), *The Maphumulo Uprising: War, Law and Ritual in the Zulu Rebellion*. Scottsville KZN: University of KwaZulu-Natal Press.

Guy, Jeff (2006), *Remembering the Rebellion: The Zulu Uprising of 1906*. Scottsville KZN: University of KwaZulu-Natal Press.

Kallaway, Peter (1986), *Johannesburg Images and Continuities: A History of Working Class Life Through Pictures, 1885–1935*. Johannesburg: Ravan.

Mwase, George Simeon (1975), *Strike a Blow and Die: The Classic Story of the Chilembwe Rising*. London: Heinemann.

Nasson, Bill (2007), *Springboks on the Somme: South Africa in the Great War, 1914–1918*. Johannesburg: Penguin.

Nasson, Bill (2014), *WWI and the People of South Africa*. Cape Town: Tafelberg.

Odendaal, André (1984), *Vukani Bantu! The Beginnings of Black Protest Politics in South Africa*. Cape Town: David Philip.

Odendaal, André (2012), *The Founders: The Origins of the African National Congress and the Struggle for Democracy*. Johannesburg: Jacana & Lexington, KY: University Press of Kentucky.

Palmer, Robin & Neil Parsons, eds. (1977), *The Roots of Rural Poverty in Central and Southern Africa*. London: Heinemann & Berkeley, CA: University of California Press.

Parsons, Neil (2018), *Black and White Bioscope: Making Movies in Africa 1899 to 1925*. Bristol: Intellect Books, Chicago, IL: University of Chicago Press & Pretoria: Protea Books.

Phillips, Howard (2012), *Plague, Pox and Pandemics: Jacana Pocket History of Epidemics in South Africa*. Auckland Park: Jacana Pocket Books.

Plaatje, Solomon Tshekisho (1916), *Native Life in South Africa: Before and Since the European War and the Boer Rebellion*. London: P.S. King & many reprints.

Ngqulunga, Bongani (2017), *The Man Who Founded the ANC: A Biography of Pixley ka Isaka Seme*. Johannesburg: Penguin Random House.

Ranger, Terence Osborn (1970), *The African Voice in Southern Rhodesia, 1898–1930*. London: Heinemann.

Samson, Anne (2006), *Britain, South Africa and the East African Campaign, 1914–1918: The Union Comes of Age*. London & New York: I.B. Tauris.

Samson, Anne (2013), *World War I in Africa: The Forgotten Conflict Among European Powers*. London: I.B. Tauris.

Shepperson, George Albert & Thomas Price (1958), *Independent African: John Chilembwe and the Origins, Setting and Significance of the Nyasaland Native Rising of 1915*. Edinburgh: Edinburgh University Press.

Stapleton, Timothy Joseph (2006), *No Insignificant Part: The Rhodesia Native Regiment and the East Africa Campaign of the First World War*. Waterloo: Wilfrid Laurier Press.

Van Onselen, Charles (1980), *Chibaro: African Mine Labour in Southern Rhodesia 1900–1933*. Johannesburg: Ravan.

Van Onselen, Charles (1996), *The Seed if Mine: The Life of Kas Maine, a South African Sharecropper 1894-1985*. New York: Hill & Wang & Cape Town: David Philip.

Willan, Brian (1984), *Sol Plaatje African Nationalist 1875–1932*. London: Heinemann, Berkeley, CA: University of California Press & Johannesburg: Ravan.

VIDEOGRAPHY

DVDs and downloads:

The African Queen (dir. John Huston, 1951): classic tale of Cockney roughneck (Humphrey Bogart) with prissy missionary lady (Katharine Hepburn) attacking Germans on Lake Tanganyika during the First World War.

Black and White in Color (dir, Jean-Jacques Annaud, 1976): Gentle comedy about French colonists' ridiculous attempt to conquer German Cameroun in the First World War.

De La Rey (dir. Henk Hugo, 1980): Afrikaans movie about the life and death of the leader of the Boer rebellion in 1914.

Namibia: Genocide and the Second Reich (BBC, 2014): documentary with historian Jan-Bart Gewald on German-Nama and German-Herero extermination and concentration camps.

Shout at the Devil (dir. Peter Hunt, 1976): English aristocrat (Roger Moore) and his American roughneck relative (Lee Marvin) combine to attack a German cruiser on the coast of East Africa.

8 Golden Years for Colonialism, 1919–1948

The imperialism of the European powers developed into the colonialism of white-settler rule in most of southern Africa after the Great War. White settlers were, in the words of the novelist John Buchan, 'a racial aristocracy in relation to the subject peoples...a democracy in relation to each other.' The colonial system in South Africa and ex-German South West Africa, Southern Rhodesia, and parts of Northern Rhodesia and Nyasaland fostered the development of settler commercial agriculture in support of mineral-exporting industries, drawing heavily on African labour throughout the region. What has been called 'the alliance of Gold and Maize', between mine capital and agricultural capital, ensured white riches and exacerbated black poverty.

Other colonies in southern Africa, notably the High Commission Territories and large parts of Northern Rhodesia and Nyasaland, came under what became known as Indirect Rule – British district commissioners supervising the everyday rule of officially recognized African chiefs and paramount chiefs. Meanwhile, Angola and Mozambique were treated as extensions of Portugal itself, in which all the former slave majority – except a culturally assimilated minority – had no intrinsic rights.

Effective 'secondary resistance' to colonial rule now came from Western-educated Africans who have too often been seen as 'collaborators' in the age of armed and violent 'primary resistance'. Schools were the incubators of a new social class, conversant in the language and laws of the colonial state. The cash nexus was spread by the demands of poll-tax and hut-tax that forced African men to sell their crops for cash as peasants or migrate and sell their labour for cash. Peasant production, however, became less viable as white settlers seized land and controlled markets to favour large commercial farms.

SOUTH AFRICA UNDER JAN SMUTS 1919–24

In 1907, white miners struck on the Witwatersrand against Africans replacing them in semi-skilled employment at a time of economic recession. Racial discrimination in the workplace was enforced by the 1911 Native Regulation Act that made industrial strikes by black workers an imprisonable offence – and by the 1911 Mines and Works Act that reserved all skilled jobs in mines and industries for whites in the Transvaal and Orange Free State.

The end of the Great War was a time of world economic depression. The authorities were alarmed by the number of demobilized white soldiers coming back from the Great War, seeking their old jobs. Conscious of socialist revolutions in Europe, ex-soldiers took the lead in organizing the white working class against the mine capitalists. In September 1918, the Witwatersrand Chamber of Mines was forced to concede a so-called Status Quo agreement reserving semi-skilled as well as skilled jobs for whites only. With post-war inflation sharply pushing up prices, there were strikes for better wages by unskilled black workers that were crushed by police. Sanitary workers and other municipal employees struck in Johannesburg in 1919. Nineteen black strikers were killed at Port Elizabeth and eleven on the Rand in 1920.

Jan Smuts, Botha's successor as prime minister since 1919, tried to balanced the interests of the Randlord mine-owners, the paymasters of his South Africa Party (SAP), against the interests of white workers who could vote out the SAP at the next elections. The mine-owners were hit by the falling world gold price, from 130 shillings per ounce in 1919 to 95 shillings by December 1921. The obvious answer was to save costs by replacing high-wage whites by low-wage blacks. In November 1921, the Chamber of Mines decided with Smuts's approval to eliminate the job colour bar for all semi-skilled positions. The jobs of thousands of white mineworkers were threatened, and they responded in outrage. The announcement led to major strikes in the gold and coal mines, escalating into a general strike in the Transvaal in early 1922, which then became armed rebellion.

Under a barrier reading 'Workers of the world unite and fight for a white South Africa', workers led by ex-soldiers marched into central Johannesburg. They attacked black workers who ignored the strike, but were opposed by armed Afrikaner commandos come in from the countryside, as well as by police. They were bombed from the air by aircraft. The Rand Revolt lasted from January to March 1922. By the end of the conflict, over 200 were dead and over 650 wounded. 800 were charged in the courts, 46 on murder charges. Eighteen were sentenced to death, and four actually executed. Foreign-born rebel leaders were deported. White miners were forced to accept lower wages and an increasing proportion of black workers in semi-skilled roles.

Emerging out of this ferment were two significant new forces – communists and black trade unionists. Inspired by the Russian Revolution, the Communist Party of South Africa (CPSA) was formed in 1921 by members of the International Socialist League that had previously broken away from the S.A. Labour Party. The failure of the 1922 Rand Revolt made the CPSA rethink its entirely white membership. Black workers should no longer be disregarded as mere slaves or 'muscle-machines'. Instead, they should be encouraged to realize their working-class identity in solidarity with white workers.

The Industrial and Commercial (Workers) Union of South Africa (ICU) was founded by a Nyasa (Malawian) migrant named Clements Kadalie in Cape Town in 1919 – after he had organized a successful dockworkers' strike with ISL assistance in December 1918. Kadalie oversaw a significant rise in African trade union activity, which benefitted from an increase in African wages between 1921 and 1925 that was not exceeded in any other period between 1900 and 1970.

Prime minister Smuts came under heavy criticism for his heavy-handed suppression of the 1922 revolt. He was also responsible for the aerial bombing and machine-gunning of Nama-Khoe people protesting new taxation at Bondelswarts in South West Africa in 1921 – killing many women and children. Similarly, Smuts authorized the police machine-gunning of members of the Israelite separatist church at Bulhoek near Queenstown, after the crowd refused to disperse. Poet Roy Campbell referred to Smuts with bitter irony as 'The saint who fed birds at Bondelswart/ And fattened up the vultures at Bulhoek.'

The Dutch Reformed Church was worried about the increasing 'poor white problem' – the influx of unemployable white Afrikaner *bywoners* into the cities, driven out of the countryside by the commercialization of farming using more capital and less labour. (There was, of course, a parallel poor-black African problem.) The number of poor whites in 1920 was estimated around 100,000. The main response of the Botha-Smuts SAP government to the problem was reduction of competition by black labour. The 1923 Native Urban Areas Act restricted urban Africans to segregated peri-urban locations. Laws required them to carry passes at all times, validated by their current employers to permit their presence in that town.

PACT & NATIONAL PARTY GOVERNMENTS 1924–36

After the 1924 elections, J.B. Hertzog's National Party and the S.A. Labour Party came together in the so-called Pact government – combining a large party of rural Afrikaners, small property-owners, and unskilled Afrikaner workers with the smaller working-class Labour Party still led predominantly by English speakers. Together they drove forward a programme of economic nationalism, defying 'free market' forces. The Pact's 'civilized labour' policy meant preferential employment of better paid white labour over lesser paid black labour in unskilled as well as semi-skilled jobs. (The term 'civilized' was a code for white that would not illegally exclude men of colour who had the vote in the Cape province.) The Pact also ensured that all white men in South Africa now had the right to vote. The Cape franchise had previously excluded poor white men without property.

The 1924 Industrial Conciliation Act established industrial councils made up of employer associations and white trade unions. Blacks were explicitly excluded from the legal category of 'employees' given rights. The Wages Act of 1925 gave the minister the right to appoint wage boards to regulate wages and conditions in employment other than agriculture and domestic service. Industries could not set wages for unskilled white workers below the level for a 'civilized' standard of living. The government also ensured jobs for thousands of unskilled poor whites on the railways, in the country's harbours, and in state institutions such as the postal services – transferring thousands of jobs from black to white. By 1929, the S.A. Railways and Harbours were employing about 25,000 previously unemployed whites. Meanwhile, the Pact government awarded preferential tariffs and government contracts to companies that employed a high ratio of 'civilized' to 'uncivilized' labour. The 1926 Mines and Works Amendment Act reversed a successful Supreme Court challenge of 1923, by re-affirming the job colour bar for all classes of skilled work.

In contrast to the Botha-Smuts government that supported large commercial farmers, the Pact government supported smaller Afrikaner farmers with subsidized inputs, guaranteed crop prices, export bonuses, and preferential railway goods tariffs – plus protection from foreign imports by high customs tariffs. The government Land Bank gave loans to poor farmers, and more land was made available for purchase by former *bywoners*.

Hertzog realized the necessity of diversifying South Africa's economy beyond reliance on income from mineral production. To protect emerging manufacturing industries and promote import substitution, the government passed the 1925 Customs Tariff Act, which imposed customs tariffs on imported industrial goods – though exceptions were made for essential capital goods and raw materials. As a result, between 1925 and 1929 the value of manufactured goods produced in South Africa increased by about 40 per cent and created much employment. Cheap and readily available electric power was seen as essential for a modern nation, and steel production was seen as the essential core for economic diversification. The Pact government extended the remit of the Electricity Supply Commission (ESCOM), set up by the Smuts government in 1923. The Iron and Steel Corporation (ISCOR), created in 1928, built the first modern iron and steel smelting and rolling works on the African continent.

Kadalies's ICU filled the gap when the S.A. Native National Congress declined in membership and influence, despite renaming itself the African National Congress (ANC) in 1923. After Kadalie vocally supported Smuts in 1920 elections, Hertzog countered by giving Kadalie funds to obtain the Cape non-white vote in 1924 elections. ICU concerns extended beyond urban-industrial workers into supporting peasant cries for land. In 1925, it shifted its headquarters from Cape Town to Johannesburg, and its membership swelled to over 150,000 with branches throughout the country by 1927–28. Its popularity attracted a wide African (both black and coloured) nationalist following, with an eclectic mix of ideas including Garveyism from America and more radical socialism. But its success brought disputes over Kadalie's autocratic leadership, as well as financial disputes over funds. In 1926 Kadalie expelled communists from the ICU and thus deprived the movement of some of its most dedicated mobilizers.

Lobbied by S.P. Bunting and Eddie Roux, the 1924 CPSA conference resolved to organize all workers – regardless of race – in a united workers' front. The party went all out to recruit African members, and by 1928 the majority of party members were black. James La Guma, the coloured South West African former ICU secretary-general expelled by Kadalie, travelled to Europe in 1927 to persuade the Communist International (Comintern) to abandon reliance on white workers for a revolution against capitalism in South Africa – and to respect African nationalism as being more than merely 'petty bourgeois'. The Comintern agreed that the CPSA should aim at a Black Republic: 'an independent native South Africa Republic as a stage towards a workers' and peasants' republic with full equal rights for all races, black, coloured and white'. Some white communists left the CPSA in protest, but it now collaborated with African nationalists, including the ANC, in setting up a front organization called the League of African Rights.

Aimed at the growing influence of communists, the 1927 Native Administration Act and the 1930 Riotous Assemblies (Amendment) Act made into a crime the 'fomenting of feelings of hostility between blacks and whites' – a phrase ironically to be used over the coming years as a method of preventing black-white cooperation!

Kadalie also went to Europe in 1927 and came back with U.K. Labour Party organizers. In 1928, the Natal ICU branch leader, A. G. Champion, declared his ICU-yase-Natal independent from Kadalie. After more splits, Kadalie himself resigned in January 1929 to run his own Independent ICU in East London.

Legal restrictions on black labour agitation and organization were now becoming very effective. By 1932, ICU was moribund as a united movement, but its influence lingered on – not only in South Africa but also in South West Africa, Basutoland, Mozambique, Southern Rhodesia, Northern Rhodesia, and Nyasaland.

Hertzog had laid out his plans for future racial segregation in a speech at Smithfield, in the Orange Free State, in 1925. The aim was to bring all black people in South Africa, regardless of their previous exemptions from regulations as 'civilized' or educated people, under a common system of administration. The Native Administrative Act, passed by parliament in 1927, reduced all black people in the Transvaal, Natal, and Orange Free State into tribesmen and tribeswomen – subject to tribal laws and a 'tribal' chief appointed by government, with the governor-general as their 'supreme chief'. The next Hertzog Bill was intended to remove the parliamentary vote and the right to own land from 'civilized' black people in the Cape province. This latter proposal, however, raised outcry not only from the ANC, ICU, and CPSA, the S.A. Indian Congress, and the African People's Organisation, but also from white liberals and even Jan Smuts. It was abandoned in the run-up to the 1929 elections.

Strengthened by the universal franchise for all white men, Hertzog's National Party won enough votes in 1929 to ditch the S.A. Labour Party. (In 1930 the franchise was extended to all white women.) Drought and the Great Depression that set in during 1929–30 drove even more white Afrikaners into towns. The number of poor whites swelled to about 300,000, i.e. one in three of white Afrikaners. Hertzog's government enforced the laws that gave poor whites preference over poor blacks. But the Broederbond (brotherhood) pressure group within the National Party was more concerned with promoting Afrikaner capitalism and bourgeois respectability. In 1929 the Broederbond founded a front organization called the Federation of Afrikaans Cultural Organisations (FAK). It promoted the idea of 'Christian National Education', i.e. education in Afrikaans along lines approved by the three Dutch reformed churches. FAK also set up cultural rivals to shadow 'English' bodies such as the Boy Scouts, the Red Cross, and the National Union of South African Students (NUSAS).

World demand for South African minerals and agricultural products fell drastically in the Great Depression. Great Britain and other countries devalued their currencies and abandoned the gold standard, against which their currencies were valued. As a matter of nationalist pride, Hertzog refused to abandon the gold standard for the South African pound. South African exports became so comparatively overvalued that demand for them dropped even further, and the mines were threatened with closure. South Africa's agricultural production dropped by almost half between 1928 and 1932, while the value of diamond exports (including from South West Africa) dropped from 16.5 million in 1928 to only 1.4 million in 1934. South Africa was threatened by a run on the banks, as investors withdrew their money to gamble on currency exchange. Hertzog finally abandoned the gold standard in December 1932.

An increase in the world gold price in 1934–35 led to a strong recovery in gold sales. An inflow of foreign investment further boosted the fortunes of the mining sector. The price of gold rose from £4 per ounce in 1932 to over £7 in 1935, and the value of gold production rose from £47 million in 1932 to £118 million in 1940. This gold boom boosted government revenue, and GDP per capita almost doubled between 1933 and 1945. The value of goods locally manufactured rose from £30.5 million in 1932 to £64 million in 1939 – mostly textiles, processed and canned food and drink, and metal goods. New mines produced copper, manganese, chrome, iron ore, and coal. ESCOM expanded with new coal-powered electricity power stations, and ISCOR made great strides under the government's generous financial support and tariff protection.

Afrikaner capitalism continued to grow in the 1930s, with the establishment of the *Volkskas* (People's Bank) in 1934 and some exclusively Afrikaner trade unions, including the railway workers union called Spoorbond, led by one of the Broederbond's pioneers, H. J. Klopper. Under the leadership of Daniel Malan and the Broederbond, which Malan joined in 1933–34, Afrikaners continued to support the Sanlam and Santam insurance and credit institutions in order to pool their resources and invest in new economic opportunities. The Broederbond also started a campaign in the 1930s to take over the white miners' trade union on the Rand.

The gold boom helped the government to address the 'poor white problem', mainly through economic diversification and industrialization, which created numerous job opportunities for the whites under the 'civilized' labour policies dating from Pact government days. Jobs were created in the Police and Defence Forces, a massive road-building programme which began in 1935, establishment of the South African Broadcasting Corporation in 1936, re-organization and expansion of South African Airways, and the creation of Marketing Control Boards for agricultural commodities in 1937. The rapidly expanding manufacturing sector also provided many job opportunities.

The boom years created the need for more black mine workers. In 1934 Portugal agreed to increase its regular supply to the Witwatersrand to 100,000 men from Mozambique. (Portugal and South Africa had signed the Mozambique Convention in 1928, which once again tied labour to South Africa with increased use of the port of Lourenço Marques.) The Witwatersrand chamber of mines revived its recruitment of labour from north of the Limpopo for the first time since 1913 through its Wenela (Witwatersrand Native Labour Association) subsidiary. Wenela recruitment depots were set up in northern Bechuanaland, Northern Rhodesia, Nyasaland, and Tanganyika. Angolans also came through these depots after walking across colonial borders.

Many poor whites initially lived alongside people of colour in makeshift shacks on the edges of towns, doing piecework or resorting to crime and prostitution to make ends meet. Notwithstanding the rise of urban racial segregation, a rich and complex culture developed in city black townships, slums, and squatter camps among a multi-cultural mix of workers, including Africans, Indians, Coloureds, Chinese, white Afrikaners, and poor Greeks, Portuguese, Italians, and Irish. New cultural forms emerged, such as the *stokvel* (Afrikaans for a savings group), the shebeen (Irish for an illegal liquor den), and *marabi* music (southern African jazz) – as also did a new urban *créole* called Fanagalo (born of Zulu and Afrikaans, with a little English) with its ever-evolving gang slang called *tsotsi-taal* or *fly-taal*. Millions were introduced to modern music and movies by travelling shows in black township halls and mine labour compounds.

The great increase in labour migration in southern Africa during the 1930s and 1940s had profound effects on family life in every part of southern Africa. Isaac Schapera's *Married Life in an African Tribe* (1940) recorded how wives were left in the countryside while men found new partners in towns. Migrant workers became jealous of élite men who remained in the countryside, notably chiefs and headmen or teachers and clerks, accusing them of adultery with the wives the migrant workers had left behind.

FUSION GOVERNMENT 1934–39

As elections approached in 1934, Hertzog lost his nerve in economics and approached his erstwhile rival, Jan Smuts, to form a Fusion government after the elections. Hertzog's National Party and Smuts's South African Party re-emerged as the United South African National Party – otherwise known as the United Party (UP). Hertzog was prime minister; Smuts was his deputy. This led to protests on both sides. The Purified National Party broke away under Daniel F. Malan, while die-hard 'English' in Natal broke away from the S.A.P. to form the Dominion Party.

The Fusion's Marketing Act of 1937 set up more agricultural marketing boards that kept up prices given to white farmers for dairy produce, meat, maize and wheat, etc. – in cooperation with farmer cooperatives that acted as monopoly purchasers of crops at higher than market prices. This raised the general cost of living by paying higher prices than for imported food crops, while farmers were given bonuses for export-quality products. This favoured large-scale well-capitalized farmers, who were represented on the marketing boards.

Hertzog now revived his Native Bills previously abandoned. The 1936 Native Representation Act finally eliminated African voters from the common voters' roll in the Cape province. In total 16,000 Cape voters were removed from the common voters' roll and placed in a separate roll – able to elect three white representatives to sit in the lower house of parliament. The African population of other provinces was henceforth to be represented by four white senators in the upper house of parliament. There also was to be a small new national body, called the Native Representative Council, consisting of 12 Africans – chiefs and headmen, plus 'educated natives' nominated through lower 'native councils'.

The 1936 Natives Trust and Land Act consolidated the segregationist provisions of the 1913 Natives Land Act. It raised the allocation of 'native' land to 13 per cent of the total land mass. The S.A. Native Trust under the Department of Native Affairs now supervised economic development of all 'native reserves'. The Native Trust Fund was empowered to acquire designated land 'released' from white farmland or ownership by the state. Trust income would be raised through poll-taxes, fees, rents, fines, and other sources. Farmland already owned by Africans in freehold title – the so-called 'black spots' within 'white' areas – were to be removed by purchase and their inhabitants packed off to the reserves.

One of the functions of the Native Trust was to oversee land conservation and 'betterment' reclamation or rehabilitation – stemming environmental degradation and improving productivity in the 'native reserves'. In the wake of the 1913 Land Act, the reserves had become overcrowded with people and their livestock evicted from white areas. Growing problems of soil degradation and soil erosion were partly due to overstocking of livestock. The Native Trust would plan future land usage, bringing dwellings together in villages for better provision of services, enforcing the maximum carrying-capacity of land by livestock, enforcing anti-squatter laws on white land, and putting an end to sharecropping by undercapitalized white farmers with black peasants. Proclamation No 31 of 1939 led to 'betterment' measures of wire fencing, resettlement of people, and stock limitation or de-stocking – by shooting cattle if necessary.

The growth of Afrikaner nationalism was orchestrated and dramatized by the centenary celebrations of the Great Trek (1935–38). The trek was re-enacted by ox-wagon parades throughout the country, culminating outside Pretoria on 16 December 1938 – the exact centenary of the battle of Blood

River. A tall Voortrekker monument was to be built overlooking Pretoria over the next decade, expunging the hill's previous name Robert's Heights that celebrated the British conquest of 1900. The centenary was accompanied by economic and political debate among Afrikaners along the lines of two divergent views – the promotion of Afrikaner private capitalism advocated by Nicolas Diedrichs and others, and an approach that favoured 'national-socialism' where a dictatorship would rule on behalf of the *volk* (race or nation). The Broederbond established a Reddings-daadbond (reconstruction society) under Diedrichs in 1939, to promote private capitalism among groups of businessmen. It persuaded the three Dutch Reformed churches to do business only with Broederbond-approved businesses and institutions.

African responses to the growing barrage of segregationist laws in the 1930s were surprisingly muted. Under the conservative leadership of Pixley Seme in 1930–37, the ANC did little to challenge the segregationist regime. Seme discouraged mass action and instead stressed individual African self-betterment. ANC membership dwindled and its newspaper, *Abantu-Batho*, collapsed. In December 1935, frustrated ANC members met with representatives of Abdurahman's African People's Organisation in an All-African Convention that spearheaded protest against the Hertzog Bills. Some people were temporarily persuaded that Hertzog's 1936 Native Representative Council might give Africans a voice in the government of their country.

HIGH COMMISSION TERRITORIES 1920–39

In both 1924 and 1927, Hertzog's Pact government requested the British government to transfer all the High Commission Territories to the Union. The Fusion government repeated the request in 1935 and 1938. Swaziland was regarded as a natural part of the Transvaal. The labour of Basutoland, much of it skilled and semi-skilled, was essential to the South African economy. The Kalahari desert would enable the Union to increase its 'native reserves' from 13 to 45 per cent of the total land mass. Transfer of the territories would also bring into line the paramount chiefs and their advisers considered politically too challenging against white-supremacy. Tshekedi Khama's 1935 *Statement to the British People and Parliament* argued that transfer to the Union would be a breach of British 'protectorate' guarantees to Africans, as South Africa would extend its repugnant 'native policy' to Bechuanaland.

Aware of strong objections among the chiefs and people of the three Protectorates, the British parliament resisted Hertzog, but began to wilt in 1935 and 1938–39 – allowing the Union government to make its case for transfer to the people of the territories over their vociferous objections. The High Commission Territories became a rallying point for opponents of Afrikaner nationalism and racial segregation in Great Britain and among Pan-Africanists overseas.

Indirect rule in the High Commission Territories was channelled through African chiefs and councils, giving them a share of the annual poll-taxes or hut-taxes that they collected. In Swaziland, the *Libandla* general assembly and its executive known as *Liqoqo* under the king (paramount chief) comprised the territory's Swazi National Council. In Basutoland, the *Pitso* general assembly of regional chiefs and headmen, with an executive under the king (paramount chief), was formally recognized by the colonial authorities as the Basutoland National Council in 1910. In Bechuanaland Protectorate, there was no single nation, but five major and two minor Tswana *merafhe* (tribal states including many non-Tswana) were officially recognized – with representatives combined in a Native Advisory Council constituted in 1919, which adopted a constitution echoing that of the S.A. Native National Congress. The two largest *merafhe*, the Ngwato and Tawana in the north, repudiated any suggestion of political connection with the Union of South Africa and boycotted the Native Advisory Council until the 1930s.

Only the Basutoland National Council had the power to discuss the whole annual colonial budget. The Swaziland and Bechuanaland 'native' councils were limited to questions of 'native welfare'. Only the European Advisory Council in each territory, representing the territorial minority of white settler farmers and traders, had the power to discuss the territory-wide colonial budget.

The Basutoland National Council came under attack from progressive commoners in the 1920s, objecting to its composition by self-interested chiefs and headmen. Basutoland had a strong progressive movement because of Protestant, Catholic, and Anglican missionary competition to win converts through educational opportunities. The colonial government was also induced to spend more money on education in Basutoland than in the other two territories. Teachers, evangelists, small traders, clerks, and other literate Basuto joined the Progressive Association or *Lekhotla la Tsoelopele*, founded in 1907 by Azariele Sekese and Simon Phamotse. It called for greater representation of commoners in all political structures, the prevention of chiefly abuse in court cases and land allocation, and an end to racial discrimination. Membership rose from 1,000 in the 1920s to over 3,000 in the 1930s. The association was given one representative in the National Council in 1919. Its best-known member was Thomas Mofolo, who published his biography of Shaka Zulu in Sesotho in 1926 – later translated into both French and English.

More radical than the Progressive Association in Basutoland was the *Lekhotla la Bafo* (people's council), founded by Josiel Lefela in 1919. An ex-migrant worker on the Rand now a small businessman, Lefela championed the cause of common village people against the tyranny of chiefs and headmen. He became a member of the Basutoland National Council because he was headman of the village that he had founded, namely Mapoteng. Somewhat of a populist and Pan-Africanist, inspired by Marcus Garvey, he was highly critical of colonial administration and questioned the legitimacy of colonial rule. The colonial government expelled Lefela from the National Council in the 1920s, accusing him of being a 'public agitator', but he was soon re-instated. In 1928, he caused panic among colonial administrators by inviting ANC president James Gumede, freshly back from the Soviet Union, to address his members. Lefela took every opportunity to resist British rule, and strongly opposed colonial administrative reforms in Basutoland in 1938.

In Swaziland, a Progressive Association was founded in 1929 by Benjamin Nxumalo, an African Methodist Episcopal teacher, representing the interests of the small Western-educated Swazi élite that had close family connections with royalty and the traditional élite.

In Bechuanaland, there were no territory-wide political bodies until the 1950s, but there were well-educated 'progressives' among chiefs and their relatives as well as school teachers and clerks. Simon Ratshosa from Serowe is a case in point. He wrote and distributed two books in longhand and typescript, attacking chieftainship as 'cruel and repulsive' and foreseeing a future for the whole of Bechuanaland under the rule of a 'party of enlightened natives'. Paradoxically, as the former master of many San or Sarwa, employed as servile herders by Ngwato cattle-owners, he championed the rights of the 'Bushmen' – denouncing their slavery to the world.

As regent chief of the Ngwato, Tshekedi Khama challenged colonial rule. His first battle was over the mineral concession owned by the British South Africa Company. The company wanted to start copper mining in Ngwato territory. Tshekedi objected to a white mining town opening the door to white settlement and incorporation into the Union. The issue was settled – until the 1950s – by a downturn in world copper prices that made the company abandon its plans.

Tshekedi's most serious tussle with the British came in 1933. The local colonial magistrate declined to prosecute a young white car mechanic named Phinehas McIntosh, a seducer of young women who got into fights with jealous young men. Tshekedi sentenced McIntosh to be judicially flogged. The news aroused white fury across Southern Africa. The acting British high commissioner at the Cape, Admiral E.R.G.R. Evans, sent his sailors and marines north by railway ('Join the Navy and See the Kalahari'). Tshekedi made his case before Evans in cool legal terms – while a machine-gun was trained on the mass of people behind him. McIntosh and his parents declared themselves loyal subjects of Tshekedi. Proceedings descended into farce, and Tshekedi was duly re-installed as regent chief three weeks later when the real high commissioner returned to Cape Town.

In 1934, Tshekedi Khama and his cousin, chief Bathoen II of the Ngwaketse, took the high commissioner to court – arguing that proposed Native Administration proclamations would contravene the agreements made with their fathers in 1885 and 1895. But the Watermeyer Judgement that came back in 1936 ruled that under Britain's Foreign Jurisdiction Acts, British power over 'native tribes' was 'unfettered and unlimited...not limited by Treaty or Agreement'. Bechuanaland Protectorate's resident commissioner Charles Rey was jubilant. But the proclamations were revised in 1940 by the next resident commissioner, Charles Arden-Clarke, rendering Tshekedi and Bathoen more content.

Bechuanaland remained the poorest of the High Commission territories. Cattle sales across the borders were inhibited between 1924 and 1941 by South African regulations favouring white commercial ranchers. The economy remained dependent on migrant workers: the number in Rand mines increased almost fivefold between 1926 and 1940. Others found employment in Southern Rhodesia, South West Africa, and on farms in South Africa.

Swaziland's rural economy was divided between a subsistence sector of Swazi households – cultivating sorghum and maize and rearing cattle – and commercial agriculture under white ownership, growing cotton, tobacco, and maize and raising sheep and cattle. Many white farm-owners were absentee landlords living in South Africa. As well as gold and tin mining, an asbestos mine was opened by a British company at Havelock (Bulembu) near Piggs Peak in 1938. It became one of the world's five biggest asbestos mines, employing local workers as well as migrants from Nyasaland and Mozambique.

The productive peasant economy in Basutoland, producing wheat and wool for sale in South Africa, suffered from the 1929 Great Depression, severe drought in 1932–33, and widespread soil erosion. The value of exports dropped to less than half of its 1929 value by 1936. This ended Lesotho's historic role as granary for South Africa, making labour migrancy all the more important. By mid-1930s, 15 per cent of Lesotho's total population was employed in South Africa.

SOUTHERN RHODESIA & NORTHERN RHODESIA 1923–39

Southern Rhodesia became a self-governing colony in 1923, after the charter of the British South Africa Company finally expired and transfer to the Union of South Africa was rejected by the Rhodesian electorate. The land partition between whites and blacks that had begun before the Great War was intensified. The 1930 Land Apportionment Act allocated 51 per cent of the land – close to roads and railways – to a white population of 50,000 people, while more than 1 million Africans were allocated 30 per cent. Africans were prohibited from buying land in white areas. The 'native reserves' were re-named Tribal Trust Lands, and a small percentage of land was set aside as African Purchase Areas with plots that could be privately owned. The remaining 19 per cent of land was designated Crown Land (i.e. state land) to be kept as public parks or state forests and for future allocation.

As in South Africa, 'betterment' programmes were set up in Tribal Trust lands under the auspices of a Native Trust Fund to counter environmental degradation. As in South Africa, the most unpopular aspect was the de-stocking of African cattle (i.e. the reduction of traditional individual wealth) to lessen soil damage from over-grazing. Manufacturing industry was slow to take off. It received a small boost from import-substitution during the Great War, geared to local consumer and producer needs – timber, fertilizer, leather, bacon, biscuits, soap, and furniture. Manufacturing picked up pace in the 1930s to service the gold-mining industry boom. Throughout this period, the colonial state left the manufacturing sector to its own devices, paying its attention instead to the mining and agricultural sectors.

Racial discrimination was loosely applied in Southern Rhodesia until after the Great Depression. Some African and coloured men had the parliamentary vote along the lines of the former Cape Colony. It was Godfrey Huggins, who became prime minister in 1934, who attempted to introduce strict racial segregation. Huggins advocated a dualistic 'two-pyramid policy': whites and blacks rising in their own separate social spheres, with the top black people equal to, but not mixing with, the lower white people.

Like in South Africa, Southern Rhodesia's 1934 Industrial Conciliation Act protected white workers from competition with cheaper black labour. The act made the job colour-bar part of the country's labour régime – providing for trade unions and industrial councils for employers and employees to negotiate wages and work conditions and pointedly excluding blacks from the definition of 'employee'. As also in South Africa, white farmers had privileged access to domestic and international markets through a Maize Control Act. A Maize

Control Board paid lower prices for African-produced maize – resulting in African farmers selling their crops to white farmers who then sold them on to the board for a profit.

Southern Rhodesia both sent labour to the South African gold mines and attracted migrant labourers from neighbouring Mozambique, Nyasaland, and Northern Rhodesia. The Rhodesia Native Labour Bureau recruited foreign labour from 1903 until 1933 – an average of about 13,000 workers each year. The government made formal agreements with neighbouring colonial authorities to supply agreed quotas. It signed the 1913 Tete Agreement with the Portuguese colonial administration of Mozambique, and it concluded a Tripartite Labour Agreement with Nyasaland and Northern Rhodesia in 1937.

Strikes by African workers during the 1918–19 period of industrial unrest, at the Globe & Phoenix mine and by sanitation workers at Wankie Colliery, were easily put down. During the 1920s–30s, what might be called proto-nationalism manifested itself through small, élitist, and relatively ineffectual organizations for mutual welfare, including burial societies and tribal-cultural clubs. The Rhodesia Native Association, the Union Bantu Vigilance Association, the Rhodesia Bantu Voters' Association (with Martha Ngano as energetic woman leader), the Amandebele Patriotic Society, the Gwelo Native Welfare Association, and the Ndebele Home Movement were focused on obtaining group concessions from the colonial government, rather than promoting mass interests. Their petition-style politics was easy for the colonial authorities to ignore. Most effective, at least temporarily, was the Southern Rhodesian branch of the Industrial Commercial Workers Union, inspired by Clements Kadalie and established by Robert Sambo in 1926. It organized workers across ethnic and parochial lines, and it adopted more militant tactics for better wages and working conditions. The 1927 African workers' strike at Shamva gold mine near Salisbury involved about 3,500 workers demanding better wages. It ended only when the army intervened. The government clamped down on the ICU, deported Sambo to Nyasaland, and arrested his local lieutenants.

Northern Rhodesia passed from the British South Africa Company to the control of Britain's Colonial Office in 1924. The two Rhodesias were kept apart by separate systems of law and administration. Northern Rhodesia used English common law; it recruited officials through the Colonial Office in London. (Southern Rhodesia retained the Cape law code; it recruited its own administrators in Southern Africa.)

Northern Rhodesia had white settler farms along the railway that ran from Livingstone (capital until 1935) at the Victoria Falls through Lusaka (capital from 1935) and Broken Hill (Kabwe) to the Katanga copperbelt in Belgian Congo. A major zinc mine was opened at Broken Hill in the 1920s, where the remains of *Homo rhodesiensis* were discovered in initial excavations. Big mining companies began to open copper mines on the Northern Rhodesia side of the Katanga copperbelt border, attracting with slightly better wages migrant workers from Nyasaland and Northern Rhodesia who had formerly worked in Katanga.

Initial boom prices for copper after the 1929–32 Great Depression then dropped dramatically, reaching a low point in 1935 when Copperbelt workers went on strike against increased tax. Six were shot dead by police. By 1936, when the market recovered, there were 15,000 black and over 10,000 white workers (mostly drawn from South Africa) on the Copperbelt. The period after 1936 saw ever-rising world demand for copper – not only for electrical wiring but also for shell-cases and bullets. In 1940 the rise in productivity and profits caused white mine workers to strike for a minimum £60 per month – way above wage levels on the Witwatersrand and even more so than in Europe. Seventeen black mine workers were shot dead while demonstrating for £12 per month.

Migrant workers brought ideas as well as goods and clothing and new food habits (such as tea-drinking and consumption of sugar) back to their rural homes. Around 1908, the Watch Tower movement (Jehovah's Witnesses) caught on among returning migrants in Nyasaland, holding that all government by man was evil and predicting that the world would end in 1914–15. The Great War gave credence to the prophesy, and Watch Tower (*Kitawala*) subsequently took fire in Northern Rhodesia and the Belgian Congo. In 1925, one Watch Tower convert, Tomo Nyirenda, set himself up as a messianic leader called *Mwana Lesa* (Child of God) near the Northern Rhodesia copperbelt and in Katanga. He claimed to be able to detect witches in water and drowned maybe 100 accused people in the process – before he was caught and hanged as a murderer in 1926.

SECOND WORLD WAR

When war broke out in 1939, white Afrikaners were divided over which side to support. Jan Smuts wanted South Africa to fulfil its obligations to the British Empire. J.B. Hertzog wanted to keep South Africa out of the war. Supporters of Daniel Malan called on South Africa to fight on Germany's side. Smuts forced Hertzog to resign and took South Africa into the war on Britain's side, some days after war was declared. Hertzog joined Daniel Malan in a Reunited National Party, but subsequently broke away when Malan insisted on eliminating English as an official language. Hertzog formed a new party, the Afrikaner Party, but died in 1941.

Former minister of defence Oswald Pirow, a great admirer of Nazi Germany, left the Reunited National Party in 1942 to found the New Order Party – not only pro-German but rabidly anti-semitic and anti-black. The New Order Party skated on the edge of wartime illegality, and it collapsed in 1943. Meanwhile the leader of the 'cultural' group Ossewa-Brandwag (OB, the ox-wagon sentinels), Johannes van Rensburg, transformed it into a paramilitary organization modelled on Nazi stormtroopers. During 1941–42, the OB conducted a sabotage campaign, blowing up railway lines and electric pylons. Many OB members were arrested for sabotage, and some were detained in camps – including future prime minister Balthazar John Vorster. The OB, however, declined as the chances of German victory in the war grew slimmer.

About 334,000 men and some women served in the South African Defence Force (SADF) during the Second World War – of whom 211,000 were white troops, and 123,000 were (usually unarmed) black, coloured, or Indian troops in labour and service corps. (Some South Africans joined the British air force, and others joined the British Army, which, however, officially declined to make men of colour into officers.) The SADF army and air force saw action in Kenya and Ethiopia, then with British and Commonwealth forces in North Africa (Egypt and Libya), and participated in the U.S.-led invasion of Italy.

The High Commission Territories insisted that their troops join the British Army, not the SADF. 21,460 men from Basutoland, 11,000 men from Bechuanaland, and 3,600 men from Swaziland served as pioneers (construction workers) and gunners in Egypt, Palestine, and Italy. In May 1943, 633 men from Basutoland died in the Mediterranean when the S.S. Erinpura was the first ship sunk by a radio-controlled glide-bomb, launched from a German plane high in the sky a few kilometres away.

Southern Rhodesia sent 9,927 white soldiers and airmen to war: future prime minister Ian Smith joined the British air force. 13,300 black men from Southern Rhodesia also served, many in armed combatant roles. 14,580 men from Northern Rhodesia and 28,000 men from Nyasaland mostly served in India and Burma as armed soldiers with the British Army and its King's African Rifles.

In 1940, the Smuts government established South Africa's Industrial Development Corporation (IDC) 'to facilitate, promote, guide and assist' in the financing of new industries and modernization of existing industries. There was no upper limit in the wartime demand for minerals such as gold and copper, food from farms, locally manufactured goods – and, of course, labour from all over. Gold from the British Empire was vital as secure payment against Britain's mounting debts to the United States for war materiel. Gold production rose from £121 million in 1941 to £145 million in 1950.

Investment, both domestic and international, poured into South African production of metals vital for the war effort and spilled into a manufacturing sector replacing imports that could no longer come across submarine-infested seas. Food processing, drink, clothing, and textile manufacturing industries grew rapidly, as also did engineering, electronics and chemical production, and building and construction work. Ship repairs at the country's ports serviced Allied naval and merchant ships. Small arms and ammunition were produced at Magazine Hill near Pretoria and elsewhere. Manufacturing's share of GDP rose from 12 per cent in 1939 to 19 per cent by 1949. ISCOR struggled to keep up with demand for iron and steel, but it was producing 58 per cent of South Africa's needs (worth £138 million) by 1945.

Between 1942 and 1945, the pass laws were relaxed in South Africa and elsewhere – to ensure the easy flow of labour to the new factories in urban centres. Large numbers of Africans, including women whose husbands were serving overseas, moved into towns and cities. The population of the Witwatersrand increased by over half a million between 1936 and the 1940s. There was similar growth in the populations of Cape Town, Durban, Salisbury and Bulawayo, and Copperbelt towns.

By the end of the war, the economy of South Africa had taken off on a pathway of self-sustaining growth – with a well-developed system of transport and communications, relatively cheap electric power from ESCOM, a ready supply of iron and steel from ISCOR, and openness to foreign investment capital – thanks to the wartime boom, a steady world gold price, and indefinite supply of cheap African labour. After pre-war scepticism about state intervention versus the free market, Southern Rhodesia also set up its version of IDC in 1940, to spearhead the growth of manufacturing. The state established key parastatals – the Cold Storage Commission (for meat), the Rhodesian Iron and Steel Commission (RISCO), a roasting plant (for peanuts etc.), and a Sugar Industry Board. By the end of the war, Southern Rhodesian manufacturing industry was on its way to continued growth, while lesser Northern Rhodesian industrialization was clustered around mining on the Copperbelt.

Prime minister Jan Smuts spent much of the war in military dress conducting British Empire affairs in England and overseas. He became, in his own estimation as well as that of others, a great international statesman and moralist. It was Smuts who drafted the high-sounding principles of the preamble to the founding charter of the United Nations Organisation (UN) at the end of the war. Ironically, it spoke of 'faith in fundamental human rights, in the dignity and worth of the human person' – while human rights among Africans and people of colour were being trampled upon in Smuts' own country. In 1943, for example, the Smuts government set up a Coloured

Affairs Department, modelled on the Native Affairs Department, to more fully segregate coloured people from whites and blacks where colour lines had been blurred. Indians were now barred from owning land or houses previously owned by whites.

The entry of the United States into the Second World War encouraged general war morale, but it was the Soviet Union's entry into the war as an ally that removed a thorn from the side of the Smuts government – the Communist Party of South Africa (CPSA) that had previously been preaching war resistance or at least neutrality.

Wartime propaganda proved remarkably effective in quelling present discontent by raising hopes of a better post-war future. Soviet films were warmly appreciated when shown in Bechuanaland. There were, however, pockets of African resistance to recruitment for the military and the mines. In Basutoland, Josiel Lefela was arrested and spent most of the war in prison for urging men not to serve in an imperialist war – especially after there was initial reluctance to give them weapons training. (The High Commission Territories Corps was disbanded in 1948 after South Africa protested at the presence of 'armed natives' on its borders.) Josiel Lefela returned to his seat on the Basutoland National Council after the war; he was then excluded and detained for the second time for his consistent resistance to British rule.

The ANC of South Africa once again became an effective body from 1940 onwards under the leadership of Dr A.B. Xuma. Students at Fort Hare and neighbouring Lovedale were attracted to it, and they joined the ANC Youth League (ANC-YL), founded by Anton Lembede at Johannesburg in 1944. Lembede espoused what he called 'African socialism' and proudly proclaimed that he was a peasant. ANC-YL members tended to gravitate either towards Africanism – promoted by the fifth Pan-African Congress held in Manchester, England, in 1945 – or towards socialism and collaboration with the CPSA.

The Second World War acted as a catalyst in raising political consciousness among African soldiers, workers, and students. Even more than during the First World War, experience of a wider world overseas and closer interaction with white people during the war destroyed myths of racial difference and white invincibility. Africans pondered the provisions of the Atlantic Charter drawn up by President Franklin Roosevelt and Prime Minister Winston Churchill in 1941, justifying the war as a struggle for democracy and the self-determination of nations. Why was Africa excluded? The ANC of South Africa responded with a proposed bill of rights for Africans titled *Africans' Claims* (1943). African political demands became more strident in tone after the end of the war, as demobilized African troops received little or no reward and found conditions back home not much better than before. Africans were struck by the contradiction between fighting a war for democracy and being denied the same rights.

A new militancy was evident in a strike by Rhodesia Railways African Employees Association in 1945, when over 80 per cent downed tools, and Bulawayo municipal workers struck in sympathy. Black mine workers on the Witwatersrand, beset by the rising wartime cost of living, were organized into the African Mine Workers' Union by African communist leader J.B. Marks and others in 1941. In 1946 the AMWU brought out 75,000 men on strike against cuts in their rations, demanding £3 per week (£12 per month) at a time of post-war super-profits by the mine-owners (£15.6 million per year). Police drove the strikers down into the mines, level by level, and nine miners were killed. The suppression of the strike was condemned as 'fascism' by the Native Representative Council, where its proposer Paul Mosaka condemned the council itself for collaboration with government:

> We have been fooled. We have been asked to cooperate with a toy telephone. We have been speaking into an apparatus at the end of which there is nobody to receive the message. Like children we have taken pleasure in the echo of our own voices.

In 1947, southern Africa hosted a tour by King George VI of Great Britain and his family, including his daughter the future Queen Elizabeth II, who reached the age of 21 at the end of the tour. The purpose of the royal tour was to thank people of all races, especially servicemen and servicewomen, for their war effort. The king was annoyed when Africans were kept far apart from him in South Africa. But he was very pleased with the Lovedale choir singing Enoch Sontonga's *Nkosi Sikelel' iAfrika* (with recent Sotho addition by Moses Mphahlele). He preferred it to the royal anthem 'God Save the King' and insisted on it instead being sung for him in the Rhodesias and the High Commission Territories – with a Setswana translation in Bechuanaland.

PORTUGUESE MOZAMBIQUE 1910–60

The 1910 revolution in Portugal had overthrown the country's last king. It ushered in a liberal republican government that lasted until 1926, when it was also overthrown in a military coup. An economics professor called António Salazar became minister of finance and subsequently became fascist leader of the *Estado Novo* (New State) from 1933 until 1968. Salazar was inspired by the fascism of Mussolini in Italy, and he kept tight control of Portugal's colonies through centralized, authoritarian rule. He suppressed democracy and political dissent both at home and in the colonies. Trade unions were replaced by state-controlled syndicates, and workers were not allowed to strike. Dissent was muzzled through press censorship and the use of informers, secret agents, the police and army, and the court system. The dreaded secret police, PIDE, terrorized all opponents, white or black.

Salazar's 1930 Colonial Act claimed that Portuguese colonialism was motivated by 'altruism, self-denial, faith, and a historic responsibility of civilisation.' But colonies existed solely for the benefit of Portugal. All raw materials were processed in Portugal; the finished products were then sold back to the colonies. Portuguese-chartered companies had plantations in Mozambique, and peasants were compelled elsewhere in Mozambique to produce annual quotas of cotton or rice. Yet Salazar always claimed that Portuguese rule, in alliance with Roman Catholicism, had a 'civilising mission' in bringing religion and higher culture to the savages of Africa. Colonial policy in Mozambique, *Regime do Indigenato*, divided indigenous people between *assimilados* and *indigena*. *Assimilados* were coloured and black Africans able to read and write Portuguese, employable in the colonial economy, and no less free than Portuguese people in Portugal – but were less than 1 per cent of Africans in Mozambique by 1961. The rest of the population was classified as *indigena*. They remained subject to the customary law of chiefs interpreted by colonial administrators. They had to carry identity cards, live outside European areas, and fulfil annual labour requirements.

Under legislation passed in 1930, it was a punishable offence for African men between 18 and 55 years old to be 'idle' – i.e. not cultivating cotton or rice, or not having worked recently in South Africa or Southern Rhodesia. The 'idle' were forced into employment for at least six months, in order to pay their taxes. The only exceptions were self-employed craftworkers and the owners of at least 50 head of cattle. Compulsory cotton cultivation was forced on peasants in the north of Mozambique from 1938 onwards, followed by compulsory rice cultivation in 1942. Colonial officials instructed the peasants on how much land to put under cotton, set production quotas, and imposed a daily work schedule. Producers were forced to sell their cotton to the state's cotton marketing board at very low prices. Failure to meet quotas was punished by beatings or imprisonment, rape of women, and sometimes by deportation to the old slave island of São Thomé. The *Regime do Indigenato* was a source for financial corruption and abuse by African agents known as *sipais*.

The *Estado Novo* of 1933–74 benefitted from 'farming out' 100,000 Mozambican workers at any one time to South Africa and an equivalent number to Southern Rhodesia. Apart from taxing direct cash remittances by workers, the colonial state benefitted from taxing South African imports and exports through Lourenço Marques and those of Southern Rhodesia through Beira. During the 1950s–70s, large areas around the Zambezi valley were marked out for settlement by small farmers or peasants direct from Portugal. They were given land, livestock, credit, and financial assistance. Portuguese farm immigration into Mozambique rose from 1,900 people per year in 1937 to 10,000 in 1959.

After more than 400 years of Portuguese rule only a handful of Africans had received Western education. The 1941 Missionary Act of 1941 gave a virtual monopoly over elementary schooling to Portuguese Catholic missions – though American and Swiss Protestant missions remained significant in Angola and Mozambique. Almost 98 per cent of the population was illiterate in 1958, and only 7.5 per cent out of a school-going age population of 3 million was attending school in 1960. Furthermore, the curriculum alienated African learners by focusing on Portuguese heroes and culture.

FURTHER STUDY

BIBLIOGRAPHY

See also books recommended in previous chapters.

Beinart, William Justin (2008), *The Rise of Conservation in South Africa: Settlers, Livestock, and the Environment 1770–1950*. Oxford: Oxford University Press.

Bloomberg, Charles (1990), *Christian Nationalism and the Rise of the Afrikaner Broederbond in South Africa, 1914–48*. London: Macmillan & Bloomington, IN: Indiana University Press.

Bunting, Brian (1975), *Moses Kotane: South African Revolutionary*. London: Ikululeko Publications.

Coplan, David (2008), *In Township Tonight: South Africa's Black City Music and Theatre*. Chicago, IL: University of Chicago Press & Johannesburg: Jacana.

Coplan, David (2012), *In the Time of Cannibals: The Word Music of South Africa's Basotho Migrants*. Chicago, IL: University of Chicago Press.

Crowder, Michael (1988), *The Flogging of Phinehas McIntosh: A Tale of Colonial Folly and Injustice: Bechuanaland 1933*. New Haven, CT: Yale University Press.

Delius, Peter Nicholas St Martin (1996), *A Lion Amongst the Cattle: Reconstruction and Resistance in the Northern Transvaal*. Randburg: Ravan Press & Portsmouth, NH: Heinemann.

Dubow, Saul (1989), *Racial Segregation and the Origins of Apartheid in South Africa, 1919–36*. Basingstoke: Macmillan Education.

Dubow, Saul (2005), *South Africa's 1940s: Worlds of Possibilities*. Cape Town: Double Storey.

Hassim, Shireen (2014), *The ANC Women's League*. Auckland Park: Jacana Pocket Books.

Hughes, Heather (2011), *First President: A Life of John Dube, Founding President of the African National Congress*. Johannesburg: Jacana Media.

Isaacman, Allen & Barbara Isaacman (1983), *Mozambique: From Colonialism to. Revolution, 1900–1982*. Boulder, CO: Westview Press.

Katjavivi, Peter (1988), *A History of Resistance in Namibia*. London: James Currey & Paris: UNESCO: James Currey.

Kuper, Hilda Beemer (1978), *Sobhuza II: Ngwenyama and King of Swaziland: The Story of an Hereditary Ruler and His Country*. London: Duckworth.

Limb, Peter (2010), *The ANC's Early Years: Nation, Class and Place in South Africa Before 1940*. Pretoria: Unisa Press.

Limb, Peter, ed. (2012), *The People's Paper: A Centenary History & Anthology of Abantu-Batho*. Johannesburg: Wits University Press.

Masilela, Ntongela (2013), *An Outline of the New African Movement in South Africa*. Trenton, NJ: Africa World Press.

Morton, Fred & Jeff Ramsay, eds. (1987) *The Birth of Botswana: A History of the Bechuanaland Protectorate from 1910 to 1966*. Gaborone: Longman Botswana.

Moyana, Henry V. (2002), *The Political Economy of Land in Zimbabwe*. Gweru: Mambo Press.

Moyo, Sam (1995), *The Land Question in Zimbabwe*. Harare: SAPES Books.

Nasson, Bill (2013), *South Africa at War 1939–1945*. Auckland Park: Jacana Pocket Books.

Ngcukaitubi, Tembeka (2018), *The Land is Ours: South Africa's First Black Lawyers* [Richard Msimang, Pixley Seme & George Montsioa] *and the Birth of Constitutionalism*. Johannesburg: Penguin Random House.

Phimister, Ian (1988), *An Economic and Social History of Zimbabwe, 1890–1948: Capital Accumulation and Class Struggle*. London: Longman.

Switzer, Les & Donna Switzer (1997), *The History of the Black Press in South Africa and Lesotho: A Descriptive Bibliographic Guide* [1836–1976]. Cambridge: Cambridge University Press.

Willan, Brian, ed. (1996), *Sol Plaatje: Selected Writings*. Johannesburg: Witwatersrand University Press.

Wylie, Diana (1991), *A Little God: The Twilight of Patriarchy in a Southern African Chiefdom* [Tshekedi Khama]: Johannesburg: Witwatersrand University Press.

VIDEOGRAPHY

DVDs and downloads:

Come See the Bioscope (dir. Lance Gewer, 1994. 26 mins): drama-documentary based on township reception of Sol Plaatje's touring 'Coloured American bioscope' in 1924.

Cry, the Beloved Country (dir. Zoltan Korda, 1951. 103 mins; & dir. Darrell Roodt, 1995. 106 mins): based on Alan Paton novel. In the 1951 version, two African clergymen (Canada Lee & Sidney Poitier), in the crime-ridden townships of Johannesburg, find a son who has murdered a white man, and a daughter turned to prostitution. In the 1995 version, there is just one clergyman (James Earl Jones), who comes to terms with the white victim's father (Richard Harris).

The Forster Gang (dir. Cedric Sundstrom, 2001): the Johannesburg bank-robbing and killing spree of the Forster Gang in 1914 culminated in a police siege, and – by coincidence – stymied the Boer rebellion.

The Grass is Singing, aka **Killing Heat** (dir. Michael Raeburn, 1981): based on a Doris Lessing novel, with Karen Black as an alienated white Rhodesian housewife in the *bundu* (outback) who has an affair with the house servant (John Kani).

In Darkest Hollywood: Cinema and Apartheid (dir. Peter Davies & Daniel Riesenfeld, 1993. 112 min): documentary with many movie clips. How cinema developed racial stereotypes supporting segregation, only later opposing apartheid.

Jim Comes to Jo'burg, aka **African Jim** (dir. Donald Swanson, 1949. 50 mins): musical tale of Jim who finds a job in a nightclub, with singer Dolly Rathebe, and foils the gangsters who mugged him.

The Native Who Caused All the Trouble (dir. Manie van Rensburg, 1989. 82 mins): based on true story of Rev Tselilo Mseme (John Kani) who in 1937 defied racial segregation to build his church on 'white' land at Cape Town.

Song of Africa: Story of a Zulu Jazz Band (dir. Emil Nofal, 1951. 58 mins): Zulu youth goes to town, falls in love with city township music (*marabi, kwela* or *mbaqanga*), and returns home to found his own band.

9 Apartheid & African Nationalism 1948–1967

Many southern Africans awoke with a start when, on 3 February 1960, the prime minister of Great Britain, Harold Macmillan, made a speech before the South African parliament: 'The wind of change is blowing through this continent, and whether we like it or not, this growth of national consciousness is a political fact. We must all accept it as a fact, and our national policies must take account of it.'

Colonial independence with majority-rule began in India and Pakistan in 1947 and by 1957 had reached Africa with the independence of Ghana (Gold Coast). The Cold War blocs of West (United States & Western Europe) and East (Soviet Union & Eastern Europe) competed to attract Asian and African nationalists towards parliamentary democracy (capitalism) or communism (revolutionary-socialism).

The white settler territories of South Africa and South West Africa, Southern and Northern Rhodesia, Portuguese Angola and Mozambique bucked the trend and clung onto power against black majority rule. Portugal denied that its colonies were colonies: they were integral parts of the mother country, under the same fascist dictatorship. Southern and Northern Rhodesia moved towards a federation with Nyasaland that claimed to be 'multi-racial': the interests of a white minority (represented by parliament) were considered equal or superior to those of the black majority (represented by traditional chiefs and colonial administrators). In South Africa, racial segregation was revived and made legally watertight by the (Reunited) National Party (NP)[1] that was elected to power in 1948. The NP doctrine of reinforced racial segregation was called *apartheid* (apartness).

SOUTH AFRICA UNDER APARTHEID

Like in the United States presidential election of the same year, racial segregation was a most vital issue at stake in the South African general elections of 1948. Jan Smuts' governing United Party had previously accepted Judge Henry Fagan's report of the 1946–47 Native Laws Commission. Fagan argued that urbanization made total segregation between whites and blacks impossible, so government should allow gradual extension of political rights to urban Africans. D.F. Malan's NP accepted the opposite viewpoint of a report by Paul Sauer, that total racial segregation was now necessary – in order to stop whites being eventually overwhelmed by blacks. Blacks could only be temporary dwellers in urban areas or on white farms while their employment lasted, and they should all return to the 'native reserves' from which they (or their ancestors) came.

The NP made their apartheid plans explicit in their 1947 manifesto and in their 1948 election campaign. The party appealed to both white farmers who wanted cheap African labour and white workers who feared African competition in the workplace. Slogans such as *swart gevaar* (black peril) and *rooi gervaar* (red peril) conflated African nationalism and communism as threats to white *baaskap* (boss-ship). Furthermore, the NP blamed the UP for the hardships arising from participation in the Second World War, including petrol rationing, high inflation, and shortages of basic commodities such as meat.

Their victory at the polls reinforced NP conviction that they were on the correct path. Malan called for the complete prohibition of racially mixed marriages, for the outlawing of black trade unions, and stricter enforcement of job reservation. Two of the first laws passed by the NP government enforced racial segregation at the family and personal level. The 1949 Prohibition of Mixed Marriages Act extended the existing ban on white-black marriages to white-coloured marriages. The 1950 Immorality Act went further to declare illegal sexual relations between all races.

The foundation of apartheid's programme of legal social engineering was the 1950 Population Registration Act, which was to classify everyone according to a defined racial category: European (white), Coloured, Indian, and native or 'Bantu'. This had tragic and sometimes farcical consequences in dividing even nuclear families into two or more different races. Newspapers carried monthly lists of names of individuals who were officially re-classified from one race to another.

The 1950 Group Areas Act restricted different races to different areas. This enabled government to remove millions of Africans from areas now declared white where their ancestors had lived. Coloured people were expelled to remote sandy flats from multi-racial District Six in Cape Town. Africans were expelled from Cato Manor at Durban when it was declared as an Indians-only area, and from Sophiatown in Johannesburg when it was declared as a whites-only area. Multi-racial Sophiatown had been unique as an urban area where Africans were allowed to own land. It was replaced by a white suburb named Triompf. Africans were removed across the open veld to Meadowlands within Soweto (South-Western Townships) in 1954–55.

The 1952 Natives (Abolition of Passes and Coordination of Documents) Act introduced a single 'reference book', i.e. a pass-book big enough to carry lots of official stamps. It was compulsory for every African man to carry a pass-book at all times. The law was initially not extended to women. Offenders could be 'endorsed out' by police from white areas back to 'homelands' that they had never known. Endorsements 'in' by employers in pass-books were an essential part of government's 'influx control' to eliminate surplus labour from white areas. Over the years, millions of people were imprisoned for either not carrying a pass-book or having the wrong stamps in them for that area and time. This law also led to widespread corruption among policemen, as injustice could only be avoided by bribery.

The 1951 Native Building Workers Act banned African construction workers any from skilled job outside their designated 'homelands'. The 1953 Native Labour Settlement of Disputes Act and the 1956 Industrial Conciliation Act restricted black trade unions, banning them from mining, government, and domestic work as well as banning strike action. Blacks were excluded from membership of non-black unions. Widened job colour-bar restrictions now applied to all industries, trades, occupations, and classes of work.

The 1953 Reservation of Separate Amenities Act introduced 'petty apartheid' into public places – by making it a punishable offence for Africans to mix with whites in parks, beaches, trains, hotels, swimming pools, theatres, post offices, railway stations, libraries, public toilets, and other facilities. Separate facilities were to be provided for each race.

The 1953 Bantu Education Act ensured that Africans received separate and inferior education. The legislation grew out of the recommendations of the 1949–51 Eiselen Commission on native education that recommended the phasing out of mission schools, the use of mother-tongue instruction, and compulsory education deferred to a future date. In the words of Bantu Affairs minister H.F. Verwoerd: 'There is no place for the Bantu in the European community above certain forms of labour...for that reason it is of no avail for him to receive a training which has, as its aim, absorption into the European community'. The 1963 Coloured People's Education Act and the 1965 Indian Education Act similarly placed these sectors under racial educational departments. Annual spending on education in 1968 was less than R15 per black child and R228 per white child (rising to R42 and R644, respectively, in 1975).

The 1951–54 Tomlinson Commission investigated the development of the old 'native reserves'. The Tomlinson Report (published in 1955) recommended enlargement and consolidation of 'Bantu homelands' – dubbed Bantustans in the media. It advocated soil conservation measures and employment generation by placing white-owned industries on Bantustan borders. Tomlinson argued that the expansion and development of black areas was crucial to the success of 'separate development' – though equitable division of land between black and white could only be achieved by incorporating the High Commission Territories.

When H.F. Verwoerd succeeded J.G. Strijdom as prime minister in 1958, he made setting up 'Bantu homelands' his main task. The 1959 Promotion of Bantu Self Government Act provided for new administrations in each Bantustan, under central white South African government supervision. Ten separate Bantustans were subsequently recognized: Transkei, Bophutha-Tswana, Venda, and Ciskei (later popularly grouped as the TBVC states), and KwaZulu, Lebowa (North Sotho), Gazankulu (Tsonga), QwaQwa (South Sotho), Kangwane (Swazi), and KwaNdebele. The development of viable Bantustans was essential to the plan of 'grand apartheid' (contrasted with everyday racial discrimination as 'little apartheid'), as labour pools from which black workers could be extracted and then returned from white areas. As well as accommodating traditional rulers, the NP government also recognized that it could divert educated élites from the cities by creating employment prospects for bureaucrats and trained professionals inside the Bantustans. The more controversial aspects of environmental 'betterment', notably limits on livestock holdings, were modified to ensure the cooperation of rich people in the Bantustans who saw cattle as their capital.

POPULAR RESISTANCE IN SOUTH AFRICA

The independence of India and Pakistan from the British Empire in 1947 gave a fillip to African nationalism. The ANC Youth League followed the Africanist ideas of its leader Anton Lembede – who died suddenly in 1947. The Youth League adopted an anti-socialist stance in its 1948 manifesto: 'the fundamental fact [is] that we are not oppressed as a class, but as a people, as a Nation.' But youth leaguers like Nelson Mandela, Walter Sisulu, and Oliver Tambo found themselves drawn as allies to the communists on the ANC executive, Moses Kotane and J.B. Marks, as well as to the S.A. Indian Congress.

After the Separate Representation of Voters Bill of 1951 had been blocked for four years in parliament and in the supreme court, prime minister J.G. Strijdom (Strydom) used the 1955 Senate Act to pack the senate with new members and got the law passed. The act ended the last vestiges of the colour-blind Cape franchise, by removing the vote for the national parliament from Coloured people.

The Communist Party of South Africa prided itself on its multi-racial membership and thus became a prime target of the state. The 1950 Suppression of Communism Act declared the party illegal and was aimed at dissidents of all races, as it applied very broadly to 'any person whom the minister deems to be a Communist'. The CPSA reorganized itself as an underground movement under the revised name of S.A. Communist Party (SACP) in 1953.

In 1952–53, the ANC and its multi-racial allies of the Congress Alliance (Coloured People's Congress, Indian National Congress, and the Congress of Democrats among whites) organized a national 'defiance campaign' – calling for 'boycott, strike and civil disobedience' against apartheid laws, inspired by the peaceful political tactics of Mahatma Gandhi in India, inviting the police to arrest demonstrators until the prisons overflowed. The 'defiance campaign' was called off in 1953, after police violence deliberately incited mob rioting. ANC leaders were arrested, and the NP government gave itself more police-state powers of detention without trial. The Congress Alliance founded the South African Congress of Trade Unions (COSATU) and the Federation of South African Women. The latter organized protests around the country against the government announcement that African women would be required to carry passes. On 9 August 1956, 20,000 women assembled outside government buildings in Pretoria, under white and coloured and Indian women leaders led by Lilian Ngoyi. The crowd sang in Zulu: *Strijdom uthinta abafazi, uthinti imbokodho* ('Strijdom, when you hit a woman, you strike a rock').

The Congress Alliance held a national convention, known as the Congress of the People, at Kliptown south of Johannesburg, on 25 and 26 June 1955. The convention adopted a Freedom Charter based on the UN Charter of Human Rights: 'South Africa belongs to all who live in it, black and white... only a democratic state, based on the will of all the people, can secure to all their birthright without distinction of colour, race, sex or belief...' Members of an Africanist Watchdog Committee in the ANC Youth League, notably Peter Mda and Robert Mangaliso Sobukwe, rejected the charter because it promised 'equal status in the bodies of the state, in the courts and in the schools for all national groups and races' – equal rights for privileged minorities over the oppressed African majority of the people.

In December 1956, 156 Congress Alliance leaders, both men and women, were arrested and later brought to court on the charge of treason. Former Nazi-sympathiser Oswald Pirow headed the prosecution; Bram Fischer, secretly the head of the SA Communist Party, headed the defence team of lawyers. Justice and the rule of law prevailed eventually. No one was convicted. The Treason Trial finally collapsed when the last 30 accused were acquitted in March 1961. Meanwhile, the ANC was split over the Freedom Charter. Africanists led by Robert Sobukwe walked out and founded their own Pan-Africanist Congress (PAC) on 6 April 1959.

There were outbreaks of popular protest in rural areas against 'tribal' authorities imposed under the Bantu Authorities Act of 1951. Disturbances among Hurutshe Tswana in the Marico district during 1957–58 began with resistance to the imposition of pass laws on women. The Sekukuneland Revolt among Pedi people in 1958 began with protests following deposition of a popular chief. The Pondoland revolt of 1960 had similar origins, rejecting government-imposed authorities in the Transkei. The government resorted to force to put these and other rural protests down.

When the ANC announced a new campaign against women's pass-laws in March 1960, the PAC moved first with its protests against all pass-laws. On 21 March 1960, thousands of men and women marched to the police station at Sharpeville, south of Johannesburg – demanding to be arrested for not carrying passes. Police officers panicked and fired into the crowd, killing 69 people and wounding hundreds of others. The Sharpeville massacre was widely condemned worldwide, as pictures were splashed across newspapers showing unarmed demonstrators being shot in the back while fleeing from the police station.

PAC protests over Sharpeville spread to other parts of the country, notably in the African townships of Langa and Nyanga in Cape Town, where five were shot dead. The ANC also organized national stay away strikes. On 30 March, government invoked a state of emergency and detained more than 18,000 people. The 1960 Unlawful Organisations Act declared both the ANC and the PAC to be illegal organizations.

Prime minister Verwoerd survived an assassination attempt by an anti-apartheid white farmer in April 1960. In October 1960, the white electorate voted 52–47 for the Union of South Africa to become a republic. After Congress members attempted to form a new organization, the government declared a 'state of emergency' that suspended the rule of law in May 1960 and arrested 10,000 more people. One of those arrested was Robert Sobukwe; he was sentenced to three years in jail. Under the barrage of international criticism, South Africa withdrew itself from the (British) Commonwealth and became the Republic of South Africa on 31 May 1961.

The 1962 Sabotage Act included political propaganda as a kind of sabotage. It gave the minister of justice the power to impose house arrest. Detainees were muzzled by 12-day, 90-day, and, later, 180-day detention without trial or access to lawyers. Both ANC and PAC activists concluded that political freedom could only be achieved by armed struggle. African nationalist

Nelson Mandela, white communist Joe Slovo, and others formed Umkonto weSizwe (MK). PAC established its own military wing known as Poqo (Xhosa for 'alone'). Mandela was arrested near Pietermaritzburg in August 1962. MK colleagues Walter Sisulu, Govan Mbeki, Raymond Mlangeni, Dennis Goldberg, and others were arrested at a suburban farmhouse in Rivonia north of Johannesburg. They were planning a sabotage campaign named Operation Mayibuye. Facing the death penalty, Nelson Mandela made a famous speech from the dock:

> I have fought against white domination and I have fought against black domination. I have cherished the idea of a democratic and free society in which all persons live together in harmony and with equal opportunities. It is an ideal which I hope to live for and achieve. But if need be, it is an ideal for which I am prepared to die.

The Rivonia trialists were sentenced to life imprisonment: eight of them on Robben Island, and Goldberg in the whites-only Pretoria Central prison. Soon after the trial Bram Fisher, who had led the defence team, was also arrested and sentenced to life imprisonment. When Robert Sobukwe of PAC completed his three-year sentence in 1963, the South African parliament periodically renewed a special law to detain him without trial. He spent six years in solitary confinement on Robben Island, and was then put under house arrest at Kimberley, where he died in 1978.

The South African régime had succeeded in quelling political protest, and the apartheid system appeared safe from danger. It maintained a ruthlessly intrusive spy-informer network that kept the security police informed. The state frequently resorted to political banning, detention without trial, and targeted political assassinations. It defied mounting international condemnation and a growing anti-apartheid movement that advocated trade and sports boycotts, an arms embargo, and other international sanctions.

The economy of South Africa prospered during the boom years that began in the later 1950s. The percentage of iron and steel used in South Africa produced by ISCOR rose from 50 per cent in 1945 to 70 per cent by 1955, and the value of locally manufactured goods rose from £138 to £482 million between these same years. The economy continued to grow throughout the 1960s into the early 1970s. White South Africans continued to live well, and they could ignore the global outcry against apartheid. The assassination of Prime Minister Verwoerd by parliamentary messenger Dimitrio Tsafendas in the House of Assembly on September 1966 was one of the few omens of turbulent times ahead.

The 1967 Terrorism Act provided for indefinite detention in solitary confinement without access to family, friends, or lawyer. The 1967 and 1968 Prohibition of (Improper) Political Interference Acts prohibited multi-racial membership of political parties – aimed at the Liberal Party which had been multi-racial hitherto. Both of the exile political parties began to prepare for armed struggle from their bases in Africa – the ANC in Zambia and the PAC in Tanzania.

TWO RHODESIAS & NYASALAND 1945–63

The Second World War accelerated the growth of mass nationalism, led by teachers or small businessmen and trade unionists – no longer confined to petitioning the colonial masters. The war had meant rapid growth of mining and manufacturing, and commercialization of agriculture producing foodstuffs for the cities and tobacco for export. Land alienation was intensified in Southern Rhodesia for new white farmers and farms. The lasting source of grievance among peasant families was their removal to the reserves from their traditional lands – where they were replaced on the farms by contract workers from Nyasaland. African soldiers returned from overseas with high expectations. But they found themselves in competition with the post-war influx of white settlers from overseas seeking higher living standards, and from English-speaking whites escaping Afrikaans language restrictions in South Africa after 1948.

As in South Africa, the rising post-war cost of living resulted in strikes. The Rhodesia Railways African Employees Association, based at Bulawayo, struck for more pay up and down the lines in 1945. Charles Mzingeli organized workers in Salisbury in his Reformed Industrial and Commercial Workers Union (RICU) in 1946. Benjamin Burombo organized people around Bulawayo in his British African Voice Association of 1947. A strike by municipal workers at Bulawayo in 1948 spread elsewhere in Southern Rhodesia. (It was never really a 'general strike' as some sources claim.) After wildcat strikes among mineworkers on the Copperbelt in 1946, the Northern Rhodesia African Mineworkers Union was founded in 1948 with aid from trade unions in Britain.

To dissociate himself from apartheid in South Africa, Southern Rhodesian prime minister Huggins abandoned his 'two-pyramid policy' in favour of multi-racial 'partnership'. White and black would develop the country as partners – but he let slip that he envisioned it as the partnership between a rider and a horse! The Federation of Southern and Northern Rhodesia and

Nyasaland, popularly known as Central African Federation, was established in 1953. It brought together the labour and mineral resources of the north with the commercial and industrial resources of the south. It was also seen as the pro-British 'multi-racial' alternative to Afrikaans apartheid social engineering in the Union of South Africa.

The idea of such a federation between colonies had been mooted among colonial officials since 1915, to reduce the duplication of administrative costs. The Hilton Young Commission of 1927–29 explored the possibility of federation from Kenya and Uganda in the north to Southern Rhodesia in the south. But it was considered a step too far, and the idea lapsed until after the Second World War. The post-1945 Labour government in Britain wanted to group colonies into federations that would become viable self-governing dominions within the Commonwealth – and would be protected markets for British imports and exports.

Plans for the Central African Federation were most strongly opposed in 1951–53 by the Nyasaland African Congress (founded 1944) and the Northern Rhodesia African Congress (founded 1946). Objections to federation were weaker in Southern Rhodesia, where human rights among Africans stood to benefit. The main focus of nationalist agitation there was against the 1951 Land Husbandry Act, which attempted to benefit a minority of productive African small farmers at the expense of the majority of peasants being driven into paid employment.

Southern Rhodesia, Northern Rhodesia, and Nyasaland all kept their separate governments and legal systems. The federal government was responsible for foreign relations and defence, customs and currency, railways and airports, electricity, broadcasting, and white education. Salisbury was the federal capital. The Central African Federation built the great Kariba hydro-electric dam on the Zambezi to supply power for mining and industrialization. It also established Central African Airways and founded the multi-racial University College of Rhodesia and Nyasaland at Salisbury. The Central African Federation was an initial economic success, but it was never acceptable to African nationalists. In Nyasaland and Northern Rhodesia, it was seen as extending white supremacy from Southern Rhodesia. In Southern Rhodesia, initial optimism among liberals, notably at the University College, turned into more radical objections as the mask of multi-racialism slipped from the face of an essentially racialist régime.

By the mid-1950s, nationalist movements in all three territories began to demand 'one-man-one vote' majority rule, inspired by the advance towards independence of the Gold Coast (Ghana) in West Africa. They were also cognizant of the Mau Mau land-and-freedom war against British rule in Kenya. Youthful leaders of the Nyasaland African Congress leaders decided to call home their countryman Dr Hastings Kamuzu Banda, who had spent 42 years overseas. Banda arrived home in 1957, demanding independence and an end to the Central African Federation. Northern Rhodesia's African Congress under Harry Nkumbula began negotiations with more amenable colonial authorities in 1955–56 but came into conflict with trade unionists organizing 'rolling strikes' up and down the mining towns of the Copperbelt.

Nationalist leaders from British Central Africa attended the All-African People's Conference convened by President Kwame Nkrumah in independent Ghana in 1958. The conference inspired greater militancy among African nationalists in the remaining colonies. Kenneth Kaunda broke with Nkumbula in 1958 to form the more militant Zambia African National Congress (ZANC). The City Youth League of Salisbury, also inspired by ANC boycotts in South Africa, came together with trade unionists at Bulawayo to form the Southern Rhodesia African National Congress (SRANC), under Joshua Nkomo, in 1958. But it was Dr Banda in Nyasaland who voiced the greatest militancy: 'Very soon I hope to have the whole of Nyasaland on fire.'

Anti-colonial riots in Nyasaland were put down by federal troops in 1959. Fifty Africans were shot dead; Banda was imprisoned; his party was banned. All three territories enacted similar security laws, along South African lines, to restrain the 'Central African Emergency'. The main nationalist parties were banned and then re-registered under new names in 1959–60: the Nyasaland African Congress as the Malawi Congress Party (MCP), ZANC as the United National Independence Party (UNIP), and SRANC as the National Democratic Party (NDP).

Meanwhile, in the Belgian Congo, the return from Ghana of nationalist leader Patrice Lumumba led to very serious rioting against Belgian rule. Belgium suddenly conceded ill-prepared 'independence' in June 1960. Only two weeks later, Belgian troops invaded, and the copper-rich province of Katanga was declared independent under Moise Tshombe – with the support of Belgium, South Africa, and the Central African Federation prime minister Roy Welensky. Lumumba was deposed and subsequently murdered, and United Nations troops imposed an uneasy peace and reunification with Katanga.

In 1961, the British government convened in London a constitutional conference for Southern Rhodesia that proposed 50 seats for whites and 15 seats for Africans in parliament. The African delegation led by Nkomo reversed their initial acceptance and rejected these proposals. They returned home to lead demonstrations for 'one-man-one-vote'. Nkomo's NDP was banned after riots and re-emerged as the Zimbabwe African People's Union (ZAPU) later in 1961. As a result, there was a mass boycott of the 1962 elections based on the 1961 constitution. A new, very right-wing, white party called the Rhodesia Front was swept into power. (Historians may ask whether acceptance of the 1961 constitution could not have been used to achieve 'one-man-one-vote' peacefully from within parliament.)

The Central African Emergency and the Congo Crisis convinced Britain and the big mining companies, which controlled the Copperbelt, to dissolve the Central African Federation. It was anyway doomed when Banda's Malawi Congress Party won the 1961 Nyasaland elections. All three territories were set on separate paths to independence in 1962–63. After a period of mass discontent (known as Cha Cha Cha), UNIP formed a coalition government with NRANC in 1962. Nyasaland and Northern Rhodesia became the independent republics of Malawi and Zambia, respectively, in 1964. Southern Rhodesia was left in the anomalous position of a white settler-dominated state with a voting franchise that excluded most Africans.

Growing dissatisfaction with the leadership of Joshua Nkomo, based in Matabeleland, led to the breakaway of ZAPU members in Mashonaland to form the Zimbabwe African National Union (ZANU) in 1963. At the same time as the banned ANC and PAC from South Africa were turning to armed struggle, ZAPU and ZANU began to smuggle arms into the country and to recruit cadres for military training abroad. Nationalist leaders did not yet envisage a prolonged armed struggle, but rather a few sharp armed attacks to bring the Rhodesia Front government to the negotiating table.

THE END OF THE HIGH COMMISSION TERRITORIES

The British parliament's 1909 pledge not to transfer the High Commission Territories to the Union of South Africa without consultation in the territories was repeated so often that 'consultation' was becoming understood as meaning 'consent'. But British governments did not rule out the possibility of transfer so long as their close ally Jan Smuts remained prime minister of the Union. When Smuts suggested in 1946 that Britain should reward South Africa for its war service with the gift of Basutoland, a junior minister in Britain's new Labour government (Douglas Dodds-Parker) resigned in protest – saying that it would be a betrayal of the people of Basutoland for *their* war service!

Historians differ as to when South Africa's claim to the territories lapsed. Some point to a speech by Conservative prime minister Winston Churchill in 1954. Others point to British government rejection of the terms of the 1955 Tomlinson Report in South Africa, or finally to 1961, when South

Africa left the Commonwealth and the three territories were advanced in self-government towards independence. That did not, however, stop South Africa's ambitions, because in 1963 prime minister Hendrik Verwoerd invited the three states to joint its own commonwealth of Bantustans. The High Commission Territories were not finally dissolved as a grouping until 1963–64, when the position of high commissioner was abolished and each territory became a full colony with its own equivalent of a governor.

The oldest, most populous, and best-educated country, Basutoland, was considered the most important by the outgoing colonial administration. The smallest but richest territory, Swaziland, was considered the second most important, as it had considerable white settlement and capital investment. Bechuanaland, the largest but poorest and least populous, was considered the 'Cinderella' of the three. The prime role of both Basutoland and Bechuanaland in the colonial system of Southern Africa was as labour reserves for the mines of the Witwatersrand.

NATIONAL FERMENT IN BASUTOLAND

Ntsu Mokhehle established a Basutoland African Congress in 1952, with the mission of fighting racial discrimination and transfer into the Union. It exploited dissatisfaction with the 1954 Moore Report, which neglected to recommend that the Basutoland National Council should become a more fully elected Legislative Council. Moore had backed the interests of the 'big chiefs' of the dominant Mokoteli-Kwena clan by recommending that the number of 'small chiefs' from other clans be reduced. Veteran nationalist Josiel Lefela of *Lekhotla la Bafo* was so outspoken in denouncing the report that he was expelled from the Basutoland National Council in 1955. Nevertheless, the council rejected the report and sent a delegation to London for constitutional talks in 1958.

Some Basutoland African Congress supporters broke away in 1957 to form a royalist party, *Marema-Tlou Party* (MTP), committed to support Bereng Seeiso (later Moshoeshoe II) when he became of age as paramount chief or king. Chiefly supporters of the existing regency, led by Chief Leabua Jonathan, formed their own Basutoland National Party (BNP) in 1958. Meanwhile, Ntsu Mokhehle attracted large numbers into his party, renamed the Basutoland Congress Party (BCP), and aligned it with Kwame Nkrumah in Ghana and the PAC in South Africa.

The Basutoland National Council was transformed into a Legislative Council in 1960, with powers of law-making subject to a colonial-appointed Executive Council that put Basutoland on the road to self-government and eventual independence. The BCP won the majority of elected seats in the Legislative Council elections of 1960. In 1965, the country held general elections based on universal adult suffrage. Leabua Jonathan's BNP won 31 out of the 60 seats in the new parliament against the 25 of Ntsu Mokhehle's BCP. Leabua Jonathan became the first prime minister. The kingdom of Lesotho gained independence on 4 October 1966, with a sovereign parliament under a virtually powerless constitutional monarch.

The majority of the people were poor, the country had few natural resources, and it depended on subsistence agriculture and remittances from migrant workers in South Africa. Though the highlands of Basutoland were once considered the wheat granary for South Africa, almost all its foodstuffs as well as manufactured products were imported from South Africa. The kingdom was completely surrounded by the Republic of South Africa, which regarded it as little better than a Bantustan. There were tensions between King Moshoeshoe II and Leabua Jonathan's government, and Lesotho could be swamped by refugees fleeing repression in South Africa.

COLONIAL DEVELOPMENT IN SWAZILAND

From the latter 1940s, Britain's Colonial Development Corporation (CDC), together with South African capital, invested in forestry, sugar, and fruit industries. The CDC planted the Usuthu forest and set up the Usuthu Pulp Company to process the timber, while the (South African) Anglo-American Corporation established a similar company called Peak Timbers Ltd. The CDC developed the Ubombo sugar plantations and sugar-mill, which also became a major employer and revenue earner for Swaziland. When the iron ore mine was established at Ngwenya, Anglo-American and the CDC entered into a contract to supply 12 million tons of ore over three years to Japan.

Benefits to Swaziland were, however, limited because of the very light taxes which business paid to the state. Many Swazi remained dependent on the migrant labour to South Africa that had previously developed during the drought of 1929–34. The unequal distribution of land between whites and blacks remained the burning issue at the heart of Swazi nation politics. Traditionalists and progressives combined to send a petition to the British government for a reconsideration of the precolonial concessions 'given' by King Mbandzeni. When this petition was ignored, Ngwenyama or King Sobhuza II delayed in licensing the Ngwenya iron ore mine until Britain recognized that all underlying mineral rights belonged to the Swazi nation. The mining company paid a peppercorn annual rent to the Swazi nation, but the CDC ensured that the Swazi nation (i.e. its royal government) became a share-holder in the forestry and sugar companies being set up.

Sobhuza regarded the militant nationalism that was sweeping across Africa as an alien idea opposed to monarchy and good order. When white settlers proposed their own Legislative Council, Sobhuza proposed instead a bi-racial council equally composed of white and Swazi representatives. Whites might have a secret vote, but Swazi should select candidates by acclamation at public gatherings. Meanwhile all Swazi would remain subject to the *Libandla* or Swazi National Council, and the Legislative and Executive Councils would be precluded from interference in Swazi law and custom – and would not have any rights over land and minerals.

Progressive Swazi nationalists, led by J.J. Nquku, Dr Ambrose Zwane, and Prince Dumisa Dlamini, responded by founding the Swaziland Progressive Party in July 1960 that called for the removal of all racial segregation and the adoption of 'one-man-one-vote'. The white settlers threw their support behind Sobhuza's proposal, which was accepted by a mass plebiscite arranged by the royal government in February 1962. The progressives were out-played by Sobhuza and the traditionalists, and they began to split and quarrel among themselves. The new party founded in 1962 by Zwane and Dumisa Dlamini, the Ngwane National Liberatory Congress (NNLC), had the strongest Pan-Africanist links.

The Swaziland constitutional conference held in London in 1963 ended in disagreement. White settler representatives demanded that control of land and mineral rights should be under the national parliament and not under the *Libandla*. Swazi nationalists stuck to their insistence on one-man-one-vote. The British-imposed compromise pleased no one — a national parliament divided equally between representatives of the Swazi nation, the white settlers, and one-third elected by universal franchise.

Sobhuza founded the Imbokodvo National Movement to fight the impending elections. The whites campaigned as a United Swaziland Association. Meanwhile, the NNLC helped to organize workers to go on strike at Big Bend sugar estates and Havelock (Bulembu) mine. The strikes spread to Mbabane and elsewhere as a general strike. Prince Dumisa was imprisoned and, with traditionalist support, the British flew in troops from Kenya to put down the strikes.

When the country went to the polls in June 1964, Imbokodvo took two-thirds of the seats, with the remainder going to the United Swaziland Association. From their unchallenged position in the Legislative Council, Imbokodvo agreed in 1965 to a future Legislative Assembly or national parliament, based on a non-racial voters' roll and one-person-one-vote. Imbokodvo overwhelmingly won the 1967 elections. It took the country to independence on 6 September 1968 – determined to overturn the few restrictions on royal power placed on it by the constitution.

COLONIAL UNDERDEVELOPMENT IN BECHUANALAND

Bechuanaland Protectorate was described as 'the country without a future' in the mid-1950s. But in 1954 the CDC established an abattoir at Lobatse, which exported chilled meat to the copper mines of Northern Rhodesia and the Belgian Congo. This improved the living standards of the larger traditional cattle-owners, while poorer families remained dependent on drought-prone subsistence agriculture at home and labour migration abroad.

Bechuanaland hit the world headlines in 1949–50 after Seretse Khama, as a student in England, married an English woman without prior notice to his uncle Tshekedi Khama, who was the regent for Seretse as chief designate of the Ngwato. Tshekedi and Ngwato elders insisted on a divorce. But youthful ex-servicemen, who had returned from the war to find themselves taxed and their labour exploited by Tshekedi to build a college and its dam, turned against Tshekedi and acclaimed Seretse rightful chief – with his wife. The South African and Southern Rhodesian governments protested at what they considered a fundamental threat to white supremacy – the prospect of a significant black ruler with a white wife in a neighbouring country that they wished to annex. British governments, both Labour and Conservative, dithered and then agreed to exile Seretse and his wife overseas – with Tshekedi exiled elsewhere in Bechuanaland. The injustice to Seretse Khama and his wife aroused African, Asian, Caribbean, and African-American political interest and support overseas. Supporters of Seretse at home, like Leetile Raditladi, formed a Bamangwato National Congress in 1952.

Tshekedi was allowed back home in 1952, and he became deeply involved in economic planning for the whole of Bechuanaland. He served in the territory's African Advisory Council and its multi-racial Joint Advisory Council. He continued to demand the establishment of a Legislative Council in preparation for self-government. The Ngwato people, however, refused to negotiate the copper mining concession with the Rhodesian Selection Trust, negotiated by Tshekedi, until Seretse Khama was allowed back home. Uncle and nephew were ultimately reconciled in 1956. Seretse Khama returned home with his wife and children – though as a private citizen and never as a chief. Together the two men worked to restore political stability and economic progress. Tshekedi died in 1959, before the opening of the copper mines and the Legislative Council that he had long worked for.

The proposed Legislative Council motivated Leetile Raditladi to found a Bechuanaland Protectorate Federal Party (BPFP) in 1959. Africanists under K.T. Motsete then founded the Bechuanaland People's Party (BPP) in 1960, demanding immediate one-man-one-vote and independence. Motsete was an old teacher who had helped found the Nyasaland African Congress in 1944.

He soon lost control of the BPP to ex-soldier Philip Matante and ex-ANC treason trialist Motsamai Mpho. PAC-supporting Matante, buoyed by mass support against the Tati Company landlords of Francistown, succeeded in expelling first Mpho and then Motsete from the BPP. Mpho founded his own Botswana Independence Party (BIP) in 1964, based in Ngamiland.

From 1958 onwards, Bechuanaland received increasing numbers of political refugees crossing the border on foot from South Africa. Most were youths seeking education abroad, and they were sent northwards through Northern Rhodesia into East Africa. There were also significant political figures, such as Oliver Tambo, who went northwards by aircraft to set up the external missions of the ANC. Nelson Mandela not only went north on the 'refugee pipeline' in 1962 but also came back south to enter South Africa clandestinely.

The Bechuanaland Democratic Party (BDP) originated among members of the Legislative Council in 1962, headed by Seretse Khama, with Quett Ketumile Masire as its main organizer. The party's strength was support from educated élites nationwide and cordial relations with more progressive colonial officials. The BDP called for universal suffrage and multi-party democracy. The first one-person-one-vote elections in the country were held in March 1965. The BDP won 28 of the 31 elected seats, against Matante's BPP with the remaining three. Seretse Khama became prime minister and then president of the independent Republic of Botswana on 30 September 1966.

Per capita income at independence was about $70, and the country had only 12 kilometres of paved road. In the first few years of independence, Botswana quietly developed non-racial political and bureaucratic institutions that would facilitate the country's economic development – which would in turn enable it to escape the political stranglehold of white-ruled South Africa and Rhodesia. The first prerequisite for the Republic of Botswana's postcolonial development was to develop its own national government headquarters and capital. The new town of Gaborone had been opened only in 1964, when the old colonial administration abandoned its quarters at Mafeking – a town inside the Republic of South Africa.

ANTI-FASCIST STRUGGLES IN ANGOLA & MOZAMBIQUE

The Portuguese colonies of Angola and Mozambique were tightly held in the grip of Portugal's fascist Estado Novo of 1933–68. After the Second World War, in which Portugal had been neutral but pro-Nazi, prime minister Salazar promoted agriculture and mining in Angola, including oil extraction, for the benefit of large-scale white immigration into the colonies. In Angola, white immigration increased by 80 per cent between 1950 and 1955, with immigrants arriving at the rate of 1,000 per month. They occupied the most productive farmlands and were supported by generous government subsidies.

However, many white immigrants were illiterate and ignorant of local climate and soils, and the agricultural scheme failed. Many drifted into urban centres to compete with African workers over menial jobs. Jobs were handed out on the basis of skin colour: whites first, *assimilado* people of colour (assimilated to Portuguese culture) second, other people of colour third, and blacks last. Whites who stayed on the land relied on the contract labour system, which compelled Africans to work on cotton and coffee plantations for part of every year, for a mere pittance. The police often rounded up the required number of Africans from villages and forced them to work on the white farms.

In both Angola and Mozambique, forced cotton cultivation by peasants fed Portugal's textile industry. Prices paid for the cotton were very low. Armed police enforced the production quotas, often with violence. Peasants who resisted were arrested or deported. All this caused a great deal of popular resentment in rural areas. The only escape for a few was provided by Protestant Christian missions of non-Portuguese origin. It is not a coincidence that the three key leaders in the anti-colonial struggle from the 1960s onwards – Holden Roberto of FNLA (Frente Nacional de Libertação de Angola), Agostino Neto of MPLA (Movemento Popular de Libertação de Angola), and Jonas Savimbi of UNITA (Uniao Nacional para a Independência Total de Angola) – were products of Baptist, Methodist, and Congregationalist mission schools, respectively.

Protest was ruthlessly suppressed by the secret police known as PIDE (Policia Internacional da Defesa do Estado). Nevertheless, several African political organizations emerged from the 1950s onwards. One of the first African political parties established in Angola in 1953 was PLUDADE (Partido Luta Unida dos Africanos de Angola), which later changed its name to FNLA. Its leader Holden Roberto had close links to anti-colonial leaders elsewhere, such as Kwame Nkrumah. Other political parties followed, notably MPLA, formed in 1956 under the leadership of Ilidio Tome Alves Machado. Though MPLA was led by *mestizos* and *assimilados*, it drew support from the mainly black population of Luanda – and had close connections with Portuguese communists and socialists.

Worried by increasing demands for social justice and national independence, the Portuguese government banned all nationalist parties in Angola in 1959. When MPLA members protested the ban, government forces shot dead 30 and wounded over 200 people. Towards the end of 1960, about 30,000 peasant cotton farmers in the Cassange area went on strike and stopped paying taxes. They then attacked government installations, offices of the official cotton purchasing agency, and a Portuguese Catholic mission station. In response, the colonial army moved in and killed more than 10,000 people.

This was the cue for African nationalists deciding to take up arms to overthrow Portuguese colonialism. On 3 February 1961, MPLA supporters attacked a radio station and the main prison in Luanda, the colonial capital. White settlers assisted by soldiers responded by killing over 3,000 Africans in the shanty town (*muceques*) of Luanda. Then, on 15 March 1961, the Kongo people of northern Angola rose against the colonial system and killed over 200 Portuguese settlers. Government forces retaliated by killing over 30,000 Africans in reprisal. FNLA and MPLA members left the country from 1961 onwards to organize armed struggle from beyond its borders. Many initially fled to the newly independent Congo. In 1966, Jonas Savimbi broke away from FNLA to form his own movement called UNITA, which drew its strength among Ovimbundu of southern Angola. FNLA drew support mainly from the Kongo people of the north, while MPLA recruited a mixture of people around the city of Luanda.

In Mozambique, as in Angola, the political consciousness of élite Africans – often with Protestant mission education – was raised by resentment of fascist repression in the 1950s. A dock strike at Lourenço Marques in 1956 led to 49 strikers being shot dead. More than 500 protesting Makonde peasants were shot dead at Mueda in the north of Mozambique in 1960. There was a proliferation of small political groups between 1956 and 1961, with names proclaiming African democracy, Mozambique liberation, progress, Catholic socialism, and socialism both democratic and revolutionary, as well as the cause of Makonde people. Other political groups were formed among Mozambican exiles in Salisbury, Mombasa, and Malawi – who came together in June 1962 to form FLELIMO (Frente de Libertaçao de Mocambique), based at Dar es Salaam in newly independent Tanganyika (afterwards united with Zanzibar as the Republic of Tanzania).

FRELIMO invited Eduardo Mondlane to be its president. Mondlane had attended a Swiss mission before passing on to the Universities of the Witwatersrand and Lisbon, and Northwestern University in the United States – where he obtained his doctorate. After working for the United Nations in Mozambique, he had become an anthropology professor at Syracuse University, from which he was recruited to Dar es Salaam by FRELIMO in 1963. Mondlane already knew the liberation leaders Amilcar Cabral of Portuguese Guinea and Agostino Neto of Angola. At its first congress, FRELIMO not only condemned Portuguese colonialism and demanded independence but also urged cooperation with sister liberation movements in Angola and Portuguese Guinea (Guinea Bissau). FRELIMO organized a dock strike at Lourenço Marques in 1963, and in 1964 launched its first armed guerrilla campaign into northern Mozambique.

CHALLENGES TO THE SOUTH WEST AFRICA MANDATE

The Union of South Africa's mandate over 'the interests of the indigenous population' of South West Africa, given by the League of Nations, lapsed in 1945 when the League was replaced by the United Nations organization. Jan Smuts pledged to continue the mandate by submitting annual reports to the UN, while he made a determined attempt get the UN to allow its incorporation as an integral part of South Africa. Herero chiefs protested. After Smuts refused them passports, paramount chief Hosea Kutako asked Tshekedi Khama in Bechuanaland to take their case to the UN. Tshekedi was then stopped from travelling to New York by the British government. Tshekedi turned to his friend Rev. Michael Scott to go instead.

Though he was banned from entering South West Africa in 1947, Scott continued to press 'the interests of the indigenous population' for many years at the UN. Between 1946 and 1960, there were no less than 120 separate petitions sent to the UN to no avail. In 1950 the International Court of Justice ruled that the Union of South Africa was still bound by the terms of the 1919 Mandate. But South Africa refused to accept the ruling and defiantly placed the Africans of South West Africa directly under the Union's Native Affairs Department. The territory was increasingly valuable to South Africa, as its exports of diamonds, sea fish, karakul wool, copper, and lead earned valuable foreign exchange.

South West African students in South Africa formed their own student union in 1952, which converted itself into the South West African Progressive Association in 1955. The first political party was the Ovamboland People's Congress, formed in 1957 by migrant workers in Cape Town, led by Herman Toivo ja Toivo. In 1958, he was deported from South Africa back to South West Africa, where he recruited Sam Nujoma to the cause. They worked closely with the South West African Progressive Association. Together they organized residents' protests against their forced removal from Windhoek's old location to the new Katutura Township, where they would pay high rents and be allocated to ethnic sections.

The Progressive Association reformed itself into a political party called SWANU (South West African National Union) in August 1959. On 18 December 1959, Windhoek old location residents began to boycott municipal beer halls, cinemas, buses, and other municipal facilities. Two days later, police shot and killed 13 demonstrators. Toivo and Nujoma concluded that SWANU was too ineffective in mobilizing the masses. They decided to found their own mass-based party in April 1960 – SWAPO (South West African People's Organisation). Encouraged onwards by Hosea Kutako, SWAPO's president Sam Nujoma escaped across Bechuanaland and Northern Rhodesia to Tanganyika, where he was helped to reach the UN at New York. He returned to set up the headquarters of SWAPO-in-exile at Dar es Salaam.

SWANU was eventually overshadowed by SWAPO as a nationalist movement, but it retained a power base in heavily populated Ovamboland in the north-west. In the north-east, the Caprivi African National Union emerged in 1963 and was soon banned. In 1964 Herero and Nama councillors in the south formed their own NUDO (National Unity Democratic Organisation), led by Hosea Kutako, Samuel Witbooi, and Clemens Kapuuo. SWAPO sent young people abroad for education and military training. It established a military wing called PLAN (People's Liberation Army of Namibia). In 1966, in cooperation with ZAPU and the ANC, SWAPO launched armed struggle through the Caprivi Strip with a PLAN attack on the colonial administrative centre of Oshikango and on a South African military base at Omugulugwombashe.

RHODESIA REMAINS A SETTLER COLONY

The 1963 split between ZAPU, under Joshua Nkomo, and ZANU, led by Rev. Ndabaningi Sithole and Robert Gabriel Mugabe, followed rival supporters fighting pitched battles in the streets of the townships. This gave the Rhodesia Front government, now under prime minister Ian Smith, the excuse to ban both parties in August 1964. Disagreement over leadership personalities and strategy gradually hardened into divisions along geographical and ethnic lines. ZAPU was generally supported by Ndebele- and Kalanga-speakers in Matabeleland, while ZANU was generally supported by Shona-speakers in Mashonaland and other provinces. The division was later deepened by the fact that ZAPU received military support from the Soviet Union and East Germany, while ZANU received a lesser amount from the People's Republic of China.

In protest against Britain's refusal to concede independence to Rhodesia under white minority rule, the Rhodesia Front government under Ian Smith declared its own UDI (unilateral declaration of independence) for Rhodesia on 11 November 1965 – with the support of the white Republic of South Africa. This rebellion against Britain appealed to right-wing supporters in Britain and especially in Southern 'rebel' states of the United States. It also justified the use of armed struggle by ZAPU and ZANU – to bring the country they called Zimbabwe back into international legitimacy. ZAPU had already established a military wing, ZIPRA (Zimbabwe People' Revolutionary Army), and had infiltrated a number of districts in the north and north-west of the country by 1964. Meanwhile, ZANU had set up its own army named ZANLA (Zimbabwe African National Liberation Army), which launched its first attack at a farm in Sinoia (Chinhoyi) in 1966.

THE NEW REPUBLICS OF ZAMBIA AND MALAWI

Northern Rhodesia became the independent Republic of Zambia on 24 October 1964. The UNIP governing party was led by Kenneth Kaunda as prime minister, soon to be made president after parliament opted for a new constitution. The international copper price was high, so the national economy – though excessively dependent on it – appeared healthy, ready for heavy expenditure on education, health, social services, infrastructure, and state employment. Rural areas desperately needed basic health and education facilities and usable roads. They also needed good prices for their produce marketed in the cities. At the same time the urban masses expected low food prices as well as improved living standards. Could all these expectations be met? Zambia faced hostile white-ruled governments on most sides: Rhodesia in the south and the South African-controlled Caprivi Strip in the south-west, Portuguese Angola in the west, and Portuguese Mozambique in the south-east.

Nyasaland became the independent Republic of Malawi on 6 July 1964, under prime minister (later president) Dr Hastings Kamuzu Banda. One of his first acts was to tell an OAU (Organisation of African Unity) conference in Cairo that it would be unrealistic to expect Malawi to cut its ties with Portugal, Southern Rhodesia, or South Africa. He refused to endorse OAU resolutions urging African states to cut ties with white-ruled southern Africa. This led to a cabinet crisis a few weeks later, when Banda dismissed three ministers from his government, and three others resigned in protest at his dictatorial tendencies. (Most of these ex-cabinet ministers went into exile, and two of them subsequently sponsored unsuccessful military invasions. One was imprisoned for life.)

Dr Banda kept a very tight rein on government and administration. He is said to have regularly inspected the books and records of all his ministries. In 1963, he created the Malawi Young Pioneers to encourage unemployed youth to work in the fields and to take up other vocational training activities. In time, the Malawi Young Pioneers became a para-military body enforcing Banda's rule. Banda was obstinately proud that Malawi was the only independent African country to open up full diplomatic relations with apartheid South Africa.

SOUTH AFRICA'S OUTWARD POLICY

Anti-apartheid movements overseas began in the mid-1950s and were campaigning for boycotts of South African exports by the early 1960s. South Africa left the Commonwealth in 1962. The UN formally condemned apartheid in Resolution 1761 – declaring that apartheid seriously endangered international peace and security and calling on member nations to terminate diplomatic, military, and economic relations with the Republic of South Africa.

In 1963 prime minister Hendrik Verwoerd of South Africa offered to 'become the guardian, the protector or the helper' of the former High Commission Territories: 'we could lead them far better and much more quickly to independence and economic prosperity than Great Britain can do.' Verwoerd also suggested the creation of a common market under South African guidance for increased trade and investment as far north as the Congo. (This was later referred to as South Africa's 'constellation of states'.) Only Leabua Jonathan of Basutoland agreed to meet Verwoerd before the latter was assassinated in September 1966.

Under the so-called 'outward policy' of Verwoerd's successor Balthazar Vorster, South Africa extended its offer of free technical and economic advice to all African countries. There were contacts with Francophone African countries, the Congo, and Liberia. The most enthusiastic response was from Dr Banda of Malawi. Malawi established full diplomatic relations with South Africa in September 1967, leading up to the exchange of official visits by Banda and Vorster in 1970. Malawi was rewarded with soft loans to build transport infrastructure and a new capital city at Lilongwe.

FURTHER STUDY

BIBLIOGRAPHY

See also books recommended in previous chapters.

Beinart, William Justin (2010), *Popular Politics and Resistance Movements in South Africa*. Johannesburg: Wits University Press.

Callinicos, Luli (2004), *Oliver Tambo: Beyond the Engeli Mountains*. Cape Town: David Philip/ New Africa Books.

Cherry, Janet (2013), *Umkhonto we Sizwe*. Auckland Park: Jacana Pocket Books.

Dubow, Saul (2014), *Apartheid, 1948–1994*. Oxford: Oxford University Press.

Green, Reginald H., K. Kiljunen, & M. Kiljunen, eds. (1981), *Namibia: The Last Colony*. Harlow: Longman.

Huddleston, Trevor (1956), *Naught for Your Comfort*. London: William Collins.

Isaacman, Allen & Barbara Isaacman (1983), *Mozambique: From Colonialism to. Revolution, 1900–1982*. Boulder, CO: Westview Press.

Johns, Sheridan & Gwendolyn Carter, eds. (1972–77), *From Protest to Challenge: A Documentary History of African Politics in South Africa 1882–1964*. Stanford, CA: Hoover Institution Press & Claremont: David Philip.

Kallaway, Peter, ed. (1984). *Apartheid and Education: The Education of Black South Africans*. Johannesburg: Ravan.

Katjavivi, Peter (1988), *A History of Resistance in Namibia*. London, Paris and UNESCO: James Currey.

Kaunda, Kenneth (1962), *Zambia Shall be Free*. London: Heinemann African Writers Series.

Machobane, L.B.B.J. (1990), *Government and Change in Lesotho, 1800–1966: A Study of Political Institutions*. Basingstoke: Macmillan.

McCracken, John (2012), *A History of Malawi: 1859–1966*. Woodbridge: James Currey.

Mandela, Nelson, with Richard Stengel (1994), *Long Walk to Freedom Volume I: 1918–1962*. Boston, MA: Little, Brown & London: Macdonald Purnell.

Marks, Shula (1987), *'Not Either an Experimental Doll': The Separate Worlds of Three South African Women. Correspondence of Lily Moya, Mabel Palmer and Sibusisiwe Makhanya*. Durban: Killie Campbell Africana Library & Pietermaritzburg: University of Natal Press.

Manson, Andrew (2014), *Land Chiefs Mining: South Africa's North-West Province Since 1840*. Johannesburg: Witwatersrand University Press.

Meli, Francis (1988), *South Africa Belongs to Us*. Harare: Zimbabwe Publishing House.

Mondlane, Eduardo (1969), *The Struggle for Mozambique*. Harmondsworth: Penguin Books.

Morton, Fred & Jeff Ramsay, eds. (1987), *The Birth of Botswana: A History of the Bechuanaland Protectorate from 1910 to 1966*. Gaborone: Longman Botswana.

Newitt, Malyn D. (1995), *A History of Mozambique*. London: Hurst & Bloomington, IN: Indiana University Press.

Nicol, Mike (1991), *A Good-looking Corpse: The World of Drum – Jazz and Gangsters, Hope and Defiance in the Townships of South Africa*. London: Secker & Warburg.

Nkomo, Joshua, with Nicholas Harman (1984), *Nkomo: The Story of My Life*. London: Methuen.

Nujoma, Sam (2001), *Where Others Wavered: The Autobiography of Sam Nujoma*. London: Panaf Books.

Pachai, Bridgal (1973), *Malawi: The History of a Nation*. London: Longman.

Phiri, Bizeck Jube (2006), *A Political History of Zambia: From the Colonial Period to the Third Republic*. Trenton, NJ: Africa World Press.

Pogrund, Benjamin (2003), *How Can a Man Die Better: The Life of Robert Sobukwe*. Johannesburg: Jonathan Ball.

Raftopoulos, Brian & Alois Mlambo, eds. (2009), *Becoming Zimbabwe: A History from the Pre-Colonial Period to 2008*. Harare: Weaver Press.

Roberts, Andrew Dunlop (1976), *A History of Zambia*. London: Heinemann.

Sisulu, Elinor (2002), *Walter and Albertina Sisulu: In This Lifetime*. Cape Town: David Philip/New Africa Books.

Sithole, Ndabaningi (1959), *African Nationalism*. Cape Town: Oxford University Press.

Tlou, Thomas, Neil Parsons, & Willie Henderson (1995), *Seretse Khama, 1921–1980*. Gaborone: Botswana Society & Braamfontein: Macmillan.

White Luise (2003), *The Assassination of Herbert Chitepo: Texts and Politics in Zimbabwe*. Bloomington, IN: Indiana University Press.

VIDEOGRAPHY

DVDs and downloads:

Come Back Africa (dir. Lionel Rogosin, 1959–60, 59 mins): drama-documentary tracing the life of a Zulu migrant man come to the big city, surviving odd jobs without a pass, oppressed by the police state, his wife murdered by a gangster. Guest appearances by *Drum* magazine journalists debating in a shebeen, and penny-whistle music by 'Lemmy Special'.

Drum (dir. Zola Maseko, 2004. 94 mins): *Drum* magazine's 'Mr Drum' Henry Nxumalo (played by American actor Taye Diggs) experiences the destruction of Sophiatown, reveals slavery of prisoners on Eastern Transvaal farms, and is murdered.

Gold (dir. Peter R. Hunt, 1974. 120 mins): Roger Moore as goldmine manager foils plot to sabotage the mine by flooding.

Katrina (dir. Jans Rautenbach, 1969. 101 mins): adapted from play *Try for White*: Katrina rejects her Coloured family and succeeds in 'passing for white' until her secret is rumbled.

Master Harold and the Boys (dir. Lonny Price, 2010. 87 mins): story based on the childhood of playwright Athol Fugard of white boy Harold (Freddie Highmore) with neglectful parents who is effectively brought up instead by African household servants Sam and Willie.

N!ai: The Story of a !Kung Woman (dir. John Marshall, 1990. 59 mins): using documentary flashbacks, N!ai filmed in 1978 looks back on her girlhood and youth on the Namibia-Botswana border in the 1950s–60s. Includes Jamie Uys actually filming *The Gods Must Be Crazy*.

The Power of One (dir. John G. Avildsen, 1992. 127 mins): white boy growing up during Word War Two and discovering the colour bar, including his training as a boxer and a scene where he is a bystander of white warders and black prisoners in Barberton Prison.

Skin (dir. Anthony Fabian, 2008. 107 mins): white Afrikaner girl Sandra Laing (Sophie Okonedo) is reclassified Coloured and denied her previous civil rights because of her skin, but finds love across the colour bar while her white family rejects her.

Spud (dir. Donovan Marsh, 2010. 103 mins): growing-up comedy about white boy nicknamed Spud (potato) and his alcoholic teacher (John Cleese) at a posh private high school.

The Wilby Conspiracy (dir. Ralph Nelson, 1975. 102 mins): the Mandela figure (Sidney Poitier) is surprisingly released from Robben Island, so that he will lead the apartheid police over the border to capture the guerrilla leader 'Wilby' (Oliver Tambo?).

A World Apart (dir. Chris Menges, 1988. 112 mins): Shawn Slovo's drama of coming to terms as a teenager with her mother (Barbara Hershey as Ruth First) and father Joe Slovo as Communist Party activists in 1950–60s Johannesburg.

10 Years of Revolutionary Insurgence 1967–1990

By the mid-1970s the entire region was in the throes of armed struggle that had begun in the 1960s, as liberation movements confronted colonial governments. Majority-ruled states already independently accommodated refugees or permitted passage for those who went on for military training in Africa and beyond.

Political and sometimes logistic support was given to southern African liberation movements at the Organisation of African Unity (OAU) that met in Addis Ababa. But more credit should be given to presidents Julius Nyerere, Kenneth Kaunda, and Seretse Khama, who shared a common vision of a non-racial but majority-ruled region of peace and prosperity. They worked closely together from about 1970. Tanzania, Zambia, and Botswana became known as the Front-Line States because of their proximity to colonial Portuguese, Rhodesian, and South African territories.

ZAMBIA UNDER PRESIDENT KAUNDA

Between 1968 and 1970, President Kaunda's UNIP government acquired majority shares in strategic companies in the mining, agriculture, retail, and manufacturing sectors. It also gained a foothold in the banking, transportation, building, and other sectors. It established parastatal corporations for mining development, industrial development, financial development, and national transport. The process peaked with the 1970 majority state ownership of the two great copper mining companies.

'Zambianization' (indigenization) attempted to replace foreign personnel in the civil service and parastatals with Zambian citizens – but was held back by shortage of skilled or highly educated manpower. Hence heavy investment in a new University of Zambia. Zambian Humanism was President Kenneth Kaunda's personal philosophy of human worth and Christian duty that was much touted and little followed. Impatient with the opposition Zambia African National Congress (ZANC), with support limited to Southern Province, and inspired by the precedent of Tanzania, UNIP declared itself to be the only political party in a one-party state in 1972. The argument was that multi-party politics promoted 'tribalism' (ethnic conflict).

The copper-dependent Zambian economy grew an average 4 per cent per year in the first decade of independence. But the 1973 world oil crisis led to a sharp decline in copper prices, and Russian copper production flooded what was left of the world market. The escalation of liberation wars in neighbouring Rhodesia and Angola strained Zambia's economy by disrupting export routes to seaports in the Indian and Atlantic Oceans. The problem was compounded by Zambia's principled gesture of closing its border with 'rebel' Rhodesia, across which the railway with most exports and imports used to flow. While awaiting the completion of the Tazara railway from the Tanzania coast to the Copperbelt, being built by Chinese engineers and workers between 1970 and 1976, copper was exported and oil was imported by trucks along the long, tortuous dirt road between Zambia and Tanzania.

The Republic of Zambia also suffered from its hosting in the 1970s–80s of refugee liberation movements from neighbouring countries. It hosted the regional headquarters for liberation movements ZAPU and ZANU from Rhodesia, ANC from South Africa, and SWAPO from South West Africa, as well as forward bases for their guerrillas. As a result, Zambia suffered frequent border incursions, and even aerial bombing of urban areas, by the military forces of colonial Rhodesia. Zambia's pride as the beacon of southern African liberation extended to assisting guerrillas of FRELIMO and, at different times, MPLA and UNITA, crossing its Angola and Mozambique borders.

Zambia argued that armed conflict was regrettable but necessary to bring the colonial régimes to the negotiating table. An active member of the Non-Aligned Movement soon after independence, Zambia also attempted to balance its relations between east and west in the Cold War. President Kaunda became a conspicuous campaigner for regional détente along with fellow Front-Line presidents Julius Nyerere of Tanzania and Seretse Khama of Botswana. When reconciliation in Angola and Mozambique suddenly became a possibility after revolution in Portugal in 1974–75, Kaunda initiated secret personal negotiations for the future of Rhodesia with prime minister Balthazar John Vorster of South Africa. Kaunda agreed to put pressure on ZANU and ZAPU, while Vorster pressured the Rhodesian prime minister Ian Smith. All parties met on board a train halted on the railway bridge over the Victoria Falls to negotiate peace, but mutual intransigence resulted in failure – and war resumed.

Zambia, having been born in 1964 during a copper boom, suffered increasing economic problems with the dramatic fall in mineral revenues from 1975 onwards into the 1980s. Nationalization of the copper mines proved to be a poisoned chalice, as the state covered losses and liabilities while the old operating companies exported profits by 'transfer pricing' agreed with overseas buyers. Urban workers were subsidized by basic food prices that discouraged peasant production of foodstuffs. Zambia was obliged to resort to an IMF economic structural adjustment program (ESAP) that reduced state expenditure on bureaucracy and provision of social services. The capital, Lusaka, experienced serious rioting in 1986 over the rising price of maize-meal after state subsidies were removed. Zambia tried to avoid ESAP prescriptions for a few years but was induced to re-adopt them by the necessity of raising loans from international banks. Between 1975 and 1990 the size of the Zambian economy declined by about 30 per cent.

MALAWI UNDER PRESIDENT BANDA

In 1971, Dr Banda was declared president for life of the Republic of Malawi. He ruled the heavily populated country as his personal fiefdom, often ignoring his cabinet ministers. The internal economy was dependent on peasant subsistence crops and subsistence fishing, with white-owned plantations in the south-east growing tea, tobacco, coffee, and cotton. Banda's rule was bolstered by the cash remittances of mass labour migration abroad and by high levels of foreign aid – distributed as if from his personal largesse. Post-colonial aid from Britain was soon outpaced by aid from apartheid South Africa. Banda initially ensured continuation of aid by manipulating GDP figures downwards, while accumulating commercial interests and plantations within his personal company, the so-called Press Holdings.

South Africa helped to construct a new capital city in Lilongwe. Portugal rewarded Malawi with funding to build a new railway to the Mozambican port of Nacala. Labour migration to South Africa helps to explain the transition of Banda from rabid African nationalist into apartheid supporter. The number of Malawian workers in South African gold mines jumped from 22,000 in 1960 to 76,000 in 1970. They were flown in and out of Malawi by Wenela aircraft until a disastrous Wenela plane crash in 1974 at Francistown in Botswana, after which they were flown by Malawi Airways – and their number fell to under 14,000 by 1980.

Peasant farmers were urged to increase productivity and to adopt new cash crops such as flue-cured tobacco. Trade unions were restricted, and wage levels on plantations were kept low in order to attract foreign investment. The economy began to grow, with GDP growing annually at 5 per cent in 1969–73 and 6 per cent in 1973–79. But this was reduced in the early 1980s by severe droughts, disruption of exports by civil war in central Mozambique, and the general world debt crisis with declining terms of trade for the Third World.

BOTSWANA UNDER PRESIDENT SERETSE KHAMA

The Republic of Botswana began independence utterly dependent on British aid even to cover the costs of its government administration, but succeeded in building up a self-financing economy by 1971–72. For some years it was the fastest-growing economy in the world, with GDP rising from an annual 10 per cent in 1965–69 to 22 per cent in 1969–74, before settling down to 8 per cent in 1975–78 and 13 per cent in 1978–89. The initial growth was largely due to beef and copper-nickel exports, but state revenue took off after Botswana initiated the 1969 renegotiation of the customs union with South Africa, and the opening of the Orapa diamond mine. Diamond sales profits were shared 50:50 with De Beers. The second boost to the economy in 1978–89 was largely due to the opening of the richest diamond mine at Jwaneng. Botswana's diamond sales – even more than South Africa's gold sales – boomed during uncertain times in the world economy as a store and shelter of individuals' wealth overseas.

The Botswana government had both the will and the means to channel new wealth into infrastructure development, education, and health – assisted by an initially small but honest state bureaucracy, a parastatal sector limited in size, budgeting limits, and sound national five-year development planning. The international stature of President Seretse Khama increased with Botswana's rise as a beacon of peaceful non-racial society – despite its being a 'hostage stage' almost totally surrounded by white-ruled Rhodesia, South Africa, and South West Africa. Much store was given to opening a new road and ferry service into Zambia across the Chobe-Zambezi confluence at Kazungula. Botswana also retained its multi-party constitution, though one party, the BDP (Botswana Democratic Party), was dominant.

President Khama's friendship with President Kaunda of Zambia was vital when Kaunda's relationship cooled with President Julius Nyerere of Tanzania. The three men worked together with President Samora Machel of Mozambique in regional politics, as the presidents of the Front-Line States. Though by then a dying man, President Khama took the lead in setting up SADCC (Southern African Development Coordination Conference) in 1980. Seretse Khama was succeeded as president in 1980 by his deputy, former economic planning minister Quett Ketumile Masire.

Botswana arranged for its copper-nickel exports to go through newly independent Zimbabwe, rather than South Africa. But relations rapidly deteriorated after the ZANU government turned on its ZAPU rivals in Matebeleland (western Zimbabwe). ZAPU leader Joshua Nkomo escaped through Botswana in 1983, and the government in Harare considered the government in

Gaborone too dominated by Nkomo's ethnic Kalanga kinsmen. Many peasant refugees fled from Matabeleland into Botswana.

The presence of South African refugees in Gaborone, most of them loyal to the ANC and some of them members of ANC's guerrilla wing Umkhonto we Sizwe (MK), led to cross-border raids by South African police saboteurs and soldiers. The most serious raid was on 14 June 1985, when houses in Gaborone were bombed and both ANC operatives and innocent civilians were killed. The sheer brutality of the raid on a successful non-racial nation caused outrage overseas that rebounded on South Africa. Pro-Botswana activists in Washington DC pressurized multinational banks not to renew the massive loans that were keeping the South African government and its security-defence establishment financially afloat.

SWAZILAND & LESOTHO UNDER KINGS SOBHUZA II & MOSHOESHOE II

The Kingdom of Swaziland had been the richest of the three former High Commission Territories. It had a relatively diversified economy at independence in 1968, based on mining, cattle ranching, sugar production, and forestry – owned by South African or British capital and dependent on cheap local labour. Most Swazi, however, were engaged in subsistence peasant agriculture, or as migrant labourers on South African mines.

Swaziland was and is ruled by two parallel governments – the 'modern' Government of Swaziland with ministers responsible for everyday administration, and the 'traditional' government of the *Liqoqo* or Swazi National Council – the king and his councillors mainly from the Dlamini clan – representing the Swazi Nation. From 1968 onwards it was the 'traditional' government, not the 'modern' one, that amassed considerable wealth from mineral royalties – since the constitution vested all mineral wealth in King Sobhuza II as personification of the Swazi Nation. The royalties that went to royalty, in the Tibiyo TakaNgwane and Tisuka TakaNgwane funds, were used to buy back lands historically lost to whites and to purchase holdings in private companies.

Swaziland welcomed South African capital setting up 'infant industries', such as beer-brewing, that were protected and promoted by the 1969 customs union renegotiation. The Government of Swaziland remained excessively dependent on the customs union with South Africa – accounting for between 48 and 67 per cent of all its income in 1981–87. Income from taxation, at rates unchanged since the colonial period, did not keep pace with the national economic growth from manufacturing and extractive industries that expanded ahead of population growth.

The Swazi Nation had formed the Imbokodvo National Movement to win the first post-independence elections in 1972, but it lost three seats to the Ngwane National Liberatory Congress. Traditionalists tried to deport one of the NNLC winners, T.B. Ngwenya, on the grounds that he was born across the border, in South Africa. The case was eventually thrown out by the appeal court. Incensed that Swaziland was subject to the rule of alien law, in April 1973 King Sobhuza II declared the 1968 constitution invalid, dissolved parliament, and banned all political parties and trade unions. In future, he would rule by decree. The king introduced a new semi-parliamentary system in 1978 – based on local *tinkhundla* meeting places where voting was conducted by public acclaim in the open. People chosen at the *tinkhundla* went to an electoral college, which then elected 40 members of parliament. The king nominated 10 additional members, and the 50 parliamentarians then chose 10 members of the senate by a secret ballot, to which the king added a further 10 senators. Together, the two houses of parliament had limited legislative powers.

King Sobhuza II died in August 1982, at the age of 83, having been monarch since boyhood. The political insecurity of an interregnum followed, with factions in the *Liqoqo* jockeying for power. Queen Regent Dzeliwe, appointed head of state in 1982, was together with her prime minister Prince Mabandla replaced in 1984 by Queen Regent Ntombi – mother of the young Prince Makhosetive, still a schoolboy in England, who had been chosen to be king from among the scores of Sobhuza's living sons. Makhosetive was duly installed as King (Ingwenyama) Mswati III on 25 April 1986. Mswati abolished the *Liqoqo* that had been exercising supreme power and instead relied on the parliament chosen through the *tinkhudla*. In 1988–89, an underground party called PUDEMO (People's United Democratic Movement) began to call for democratic reforms and curbs on royal autocracy.

ANC members had been generally welcome in Swaziland. (Sobhuza remembered that his grandmother had been a founder of the ANC.) But in 1982, Swaziland was obliged to sign a mutual security pact with South Africa that made ANC members leave for Mozambique. MK operatives, however, easily crossed the borders with South Africa and Mozambique, and South African police squads crossed over for explosive attacks on guerrilla hideouts inside Swaziland.

The Kingdom of Lesotho, populous but impoverished, with an unsustainable economy, and totally surrounded by South Africa, remained very heavily dependent on labour migration to South Africa and on British budgetary aid.

Independence brought no obvious gains, and the right-wing Basutoland National Party government, under prime minister Leabua Jonathan, saw rising popular support for the left-wing Basutoland Congress Party, led by Ntsu Mokhehle. When, in January 1970, the BNP was losing to the BCP in general elections, Jonathan stopped the count and announced: 'I have seized power. And I'm not ashamed of it. I have the support of my people.' King Moshoeshoe II, who stood up for the rule of law under the constitution, was temporarily deposed.

The constitutional coup of 1970 halted British aid essential to keep the government solvent. It drove the BNP government into the hands of the South African government. There was also the unexpected boost to government coffers of rising income from the 1969 customs renegotiation. But this was to change after the 1976 Soweto uprising in South Africa, which led to an influx of youthful refugees, who aroused the conscience of the world. World Food Programme, U.S., Swedish, German, and other European aid began to pour into Lesotho. Leabua Jonathan realized that there was more profit in posing as a critic than as a friend of South Africa. How far this 'anti-politics machine' actually raised productivity and eliminated poverty in Lesotho can be debated. It certainly infuriated the South African government.

In 1982, South Africa launched a military commando attack in and around Maseru, the capital, a few minutes from the South African border. Forty-two people, both ANC-MK operatives and local sympathisers, were killed. A second military incursion, in December 1985, led to the deposition of Leabua Jonathan in 1986 and his replacement by a local military régime headed by Justin Metsing Lekhanya.

REVOLUTIONS IN PORTUGUESE ANGOLA & MOZAMBIQUE

In Angola, armed conflict with Portuguese forces raged continuously from 1961 until independence in 1975. By that time, armed conflict had arisen between rival liberation movements. FNLA received support from Kongo people in the far north. It was headquartered in Zaïre (former Belgian Congo), where it received assistance from the government of Mobutu sese Seko and some U.S. help through the CIA. MPLA was equipped by the Soviet Union (Russia) and its allies. UNITA was helped on occasion by China and Zambia but had little external aid – until South Africa picked it as an ally in the later 1970s.

The fascist regime in Portugal (1926–74) had no intention of ever relinquishing Angola. It tried to separate peasants from guerrilla forces by relocating them into *aldeamentos* ('protected villages'). MPLA intensified its armed struggle from 1966 onwards. Hence, the OAU recognized MPLA instead of FNLA as the 'sole and authentic' representative of the Angolan people.

In Mozambique, FRELIMO underwent great changes after its first president, Eduardo Mondlane, was assassinated by a parcel bomb at Dar es Salaam in 1969. Samora Machel took over as leader in 1970 and extended guerrilla activity from the north to the centre of the country. He opened up the Tete front on the Zambezi, where the Portuguese army was protecting the multi-million dollar Cahora Bassa dam under construction on the Zambezi. The dam was designed to supply electricity to the Witwatersrand. It was the king-piece of an enormous settlement scheme for small farmers brought out of poverty in Portugal. As in Angola, the Portuguese responded by setting up *aldeamentos*. In 1973, 400 villagers south of Tete were killed, in reprisal for their support for FRELIMO, in what became known as the Wiriyamu Massacre.

The economic and social strain of colonial wars in Angola, Mozambique, and Portuguese Guinea proved too much for Portugal. Rebellious soldiers in Lisbon formed the Armed Forces Movement, which overturned the Portuguese government in a coup on 24 April 1974 – and immediately began to negotiate the end of Portuguese rule in Africa. On 7 September 1974, agreement was reached to transfer power to FRELIMO. Mozambique became independent on 25 June 1975, under Samora Machel as president.

ARMED STRUGGLE IN RHODESIA-ZIMBABWE

After the unilateral declaration of independence (UDI by the Rhodesia Front government of prime minister Ian Smith declared in 1965, the British government declined to intervene militarily against the rebels. There was a strong political lobby in Britain, possibly even plotting a military coup to overturn the British government, which declared the rebel whites of Rhodesia to be 'our kith and kin'. The Labour government in Britain failed to negotiate any peaceful resolution of the rebellion in negotiations with Ian Smith on board naval ships in neutral waters – HMS Tiger in December 1966 and HMS Fearless in October 1968. United Nations sanctions blocking international trade with Rhodesia were imposed to push the Smith regime towards negotiations. Sanctions proved ineffective so long as Rhodesia was supported and supplied by South Africa to the south and Portuguese Mozambique to the east.

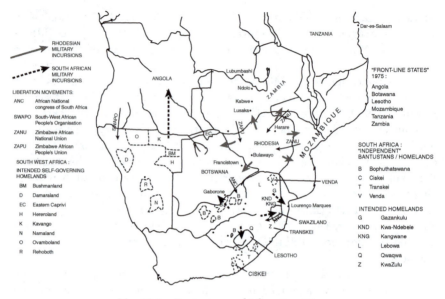

Map 10.1   Bantusans and Liberation Wars

ZAPU and ZANU infiltrators crossing the Zambezi from Zambia had little success with armed struggle in Rhodesia during the 1960s. They had, as yet, limited support from the rural population. Between June 1967 and July 1968, guerrillas of the ZIPRA military wing of ZAPU and the MK military wing of South Africa's ANC crossed the Zambezi near the Victoria Falls in what became known as the Wankie (Hwange) campaign. The campaign was symbolic rather than successful. It resulted in South African armed police reinforcements arriving to assist the Rhodesian army to capture or repel the invaders. Criticism of the continuing inertia of ZAPU and ZANU leaders, living luxuriously in Zambia, led to an unsuccessful 1971 attempt to unite the parties by James Chikerema in FROLIZI (Front for the Liberation of Zimbabwe).

The 1970 declaration of Rhodesia as a republic by Ian Smith put an end to any hope of its restoration as a British possession. Despite this, a new Conservative government in Britain renewed negotiations in late 1971. The agreed package to reduce racial discrimination and increase African representation in politics was put before the people of Rhodesia by a commission under a British judge, Lord Pearce. Because ZAPU and ZANU were banned inside Rhodesia, a body called the African National *Council* was founded under the leadership of a Methodist bishop, Abel Muzorewa. It delivered a thundering 'No' on behalf of the African majority to the Pearce proposals.

ZAPU and ZANU had different strategies to intensify the war. The ZAPU/ZIPRA strategy was to limit guerrilla incursions into Matebeleland and to build up conventional forces, with Soviet equipment, ready for invasion across the Zambezi. The ZANU/ZANLA strategy was to infiltrate guerrillas through Mozambique, preceded by propaganda teams to prepare rural Africans to work closely with incoming guerrillas. Local people became the eyes and ears of the guerrillas and provided them with food and shelter – often at great cost, as government forces punished them for supporting the insurgents. Many youths, including schoolchildren, also crossed the borders of Rhodesia via Mozambique and Botswana to seek recruitment by ZANLA or ZIPRA. Rhodesian radio programmes and newspapers attempted 'to win the hearts and minds' of the African majority. The Rhodesian government resorted to 'protected villages' like the Portuguese *aldeamentos*, to starve guerrillas of food and information. Peasants were locked behind barbed-wire at night. Rhodesian propaganda to discourage peasant support of guerrillas included displaying the dead bodies of liberation fighters.

ZANU/ZANLA and ZAPU/ZIPRA created a joint military command (JMC) in 1972 under the joint leadership of Herbert Chitepo for ZANU and Jason Ziyapapa Moyo for ZAPU. Its first notable success, the attack on Altena farm in Centenary district by ZANLA guerrillas led by Solomon Mujuru, on 21 December 1972, is generally regarded as the beginning of the 'Second *Chimurenga*' or freedom war. However, JMC coordination collapsed in 1974, and there were dangerous splits in the leadership within ZANU/ZANLA as the scale of recruitment and military activity expanded. In 1974, young ZANLA recruits both male and female, led by Thomas Nhari, rebelled against negligence, incompetence, and sexual harassment by high-living ZANU leaders. After failing to kidnap ZANU leaders in Lusaka, the Nhari rebels were routed at Chifombo Camp by ZANLA commander Josiah Tongogara, and their leaders were executed.

The temporary ceasefire in the Zimbabwe-Rhodesia war of 1974–75 achieved by Kaunda and Vorster led to the release of ZANU leaders imprisoned in Rhodesia in November 1974. It only now became clear that Robert Gabriel Mugabe had deposed fellow-prisoner Rev. Ndabaningi Sithole as ZANU internal party leader. As Mugabe prepared to move to newly liberated Mozambique as the main ZANU/ZANLA base in March 1975, ZANU leader-in-exile Herbert Chitepo was assassinated at Lusaka by a bomb planted in his car. A Zambian commission of enquiry blamed the assassination on jealousies and rivalries between ZANU factions. Rhodesian intelligence, of course, also claimed credit. In any case, suspicions lingered on for decades in the ranks of ZANU.

In January 1976, Presidents Machel and Nyerere made yet another attempt to merge ZANU/ZANLA and ZAPU/ZIPRA forces into one army – the Zimbabwe Independence People's Army (ZIPA). Within a few months, ZANLA and ZIPRA soldiers, in training at Morogoro in Tanzania, quarrelled with each other over petty matters such as food. Fifty soldiers died, and many withdrew to Zambia. ZIPA soldiers formed a so-called *Vashandi* (workers) group that espoused radical 'leveller' ideas of equality with officers and between ranks. By 1977 Mugabe had sufficient power, with the help of the Mozambican army, to crush the *Vashandi* movement – 600 men and women were detained.

U.S. Secretary of State Henry Kissinger was the next to revive peace talks. ZAPU and ZANU combined as the Patriotic Front (PF), jointly led by Robert Mugabe and Joshua Nkomo, for purposes of negotiation at Geneva in Switzerland. The Geneva talks between the PF and Ian Smith broke down after a fruitless seven weeks in December 1976. Smith took the next initiative two years later, by negotiating his own 'internal settlement' in 1978 with Bishop Muzorewa and Rev. Sithole, plus two government-appointed chiefs, Chirawu and Ndiweni. Rhodesia was re-christened the Republic of Zimbabwe-Rhodesia and went to the polls on a bi-racial franchise in April 1979. Bishop Muzorewa became nominal prime minister, while whites retained control of the judiciary, civil service, police and armed forces, and the economy at large. The 'internal settlement' satisfied neither the liberation movements nor the international community. Civil war continued. The Rhodesian air force bombed ZANU camps in Mozambique, at Chimoio (1976) and Nyadzonya (1977), and ZAPU camps at Mkushi and near Lusaka in Zambia (1978).

By 1979 all sides had reached the point of exhaustion. South Africa was no longer prepared to finance wars in both South West Africa and Rhodesia. The Front-Line presidents, whose countries were suffering from Rhodesian military incursions, exerted pressure on the Zimbabwe liberation movements to come to terms with Zimbabwe-Rhodesia. There was also a forthcoming Commonwealth heads of state meeting to be held in Lusaka, bringing the prime ministers and presidents of every Commonwealth nation together with Queen Elizabeth II.

The Commonwealth leaders put pressure on British prime minister Margaret Thatcher's Conservative government in Britain to issue invitations to a conference that the protagonists had no choice but to attend. Chaired by Lord Carrington, the conference was held at Lancaster House in London in 1979. Smith and Muzorewa represented Zimbabwe-Rhodesia. Mugabe and Nkomo represented the Patriotic Front. After much debate, the Conference adopted the Zimbabwe independence constitution and agreed on the terms for a ceasefire – to be monitored by a commission of both the Rhodesian security forces and the liberation movements. Zimbabwe-Rhodesia would temporarily assume the status of a full British colony. A general election was to be supervised by international observers.

The agreement was signed on 21 December 1979. Five days later, the long-time military commander of ZANLA, Josiah Tongogara, died in a car accident – never fully explained. Zimbabwe-Rhodesia went to the polls in February 1980. ZANU-PF won a majority of seats in the new parliament. Robert Mugabe was prime minister in a new government of national unity, headed by President Canaan Banana. Joshua Nkomo chose to become minister of home (internal) affairs.

POST-COLONIAL ANGOLA

MPLA, FNLA, and UNITA all signed the Alvor Accords with Portugal on 15 January 1975. Until elections could be held, the transitional government combined Agostinho Neto of MPLA, Holden Roberto of FNLA, and Jonas Savimbi of UNITA. But before elections could be held, the three liberation movements fought among themselves for control of Luanda, the capital city. Antagonism between the three movements was complicated by the Cold War between East and West. MPLA couched its opposition to the other two as a struggle against capitalist neo-colonialism, while the other two parties claimed they were fighting communism.

Supported by Mobutu's soldiers from Zaïre, FNLA forces attacked MPLA-controlled Luanda. MPLA received military support from Cuba. Cuban soldiers helped to defeat the FNLA attack and also to expel members of UNITA with their South African mercenary allies. Having secured control of Luanda, and subsequently major urban centres along railway lines, MPLA declared Angola's independence on 11 November 1975 – without any general elections having been held. FNLA and UNITA responded by proclaiming their own independent government at Huambo in eastern Angola. The OAU recognized the MPLA as the legitimate government of Angola. Nevertheless, civil war was to rage for 27 years, costing 1.5 million lives and displacing many more.

Cuba sent 30,000 people to Angola in 1975–76 to support the MPLA in both military and civil roles – particularly in public health. By 1982, there were 35,000 Cubans in Angola, of whom 27,000 were combat troops. By 1988, the number had risen to 50,000. Meanwhile, South Africa became increasingly involved on the side of UNITA behind the façade of an anti-communist crusade. South African military forces intervened on behalf of UNITA because

PLAN (People's Liberation Army of Namibia), the military wing of SWAPO, was hosted by MPLA and – together with ANC military camps in Angola – was supplied with food and equipment by East Germany. After Rhodesia fell to ZANU and ZAPU in 1980, the South African Defence Force was strengthened by former Rhodesian soldiers with counter-guerrilla experience. FNLA gradually faded from the scene, discredited by its association with the Mobutu kleptocracy in Zaïre/'Democratic Republic of the Congo'. The Angola civil war became a straight conflict: MPLA and Cuban forces advancing from the north, against UNITA and South African forces advancing from the south. The climax of the war was the battle of Cuito Carnavale in September 1987 – to which we will return below.

NAMIBIA'S LIBERATION WAR

South West Africa was rocked by a wave of workers' strikes, demanding better working conditions, in 1971 and 1972 at Windhoek and the port city of Walvis Bay. The strikes almost brought the colony's economy to a standstill. SWAPO and other liberation movements in exile also waged an incessant international diplomatic campaign for the independence of Namibia.

In January 1976, the United Nations general assembly condemned South Africa's continued illegal occupation of South West Africa and the application there of apartheid laws. But UN security council permanent members supplying arms to South Africa – France, the United Kingdom, and the United States – frustrated any sanctions being applied against South Africa. Meanwhile, the OAU recognized SWAPO over other Namibian liberation movements as the 'sole and authentic' representative of the Namibian people.

With the independence of Angola in 1975, SWAPO's military branch PLAN was able to launch attacks across the Angolan border. Under increasing international and guerrilla pressure, South Africa was driven towards an 'internal settlement' in South West Africa/Namibia. A new constitution adopted at the Turnhalle in Windhoek in 1977 gave the colony three tiers of government – national, regional-ethnic, and local. This system of divide-and-rule balanced Nama-Khoe, Herero, whites, and others in the south of the country against the perceived threat of SWAPO-supporting Ovambo masses in the north. SWAPO denounced Turnhalle as a sham designed to perpetuate South African rule.

The UN's resolution 435 in 1978 demanded South Africa's withdrawal from Namibia and the holding of free elections. Supported by President Ronald Reagan's administration in the United States, South Africa refused to comply if Cuban forces were not withdrawn from Angola. South Africa continued to fight PLAN on either side of the Angola-South West Africa border for a decade more. The war eventually reached its climax in September 1988 when a joint offensive by the South African army and air force, with UNITA allies, penetrated deep into Angolan territory – pushing back Cuban, MPLA, and SWAPO forces to Cuito Cuanavale. But the South African advance fell apart, and it could not counter Cuban counter-attacks. South African jets and other equipment were running out of munitions and spare parts – because of the credit boycott of South Africa by international banks – and the tactical advantage was lost.

South Africa had to strategically retreat from the Battle of Cuito Cuanavale. South Africa agreed to implement UN resolution 435. Following a UN-supervised general election, Namibia became independent in 1990, under a SWAPO government headed by President Sam Nujoma.

DESTABILIZATION IN MOZAMBIQUE

Centuries of Portuguese rule left independent Mozambique in 1975 with mass illiteracy, poverty, and racial and ethnic divisions – and some impressive architecture in the capital. FRELIMO was determined to find socialist solutions to the country's main challenges, but the first problem was to promote a unified national identity. Convinced that ethnicity had to be eradicated, President Machel insisted on the use of Portuguese as the language of national unity – declaring that FRELIMO did not recognise tribes, regions, races, or religious beliefs, only Mozambicans. This did not reassure 150,000 whites who left Mozambique for South Africa or Portugal within a year of independence.

The capital, Lourenço Marques, was renamed Maputo. Full of naïve socialist enthusiasm, FRELIMO created 'dynamising groups' of 12 members, who crisscrossed the countryside to 'raise the political consciousness of the masses' by collective economic, social, and cultural activities. Private schools were abolished and free education was provided by the state to all citizens. Between 1974 and 1981, the number of children attending primary school increased from 700,000 to 1,376,000 and those in secondary schools from 20,000 to 135,000. The national rate of literacy climbed from 5 per cent to 25 per cent during the first five years of independence.

FRELIMO nationalized private hospitals, and it initiated nationwide public health and preventive medicine campaigns. Health brigades dispersed across the country to educate the masses. Because there were only 73 doctors in the country, the government imported over 500 from neighbouring countries as well as from Cuba. They embarked on a national vaccination campaign against measles, tetanus, and smallpox. Over the first five years of independence, infant mortality rates dropped by 20 per cent. The government also nationalized all houses not used by owners as family homes, and it gave these to those without houses. By 1978, more than 160,000 Mozambicans living in the shacks of shanty towns had been rehoused into proper city dwellings.

While these sweeping measures improved the quality of life, they also created new problems. Rapid increase in education strained national resources, resulting in shortages of books, supplies, and teachers. Newly built rural clinics often lacked trained staff and adequate medical supplies. The nationalization of housing resulted in corruption and nepotism on the part of bureaucrats charged with allocating housing. Talking about socialism became an excuse for not working towards it.

Mozambique depended heavily for food supplies on imports from South Africa. The exodus of whites deprived the country of much-needed skills of engineers, technicians, doctors, accountants, and other professionals. Some whites had sabotaged equipment and machinery before they fled. The Mozambican economy also took heavy strain when FRELIMO enforced international economic sanctions against Rhodesia – its third trading partner after Portugal and South Africa.

FRELIMO took over 2,000 farms abandoned by white owners. It turned them into state farms that employed more than 2 million workers by 1982. State farms, however, generally suffered from poor management and lack of technical skills and equipment. FRELIMO also took control of the production, processing, and marketing of all key cash-crops – cashew nuts, sugar, copra, and rice. Elsewhere, the government brought scattered small villages into central communal villages – to facilitate the provision of roads, wells, schools, and clinics. By 1982, over 2 million peasants (20 per cent of the total population) were living in communal villages, encouraged to work in and for agricultural cooperatives. FRELIMO nationalized strategic industries – coal mining, petroleum refining, the principal banks, and all insurance companies. By 1981, the state controlled over 75 per cent of industrial production but was hampered by endemic shortages of skills, investment, and managerial expertise. Western capitalists were reluctant to invest in Mozambique, which turned instead for key investments and personnel to the Soviet Bloc. FRELIMO declared itself a Marxist-Leninist party in 1977, signing cooperation agreements with the Soviet Union and its allies – and scaring the living daylights out of the ruling regimes in South Africa and Rhodesia with the spectre of communism on their doorstep.

Independent Mozambique made no secret of its hostility to white-ruled Rhodesia and South Africa. It welcomed to Maputo the representatives of ZANU and ANC, whose guerrillas now had long borders for infiltration. Mozambique closed its borders to trade with Rhodesia, and thus blocked Rhodesia's nearest access to the ocean at Beira – though there was no question of blocking the city of Maputo as a major outlet for oceanic trade with the Witwatersrand! Rhodesia responded with cross-border raids against ZANU/ZANLA camps in Mozambique, and its Central Intelligence Organisation (CIO) set up RENAMO (Resistência Nacional Moçambicana) among Mozambican exiles living in Rhodesia – led by André Matsangaissa, who had previously been expelled from FRELIMO. RENAMO sabotaged FRELIMO installations and successfully spread anti-FRELIMO dissidence and hostility to ZANU/ZANLA among the peasants of central Mozambique.

When Zimbabwe became independent in 1980, South Africa stepped in and took on sponsorship of RENAMO – now led by Alfonso Dhlakama. RENAMO spread its activities secretly southwards among peasants and urban workers. South Africa provided the financial and logistical support for RENAMO as a key element in its regional 'destabilization' campaign – aimed at discouraging Mozambique from support of ANC/MK. As well as cross-border incursions through the Kruger National Park, South Africa launched air raids on ANC facilities at Matola and nearby Maputo in 1981 and 1983. When RENAMO blocked independent Zimbabwe's access to Beira by road and rail, Zimbabwe and Tanzania sent troops to clear the way.

The strain of endless conflict on everyday life was made worse by severe drought in 1982, resulting in mass starvation in some places. Mozambique was obliged to respond to the blandishments of South Africa for a peace treaty. The Nkomati Agreement between President Machel and South African prime minister P.W. Botha was signed on 16 March 1984. Both countries agreed no longer to harbour forces hostile to each other or to allow their territories to be used to launch attacks. Mozambique was to expel the ANC, while South Africa would disband RENAMO. All ANC military bases were removed from Mozambique, but Botha continued to support RENAMO clandestinely. When Samora Machel died in an air crash in October 1986, ironically close to the Nkomati peace talks venue, Joaquim Chissano succeeded him as president. (It is believed that Machel's Soviet-piloted aircraft was the victim of fake air-traffic control instructions from a covert South African radio transmitter.)

INDEPENDENT ZIMBABWE'S DECADE OF PROSPERITY

Zimbabwe enjoyed economic prosperity for most of its first decade of independence, with real GDP growth averaging 5.3 per cent from 1985 to 1991. After 15 years of international economic sanctions, the country was open to foreign direct investment. Government's redistributive measures also stimulated the economy. Former refugee peasants returned to productive agriculture, with government inputs and extension services, and together with years of good rainfall achieved an agricultural miracle. Free primary and secondary school enrollments increased by 80 per cent, benefitting previously neglected girls in particular. By 1990, Zimbabwe had educated more Africans in one decade than had been educated in the 90 years of colonialism. There was also huge expansion in health services, clinics and hospitals, health awareness, child immunization, infant feeding, and family planning.

The 1980 Minimum Wages Act, the 1981 Employment (Conditions of Service) Regulations, and the 1985 Labour Relations Act strengthened workers' bargaining power and improved working conditions. Women were no longer treated as perpetual minors in law, with no right to enter into legal contracts without the permission of a male 'guardian'. The Legal Age of Majority Act in 1982 defined 18 years as the age at which people, regardless of gender, attained full legal rights as adults. The 1983 Maintenance Act and the 1987 Deceased Persons Family Maintenance Act respectively made provision for financial support of children by absentee fathers and gave women inheritance rights over property.

The dominant ZANU party in the PF government of national unity became increasingly intolerant of political dissent. It turned against its ZAPU partner and harassed other 'progressive' organizations including church bodies. Some former ZIPRA guerrillas, precluded from employment in the new national army, turned bandit and began to raid government institutions. They were incited by ex-Rhodesian agents working for South Africa, which was anxious to stop Zimbabwe hosting ANC-MK guerrillas. The Zimbabwe government's response was to deploy into Matebeleland the new Fifth Brigade of the army, trained by North Korean instructors. The Fifth Brigade unleashed a reign of terror and torture in 1982 that left over 20,000 people dead and masses traumatized. This tragedy, known as *Gukurahundi*, was hidden from the world by government media, until it was revealed by the 1999 report, titled *Breaking the Silence*, by the Catholic Commission for Justice and Peace.

ZAPU leader Joshua Nkomo was hounded out from the government of national unity and escaped abroad via Botswana – crossing the border, it was said, dressed as a woman. He returned home in 1983 under a guarantee of personal safety. But the Zimbabwe army was only withdrawn from its military occupation of Matebeleland after ZANU and ZAPU signed a new Patriotic Front (PF) unity agreement, with ZAPU-PF as junior partner to ZANU-PF.

South Africa continued to try to 'destabilize' Zimbabwe by giving logistical support to so-called Super-ZAPU guerrillas, arousing Ndebele and Kalanga peasant resentment in rural Matebeleland against corrupt rule by ZANU-PF in Harare. Corruption became a public issue in the so-called Willowgate scandal of the late 1980s. High-ranking government officials had been buying cars at privileged low prices from the government-owned Willowvale car assembly plant in Harare, to sell them on at inflated prices on the open market. This Willowgate scandal caused great outrage when it was revealed by a commission of enquiry. It led to the public breakaway from ZANU-PF of Mugabe's old guerrilla comrade Edgar Tekere in 1989. He founded a new Zimbabwe Unity Movement (ZUM) that failed to attract many followers because of intimidation by government security services.

FRONT-LINE STATES, SADCC & REGIONAL 'DESTABILIZATION'

The three Front-Line presidents (Nyerere, Kaunda, and Khama) were joined by President Samora Machel of Mozambique in 1975. (Relations with President Agostinho Neto were less close, as Luanda was made even more geographically remote by the Angolan civil war.)

With the independence of Zimbabwe in sight, the foreign and finance ministers of the five Front-Line States met at Gaborone and Arusha in May and July 1979, to make plans for regional cooperation using Zimbabwe as the vital rail and road hub for the Mozambique ports – to promote disengagement from South Africa's regional hegemony. The result was the Southern African Development Coordination Conference (SADCC), convened for the first time at Lusaka in April 1980. Lesotho, Swaziland, and Malawi, as well as independent Zimbabwe, were welcomed into SADCC. Key communication links and areas of the economy were identified for coordination: Zimbabwe with a strong agricultural economy was responsible for the food security portfolio; Botswana for livestock disease control and semi-arid crop research; Malawi for fisheries, forestry, and wildlife; Mozambique for transport and communications; Zambia for mining; Tanzania for industrial development; and Angola for energy conservation and security.

SADCC planned the 'Beira corridor' development to take more trade in and out of Zambia and Botswana through Zimbabwe. But Botswana could not fully disengage itself from South Africa, as it remained a member of a common customs union with South Africa. And Zambia had other fish to fry. In 1981–82 Zambia was persuaded by the UN Economic Commission for Africa (Addis Ababa) to host an alternative regional organization, the Preferential Trade Area (PTA) for Eastern and Southern Africa (PTA). Botswana, Tanzania, and Mozambique refused to join the PTA. Meanwhile, Angola, Malawi, Mozambique, and Zimbabwe were all distracted by internal security concerns.

South Africa's 'destabilization' of countries in the region, to get them to expel the liberation movements, was not confined to cross-border raids by the army and air force. (Its small navy was later discredited by the discovery in 1993 that its commander, Dieter Gerhardt, was in fact an East German agent!) In 1986 the South African government set up a secret police squad, given the innocent name of Civil Cooperation Bureau (CCB). Among its operatives, the best-known was Craig Williamson, who had previously penetrated anti-apartheid movements in Sweden and Switzerland until uncovered in 1980. Some ANC leaders and their families were targeted and killed by parcel-bombs through the mail. Covert attacks greatly increased in 1986–88. ANC offices were targeted in London, Stockholm, Brussels, Harare, Gaborone, Lusaka, and Paris. The CCB may have had a hand in the assassination of the Swedish prime minister Olaf Palme in 1986, after he had made anti-apartheid speeches. But the main activity of the CCB was sending death squads to attack and kill activists inside South Africa and across its immediate borders in Swaziland, Lesotho, and Botswana.

One of the last projects of the 'destabilization' campaign was the financing of an American movie, *Red Scorpion* (1988), designed to discredit MPLA in Angola and its SWAPO ally as Soviet dupes.

BLACK CONSCIOUSNESS & MOVES TOWARDS LIBERATION IN SOUTH AFRICA

After a period of economic prosperity in the 1960s, damping down ANC and PAC activity, African discontent in South Africa was reawakened in the early 1970s by worker strikes protesting low wages and high cost of living. A wave of strikes in the port city of Durban in 1973 involved nearly 1 million workers, and 100,000 were arrested.

The South African government recognized that the economy had become more complex with the rise of electronics and engineering industries, and that Africans needed industrial recognition as skilled workers – in order to avoid wildcat strikes. The government began to relax (not yet to abolish) 'colour bar' job reservation. The Bantu Labour Relations Regulation Act of 1973 extended limited union recognition to Africans after 60 years of restriction. The Metal & Allied Workers Union and the National Union of Textile Workers could now bargain legally for better wages and working conditions. While in 1971, the average white wage had been nearly 20 times the average African wage, by 1979 the gap had been narrowed to 7 times higher.

The education gap was also beginning to narrow. There were new universities besides Fort Hare (now limited to Xhosa students) that were designed to cater for different ethnic groups. The University of the North (Turfloop) was reserved for Sotho-Tswana students, the University of the Western Cape (UWC) for Coloured students, the University of Zululand for Zulu students, and the University of Durban-Westville (UDW) for Indian students. These universities, however, proved to be incubators for a pan-ethnic sense of identity for all people of colour seeing themselves as 'black'. Black Consciousness, with a philosophy of race pride and self-reliance, was inspired by trends in the United States and by Négritude in African literature and culture.

Black student leaders, notably Abram Tiro at the University of the North and Steve Biko at medical school in Natal, broke away from the predominantly white English-speaking National Union of South African Students (NUSAS) – in which the African voice was not absent but muted. They founded the South African Students Organisation (SASO) in 1969. Other groups which together constituted a Black Consciousness Movement (BCM) were the Black People's Convention (BPC), the South African Students Movement (SASM), and the National Youth Organisation (NAYO). SASM was founded in 1970 when black consciousness spread to high schools in Soweto, the segregated commuter-townships outside Johannesburg. New urban schools were part of government's new policy of 'stabilization' of the urban labour force, to get children off the streets while their parents were at work. But the apartheid government (notably minister Andries Treurnicht, ironically echoing Milner's Anglicization policy) attempted to restrict key subjects, notably mathematics as the basis for science and 'social studies' (controlled dollops of civics, geography, and history), to be taught only in Afrikaans – no longer in English. Afrikaans was regarded by Africans as 'the language of the oppressors'.

On 17 May 1976, students at Phefeni secondary school in Orlando West (Soweto) refused to attend classes until Afrikaans was dropped as medium of instruction. On 8 June 1976, students at Naledi high school burnt a police car on the school grounds. Other schools took up the call to boycott classes, culminating on 16 June 1976, when thousands of students marched through Soweto, chanting, singing, and calling for an end to Afrikaans in schools. The police shot into the crowds, wounding many, and caused the peaceful demonstration to turn into a violent riot. Probably many more than the official figure of 23 school children died that day. An iconic photograph of dying schoolboy Hector Peterson was splashed across newspapers around the world.

Rioting and general unrest spread from Soweto to schools throughout the country over the following eight months. Hundreds died and thousands were wounded – with widespread destruction of state property, municipal-owned beer halls, and administrative buildings. The Soweto Students Representative Council (SSRC) successfully organized work and consumer boycotts in October 1976 and spearheaded condemnation of so-called independence given to the Transkei Bantustan under Chief Kaizer Matanzima in that month. The SSRC demanded the release of leaders in prison and the scrapping of the separate and inferior state system of Bantu Education that had oppressed Africans since the 1950s. The Black Consciousness Movement as a whole had been banned as an organization in 1973, and its leaders remained the targets of state security. Abram Tiro was killed by a parcel-bomb at a Catholic mission in Botswana in 1974. Steve Biko died on the floor of a travelling police truck after interrogation in September 1977, the 46th person to die in police custody around that time.

Soweto and the death of Biko turned world opinion against South Africa to an extent not seen since Sharpeville. Many thousands of students fled through Swaziland and Botswana to Mozambique, Zambia, and Tanzania, where they hoped to receive guerrilla training or free education from the PAC and ANC in exile. The Africanism of the PAC was more appealing to them, but only the ANC and its military wing MK had effective organization, facilities, and good leadership under Oliver Tambo. This highly principled man – president of the ANC from 1967 to 1991 – directed the ANC's anti-apartheid struggle from exile when the other leaders were in prison. Over the course of the late 1970s and early 1980s former Black Consciousness youths, at home and abroad, were converted into supporters of the ANC. Bolstered by new recruits, ANC/MK increased sabotage in South Africa – targeting police stations, government offices, etc. In June 1980, the apartheid establishment was shaken by MK's blowing up of SASOL, the oil-from-coal refinery near Pretoria.

Anti-apartheid groups were further galvanized by the 1980 independence of Zimbabwe. The Congress of South African Students (COSAS), inspired by the ANC and formed in June 1979, led class boycotts and boycotts of white shops in the 1980s. The Azania Students Movement (AZASM) and the Azanian People's Organisation (AZAPO) were similarly inspired by the PAC and BCM, respectively. COSAS and other organizations were declared illegal in 1985. Calling themselves 'comrades', youths attacked anyone in the townships suspected of being a government collaborator, 'sell-out', stooge, or stoolpigeon. The most gruesome punishment was 'necklacing' – pulling a car-tyre over the victim's head and shoulders, pouring petrol, and setting it all alight. The dark plume of smoke could be seen for miles around.

By the end of the 1970s, prime minister (President after 1984) P.W. Botha had realized that apartheid must 'adapt or die'. The requirement for Afrikaans in schools was dropped. The word 'Bantu' disappeared from the names of government departments. 'Petty-apartheid' was relaxed in Sports, hotels, restaurants, and theatres to accommodate international pressures and the rising aspirations of the urban black middle class. The Wiehan and Riekert commissions of 1979 recommended that black workers should now be fully recognized as 'employees' in terms of the Industrial Conciliation Act. The 'colour bar' of job reservation in industry and training was finally eliminated in 1984. The game-plan of the apartheid regime in 1983–84 was a new, tri-partite national constitution, to replace the 1961 republican constitution – three houses of parliament under an executive president: one for the whites, one for the Coloureds, and one for the Indians.

The exclusion of black people from the new constitution produced its own response. Backed by the ANC in exile, anti-apartheid groups came together in August 1983 to form the United Democratic Front (UDF). Rev. Allan Boesak launched the UDF in Cape Town with representatives of trade unions, churches, student organizations, and even sports bodies. ANC veterans, both in and out of jail, were defiantly voted honorary positions, while Soweto-stalwart Popo Molefe became general-secretary. The UDF demanded the release from prison of political leaders, the unbanning of liberation movements, the return home of South African exiles, and negotiations for a non-racial and non-sexist democratic society. Its first task was the successful boycott of the Coloured and Indian elections for the tri-cameral parliament. (The rival National Forum founded in 1983, in the PAC/BCM tradition, attracted a much smaller following than the UDF.)

There was widespread rioting over the introduction of the new tri-cameral parliament. Black and Coloured townships around the cities became 'ungovernable' during 1984–85. People refused to pay rent to local municipalities and service charges for water and electricity. Police vehicles were petrol-bombed. Black and Coloured businessmen who became councillors were denounced as collaborators. The slogan 'Liberation before Education' and the Pink Floyd song 'Another brick in the wall' gained popularity among youths. In the universities, NUSAS played a key role among white students in campaigning for a non-racial democratic South Africa. The South African government responded with further repression, political trials, banning and restricting activists, arranging death threats and actual assassinations. Violence and the 'necklacing' of presumed informers or 'sell-outs' peaked in 1985, as increasing numbers of Defence Force troops were brought in in armoured vehicles to patrol the townships. Funerals themselves became scenes of violence and led to further funerals. Where moral order was restored, it was by churchmen such as Bishop Desmond Tutu.

In response, Botha tried to undermine the revolution by creating 'property-owning democracy' among black urban dwellers – permitting them to take out 99-year leases on their township houses. The key apartheid principle that blacks had no rights in urban areas was now abandoned. Plans were mooted for a fourth house of parliament at Cape Town – to occupy the South African Library building – to represent urban blacks who had no rights in the 'independent' Bantustan republics of Transkei, Bophuthatswana, Venda, and Ciskei. In 1985 the so-called Immorality Act was abolished, and in 1986 the notorious pass laws – and thus the influx control system they served – were abolished.

The high world price of gold (as a 'hedge' against inflation) had protected South Africa from the world economic downturn that followed the 1973 oil crisis. But during the 1980s the security crisis of 'ungovernability', a weak world gold price, growing inflation, and trade sanctions were 'beginning to bite'. International sanctions against South Africa had been initiated by overseas anti-apartheid movements, becoming stronger after the 1976 Soweto rising brought apartheid back to the world's attention. Backed by the Afro-Asian bloc at the United Nations, Commonwealth nations cut sporting links with South Africa under the 1977 Gleneagles agreement. Sanctions at the Olympics and other world sporting and cultural events followed. During the 1980s, anti-apartheid activists in North America, Britain, the Netherlands, Ireland, Australia, and elsewhere pressed for 'divestment' of multinational corporations from South Africa – General Motors, Ford Motor Company, IBM, Shell, Kodak, etc.

In August 1985, multinational American banks agreed to stop loans to the South African government. During 1986 trade bans and sanctions on loans and investments were applied by the European Community and the United States. In 1987, a number of American corporations – including giants General Motors and Kodak – decided to withdraw from South Africa. More international withdrawals followed. Then came the body blow, the demand by Chase Manhattan and other big banks for the repayment by the South African government of outstanding loans. Because tactical supplies of aircraft parts and war materiel had dried up, South Africa was forced to retreat from Angola after the battle of Cuito Cuanavale in September 1987. In the words of a South African minister of finance, Barend du Plessis, these investment sanctions by big banks were 'the dagger that finally immobilised apartheid.'

FURTHER STUDY

BIBLIOGRAPHY

See also books recommended in the previous chapter.

ALUKA, *Struggles for Freedom, Southern Africa*. Ithaca's Aluka on-line collection of digitized documents on the liberation struggles across southern Africa <http://www.aluka.org/struggles>.

Bundy, Colin (2012), *Govan Mbeki*. Auckland Park: Jacana Pocket Books.

Callinicos, L. (2004), *Oliver Tambo: Beyond the Engeli Mountains*. Claremont: David Philip.

Chung, Fay (2006), *Re-living the Second Chimurenga Memories from the Liberation Struggle in Zimbabwe*. Harare: The Nordic Africa Institute and Weaver Press.

Dubow, Saul (1995), *Segregation and Apartheid in Twentieth-Century South Africa*. London: Routledge.

Dubow, Saul (2014), *Apartheid, 1948–1994*. Oxford: Oxford University Press.

Ferguson, James (1990), *The Anti-Politics Machine: Development, Depoliticization and Bureaucratic Power in Lesotho*. Cambridge: Cambridge University Press.

Gill, Stephen J. (1993), *A Short History of Lesotho: From the Stone Age until the 1993 Elections*. Morija: Morija Museum & Archives.

Hanlon, Joseph (1984), *Mozambique: The Revolution Under Fire*. London: Zed Books.

Hanlon, Joseph (1986), *Beggar Your Neighbours: Apartheid Power in Southern Africa*. London: London Catholic Institute for International Relations.

Johns, Sheridan & R. Hunt Davis, eds. (1991), *Mandela, Tambo, and the African National Congress: The Struggle Against Apartheid, 1948–1990, A Documentary Survey*. Oxford: Oxford University Press.

Johnstone, Frederick A. (1976)., *Class, Race, and Gold: A Study of Class Relations and Racial Discrimination in South Africa*. London: Routledge & Kegan Paul.

Jordan, Pallo Z. (2007), *Oliver Tambo Remembered*. Johannesburg: Pan Macmillan.

Kallaway, Peter (2002), *The History of Education Under Apartheid, 1948–1994: The Doors of Learning and Culture Shall be Opened*. New York: Laing & Cape Town: Pearson Education.

Katjavivi, Peter (1988), *A History of Resistance in Namibia*. London: James Currey & Paris: UNESCO.

Lodge, Tom (1983), *Black Politics in South Africa Since 1945*. London: Longman & Johannesburg: Ravan.

Macmillan, Hugh (2013), *The Lusaka Years: The African National Congress in Exile in Zambia, 1963–94*. Auckland Park: Jacana Media.

Macmillan, Hugh (2016), *Jack Simons: Teacher, Scholar, Comrade*. Auckland Park: Jacana Pocket Books.

Macmillan, Hugh (2017), *Oliver Tambo*. Auckland Park: Jacana Pocket Books.

Mandela, Nelson with Richard Stengel (1994), *Long Walk to Freedom: The Autobiography of Nelson Mandela*. Boston, MA: Little, Brown & London: Macdonald Purnell.

Minter, William (1994), *Apartheid's Contras: An Inquiry into the Roots of War in Angola*. London: Zed & Johannesburg: Witwatersrand University Press.

Mondlane, Eduardo (1969), *The Struggle for Mozambique*. London: Penguin.

Nkomo, Joshua (1984), *The Story of My Life*. London: Methuen.

Noor, Nieftagodien (2014), *The Soweto Uprising*. Auckland Park: Jacana Pocket Books.

Sampson, Anthony (1999), *Mandela: The Authorised Biography*. London: HarperCollins.

Sapire, Hilary & Chris Saunders, eds. (2012), *Southern African Liberation Struggles*. Cape Town: UCT Press.

Simpson, Thula (2016), *Umkhonto we Sizwe: The ANC's Armed Struggle*. Cape Town: Penguin Random House.

Temu, Arnold & Joel das Eves Tembe, eds. (2015), *Southern African Liberation Struggles*. Dar es Salaam: Mkuki na Nyota Publishers.

Wilson, Lindy (2011), *Steve Biko*. Auckland Park: Jacana Pocket Books.

VIDEOGRAPHY

DVDs and downloads:

The Bang Bang Club (dir. Steven Silver, 2010. 106 mins): drama of four photo-journalists documenting the South African township revolution of the mid-1980s.

Bopha (dir. Morgan Freeman, 1993. 120 mins): Danny Glover as black police sergeant under apartheid, torn between loyalty to the apartheid state and to his community, tested by his son's joining the Soweto uprising.

Cry Freedom (dir. Richard Attenborough, 1987. 157 mins): Steve Biko (Denzel Washington) converts white journalist Donald Woods (Kevin Kline) to the anti-apartheid cause, and is then murdered by the police. The rest of the movie is about Woods' escape abroad.

A Dry White Season (dir. Euzhan Palcy, 1989. 97 mins): from André Brink's novel set in 1976: a black gardener (Winston Ntshona) is tortured by the police and his white employer (Donald Sutherland) becomes involved in underground politics. Marlon Brando as lawyer.

Endgame (dir. Pete Travis, 2009. 109 mins): Chiwetel Ejiofor as Thabo Mbeki and John Kani as Oliver Tambo in secret talks with South African businessmen in an English country house.

Flame (dir. Ingrid Sinclair, 1996. 85 mins): Florence, re-branded 'Flame' as a liberation fighter, undergoes great hardships, including rape, in guerrilla training and actual warfare, but is unappreciated by former comrades after the war.

The Gods Must be Crazy (dir. Jamie Uys, 1980. 109 mins): late apartheid comedy filmed in South Africa and Namibia about a Bushman dealing with incomprehensible but well-meaning whites and incompetent blacks.

Hold Up the Sun/ Ulibambe Lingashoni (prod. Toron/ Thebe, 1992, 5-part series): 'The ANC and popular power in the making'.

Jerusalema: Gangster's Paradise (dir. Ralph Ziman, 2008. 119 mins): Lucky Kunene (Rapulana Seiphemo) graduates from petty crime to violent hi-jacking of vehicles and whole buildings from white owners during the dying days of apartheid law and disorder.

Last Grave at Dimbaza (dir. Chris Curling & Pascoe Macfarlane, 1974. 55 mins): clandestine-made documentary film about black people removed from urban homes and dumped in remote open countryside, where many die of malnutrition and disease.

Mama Afrika (dir. Mika Kaurismaki, 2011. 90 mins): documentary on the life of singer Miriam Makeba in South Africa, the U.S., and West Africa.

Mandela: Long Walk to Freedom (dir. Justin Chadwick, 2013-14. 141 mins): Idris Elba as young lawyer Nelson and Naomie Harris as intriguing beauty Winnie, charting his rise to fame in gaol and hers to notoriety, over three decades.

Mapantsula (dir. Oliver Schmitz, 1988. 100 mins): Panic (Thomas Mogotlane) is a *pantsula*, a dandy young thief, who becomes politicized when thrown into gaol, with flashbacks to anti-apartheid struggles and police brutality.

Master Harold and the Boys (dir. Lonny Price, 2010. 87 mins): coming of age movie about white boy (Freddie Highmore), neglected by drunken racist dad, and effectively brought up by two surrogate black fathers, both waiters.

Otelo Burning (dir. Sara Blecher, 2011. 97 mins): surfing movie set in late apartheid times about young black boys torn and exploited between black township life and the influence of an ageing white surfer on the beach.

Red Scorpion (dir. Joseph Zito, 1989. 105 mins): Soviet operative Rachenko in Angola, played by muscleman Dolph Lundgren, is 'turned' to use his assassination skills against his superiors after living among the Bushmen.

Sarafina (dir. Darrell Roodt, 1992. 117 mins): ex-Broadway exuberant musical movie dramatizing the 1976 Soweto youth uprising. Leleti Khumalo as Sarafina the student leader who outperforms Whoopi Goldberg as a teacher.

Spear of the Nation: The Story of the African National Congress (dir. Ian Stuttard, 1986. 52 mins): emphasises current events of the 1980s.

Tsotsi (dir. Gavin Hood, 2005. 94 mins): Oscar-winning movie, adapted from an Alan Paton tale, about a callous young *tsotsi* (Presley Chweneyagae) who hi-jacks a car with a baby still strapped in the back. He then finds redemption as a caring individual until he is confronted by the law.

Winnie (dir. Pascale Lamche, 2017. 98 mins): documentary on the rise and fall of the widely misunderstood Winnie Madikizela, second wife of Nelson Mandela who acquired sainthood in gaol while Winnie sinned outside.

Winnie Mandela (dir. Darrell Roodt, 2011. 104 mins): doughty Winnie (Jennifer Hudson) wins the heart of Nelson Mandela before he is imprisoned for 27 years. Harassed by police, she survives rustication and betrayal, but is rejected by Mandela after his release.

11 Southern Africa since 1990

The fairly well-developed economies of colonial Rhodesia and South Africa had been designed to serve the interests of the ruling settler minority, rather than those of the indigenous majority. Africans had participated in the colonial economy as suppliers of cheap labour. Other Southern African countries, with smaller settler minorities, also inherited underdeveloped economies, servicing the needs of the colonizing power – focused on production of one or two commodities for export overseas. All newly independent countries were faced with the problem of how to combine politically inclusive government with economic development that would cater to the needs of the majority – excluded in the past. Previously racially exclusive economies suffered from uneven development, with small islands of relative prosperity floating on a sea of permanent poverty. There were low levels of general literacy, a shortage of educational and health facilities, and dependency on exporting unprocessed raw materials. With the exception of South Africa, and to some extent Zimbabwe, countries lacked investment by local capital and the local knowledge and skilled manpower necessary to drive economic development.

There have been mixed fortunes in the progress of democracy. Many politicians, initially elected by open democracy, have clung onto power to permanently entrench their rule and their enrichment. Jean Francois Bayart, in a study of West African politics, has identified this as 'the politics of the belly'. 'Big men' fill their own bellies and line their own pockets, thereafter dispensing goods and favours from state resources to their relatives, clients, and hangers-on. Political opposition has become too often based, not on social and ethical principles, but on if and when 'it is also our time to eat'.

Public funds have been looted and privatized into ownership by companies or individuals. Closely related to 'the politics of the belly' has been 'crony capitalism' in the expanding private sector of the economy. Success in business has often depended on close relations between entrepreneurs and government officials. Select business people are favoured with government tenders, legal permits, government grants, and other preferential treatment. Politicians receive loyalty in return, and government officials receive kickbacks. In post-apartheid South Africa this has been called 'tenderpreneurship'.

The most explosive problem facing former white-ruled Zimbabwe, South Africa, and Namibia has been the ownership of vast tracts of farm land – alienated for productive private use by white settlers in the colonial era, while Africans were confined to marginal 'native reserves'. Popular grievance over the loss of hereditary communal property was at the heart of anti-colonial struggle. Post-colonial solutions to the 'land question' have ranged from South Africa's land restitution and redistribution programme to Zimbabwe's violent land reforms of the 2000s.

Southern African countries all face the demographic challenge of rapidly growing populations, especially in urban areas, demanding civic services and access to fashionable consumer goods. This challenge has been, however, in part mitigated by countries – beginning with Botswana in the 1990s – rounding the 'demographic corner' into more balanced overall population growth. People now have fewer children, in part because of the high cost of raising children, but also because improved health facilities mean that it is no longer necessary to have many children in case some die in childhood. Meanwhile, for those lucky enough to earn a decent living, there has been the arrival of modern global consumerism – designer clothes and trainer shoes, 'smart' cell (mobile) phones, and 4 x 4 family vehicles among the urban rich.

THE END OF APARTHEID

Verligte ('enlightened') F.W. de Klerk succeeded *verkrampte* ('narrowminded') President Botha in 1989, after Botha suffered a debilitating stroke. De Klerk moved swiftly to negotiate an end to the apartheid system. He announced that he would repeal discriminatory laws and lift the banning of the ANC, PAC, SACP, and UDF. He promised to release Nelson Mandela, after 27 years of incarceration. Mandela was finally released from prison on 11 February 1990, and the country was poised to enter a new era. Negotiations between the South African government and the ANC proceeded apace for the political transition to democracy. The Convention for a Democratic South Africa (CODESA) first met in December 1991 to negotiate a multi-racial transitional government and a new constitution for South Africa. The agreed principles were approved in by the overwhelming majority in a whites-only referendum in March 1992. CODESA then reconvened to haggle over details of transition.

Secretive white and black forces tried to undermine ongoing CODESA negotiations by inciting so-called 'black-on-black' violence. A clash between single male hostel-dwellers of the Zulu royalist Inkatha Freedom Party (IFP) and ANC township residents at Boipatong on 17 June 1992, resulted in 45 deaths. On 7 September 1992, the Ciskei Bantustan's army killed 29 people when they fired on ANC demonstrators at Bisho. On 10 April 1993, the assassination of SACP secretary-general Chris Hani by a white-supremacist Polish refugee, Janusz Walus, almost derailed the whole CODESA process by inciting mass revenge on whites. Calm was reassured only after Mandela made a passionate appeal for peace. When white-supremacists crashed a truck through the glass front of the CODESA talks venue (Kempton Park World Trade Centre) in June 1993, it appeared merely ludicrous. But real tragedy struck on 25 July 1993, when soldiers of the PAC's armed wing, the Azanian People's Liberation Army's (APLA), gunned down worshippers of all colours in St. James' church at Harfield in Cape Town, killing 11.

In a desperate last-minute move, white right-wing militants failed to incite mutiny in the Bophuthatswana Bantustan army. Three of them were killed in a clash with security forces on 11 March 1994. South Africa ushered in its new democratic dispensation on 29 April 1994, following a peaceful election process on 26–28 April, in which the ANC had won convincingly with 62.65 per cent of the vote.

SOUTHERN AFRICAN DEVELOPMENT COMMUNITY (SADC)

SADCC accommodated the liberation of Namibia and South Africa by transforming itself into the Southern African Development Community (SADC) by a treaty signed at Windhoek, Namibia on 17 August 1992. South Africa joined SADC as its 11th member in 1994, and Mandela was unanimously elected chairman – while the secretariat remained in Gaborone, Botswana. Like its European Union (EU) model, SADC's aim was an integrated regional economy to promote peace and security, advancing towards a free trade area and a customs union.

South Africa took portfolio responsibility for SADC finance, investment, and health, but in practice cynically saw SADC as one of the expanding rings of its regional policy. The innermost ring was South Africa's currency union with Lesotho, Namibia, and Swaziland. The intermediate ring was its customs union (SACU) including Botswana as well as the currency union members. SADC was regarded as an expanding free trade area, within which the nearest states might be persuaded to eventually join the customs union. South African-based multinational retail chains, beer manufacturers, and telecommunications extended themselves into SADC and beyond, paying particular attention to the English-speaking major powers of West and East Africa, Nigeria, and Kenya. As the super-power of the region, South Africa conducted trade negotiations with foreign powers, such as the EU, that did not necessarily take the interests of other SACU and SADC members into account.

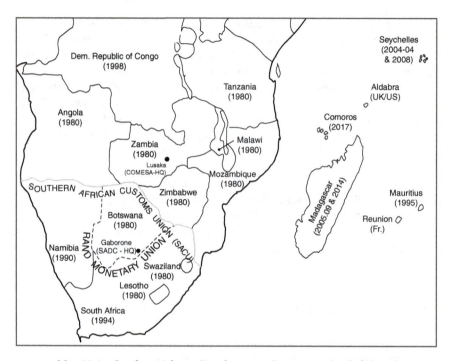

Map 11.1   Southern African Development Community (with dates of joining SADCC/ SADC)

Under Mandela's SADC presidency, new member states were admitted that had little or no economic-geographical contiguity with other SADC states. Though its territory included part of the Zambia-Angola railway, the Democratic Republic of Congo (DRC) had not previously been admitted to membership. Beginning with the admission of Mauritius in 1995, a number of countries were admitted to SADC for reasons of political sentimentality, though they did not become effective economic participants within SADC – DRC and the Seychelles in 1998 and Madagascar in 2005. More seriously, Gaborone-based SADC was weakened by rivalry with the Lusaka-based COMESA and by Zimbabwe's initiative in getting defence and security added to its portfolio of coordinating regional agriculture.

COMESA (Common Market for Eastern and Southern Africa) was the rival free-trade project of the U.N. Economic Commission for Africa's PTA (preferential trade area). Botswana and South Africa declined to join COMESA. Mozambique, Tanzania, Namibia, Angola, and Lesotho all subsequently withdrew. COMESA was considered an impractical step-too-far, creating confusion and duplication of effort, as its membership stretched from Libya and Egypt, Sudan and Ethiopia, via Zambia and Zimbabwe, to Swaziland.

Zimbabwe called on all SADC members to assist its military intervention in the Congo (DRC) civil war in 2008. Only Angola and Namibia responded with troops. Soon afterwards, South Africa and Botswana sent troops to nip in the bud a threatened military coup in Lesotho. In both cases, other SADC states criticized the lack of prior consultation. Cynics pointed out that South Africa was defending its economic interests in Lesotho, while senior officers in the Zimbabwe military had been rewarded with ownership of mines in the DRC's mineral-rich Katanga province. A further source of tension within SADC in 2008 was Zimbabwe's defiance of the SADC tribunal ruling that white farmers in Zimbabwe should be compensated financially for recent farm seizures. Zimbabwe argued that the SADC Tribunal breached the powers of its sovereign constitution. The tribunal was duly abolished in 2011.

THREE REPUBLICS: BOTSWANA, ZAMBIA & MALAWI

In Botswana, general elections followed like clockwork every five years since the 1960s, and presidents have been succeeded by their vice-presidents: Quett Ketumile Masire by Festus Mogae in 1998, Ian Khama (son of the first president) in 2008, and Mokgweetsi Masisi in 2018. The ruling Botswana Democratic Party has never been defeated, and opposition parties have waxed and waned from almost 40 per cent of the vote downwards. In 2012, the four opposition parties joined together as an electoral pact, known as the Umbrella for Democratic Change, to fight the 2014 and subsequent elections.

By 2001 per capita income stood at $7,820, more than four times the average in sub-Saharan Africa, making Botswana an upper-middle-income country in world terms. But Botswana's breakneck 30-year record of annual GDP growth had slowed down in the 1990s. Central state planning on five-year 'rolling' national plans had become less effective. The economy had expanded beyond mere redistribution of state income, from the dividends of mineral production, into a period of private capitalism. Earlier state investment in basic health and education had resulted in improved living standards and the expansion of an urban middle class in cities and rural towns. But newly accumulated capital was frittered away by rampant consumerism or sunk into the inflation of urban property values, rather than being invested into productive employment and diversification.

Botswana faced its greatest challenge during the 1990s: the infection of about one-quarter of its population by HIV-AIDS. Reduction of the epidemic, by a mixture of public propaganda and effective distribution of medication, became national priority No.1 under Festus Mogae as vice-president and president. Growing youth unemployment in urban areas was exacerbated by the influx of economic refugees from western Zimbabwe in the 1990s, though many then proceeded onwards to South Africa.

There were also significant pockets of rural poverty, particularly in the remote areas of the Kalahari and around the Okavango delta. A point at issue was the expulsion of indigenous people from the Central Kalahari Game Reserve (CKGR). Under the misapprehension that they would only hunt with bows-and-arrows, and not with guns and dogs, Khoe-speaking San people had been encouraged to settle at Xade in the CKGR, where – until the government's sudden decision to remove them – a well was dug with Japanese aid and the government supplied a clinic and basic schooling. The situation was exacerbated when the articulate spokesman among the Kalahari San, Oxford graduate John Hardbattle, died, and was replaced by an uneducated leader beholden to an international human rights organization.

The years of President Ian Khama's presidency, from 2008 until the end of his second term in 2018, were marked by his popularity abroad – because of his open criticism of President Mugabe and his rebuke to China 'We are not your colony' – and rather more muted respect at home for his decisive, if not always well-advised, executive actions. He was faulted for obsession with military security and favouritism towards relatives and old army comrades. The face of the capital city and country has been changed by a construction boom, but GDP growth has fluctuated wildly given the vagaries of the world diamond market and the abrupt closure of effectively bankrupt copper-nickel mining in 2016.

The liberation of Namibia and South Africa completed Botswana's loss of favoured international political status in the early 1990s. American and European expatriate aid personnel decamped over the borders. Though protected somewhat by having its own currency, Botswana largely reverted to economic dependence on South Africa. Longstanding dreams of alternative rail links to west and east coasts via Namibia and Zimbabwe have remained unfulfilled.

In Zambia, the downward economic spiral that had begun in 1975 continued. The one-party-state rallying cry of 'One Zambia! One Nation! One Leader!' was answered by the popular response *njala yeka* ('only hunger'). In 1990 there were more food riots: at least 30 people were killed. President Kaunda responded by lifting the ban on other political parties. The subsequent 1991 elections were won by the Movement for Multiparty Democracy (MMD) headed by Kaunda's nemesis former trade-unionist Frederick Chiluba. The MMD was to remain in power for the next 20 years under Chiluba (1991–2002), Levy Mwanawasa (2002–08), and Rupiah Banda (2008–11).

The MMD government implemented even more vigorously the IMF's economic structural adjustment program (ESAP) with privatization of state assets. After some government reluctance to re-privatize the mining sector, copper mines were closed if they could not be sold and revived by foreign capital. Chinese company investment in mines was initially successful in reviving mine production, but then came under fire for low wages and poor working conditions.

The MMD accused opposition parties of fomenting unrest. Chiluba tried to stop the return to politics (from retirement) of Kenneth Kaunda, by declaring him a non-citizen – on the grounds that Kaunda's parents had been born in Malawi. Kaunda was detained under house arrest for seven months after a botched *coup d'état* by a small group of soldiers in 1997. (He regained his citizenship in 2000.) The MMD replaced Chiluba by Levy Mwanawasa as president in 2002 – promising an end to Chiluba's wild extravagance and state corruption. But Mwanawasa himself could not brook criticism from the free press, especially one cartoonist – and was only constrained by the fact that the rule of law still persisted in Zambia.

By the time of Mwanawasa's death in 2008 Zambia was regarded as having weathered the worse of its economic woes, on a slow road to recovery. But his MMD successor, Rupiah Banda, lasted only three years before defeat in elections by the Patriotic Front of Michael Sata. President Sata died in 2014, and he was succeeded temporarily by Guy Scott (a white Zambian) before Edgar Lungu became president in 2015. Lungu has since been criticized for ordering arbitrary arrests to intimidate opposition parties.

In Malawi, the 'politics of the belly' have been equally evident. The family of Cecilia Kadzamira effectively ruled the country while Kamuzu Banda held onto the presidency until 1994, when he appears to have been 96 years of age. The one-party state came under increasing pressure to democratize from post-Cold War donors, the Catholic church, and local trade unionists. The Malawi army took the initiative to disarm the régime's network of official bodyguards and enforcers known as Young Pioneers. A referendum in 1993 chose a multi-party constitution, and Banda was succeeded by Elson Bakili Muluzi, southern Africa's only Muslim president so far, after the presidential election held in 1994. Muluzi abandoned the attempt to stand for a third term in 2004 and was succeeded as president by his nominee, Bingu wa Mutharika. The two men then quarrelled. When Muluzi stood again for president in 2009, Mutharika had Muluzi arrested and charged with massive corruption.

The main achievement of Mutharika's first term of office was state subsidization of peasant agriculture that resulted in bumper harvests and a food surplus that rose to 1.3 metric tonnes in 2009. The president, however, alienated food-short Mozambique and Botswana by refusing to sell the surplus to them. Posing as an ally of Libya and Zimbabwe, he also alienated the donor countries in Europe and the United States, on which Malawi had been so reliant. After the IMF ruled that state subsidies for agriculture contravened the terms of structural adjustment financial aid, Mutharika told these countries, in no uncertain terms, to 'go to hell'.

Just before he died in 2012, President Mutharika nominated his brother Peter as his successor, but the cabinet preferred the vice-president and former minister of foreign affairs, Joyce Banda, southern Africa's first woman president. A human rights activist, she set about repairing relations with countries such as Mozambique and Botswana. However, she was heavily defeated in the presidential election of 2014 by international lawyer Peter Mutharika, who promised to clean up corruption by more efficient tax-collection and respect for human rights.

TWO KINGDOMS: LESOTHO & SWAZILAND

In Lesotho, Leabua Jonathan's Basutoland National Party government was overturned in a South African-supported military coup, led by Justin Lekhanya, in January 1986. The military eliminated the presence of ANC/MK operatives in Lesotho. In return, Lesotho secured an agreement with South Africa in October 1986 for a massive highland scheme to supply water, and to a lesser extent electricity, to South Africa. To secure its end of the agreement in providing international finance, Lesotho signed up with the IMF for an economic structural adjustment program. Though the coup had theoretically been in the name of the king, Moshoeshoe II himself was stripped of his powers and exiled in 1990. After an internal coup within the military in 1991, deposing General Lekhanya, Moshoeshoe's eldest son was installed as King Letsie III in 1992.

In 1993, Lesotho held multi-party elections that brought the Basotho Congress Party (BCP) to power, with every seat in the national assembly, under veteran politician Ntsu Mokhehle. The BCP inherited and continued with the economic structural adjustment program, but mutinies in the army, police, and prison service followed BCP attempts to 'purge' them. King Letsie himself led a temporary military coup in 1994 that was forced to restore the BCP government by fellow SADC member states. In 1995 Letsie handed the crown back to his father Moshoeshoe, but Moshoeshoe died in a car crash the following year, and Letsie resumed his place as virtually powerless constitutional monarch.

Mokhehle lasted as prime minister until 1998, despite quarrelling with BCP members and setting up a new party, the Lesotho Congress for Democracy.

His deputy, educationist Pakalitha Mosisili, succeeded him as prime minister. Opposition protests at corruption in high places degenerated into widespread rioting and looting in 1998. When the military threatened yet another mutiny, the capital, Maseru, was invaded by South African and Botswana troops restoring order on behalf of SADC.

The succeeding years saw political intrigues of almost Babylonian proportions, including two opposing individuals alternating as prime minister. Mosisili was restored to power until Lesotho's first peaceful elections in 2002, and was then elected again until 2012, when he was succeeded as prime minister by veteran politician Tom Thabane (All Basotho Convention). Thabane eventually fled abroad in 2015. Mosisili survived an assassination attempt in 2009 to be re-elected as prime minister in 2015. He was defeated and replaced as prime minister again by Tom Thabane in June 2017.

In Swaziland, the economy has continued to be dominated by South African and British capital invested in forestry, sugar and pineapples, and tourism. There has been some local manufacturing development, particularly at Manzini, but the country has remained in the double lock of South Africa as a member of the Rand currency union as well as the customs union. Its main export earner outside SACU was sugar.

English-educated Mswati III, who was crowned king (*Ingwenyama*) at the age of 18 in 1986, took time to assert power and authority as an absolute monarch over his council of ministers – his hereditary uncles, well-established local chiefs, and the queen-mother. In traditionally correct fashion, he presided over annual festivals and married a number of wives – though he offended traditionalists by taking those he personally preferred rather than those with the right family linkages. Swaziland's dual system of government persisted, with an ex-colonial administration of government ministers at Mbabane subject to the royal government at Lobamba. National elections, such as there were, were by the *tinkundla* system of open choice in open air latterly established by Mswati's father. Mswati experimented with a trade unionist, Obed Dlamini, as his prime minister in 1989–93 but then replaced him with a prince once again.

Despite the continuing ban on political parties, the People's United Democratic Movement (PUDEMO) called for democracy and criticized the king in 1988–89. South Africa's advance towards democracy raised political expectations in Swaziland – which semi-elections in 1993 failed to satisfy. Serious unrest and rioting in 1997 raised the concerns of Swaziland's immediate neighbours, South Africa and Mozambique, but led to reaffirmation of the bans on political parties and trade unions. Nevertheless, sporadic bursts of political and trade union activism continued, notably in 2007.

In response to human rights concerns, preferential tariffs on textile exports from Swaziland were withdrawn by the United States in 2015. But the inward-looking, neo-traditional élite has been more exercised by the fact that Swaziland had suffered the highest rate of HIV-AIDS infection in the world. It remains to be seen how effective has been the king's recognition that the basic problem lies in the coercive treatment of young females by promiscuous older males.

ANGOLA & MOZAMBIQUE

In Angola, the MPLA president José Eduardo Dos Santos began negotiations for a ceasefire with the UNITA leader Jonas Savimbi in June 1989. Agreement was reached in 1991, by which the MPLA undertook to adopt a multi-party democratic system. But when MPLA won the general election in September 1992, UNITA refused to accept this and resumed the civil war. The two parties eventually came together again in the Lusaka Accord on 20 November 1994. UNITA ceased to fight MPLA, and it joined a government of national unity in 1996. Except that Savimbi himself boycotted the new government, and UNITA representatives were soon expelled – and civil war resumed. UNITA increasingly relied on child soldiers.

It was only after Savimbi was killed in combat in February 2002 that UNITA agreed to stop fighting, and the 27-year-long civil war finally came to an end. Maybe a million lives had been lost in the conflict, and millions of land-mines were strewn across the land. In 2008, Angola held general elections, which the MPLA won with 82 per cent of the votes cast.

Exacerbating conflict between MPLA and UNITA were regional and ethnic differences. MPLA's source of unending wealth was the oil exported overseas from the Cabinda enclave and offshore. UNITA's less reliable source of wealth was in the smuggling of diamonds – found in southern Angola or possibly smuggled from Namibia and Botswana. In 2006, Transparency International confirmed the corruption in the accumulation of extraordinary wealth at Luanda, by contrast with the grinding poverty of people elsewhere. Public servants demand *gasosas* or bribes as a matter of routine. The 12 richest Angolans were all top members of the MPLA élite, including reputed billionaire Isabel Dos Santos, the daughter of President Dos Santos.

In September 2017, Dos Santos stood down as president of Angola after bouts of ill health, and he was succeeded by his nominee João Lourenço. The new president promised to clear away kleptocracy. One of his first moves was to fire Isabel Dos Santos as head of the state oil company, Sonangol.

In Mozambique, FRELIMO under President Joaquim Chissano changed the country's one-party constitution in 1998–90 to allow for a multi-party political system. Peace talks with RENAMO under Afonso Dhlakama – no longer supported by South Africa – resulted in peace between the two parties signed in Rome, Italy, in 1992. RENAMO contested the 1994 elections and lost out to FRELIMO by only a narrow margin of parliamentary seats. Thereafter, popular support for Dhlakama declined, but he and his party remained irritants for the FRELIMO government, threatening boycotts and temporarily resorting to armed conflict in 2014–15.

The FRELIMO government concentrated on restoring popular and international confidence. In 1995, Mozambique recognized its close relationships with English-speaking countries by becoming a member state of the (ex-British) Commonwealth. Also in that year, almost two million Mozambicans gave the régime a vote of confidence by returning from exile in neighbouring countries. The economy recovered with the revival of foreign capital investment from South Africa, Portugal, and elsewhere, in sectors including offshore petroleum gas. There were, however, popular suspicions of corruption at the highest level, resulting in the murder of an investigative journalist in 2001.

Chissano associated himself with the presidents of South Africa and Botswana rather than those of Zambia and Zimbabwe – whom he criticized for hanging onto power after the due date on their term of office. (It may also be remarked that Nelson Mandela had married the widow of former Mozambican president Samora Machel.) In 2004–05 Chissano gave way to his deputy Armando Guebuza, millionaire brewer and banker, as the next president of Mozambique. In 2015 Mozambique was declared free of the land mines that had plagued the development of rural areas since the 1960s. After serving the statutory two terms of office, Guebuza gave way to engineer Filipe Nyusi as the fourth FRELIMO president of Mozambique in January 2017.

INDEPENDENT NAMIBIA

The Republic of Namibia was recognized as an independent state on 21 March 1990 by the presence of President De Klerk of South Africa, the colonial power that had had *de facto* ownership of the territory, and the secretary-general of the United Nations, which had claimed guardianship in international law. The SWAPO leader Sam Nujoma was sworn in as president, watched by Nelson Mandela who had recently been released from prison in Cape Town. The SWAPO government included cabinet members of opposition parties in a government of national unity, and the new army contained soldiers of both SWAPO's guerrilla wing PLAN and the colonial South West Africa Territorial Force (SWATF). In the spirit of reconciliation, there were no war trials of the victors over the vanquished.

In 1991, SWAPO welcomed capital investment from South Africa by announcing its pragmatic conversion from socialist to free-market liberal principles in ownership of mines and industries. The new Namibia dollar also remained a member of South Africa's Rand monetary area. Protracted negotiations with South Africa led to the transfer to Namibian sovereignty in March 1994 of Walvis Bay, the country's only deep-sea port, which had never been part of German South West Africa or of the subsequent mandate.

Similar to Zimbabwe and South Africa, Namibia inherited a highly skewed distribution of agricultural land between whites on the one hand and Coloured or black people on the other hand. Land reform was slow because of the willing-buyer-willing-seller principle in the independence constitution, and the reluctance of white farmers and ranchers to sell land at lower than the highest market prices. However, while Nujoma threatened on occasion to follow the post-2000 example of his comrade president Mugabe in seizing white farms by violence, this did not happen. Instead, the Namibian government expended resources on widespread provision of education and of health services to tackle the HIV-AIDS epidemic.

Namibia also adopted a more conciliatory policy towards its Khoe-San population, including Kalahari Bushmen. The Khoe Nama language was recognized alongside Afrikaans (the native tongue of most whites and Coloureds) and Ovambo (spoken by the black majority in the north). English, not the native tongue of any indigenous group, was adopted as the neutral official language, and Namibia became a member of the Commonwealth – like Mozambique despite never having been a British colony.

President Nujoma was a vocal supporter of the actions and beliefs of President Mugabe in Zimbabwe. He and his SWAPO party also maintained their close wartime relationship with Angola's ruling MPLA and their mutual hostility to the UNITA rebels of Angola. In 1998, Namibia joined Zimbabwe and Angola in sending soldiers to Congo (DRC) to assist President Laurent Kabila, who was facing civil war. In 1999 Namibia signed a mutual defence pact with Angola, allowing MPLA forces to cross Namibia's borders in their war with UNITA rebels.

Relations were not so cordial with Botswana. In 1992 Namibia claimed possession of Kasikili/Sedudu, a seasonally flooded island in the Chobe river border between Botswana and Namibia's Caprivi Strip. The island had appeared to be on the Namibia side of the river in a 1936 map, but the International

Court of Justice in 1999 confirmed that the Anglo-German (Heligoland-Zanzibar) treaty of July 1890 had placed the island on the Botswana side. Meanwhile there was sporadic revolt by the so-called Caprivi Liberation Army, representing people in the Strip who felt greater kinship with Zambia or Botswana than with Namibia. The revolt was crushed by Namibian forces in 1999.

In 1998, SWAPO ruled that President Nujoma could stand for a further term beyond the two stipulated in the constitution. Faced by a new opposition party, the Congress of Democrats, he was re-elected in 1999 by 77 per cent of voters. In 2004–05 Nujoma handed over the presidency to Hifikepunye Pohamba, who made moves to root out corruption in government and initiated more friendly relations with Zambia and Botswana. After the prescribed two terms in office, Pohamba was succeeded by former prime minister Hage Geingob as president in 2015. Geingob opened negotiations with Germany about reparations for the 1904–08 genocide in German South-West Africa.

ZIMBABWE IN DECLINE UNDER ROBERT MUGABE

By the end of the first decade of independence, it was becoming clear that there was insufficient economic growth to maintain the Zimbabwe government's populist policies of re-distribution. In 1990–95, Zimbabwe turned to the IMF and World Bank, which prescribed the harsh medicine of an economic structural adjustment programme (ESAP), cutting state expenditure or privatizing state assets, liberalizing trade and finance, and devaluation of the Zimbabwe dollar. By 1995, the economy was worse off than before the reform. The country had suffered considerable de-industrialization. Unemployment was high, as workers were retrenched and sought a living in the informal sector. Poverty levels and child mortality rates were rising, and popular discontent against the government was growing. ESAP was followed by ZIMPREST (Zimbabwe Programme for Economic and Social Transformation) – any success of which was completely undermined by two unanticipated items of heavy state expenditure in 1997–98.

In 1997, the Zimbabwe government caved in to the shrill discontent of 70,000 veterans of the liberation struggle and their dependents. Only 20,000 of the 36,000 liberation fighters demobilized in 1980 had found employment by 1985. The veterans' association, formed in 1989, pressed government into enacting the War Veterans Act of 1992 and the War Victims Compensation Act of 1993, both of which set aside funds. In May 1996, a newspaper revealed that the post-colonial ruling élites were systematically draining these funds for themselves. This caused a mass run on the remaining funds that ran dry by April 1997. The government was then harassed so much by the veterans that President Mugabe announced that each veteran was to be awarded 50,000 Zimbabwe dollars in cash. The government 'printed more money' to cover the unbudgeted cost to the exchequer, and the value of the Zimbabwe dollar took another sharp downward turn.

But worse was yet to come. In August 1998, without prior consultation of parliament, President Mugabe ordered the army and air force to intervene in the Congo (DRC) civil war, in support of President Laurent Kabila. The armed forces were rewarded by Kabila with ownership of copper mines in Katanga, but the costs that were borne by the Zimbabwe state rendered the Zimbabwe dollar virtually worthless. Faced with falling standards of living, rising inflation, a runaway cost of living, and growing unemployment, workers downed tools and took to the streets in protest. For the first time since independence, Zimbabwe experienced bread riots – forcing the government to resort to use force to put down popular discontent.

Out of this wave of urban-industrial mass disgruntlement with the 'fat cats' of Harare emerged the Movement for Democratic Change (MDC) in 1999. It was led by the former general secretary of the Zimbabwe Congress of Trade Unions, Morgan Tsvangirai, and received the support of churches and human rights organizations upholding the rule of law. The government responded by proposing a new constitution that would increase the powers of the presidency and would, amongst other things, give it the right to seize white-owned land without compensation – a final nail in the coffin for the 1979 Lancaster House agreement. Under the terms agreed at Lancaster House, the Zimbabwe government had to acquire land from white farmers on a willing-buyer-willing-seller basis – using funds provided by the British government. The process was slow, partly because the government was required to pay market prices for land, and because few white farmers were willing to sell prime land – preferring to sell off marginal land. Some farms went to productive African farmers; other farms went to politicians and 'fat cats' not really involved in agriculture.

The process of farm acquisition had ground to a halt. This gave the Labour government of prime minister Tony Blair in Britain a pretext to stop funding farm acquisitions after 17 years. It infuriated Mugabe, and the offence was compounded by the abrupt communication of the British minister in question, Clare Short, on 5 November 1997: 'I should make it clear that we do not accept that Britain has a special responsibility to meet the costs of land purchase in Zimbabwe. We are a new Government from diverse backgrounds without any links to former colonial interests. My own origins are Irish and, as you know, we were colonised not colonisers.'

A national referendum for acceptance of the proposed new constitution was held in 2000. The MDC mobilized people and the constitution was over-whelmingly rejected. In general elections later that year, the MDC unexpect-edly won 57 of the 120 contested seats. The ruling party hit back by tackling the white farmers who were suspected of being the MDC paymasters, with a so-called Fast-Track Land Reform Programme. ZANU-PF supporters, including war veterans, started invading white-owned farms, and driving the farmers away – what became known as the *jambanja* (mayhem) or third *Chimurenga*. The main support for MDC, however, lay in the urban masses. In May 2005, the Zimbabwe government embarked on Operation *Murambatsvina* ('reject fifth'), demolishing temporary or unlicensed shanty-towns in the name of urban renewal. This left more than 700,000 people homeless.

MDC continued to do well in elections, despite the government crackdown. In March 2008 elections, the party won 100 seats to ZANU-PF's 99, with the remaining 10 seats going to an MDC-breakaway party. MDC leader Tsvangirai won 47.8 per cent of the vote, while Mugabe won 43.2 per cent. However, Tsvangirai was forced to surrender the presidency by personal violence and intimidation. Under South Africa's leadership, SADC intervened and patched up a compromise government of national unity (GNU). The GNU lasted until ZANU-PF proclaimed overwhelming victory in the 2013 elections.

Farm invasions and political turmoil, and punitive sanctions imposed upon some ZANU-PF leaders and companies by Western powers, contributed to a progressive decline of the national economy. Agricultural production, hitherto the mainstay of Zimbabwe's economy, was depleted. This had a knock-on effect on manufacturing industry, which depended on agricultural producers for inputs and as a market for processed goods. Drug shortages in the coun-try's hospitals came at a time the country faced the major health challenge of the HIV-AIDS pandemic. Lack of foreign exchange due to declining exports, ostracism by Zimbabwe's traditional trading partners, and poor financial poli-cies led to runaway inflation. In 2008 the government was obliged to abandon the worthless national currency and adopt instead seven foreign currencies as legal tender.

From breadbasket to basket-case, Zimbabwe offered a case study in how erstwhile liberators could become oppressors, and how a once-thriving economy could be brought to its knees by bad governance. National unem-ployment spiralled until, by 2015, it stood at an estimated 90 per cent. Millions fled to seek work in neighbouring countries. Thus, from being the proud inheritors of an industrial hub, second only to South Africa in 1980, Zimbabweans were reduced to a nation of street vendors selling trinkets, second-hand clothes, and other items.

On 15 November 2017, the Zimbabwe National Defence Forces dramatically deposed Robert Mugabe, placed him under house arrest and pressured him into resigning the presidency on 18 November. His former deputy, Emmerson Mnangangwa, who had recently recovered from attempted assassination by poisoning and had sought refuge from Mugabe's 'hunting dogs' in Mozambique, took over the presidency. The forces were unhappy that 94-year-old Mugabe, in power for 37 years, was being manipulated by cronies gathered round his wife and her family. But Mugabe still retained status as 'father of the nation'.

THE 'RAINBOW NATION' UNDER NELSON MANDELA

April 1994 saw the emergence of an all-inclusive democratic non-racial South Africa. Nelson Mandela became president. F.W. de Klerk and Thabo Mbeki of the ANC became deputy presidents in a government of national unity (GNU) that included Mangosuthu Buthelezi's Inkatha as well as the ANC and the National Party. A new constitution was fully agreed in 1995, and a Truth and Reconciliation Commission (TRC) was set up in 1996, under the chairmanship of Bishop Desmond Tutu, to expose the crimes committed by all sides in the conflict during the apartheid era.

The GNU was faced by the urgent and sometimes contradictory problems of how to reverse South Africa's economic decline since the 1970s and how to provide equal social and economic opportunities for all citizens regardless of race. Many years of protectionism through high tariff barriers had cultivated inefficiency in commerce and industry. The economy was also constructed for the benefit of the white minority, leaving the overwhelming majority of Africans marginalized except as sources of cheap labour.

The Reconstruction and Development Programme (RDP), introduced in 1994, was a socialist-inspired initiative focused on poverty alleviation and the provision of services – education, health, water, electricity, transport, telecommunications – previously denied to the African majority. The aim was to develop 'human resource capacity' by eliminating all discrimination in the workplace and training, developing an economy balanced between regions, and democratizing the whole of the state and society. But, to achieve these aims, there were 'free market' measures to stimulate economic growth – through lowering some taxes, liberalizing trade barriers, and reducing government debt, as well as ensuring prudent government fiscal spending.

Under the RDP, measures were taken to provide affordable housing, clean water, access to health clinics, and the construction of roads, water reticulation, and sanitation. A start was made in a welfare system that covered the aged, the disabled, and underprivileged children. However, there was insufficient growth in the national economy to advance these services further. In 1996, the RDP was replaced by a macroeconomic policy called Growth, Employment and Redistribution (GEAR). This was much more aligned with the neo-liberal capitalist or 'free market' principles of structural adjustment programs propagated by the International Monetary Fund (IMF) and the World Bank. GEAR trimmed state expenditure and reduced the budget deficit by intensifying fiscal reform, reducing bureaucracy, restructuring some state assets, and selling others to private individuals. The delivery of services to the poor was restrained but continued. Unsurprisingly, the abandonment of socialist ideals came under bitter criticism by the Congress of South African Trade Unions (COSATU).

The incoming government in 1994 promised to reverse the systematic dispossession of Africans from the soil by the Natives' Land Act of 1913, the Native Trust and Land Act of 1936, and the Group Areas Acts from 1950 to 1966. The process of dismantling apartheid land legislation had begun in 1991 when de Klerk's Abolition of Racially Based Land Measures Act followed the release of Mandela from prison. It allowed people to acquire land wherever they wished, regardless of their race, colour, or creed. Under the Restitution of Land Rights Act 22 of 1994, people who had been dispossessed of land after 19 June 1913, as a result of racially discriminatory laws, had the right to restitution of that property or to fair compensation. In 1997 a 'white paper' on land policy spelt out government's future land policy. Claimants could lodge their claims with a Land Claims Court. (The deadline for lodging claims was set for 2005, extended to 2011, and later to 2019.)

In 1999 President Mandela indicated that he would not be standing for a second term. After the ANC won the second democratic elections of June 1999, his deputy, Thabo Mbeki, replaced him as president. The National Party of de Klerk remained in uneasy alliance with the ANC. The recently established Democratic Party, later Democratic Alliance (DA), became the official parliamentary opposition to the ANC. In 2004, Mbeki was returned as president again when the ANC won the third national elections.

SOUTH AFRICA UNDER THABO MBEKI & JACOB ZUMA

The Black Economic Empowerment (BEE) policy, based on a parliamentary Act of 2003, targeted previously disadvantaged people of colour, including

Coloureds, Indians, and local Chinese as well as African citizens – to change 'the racial composition of ownership and management structures and in the skilled occupations'. BEE would enable 'more black people to own and manage enterprises' through access to finance by ensuring that 'black-owned enterprises benefit from the government's preferential procurement policies'.

The emergent black middle class, including the now well-educated children of former exiles and former Bantustan bureaucrats, grew rapidly in numbers. Some became very wealthy, particularly as 'tenderpreneurs' – taking advantage of BEE preference and personal connections to be given national, provincial, or local government contracts. Corruption has inevitably crept in, as some officials connive with applicants to award contracts at inflated prices in return for kickbacks. Is this producing a productive black middle class adding to the sum of human wealth, or a greedy oligarchy of wealthy crony-capitalists?

By 2005 it was clear that GEAR had only achieved modest economic growth, and it had failed to reduce poverty or to generate significant new employment. GEAR was replaced by the Accelerated and Shared Growth Initiative for South Africa in 2005, which was replaced by the New Growth Path (NGP) in 2010. The 20-year long National Development Plan (NDP) announced in 2013 attempted to revive some of the principles of the original 1994 RDP. The quality of successive South African ministers of finance has been compromised by political interferences causing their sudden replacement.

With millions still living in poverty, South Africa is obviously one of the most unequal countries in the world. In May 2008, such resentments burst out in xenophobic violence, starting at Alexandra township in Johannesburg and spreading to the peri-urban townships of major centres. Black foreigners were accused of crowding black South Africans out of housing, employment, and other services and opportunities. Economic refugees from Zimbabwe, Mozambique, Somalia, and Congo were derogatorily referred to as *Makwerekwere* (speakers of incomprehensible tongues). Fifty-six died, hundreds were injured, and there was considerable destruction of property.

President Mbeki lost much support from the old ANC élite over his denial of HIV-AIDS science, and his much too quiet 'quiet diplomacy' with Zimbabwe. Mbeki then clashed with his deputy president Jacob Zuma and sacked him over revelations of Zuma's involvement in corruption with black, white and Indian 'tenderpreneurs' receiving bribes or illegal paybacks from multinational companies. In particular there was scandal over the supply of

French-German naval vessels and of British-Swedish fighter-jets to the South African National Defence Force.

Now seen as a remote figure, Mbeki lost the presidency of the ANC at a party congress to grassroots supporters of Zuma. Mbeki resigned from the state presidency in September 2008. Kgalema Motlanthe was the caretaker president until the next general elections in April 2009. Jacob Zuma then became president, solidly backed from his home province of KwaZulu-Natal. Upset by Mbeki's 'recall', some of his supporters broke away from the ANC to establish the Congress of the People (COPE).

Land restitution was slowed down by the willing-buyer-willing-seller principle. Few white farmers were willing to sell land at prices affordable by the government. Hence, in February 2014, the government proposed to buy land at 50 per cent of its current market value or at a 'fair productive value'. If white farmers agreed to sell their land at the proposed value, they would be rewarded with preferred status for state tenders. Land restitution was also complicated by chiefly claims. Traditional leaders were officially recognized and paid a stipend in the New South Africa, after being left out of the CODESA negotiations. This has resulted in personal rivalries and dynastic disputes claiming revived feudal authority over land distribution. Up to around 2010, only approximately 9 per cent of farmland had been transferred to African ownership through restitution and redistribution. Ironically, most of the farmland restored to African farmers has not been used for productive commercial agriculture, and it has even been sold back to white commercial farmers.

In the fourth general elections of 2009, the ANC won with a slightly reduced majority, with the opposition DA making notable gains. The pattern was repeated in the fifth general elections of 2014, when the newly established Economic Freedom Fighters (EFF), a populist but anti-Zuma breakaway from the ANC, emerged as a serious contender in the national political stakes. Popular protest was fed by news of the Marikana massacre in 2012, when 34 striking platinum miners were shot dead by police.

President Zuma was dogged by allegations of corruption, focusing on state expenditure on his Nkandla rural home. In April 2016 the High Court ruled that Zuma might be charged with 783 counts of alleged corruption, fraud, and racketeering. Zuma, however, remained confident of avoiding prosecution even after December 2017, when the ANC party congress replaced Zuma as its party leader with Cyril Ramaphosa. Ramaphosa was elected president by parliament in February 2018, in the expectation that he would clean out the Augean stables of Zuma corruption.

SOUTHERN AFRICA'S HIV-AIDS EPIDEMIC

The HIV-AIDS disease was unknown in southern Africa until the early 1980s. It became epidemic by the early 1990s. The routes and reservoirs of infection may be traced along the trucking routes from Tanzania via Zambia and Botswana into South Africa's Gauteng and KwaZulu-Natal provinces, spreading significantly into Malawi, Zimbabwe, and Mozambique, and elsewhere in South Africa and Namibia. The primary agents were adult men. Adults of all classes were hard hit north of the Zambezi, where the epidemic began earlier. Middle-class infection south of the Limpopo was restrained by access to ARV medication.

Botswana under President Mogae was the first sub-Saharan African country to provide universal free ARV treatment to people living with HIV, placing special emphasis on prevention of mother-to-child infection. Other national governments followed, with the assistance of international partners. New infections among adults have been radically reduced in Botswana, Malawi, Namibia, Zambia, and Zimbabwe, with Mozambique, South Africa, and especially Swaziland, lagging behind. The latter laggards can be explained by widespread denialism of the scientific nature of HIV infection, and therefore of the medical cure for AIDS. In the case of South Africa, President Thabo Mbeki was so persuaded by on-line quackery. He was reluctant to allow ARV treatment but was overruled by his cabinet. On coming to power in 2009, President Zuma immediately acknowledged the challenge facing the country, and accelerated the provision of ARV medication.

Average life expectancy at birth in South Africa, Namibia, Botswana, Swaziland, and Lesotho had stood at 64 years for women and 59 years for men in 1990–95. The rate fell to 51 for women and 49 for men in 2000–05, before recovering slightly to 52 for women and 51 for men by 2005–10. By 2016, South Africa's rate had risen to 61.6 years for men and 64.6 years for women. The rate had also risen in neighbouring countries. There is no doubt that such recovery can be attributed to widespread availability of ARV medication.

SOUTHERN AFRICA'S GLOBALIZATION & CLIMATE CHALLENGES

Southern Africa has experienced the positive effects of recent globalization – the revolution in information technology (particularly the universality of cell-phones), solar energy capture, new consumer tastes, cultural and linguistic trends (particularly text language), and possibly an enhanced awareness of human rights. All these have influenced and changed the way in which southern Africans perceive their identity and their role in societies and nations.

There have also been costs of recent globalization: the most obvious being the negative impact of global 'warming' or 'weirding' of the climate. The region is experiencing increasing frequency of hot days and decreasing frequency of cold days, as well as unusually variable rainfall patterns – both extremely wet periods and more intense droughts than in the past. Records show a declining trend in rainfall since 1950, interspersed with periodic floods. Notable floods in the years 1984 and 2000 caused untold damage in central Mozambique. Cyclones named Eline and Gloria caused US $700 million-worth of damage to food supplies in Mozambique in 2000. Regional droughts since the 1970s have wreaked havoc and resulted in a 60 per cent decline in regional grain production. A particularly severe drought in 1991–92 affected approximately 86 million people, with 20 million reported at risk of starvation. Another severe regional drought followed in 2002. 2016–17 saw southern Africa in the throes of the worst drought for 70 years. The city of Cape Town almost ran dry. Droughts and floods not only damage property but have impacts on health through malnutrition and waterborne diseases.

Much controversy has surrounded the acceptance or rejection of genetically modified (GM) crops. In 2002, in the midst of severe famine, Zambia, Zimbabwe, Mozambique, and Malawi all refused to accept thousands of tons of maize corn donated by the United States. Zambia returned approximately 35,000 tons of maize delivered to the country by the World Food Programme (WFP), while an estimated 3 million Zambians were on the verge of starvation. Malawi, Mozambique, and Zimbabwe later permitted the importation of GM maize, provided it was milled first into porridge meal outside their borders. This was not simply a matter of consumer preference for local white rather than imported yellow maize. GM maize was generally sterile and unsuitable for planting, but still posed the danger of genetic cross-breeding with local maize. If local maize strains were contaminated or died off, local farmers would be obliged to pay royalties every year to multinational companies. Zambia and Zimbabwe were also worried about losing future markets in the European Union if they allowed their domestic maize genes to be contaminated by GM strains that were banned in the EU.

Globalization has been a two-way process. Southern Africa boasts world class universities, hospitals, and research institutions, contributing innovative skills that are used universally. The region continues to send scientists and academics, movie stars and musicians and other artists, to work overseas. Trans-national corporations born in Southern Africa operate throughout the world: Anglo-American Corporation and De Beers began in Kimberley, Stagecoach (owners of Megabus in America, bus services and railways in Britain) began in Malawi, South African Breweries (SAB-Miller, later part of Anheuser-Busch InBev) began at the Newlands spring in Cape Town, and the *peri-peri* chicken chain Nando's began among Portuguese-Mozambican exiles in Johannesburg. Plants such as *rooibos* (red-bush), honey-bush, and grapple (devil's claw) provide health teas, and Cape flowers adorn many a garden and greenhouse round the world.

Southern African countries face many challenges in the post-colonial/post-apartheid period. What they have had in common is the need to develop their economies to meet the basic needs of growing populations and the consumer wants of modern society.

Independent Angola and Mozambique have suffered civil wars with consequences that have lingered. Both Zambia and Zimbabwe have undergone testing times after dissipating initial post-independence economic booms. Zimbabwe has declined from regional breadbasket into proverbial basket-case, as the state repressed alternative cultural and political voices, but may yet recover. Malawi has remained critically dependent on exporting its labour abroad and on lakeside tourism.

Botswana, with less political flourish and a more open society, has been transformed by meat and mineral exports out of poverty into a middle-income country. Lesotho has remained an enclave supplying labour within South Africa, dependent on foreign aid. Swaziland still combines heavy penetration by South African capital investment with the political inhibitions of a neo-feudal monarchy – which suddenly announced the re-naming of the country as eSwatini in April 2018. South Africa has not yet succeeded, and may even have slipped backwards, in reversing the ills of underdevelopment and apartheid – by more equitable development and distribution of wealth, health, education, and mutual understanding of its diverse cultural inheritances. The accession to power of new presidents in 2017–18 has renewed hope. The future is never predictable, but understanding of the present may be found in knowledge of the past.

HEADS OF STATE AND GOVERNMENT		
ANGOLA	President Joao Lourenco	Sept. 2017
BOTSWANA	President Mokgweetsi Masisi	April 2018
eSWATINI (SWAZILAND)	King Mswati III Prime Minister Barnabas Sibusiso Dlamini	April 1986 Oct. 2008
LESOTHO	King Letsie III Prime Minister Tom Thabane	Oct. 1997 June 2017
MALAWI	President Peter Mutharika	May 2014
MOZAMBIQUE	President Filipe Nyusi	Jan. 2015
NAMIBIA	President Hage Geingob Prime Minister Saara Kauugongelwa-Amadhika	Nov. 2014 March 2015
SOUTH AFRICA	President Cyril Ramaphosa	Feb. 2018
TANZANIA	President John Magufuli	Nov. 2015
ZAMBIA	President Edgar Lungu	Jan. 2015
ZIMBABWE	President Emmerson Mnangagwa	Nov. 2017

FURTHER STUDY

BIBLIOGRAPHY

See also books recommended in the previous chapter.

Baxter, Daniel (2017), *One Life at a Time: A Doctor's Memoirs of AIDS in Botswana*. Braamfontein: Picador/Macmillan.

Bundy, Colin (2016), *Nelson Mandela*. Auckland Park: Jacana Pocket Books.

Barnard, Rita, ed. (2014), *The Cambridge Companion to Nelson Mandela*. New York: Cambridge University Press.

Ciment, James (1997), *Angola and Mozambique: Post-Colonial Wars in Southern Africa*. New York: Facts on File.

Dubow, Saul (2000), *The African National Congress*. Stroud: Sutton/History Press & Johannesburg: Jonathan Ball.

Gewald, Jan-Bart, Marja Hinfelaar, & Giacomo Macola, eds. (2008), *One Zambia, Many Histories: Towards a History of Post-Colonial Zambia*. Leiden: Brill.

Glijeses, Piero (2013), *Visions of Freedom: Havana, Washington, Pretoria and the Struggle for Southern Africa*. Chapel Hill, NC: University of North Carolina Press.

Lodge, Tom (2006), *Mandela: A Critical Life*. Oxford: Oxford University Press.

Macmillan, Hugh (2014), *Chris Hani*. Auckland Park: Jacana Pocket Books.

Mandela, Nelson (2010), *Conversations with Myself*. New York: Farrar, Straus and Giroux & Johannesburg: Pan Macmillan.

Marinovich, Greg (2016), *Murder at Small Koppie: The Real Story of the Marikana Massacre*. Cape Town: Penguin Random House Books.

Mbone, Guy, ed. (1993), *Malawi at the Crossroads: The Post-Colonial Political Economy*. Harare: SAPES Books.

Melber, Henning (2003), *Limits to Liberation in Southern Africa: The Unfinished Business of Democratic Consolidation: South Africa*. Pretoria: HSRC Press.

Melber, Henning (2014), *Understanding Namibia: The Trials of Independence*. London: Hurst.

Mlambo, Alois S. (2004), *A History of Zimbabwe*. New York: Cambridge University Press.

Ndlovu-Gatsheni & Finex Ndhlovu, eds. (2015), *Nationalism and National Projects in Southern Africa: New Critical Reflections*. Pretoria: Africa Institute of South Africa.

Palotti, Arrigo & Ulf Engel, eds. (2016), *Policies and Challenges of the Democratic Transition*. Leiden: Brill.

Pauw, Jacques (2017), *The President's Keepers: Those Keeping Zuma in Power In and Out of Prison*. Cape Town: Tafelberg/NB Publishers.

Stengel, Richard (2010), *Mandela's Way: Lessons on Life, Love, and Courage*. London: Virgin Books.

VIDEOGRAPHY

DVDs and downloads:

A Reasonable Man (dir. Gavin Hood, 1999. 103 mins): a lawyer (Gavin Hood himself) defends in court and justifies the action of a young man who killed a child believing it was an evil spirit or *tokoloshe*.

Behind the Rainbow (dir. Jihan el-Tahri, 2008. 124 mins): how Jacob Zuma's faction came to power within the ANC after 1994.

Boy Called Twist (dir. Tim Greene, 2014. 95 mins): based on Dickens' classic *Oliver Twist*: a Cape Town street kid named Twist, a Rastafarian 'Fagin', friend Dodger, local Bill Sykes and Nancy, and unexpected grandfather Ebrahim.

Children of the Light (dir. Dawn Gifford Engle, 200. 92 mins): documentary life of Desmond Tutu with family and Nelson Mandela interviews.

Country of My Skull (dir. John Boorman, 2004. 103 mins): a white South African and a black American journalist (played by Juliette Binoche & Samuel L. Jackson) go beyond Truth and Reconciliation to dig out the truth about apartheid torture.

District 9 (dir. Neil Blomkamp, 2009. 112 mins): satirical science fiction about apartheid and AIDS: sick aliens are confined, removed, and then interned by brutal mercenaries.

Forgiveness (dir. Ian Gabriel, 2004. 92 mins): white police constable Coetzee, granted amnesty by the Truth and Reconciliation Commission, tries to obtain forgiveness from his dead victim's family in a fishing village.

Invictus (dir. Clint Eastwood, 2009. 113 mins): elected president of the Rainbow Nation, Mandela (Morgan Freeman) struggles to include and enthuse the all-white national Rugby team (captain Matt Damon).

Mandela and De Klerk (dir. Joseph Sargent, 1997. 116 mins): Sidney Poitier impersonates Mandela and Michael Caine impersonates De Klerk.

Max and Mona (dir. Teddy Mattera, 2004. 98 mins): comedy about Max trying to start a medical degree at university, held back by his extraordinary skill as a professional mourner, by his wily uncle, and by Mona the sacred goat.

No 1 Ladies Detective Agency (dir. Anthony Minghella, 2008. 109 mins — plus 6-part series, 2008–09, 57 mins each): based on Alexander McCall Smith comic novels, Botswana-based detective Mma-Ramotswe (Jill Scott) solves unlikely crimes and misdemeanours.

Red Dust (dir. Tom Hooper, 2004. 140 mins): based on Gillian Slovo's Truth and Reconciliation Commission novel, with Hilary Swank as Chiwetel Ejiofor's lawyer confronting a former apartheid police torturer at Graaff-Reinet.

United Africa (dir. Debs Paterson, 2010. 88 mins): comedy-drama adventure about Rwandan children who travel 3,000 miles to get to the 2010 World Cup soccer tournament in South Africa.

Yesterday (dir. Darrell Roodt, 2004. 96 mins): 'Yesterday' is the name of a rural Zulu woman, afflicted with AIDS, who finds the strength to nurse her dying miner husband and to send her daughter to school.

Notes

3 LATER IRON AGE SOCIETIES TO C.1685

1. European beads came from Venice (large red on green, white, and some striped), Bohemia (hexagonal), or Germany (ring-shaped).

4 EARLY STATES & EUROPEAN COLONIES C.1600–C.1790

1. Towerson's subsequent death in Indonesia in 1623 was dramatized in John Dryden's play *Amboyna, or the Cruelties of the Dutch to the English Merchants,* which was used as propaganda for the English seizure of New Amsterdam (New York) in 1664–67.
2. The story of Christoffel Snyman at Zandvliet (now Museum van de Caab) is told at <www.solms-delta.co.za>.
3. Dates are approximate, and subject to revision, as they are usually based on interpretation of oral traditions. The main synthesis is Martin Legassick's chapter in Thompson (1970).
4. Demand for soft and easily carved African ivory was steadily rising in Europe and North America for knife and pistol handles and even piano keys.

5 COASTAL & INTERIOR FRONTIER WARS C.1790–C.1868

1. The origin of the word 'Mfecane' is disputed. South Sotho people called the disruptive raiders the *fetcani* or *difaqane* ('the crushings'?) while Northern Nguni referred to *izwekufa,* meaning 'destruction of the nation'.
2. The name Tshwane, more correctly *Kgomo-e-tshwana* (the black cow), is also given to the Apies River.
3. Villagers at Lepalong in the Gatsrand survived by building clay-walled housing inside underground caves.

7   SCRAMBLE FOR AFRICA PART 2, 1902–1919

1. Kaiser Wilhelm II had issued a similar *Vernichtungsbefehl* or 'extermination order' on 27 July 1900 for German troops fighting Chinese 'rebels' in the Boxer War.
2. Other translations more correctly render the original Hebrew word as 'Cush' (Northern Sudan) rather than 'Ethiopia'.

9   APARTHEID & AFRICAN NATIONALISM 1948–1967

1. The Herenigde Nasionale Party (Reunited National Party) is usually given the initials NP to distinguish it from its Herstigte Nasionale Party (Reconstituted National Party) breakaway of 1969 (HNP).

General Bibliography

JOURNALS

Important journals available in major libraries and/or on-line by subscription:

African Affairs (Royal African Society, London).

African Historical Review formerly 'Kleio' (UNISA, Pretoria).

African Studies Review (African Studies Association of USA, Tucson, Arizona).

Australasian Review of African Studies (African Studies Association of Australasia and the Pacific, Adelaide).

Botswana Notes and Records (Botswana Society, Gaborone).

Bulletin of the National Library of South Africa (Cape Town).

Historia (Historical Association of South Africa, Pretoria).

History in Africa: A Journal of Debates, Methods, and Source Analysis (African Studies Association of USA).

International Journal of African Historical Studies (Boston University, Boston, MA).

Journal of African History (Cambridge University Press).

Journal of Southern African Studies (Taylor & Francis, Oxford).

South African Archaeological Bulletin (South African Archaeological Society, Cape Town).

South African Historical Journal (Southern African Historical Society, Johannesburg).

Southern African Humanities, formerly 'Natal Museum Journal of Humanities' (Pietermaritzburg).

Zambezia (University of Zimbabwe, Harare).

BOOKS

Beck, Roger (2000), *The History of South Africa*. Westport, CT: Greenwood Press.

Beinart, William Justin (1995), *Environment and History: The Taming of Nature in the USA and South Africa*. London: Routledge.

Beinart, William Justin (2001), *Twentieth-Century South Africa*. Oxford: Oxford University Press.

Beinart, William Justin (2003), *Social History and African Environments*. Oxford: James Currey, Athens OH: Ohio University Press & Cape Town: David Philip.

Berger, Iris (2009), *South Africa in World History*. New York: Oxford University Press.

The Cambridge History of the British Empire, Volume VIII: South Africa, Rhodesia and the Protectorates (1936), ed. Eric Anderson Walker. Cambridge: Cambridge University Press.

The Cambridge History of South Africa, Volume 1: From Early Times to 1885, ed. Carolyn Hamilton, Bernard Mbenga & Robert Ross (2009). Cambridge: Cambridge University Press.

The Cambridge History of South Africa, Volume 2: 1885–1994 (2011), ed. Robert Ross, Anne Kelk Mager & Bill Nasson. Cambridge: Cambridge University Press.

The Cambridge History of South African Literature (2012), ed. David Attwell. Cambridge: Cambridge University Press.

Cornwell, Gareth, Dirk Klopper, & Craig Mackenzie (2014), *The Columbia Guide to South African Literature in English Since 1945*. New York: Columbia University Press.

Denoon, Donald & Balam Nyeko (1972), *Southern Africa Since 1800*. London: Longman.

Denoon, Donald (1983), *Settler Capitalism: The Dynamics of Dependent Development in the Southern Hemisphere*. Oxford: Clarendon Press & New York: Cambridge University Press.

Dlamini, Jacob S.T. (2012), *Putting the Kruger Park in its Place: A Social History of Africans, Mobility and Conservation in a Modernizing South Africa, 1900–2010*. New Haven, CT: Yale University Press.

Dovers, Stephen, Ruth Edgecombe, & Bill Guest, eds. (2002), *South Africa's Environmental History: Cases and Comparisons*. Athens, OH: Ohio University Press & Cape Town: David Philip.

Dubow, Saul (1995), *Scientific Racism in Modern South Africa*. Cambridge: Cambridge University Press & Johannesburg: Witwatersrand University Press.

Dubow, Saul (2006), *A Commonwealth of Knowledge: Science, Sensibility, and White South Africa 1820–2000*. Oxford: Oxford University Press & Cape Town: Double Storey.

Dubow, Saul (2009), *Science and Society in Southern Africa*. Manchester: Manchester University Press.

Dubow, Saul (2012), *South Africa's Struggle for Human Rights*. Auckland Park: Jacana Media.

Du Plessis, Johannes (1911), *A History of Christian Missions in South Africa*. London: Longmans Green.

Elphick, Richard (2012), *The Equality of Believers: Protestant Missionaries and the Racial Politics of South Africa*. Charlottesville, VA: University of Virginia Press & Scottsville, KZN: University of KwaZulu-Natal Press.

Etherington, Norman, ed. (2005), *Missions and Empire*. Oxford: Oxford University Press.

Etherington, Norman (2007), *Mapping Colonial Conquest: Australia and Southern Africa*. Crawley: University of Western Australia Press.

Feinstein, Charles H. (2005), *An Economic History of South Africa: Conquest, Discrimination and. Development*. Cambridge: Cambridge University Press.

Fredrickson, George M. (1982), *White Supremacy: A Comparative Study in American and South African History*. Cape Town: Oxford University Press.

Giliomee, Hermann (2003), *The Afrikaners: Biography of a People*. Charlottesville, VA: University of Virginia Press.

Giliomee, Hermann & Bernard Mbenga (2007), *New History of South Africa*. Cape Town: Tafelberg.

Grundlingh, Albert, André Odendaal & Burridge Spies (1995), *Beyond the Tryline: Rugby and South African Society*. Johannesburg: Ravan & Berkeley, CA: University of California Press.

Houghton, Desmond Hobart & J. Dagut, comp. (1972–73), *Source Material on the South African Economy, 1860–1960*. Cape Town: Oxford University Press, 2 vols.

Jacobs, Nancy J. (2003), *Environment, Power, and Injustice: A South African History* [Kuruman area]. Cambridge: Cambridge University Press.

Jacobs, Nancy J. (2014), *African History Through Sources, 1850–1945: Experiences and Contexts*. New York: Cambridge University Press.

Kuper, Adam (1982), *Wives for Cattle: Bridewealth and Marriage in South Africa*. London: Routledge & Kegan Paul.

Lamar, Howard & Leonard Thompson, ed. (1981), *The Frontier in History: North America and Southern Africa Compared*. New Haven, CT: Yale University Press.

Landau, Paul Stuart (2010), *Popular Politics in the History of South Africa, 1400–1948*. Cambridge: Cambridge University Press.

Lekhela, Simon M.M. (2014), *Owning the Land: A History of South Africa from Jan van Riebeeck to John Balthazar Vorster*. Johannesburg: Ukuzazi Communications.

Lewis-Williams, David (2002), *The Mind in the Cave: Consciousness and the Origins of Art*. London: Thames & Hudson.

Marks, Shula (1994), *Divided Sisterhood: Race, Class, and Gender in the South African Nursing Profession*. Basingstoke: Macmillan & New York: St Martin's Press.

McCracken, John (2012), *A History of Malawi, 1855–1966*. Oxford: James Currey & Rochester: Boydell & Brewer.

McKenna, Amy, gen.ed. (2011), *The History of Southern Africa*. New York: Rosen Educational Services for Encyclopaedia Britannica.

Mitchell, Peter (2002), *The Archaeology of Southern Africa*. Cambridge: Cambridge University Press.

Mitchell, Peter (2006), *People and Cultures of Southern Africa*. New York: Chelsea House/ Infobase Publishing Facts on File.

Mlambo, Alois S. (2014), *A History of Zimbabwe*. New York: Cambridge University Press.

Morris, Alan G. (2011), *Missing & Murdered: A Personal Adventure of Forensic Anthropology*. Johannesburg: Penguin Random House.

Nasson, Bill (2017), *History Matters: Selected Writings 1970–2016*. Johannesburg: Penguin Random House.

Nattrass, Gail (2017), *A Short History of South Africa*. Johannesburg: Jonathan Ball.

Newitt, Malyn (2017), *A Short History of Mozambique*. Johannesburg: Jonathan Ball.

Odendaal, André (2012), *The Founders: The Origins of the African National Congress and the Struggle for Democracy*. Johannesburg: Jacana Media & Lexington, KY: University Press of Kentucky.

Odendaal, André (2016 & 2018), *The History of South African Cricket Revised*: Vol. 1, 1795–1914 *Cricket and Conquest*; Vol. 2, 1914–1960 *Divided Country*. Pretoria: HSRC Press.

Omer-Cooper, John D. (1994), *History of Southern Africa*. London: James Currey, Cape Town: David Philip & Portsmouth, NH: Heinemann.

The Oxford History of Africa (1975–84), Volume I (*From the Earliest Times until c.500 BC*, ed. J Desmond Clark), II (*From c.500 BC to AD 1050*, ed. John D. Fage), III (*From c.1050 to c.1600*, ed. Roland Oliver), IV (*From c.1600 to c.1790*, ed. Richard Gray), V (*From c.1790 to c.1870*, ed. John E. Flint), VI (*From 1870–1905*, ed. Roland Oliver & G.N. Sanderson), VII (*From 1905 to 1940*, ed. Andrew Dunlop Roberts), VIII (*From 1940 to c.1975*, ed. Michael Crowder).

The Oxford History of the British Empire (1999), Volume III (*The Nineteenth Century*, ed. Andrew Porter), IV (*The Twentieth Century*, ed. Judith M. Brown & William Roger Louis), V (*Historiography*, ed. Robin W. Winks). Oxford: Clarendon Press & Oxford University Press.

The Oxford History of South Africa, Volume 1 South Africa to 1870 (1969) & *Volume 2 South Africa, 1870–1966* (1971), ed. Leonard Thompson & Monica Wilson. Oxford: Clarendon Press.

Packard, Randall M. (1989), *White Plague, Black Labor: Tuberculosis and the Political Economy of Health and Disease in South Africa*. Pietermaritzburg: University of Natal Press & Berkeley, CA: University of California Press.

Parsons, Neil (1982), *A New History of Southern Africa*. Basingstoke: Macmillan, New York: Holmes & Meier & Harare: College Press.

Pretorius, Fransjohan (2014), *A History of South Africa; from the Distant Past until the Present Day*. Pretoria: Protea.

Raftopoulos, B. & A. Mlambo (2009), *Becoming Zimbabwe: A History from the Pre-colonial Period to 2008*. Harare: Weaver Press.

Ross, Robert (1994), *Beyond the Pale: Essays on the History of Colonial South Africa*. Johannesburg: Witwatersrand University Press.

Ross, Robert (1999), *A Concise History of South Africa*. Cambridge: Cambridge University Press.

Ross, Robert (2008), *Clothing: A Global History: Or, The Imperialists' New Clothes*. Cambridge: Polity Press.

Saunders, Christopher C. (1988), *The Making of the South African Past: Major Historians on Race and Class*. Cape Town: David Philip.

Saunders, Christopher C. & Colin Bundy, eds. (1988), *Reader's Digest Illustrated History of South Africa: The Real Story*. New York & Cape Town: Reader's Digest.

Saunders, Christopher & Nicholas Southey (1998), *A Dictionary of South African History*. Cape Town: David Philip.

Shain, Milton and Richard Mendelsohn (2008), *The Jews in South Africa: An Illustrated History*. Jeppestown: Jonathan Ball.

Shillington, Kevin (1987), *History of Southern Africa*. Harlow: Longman.

Soodyall, Himla, ed. (2006), *The Prehistory of Africa: Tracing the Lineage of Modern Man*. Johannesburg & Cape Town: Jonathan Ball Publishers.

Stapleton, Timothy (2010), *A Military History of South Africa: From the Khoi-Dutch War to the End of Apartheid*. Santa Barbara, CA: Praeger.

Suzman, James (2017), *Affluence Without Abundance: The Disappearing World of the Bushmen* [Ju'/hoansi]. London: Bloomsbury Publishing.

Thompson, Leonard Monteath (1995), *A History of South Africa: Human Habitation to the Present*. New Haven, CT: Yale University Press.

Tlou, Thomas & Alec C. Campbell (1984), *History of Botswana*. Macmillan Botswana.

UNESCO *General History of Africa* (1981–93), Volume 1 (*Methodology and African Prehistory*, ed. J.Ki-Zerbo), II (*Ancient Civilisations of Africa*, ed. Gamal Mokhtar), III (*Africa from the Seventh to the Eleventh Century*, ed. Muhammad al-Fasi & Ivan Hrbek), IV (*Africa from the Twelfth to the Sixteenth Century*, ed. D.T. Niane), V (*Africa from the Sixteenth to the Eighteenth Century*, ed. Bethwell A. Ogot), VI (*Africa in the Nineteenth Century*, ed. J.F. Ade Ajayi), VII (*Africa under Colonial Domination, 1880–1935*, ed. A. Adu Boahen), VIII (*Africa Since 1935*, ed. Ali Mazrui). Paris: UNESCO, Oxford: James Currey & Berkeley, CA: University of California Press.

Van Jaarsveld, Floris Albertus (1964), *The Afrikaner's Interpretation of South African History*. Cape Town: Simondium.

Wallace, Marion & John Kinahan (2011), *A History of Namibia: From the Beginning to 1990*. London: Hurst & Company.

Walker, Eric Anderson (1957), *A History of Southern Africa*. London: Longmans Green [5th edn? 1st ed. *A History of South Africa*, 1928 – previously *A Modern History for South Africans*. Cape Town: Maskew Miller, 1926].

Walsh, Frank (2000), *A History of South Africa*. London: Harper Collins.

Wilson, Francis (2017), *Dinosaurs, Diamonds and Democracy: A Short, Short History of South Africa*, 3rd edn. Johannesburg: Penguin Random House.

Witz, Lesie, Gary Minkley, & Ciraj Rassool (2017), *Unsettled History: South African Public Pasts*. Ann Arbor, MI: University of Michigan Press.

Worden, Nigel (2007), *The Making of Modern South Africa: Conquest, Apartheid, Democracy*. Oxford: Blackwoods.

Wright, Harrison M. (1977), *The Burden of the Present: Liberal-Radical Controversy over Southern African History*. Cape Town: David Philip.

INTERNET

http://history-compass.com/africa-section (Wiley On-Line Library).

https://networks.h-net.org/h-safrica (H-Africa/H-SAfrica Net).

www.saha.org.za/ (South African History Archive).

Departments of History or Historical Studies at various Southern African universities also have informative websites, e.g., University of Botswana History (UBH) www.thuto.org/ubh/

NEWSREEL FILMS: British Pathé (1896–1976) is the most comprehensive newsreel freely available on-line. Other newsreels available in part or by subscription include British Movietone, Fox Movietone, Hearst Metrotone, and Universal Newsreel. Issues of the world's longest lasting cinema newsreel, *The African Mirror* (1913–1984), from 1919 onwards, may at some time be made available through the Gauteng Film Commission (Johannesburg).

Index

CPSIA information can be obtained
at www.ICGtesting.com
Printed in the USA
LVHW052352151220
674262LV00014B/1500